# SHIMMERING MIRRORS

# SHIMMERING MIRRORS

Reality and Appearance in
Contemplative Metaphysics
East and West

## PATRICK LAUDE

SUNY PRESS

© 2017 State University of New York

Printed in the United States of America

For information, contact State University of New York Press, Albany, NY
www.sunypress.edu

Production, Eileen Nizer
Marketing, Fran Keneston

**Library of Congress Cataloging-in-Publication Data**

Names: Laude, Patrick, 1958– author.
Title: Shimmering mirrors : reality and appearance in contemplative metaphysics East and West / Patrick Laude.
Description: Albany : State University of New York, [2017] | Includes bibliographical references and index.
Identifiers: LCCN 2016051109 (print) | LCCN 2017039127 (ebook) | ISBN 9781438466835 (ebook) | ISBN 9781438466811 (hardcover : alk. paper) | ISBN 9781438466828 (pbk. : alk. paper)
Subjects: LCSH: Religions. | Contemplation. | Metaphysics. | Philosophy and religion.
Classification: LCC BL80.3 (ebook) | LCC BL80.3 .L378 2017 (print) | DDC 200—dc23
LC record available at https://lccn.loc.gov/2016051109

10 9 8 7 6 5 4 3 2 1

The attitude of staying in a deep valley while avoiding great mountains, or loving emptiness while hating existence is just like the attitude of going into a forest while avoiding trees. But one should be aware of the fact that green and blue are identical in essence, and ice and water are identical in origin; a single mirror reflects myriad forms, and parted waters will perfectly intermingle once they are reunited.

—Wŏnhyo

If there were no water whose wet nature were unchanging, how could there be the waves of illusory, provisional phenomenal appearances? If there were no mirror whose pure brightness were unchanging, how could there be the reflections of a variety of unreal phenomena?

—Tsung-mi

Just as earth, water, etc. get reflected in a clean mirror even so all events and objects of the world get reflected unmixed in the one Lord Himself.

—Abhinavagupta

*Māyā* is like a magic fabric woven from a warp that veils and a weft that unveils; a quasi-incomprehensible intermediary between the finite and the Infinite—at least from our point of view as creatures—it has all the shimmering ambiguity appropriate to its half-cosmic, half-divine nature.

—Frithjof Schuon

# Contents

# Acknowledgments

My deep gratitude goes to Alex Minchinton and John Paraskevopoulos for their thorough reading of the manuscript, as well as their substantive and editorial work and remarks. Many thanks also to André Gomez, Jean-Pierre Lafouge, Patrick Meadows, and Reza Shah-Kazemi for their intellectual support, advice, and editorial suggestions at several stages of my work on this book.

I also wish to thank the Faculty of Georgetown University School of Foreign Service in Qatar for awarding me two Faculty Research Grants in support of my research on this book.

My sincere thanks to Daniela Boccassini and Carlo Saccone, editors of *Quaderni di Studi Indo-Mediterranei*, for their kind permission to reproduce an earlier version of chapter 6, and to Roger Ames, editor of *Philosophy East and West*, and the University of Hawaii Press, for allowing me to reproduce the essay "Shimmering Reality: The Question of Metaphysical Relativity in Mystical Theology" as chapter 1 of this book.

Finally, a first version of chapter 2 of this book, copyrighted with the Indian Council of Philosophical Research, was used with the kind permission of the Indian Council of Philosophical Research and Springer.

# Introduction

Why write a new book on metaphysics in contemplative traditions and, first of all, what is to be understood by those terms? Leaving aside, for now, the discussion of the intended meaning of the adjective *contemplative,* it may be in order to point out that metaphysics is not uncommonly considered today a matter of "unreal" speculations, something like an obsolete luxury in a world of scientific "hard facts" and sociopolitical imperatives. In this respect, one of the major sources of misunderstanding lies no doubt in the literal implications of the Greek prefix *meta.* Whether it be understood, in the Aristotelian sense, as referring to a matter of sequence, that is as pertaining to that which comes *after* physics, or—as is more often the case—as alluding to a domain situated *beyond* physical reality, it remains at any rate true that metaphysics can hardly arise as a priority in a world in which the tendency to treating "the urgent as essential" tends to translate, arguably, into forgetting "the urgency of the essential," to paraphrase Edgar Morin's felicitous formula.[1] Much of contemporary thought and action is predicated upon the sense that metaphysics may be dealt with *later,* when what matters first and foremost has been settled. Many have even gone a step farther in arguing that metaphysics may remain postponed indefinitely since it deals with a beyond that is deemed out of reach, if not illusory, and above all undecidable as demonstrated, in their eyes, by the diversity of its historical forms and concepts. As the reader will have opportunities to infer from many pages of this essay, those widespread contemporary perceptions may be evaluated as misreadings of metaphysical teachings, since it is quite apparent that the latter have been articulated by their contemplative proponents as being as pertinent to the here as to the beyond, as relevant to the now as to the later.

Aristotle referred to metaphysics as the science of being qua being, while some contemporary thinkers have also characterized it as the knowledge of universal principles, although it cannot properly be defined since it has no limits.[2] Both statements are very rich in meaning. That metaphysics deals with being qua being simply means that it considers that which is the very precondition for anything else. It is not as much concerned with beings as it is with being as such, or with Being, should one deem it necessary to capitalize the term to distinguish it unequivocally from beings, in the ways in which Thomism contrasts *esse* and *ens,* or in the manner Heidegger understands the distinction between *Sein* and *das Seiende.* Even understood in the most universal and non-delimited manner, being can be, and has been, experienced, understood, conceptualized or expressed in different ways, including through the very absence, or negation, of its concept. While definitely not an object that could be analyzed and reified as *a* being, "being," or "Being," has variously been approached as Act, Stream, Presence, Light, or even as Consciousness and Subject, in all cases a reality more intrinsic to beings than themselves, to paraphrase Augustine's famous mystical intimation, *intimior intimo meo,* in *Confessions* 3:6. While stating that it is not an object, nor even the Supreme Object, we are suggesting that Being is presumably not fathomed, nor is most often even truly considered, by ordinary religious consciousness. This is so to the extent that the latter is generally content to understand it, for better or for worse, as the largest, highest, most powerful being, or Being as first being among all beings. In doing so, it all too often fails to sense that Being springs forth at the very source of any and all beings, as testified by the intuitions and formulations of a number of traditional metaphysicians, albeit in very different contexts and languages, and sometimes with divergent spiritual intents. This is precisely why metaphysics could also be considered as the science of the universal since it encompasses everything in light of that which gives reality to the whole of existence. It could be proposed, therefore, that metaphysics is simply the science of reality in its most encompassing sense, or the science of reality as such, or that of Reality.

Now, reality, whether understood relatively or absolutely, has been thoroughly questioned as a normative concept with the advent of postmodern moods of thinking and living. In our world perhaps more than ever there is widespread skepticism about any universal concept of reality, and it is widely held, practically if not theoretically, that what is "illusion" for one is "reality" for another, and conversely; and this is as true for collectivities as it is for individuals. The demise of modern ideologies is not for nothing in this state of affairs, as it highlighted the end of the so-called grand narratives which were founded on fundamental and systematic concepts of reality. The result is that reality has been more and more understood in terms of individual representations, when it is recognized as having any validity at all. Moreover, the exponential development of so-called virtual reality has contributed to blurring the lines between the immediate sense of ordinary reality, such as had been mostly shaped by materialism and positivism, and that which, until recently, would have been deemed to be nothing but an illusory universe of technological and mediatic productions. This expansion and pandemic use of the virtual world has thereby opened wider the doors to a diffuse postmodern skepticism over the very notion of reality.

In spite of these developments, or perhaps because of them, perceptions of reality and appearance still shape the existence of contemporary men and women. Whether as individuals or as groups, human beings do not seem ever closer to cease "absolutizing," if only subjectively and emotionally, that around which they build their lives, whether unawares or in full awareness. Appearance and reality may be inextricably blended to the point of calling into question the very distinction between the two, but their concepts remain at least *practically* relevant inasmuch as any human life presupposes and entails existential and moral choices based on representations of "reality."

One of the most obvious characteristics of religious traditions, and particularly contemplative currents within them, is their keenness to discriminate between reality and illusion, or at least between a reality that they hold to be *deceptive* and one which they characterize as *fulfilling*. It is along these lines that a number of contemporary commentators, and in a sense the whole pervasive vision that presides over the modern enterprise, have claimed that religions tend to depreciate terrestrial realities, and therefore open the way to indifference or neglect of the practical and socioeconomic tasks at hand, when they are not deemed to amount to the fanatical rejection of the world in the name of the transcendent. Others, on the contrary, have seen religious life as the only way of giving full weight to the seriousness and beauty of our life on this earth. So it is plain that the question of the religious vision of reality and appearance touches upon debates that are far from being merely academic.

Reality and Truth are terms that have translated, or can translate, a host of traditional and religious concepts East and West, such as the Arabic *al-Haqq*, the Sanskrit *Sat*, the Chinese *Tao*, and others. These terms hold profoundly different connotations and denotative contexts, and they refer to extremely diverse perspectives on "what is." And still, it is significant to note that Truth and Reality, or the True and the Real, often arise as the most suitable, or the least unsuitable, and certainly most expedient, ways of conveying something of all the aforementioned terms in English, as do their equivalents in other European languages. Now, although the two terms overlap, truth tends to lie in opposition to error, while reality "faces" vanity and illusion. The first points to adequation with things as they are, whereas the second refers directly to things as they are. In a sense, reality can be either a synonym of truth, or the foundation thereof. Thus, truth is a matter of correspondence whereas reality is one of "substance," in the etymological sense of "that which stands under" because it is deepest and innermost, and in a way irreducible by, and to, anything else. Reality in the fullest sense is that which cannot be reduced to anything else, or to put it experientially and axiologically—in the terms of Eliot Deutsch commenting upon the *Advaitin* Reality—that which cannot be "subrated." Even without taking reality in such an absolute and ultimate sense, any kind of reality entails a sense of irreducibility, if not in terms of its being, at least as quiddity and therefore in terms of its difference from other realities.

As for the concept of appearance, together with its various cognates in European languages, it stems from the root of the Latin verb *apparere*. The term seems to have accrued the negative connotation of semblance only in the last five centuries. The most interesting characteristic of its contemporary use is that it both implies—and therefore may affirm—reality *and* denies it. An appearance is literally an appearance of something so that the term denotes the manifestation, visible or otherwise, of some "reality." However, the term has come to be used increasingly in contradistinction with reality, so as to refer to an actual lack of genuine reality. Appearance tends to connote "semblance" rather than "manifestation," especially, of course, when used in conjunction with reality. Interestingly, the Greek verb for "to appear," *phainomai,* refers to the same meaning of manifestation, but its philosophical and ordinary denotations have conglomerated around the concept of phenomenon, which is, by and large, used in a neutral sense to refer to something perceived, or something happening, without implying any sense of semblance, indeed quite the contrary. In ordinary usage, the term may be deemed to refer to the immediate unity of reality, whereas its technical philosophical usage emphasizes its aspect of reality *for* a consciousness apprehending it. In both cases, however, none of the epistemological implications of semblance seem to be primary.

It is interesting to note that key concepts that are akin in meaning to the concept of appearance in some religious traditions, sometimes do and sometimes do not connote a lack of reality. We should mention, first of all, the Sanskrit concept of *Māyā*. Although its most common interpretations connote a sense of illusory and delusional appearance, as in *Advaita Vedānta*, it holds also true that the etymology and early Upanishadic uses of the term refer to a sense of creative "art" and "measure." Let us note briefly, as another example, that the Arabic terms *zāhir* and *zuhūr* tend to refer to appearance as manifestation. These terms are so positive, in fact, that one of the Quranic Names of God is *az-Zāhir,* often translated as the Outer or the Manifest.

We now need to address the question of our delimitation of the adjective *contemplative* and our choice to use it in preference to alternative terms. In point of fact, this choice is very directly connected to the various dimensions and aspects of the concept of appearance, since the latter implies a "contemplative" consideration of its "reality" or lack thereof. We use the term *contemplative* in the Platonic sense of *theōria,* but also with some of the implications of the notion of *contemplatio* in the Western Christian tradition. This means that we wish to highlight the intellectual, or intellective, dimension of the term, while removing from it the limitations inherent to discursive thought as such, thereby suggesting its intrinsic association with spiritual disciplines of realization or assimilation. Even though the following pages bear witness to a re-occurring use of the adjective *mystical* as a quasi-equivalent of contemplative, we have come to acknowledge a preference for the latter in the final analysis. However, our occasional use of the word *mystical* indicates that we are not unaware of its specific merits and suggestive power. Overall, though, we tend to favor contemplative and have opted for its use in the title of this work. This is because, unfortunately, the term *mysticism* all too often entails, in the modern world, suggestions of irrationality and emotional exaltation, when it does not imply an emphasis on extraordinary phenomena. As for the adjective *spiritual,* it has the inconvenience of connoting subjective vagueness and informality, if not an implicit antagonism vis-à-vis the intellectual domain understood as pertaining to sterile mind games deprived of any existential relevance. Finally, *speculative* would beautifully convey the mirror-like receptivity—from the Latin *speculum,* or mirror—of the type of metaphysical meditations that are the focus of the following essays. Sadly, the term has accrued strong connotations of imaginative insubstantiality and arbitrariness, while evoking a sense of intellectual illusoriness, at least within the range of the most common contemporary lexicon.

The works and texts that are analyzed and set into parallels and contrasts in the following pages are indeed mystical inasmuch as they postulate a sort of "unitive knowledge" as the final end toward which their central concepts converge. However, these perspectives and approaches have less to do with a desire for union, in the mystically "erotic" and devotional sense of the term, than with an inner consideration of the nature of Reality as they see it. There lie accounts of the Real that are not only "objective" in their focus, as markers of a metaphysical "space" of observation—as in the Latin etymology of *contemplari*—but also paths of "subjective" assimilation of the latter, or ways of "taking in and with oneself" that are quite plausibly mystical. In all cases, albeit within a wide spectrum of contexts, intents, and emphases, it is a matter of vision, recognition, realization, unveiling, or awakening, as well as one of adequate consideration and proper integration of the nature of Reality. It is important to keep this contemplative dimension as a background because it allows one to avoid the pitfalls of treating metaphysical concepts with excessive fixity or theological absoluteness.

With respect to the actual metaphysical "objects" under consideration, all the themes and major questions that are addressed in the following pages do relate, in one way or another, to the central concerns that have been sketched in the previous paragraphs. They all pertain to matters of understanding reality and appearance. More specifically, they range over three kinds of subheadings, which could be defined very broadly as metaphysical representations of Reality, interpretations and implications of relativity, appearance, and illusion, and spiritual realization of that which those various concepts denote. Chapter 1 provides a general overview of what is metaphysically at stake in the distinction, and relationship, between the Absolute and the relative, and the ambiguous status of the latter in relation to the former. It is, in a sense, a cross-religious examination of the implications of the dimensions of necessity, freedom, and self-determination inherent to most concepts of the Absolute. It amounts to a meditation on the major question of the exclusiveness of the concept of absoluteness and its compatibility, or lack thereof, with any reality "other" than itself. Chapter 2 considers the same set of issues from the point of view of a comparative study of what one could refer to as "metaphysics of salvation." In the perspective of comparative religion, this leads us to delineate two kinds of religious and contemplative traditions, with an emphasis on Buddhist and Christian metaphysical themes as representative of a particular emphasis on the soteriological vector of the envisioning of absoluteness and relativity in these two traditions, by contrast with contemplative traditions in which the concept of the Absolute "contains" or "entails" salvation rather than being determined by it. In other words, our intent in this chapter is to assess the ways in which religious "myths" and messages of salvation or emancipation can mold, and sometimes even alter, the concept of the Absolute. Chapter 3 tackles the same type of concerns from the vantage point of the metaphysics of evil. The latter is considered as inherently connected, in contemplative traditions, to the status of the Absolute, which means that it raises the very question of the reality of evil, since the attribution of being to the latter tends to involve a contradiction, or at least a tension, with the idea of an unconditioned Reality. Can the Absolute be absolute if there *is* evil, which amounts to asking whether there can be evil when there is an Absolute? As an extension of some of the core considerations developed in chapter 1, chapter 4 delves into the representation of the zones of contact between the Absolute and the relative. More specifically, it consists of a study of the ways in which two spiritual traditions, in various schools and currents of Hindu metaphysics and Sufi theosophy, articulate the ontological imperatives of Unity and non-Duality and the reality of diversity and difference. In other words, what is tackled here is the question of the apparent gap between principial Unicity and manifested multiplicity. Finally, chapters 5 and 6 deal with issues of representation, transmission, and assimilation of nondual Reality within the context of Hindu, Buddhist, and Islamic contemplative traditions. Chapter 5 consists of an examination of two concepts that function as ways and means of knowledge of the Unknowable, namely, the Buddhist *upāya* and Ibn al-'Arabī's "god of belief." It could be encapsulated in the question: How can one represent or teach That which can neither be presented nor taught? Chapter 6 looks more closely, and more directly than the previous chapters, at two major dimensions of contemplative methods of spiritual realization by analyzing two of their components, that is, invocatory means of return to the One through linguistic supports of meditation, and methodical considerations of the "feminine" as a central transforming agency in the process of spiritual reintegration.

As it has already been intimated through the above survey of the central concerns and questions of this study, much, if not all, of what is at stake in what follows pertains to the paradoxes of unity and diversity in contemplative teachings and practices. This is the meaning of the symbolic allusions included in our title. On the one hand, the image of shimmering phenomena suggests the perception, or presence, of unity within multiplicity.[3] The same light is transformed or manifested into countless flickering appearances. Thus, it evokes both the reality of appearance and the appearance of reality. By contrast, or as a complement, the pervasive symbol, and metaphor, of the mirror, one of the most reccurring imaginal tropes in mystical language East and West, refers to the enigma, mystery, or riddle of multiplicity in unity. It suggests the way in which the many may appear as one within the "reflecting" metaphysical "frame" of the Ultimate. It is in the subtle, complex, often paradoxical, and ever mobile meditation on this interplay of continuity and discontinuity, identity and difference, reality and appearance that lie the richness and fruitfulness of contemplative metaphysics, and the practical effectiveness of its approaches. As will appear in some of the pages of our essay, our suggestion is that therein is to be found, for contemporary readers and seekers who are ready to take contemplative metaphysics seriously, the most fundamental and encompassing responses to the current acute predicaments of religious and spiritual consciousness.

# 1

## Shimmering Reality

### *Contemplative and Mystical Concepts of Relativity*

It can be argued that what most clearly sets contemplative metaphysics apart from ordinary religious consciousness and rational[1] or apologetic theology is its treatment of the relationship between the Ultimate Reality and the non-ultimate. In fact, the various forms of mystical theology and metaphysical teachings that are the focus of the current chapter tend to combine the strictest concept of the Absolute, one that points to transcending any polarity, duality, and distinction, and a vision of relativity that both denies the reality of the world of manifestation, when considered independently from its Source, and affirms an essential continuity or unity between the Ultimate and that which is not in an ultimate sense.

The Absolute is literally *ab-solutum*, which means that it is "unbound," "detached," and "free." Although most often understood as complete and self-sufficient, and therefore also cause of itself, the Absolute must also and consequently be approached in terms of its perfect freedom, which is itself a dimension of its transcendence vis-à-vis any relationality. In this connection, relationality entails an aspect of "obligation" or reciprocity by virtue of the relationships and relations it involves. Therefore, our understanding of absoluteness as utter freedom immediately brings the central question of this inquiry to the fore by highlighting the apparent logical impossibility of positing concurrently the ontological reality of both the Absolute and non-absolute realities—including ourselves. In other words, is the Absolute conceivable side by side with the existence of a myriad of "non-absolute" realities given that such a mode of "co-being" or "co-existence" would perforce imply some sort of relationality between the former and the latter, and thereby run contrary to the very notion of an *ab-solutum*? It is this question that we would like to ponder in the current chapter through a liminal survey of some of the most rigorous concepts of the Absolute provided by a cross-religious spectrum of teachings representative of mystical theology and contemplative metaphysics. We readily acknowledge that the term *mystical* is approximative, possibly even misleading, and given to likely misunderstandings. We consider nonetheless the use of this term suitable, in parallel to the adjective *contemplative,* as a distinct indication that we will be considering doctrines and teachings that are not understood by their proponents as mere conceptual descriptions of Reality, but are also intimately associated with them to ways of spiritual realization, thereby highlighting the vital coalescence of epistemology, ontology, and soteriology.

Within the manifold tradition of Hinduism the *Advaitin* or nondual perspective of Shankara (AD 788–820) provides a fitting starting point for an analysis of the ontological status of relativity, or "other-than-the-Ultimate," when characterizing *Māyā*—which has been variously translated as "veil," "illusion," "art," "wonder," or "appearance"—as "neither real, nor unreal"[2] in his *Vivekacūḍāmaṇi*[3] or *Crest Jewel of Discrimination*. We will use these perplexing words as keys to argue that wisdom and mystical traditions, across religious boundaries, tend to assign an ambiguous ontological status to phenomenal realities as apprehended "outside" of the realm of the Ultimate Reality or Recognition. Furthermore, we propose to show that each of these traditions does emphasize one of the two aforesaid characterizations in its approach to the mystery of universal metaphysical relativity, or universal existence: neither being or real, nor nonbeing or unreal.[4] It bears specifying that the words *is, real,* and *being* are used alternatively in this essay without significant difference in meaning to imply ontological substantiality and permanence. The term *existence* will sometimes be understood in a similar sense, sometimes more technically with the specific nuance of the Latin *exsistere,* from *ek-sistere,* which connotes manifestation as in "phenomenon" or a coming into being out of nothingness that is contingent upon a higher existentiating agency. To put it otherwise, the words *being, real,* and *reality* will point to ontological substance and the term *existence* to phenomenal manifestation. We will also keep to the principle that such emphases do not amount to exclusive doctrinal propositions since mystical and contemplative teachings should not be understood as philosophical systems rationally denoting realities, but rather as symbolic approaches by way of conceptual representations intended to open the mind to a spiritual, existential, experiential realization or assimilation of Reality. This means that some teachings lay emphasis on the "not real" dimension of relativity, while others stress its being "not unreal," and others still its being both "not real and not unreal"; but at any rate, such conceptual characterizations can never be totally exclusive of their counterpart positions since they tend to suggest ontological aspects and epistemological points of view, being thereby akin to the Jain principle of *Anekāntavāda,* or limitless plurality of perspectives.[5] The need to consider these perspectives in a nonexclusive fashion stems from their implying a gap between their doctrinal formulations and the ontological and existential realities they denote.

## Dispelling Appearance

The first approach of metaphysical relativity consists in predicating it primarily as "not real." Among all the expressions of this approach, two of the most powerfully suggestive are undoubtedly Shankara's *Advaita* and Nāgārjuna's Mahāyānic *Madhyamaka*. Two words of caution are in order before we move farther: first, it bears stressing from the outset that these two doctrines are traditionally at odds on fundamental points touching upon their respective understandings of Ultimate Reality, and secondly they both can be read—as we will see later and as we have already intimated—in a way that qualifies their overall "nonrealism." While Shankara's perspective is a priori epistemological, in the sense that its chief concern is to dispel ignorance or *avidyā* to reveal the true nature of being and consciousness, Nāgārjuna's perspective can be deemed to be primarily soteriological since its ontology chiefly responds to the central question of Buddhism, that is, suffering and the way to free oneself from it. This being said, it is in fact nearly impossible, in both cases, to disconnect epistemology, soteriology, and metaphysics or ontology: as we will see, Shankara can at times approach the problem of *Māyā* in onto-cosmological terms, and Nāgārjuna's concepts of emptiness and codependent origination are intrinsically connected to ontological and epistemological stances that are aligned with a spiritual intent.[6]

As aforementioned, metaphysical relativity is, in *Advaita Vedānta*, primarily identified with *Māyā*. Now, *Māyā* is most often approached by Shankara as an epistemological phenomenon of superimposition upon Reality. In other words, *Māyā* is that which makes us mistake "the rope for the snake."[7] It is a principle of distortion of Reality that stems from one's inability to recognize Reality as it is, that is as the nondual Self or *Ātman*. On the one hand, *Māyā* is the epistemological fruit of a false identification of the Self with the body; on the other hand, it is *Māyā* itself, or more specifically *tamas*—the lowest, most opaque of the three cosmological elements that enter into the composition of *Māyā*'s world of relativity, which is constitutive of delusion as such:

> The power of *tamas* is a veiling power. It makes things appear to be other than what they are. It is this which is the original cause of an individual's transmigration and is the cause of the origination of the action of the projecting power.[8]

It must be noted, furthermore, that the ontological status of *Māyā* is incomprehensible: "She is most strange. Her nature is inexplicable," to use Shankara's words.[9] *Māyā* is fundamentally *the* unintelligible, and this lack of intelligibility is a function of the obscurity or uncertainty of its origin, as well as being bound to the undecidability of its ontological status. Although *Māyā* is most often not accounted for in terms of creation or emanation, since it is an "inexplicable wonder," some *Advaitin* authoritative texts do relate *Māyā* to a creative process on the part of the Lord.[10] In such cases, *Māyā* tends to be identified with *līlā*, or the divine sport or play that "symbolizes" creation. In Shankara's *Daksināmūrti Stotra*, for example, we read that "Īśvara amuses Himself assuming, of His own accord, the forms of the worshiper and the worshiped, of teacher and disciple, of master and servant, and so on."[11] Inasmuch as these dualities pertain to *Māyā*, the latter may be read to be implicitly ascribed to the Lord, or to the Personal God, as its Originator. In fact, the very consideration of the Lord entails a duality or a relationship between the One Lord and the multiplicity that relates to Him.[12] This deluding duality and multiplicity that is in the very nature of *Māyā* is sometimes compared by *Advaitin* authors to a fishing net that expands or contracts depending upon the will of the Lord. The fishing net is to be understood here as a power of allure and delusion, and its contraction to a divine grace, so that *Māyā* is in such cases considered as being under the control of a sometimes misguiding—i.e., "expanding" *Māyā*—sometimes liberating—i.e., "contracting" *Māyā*—Lord.[13] However, the main focus of *Advaita* is not on the origin or cause of *Māyā*, which is in a way an ever open question, but rather on its end, or its being dispelled by knowledge. It could actually be said that the only fully satisfactory definition of *Māyā* is to be found in the words "that which can be nullified," or to use Eliot Deutsch's terminology "that which can be subrated by other experience."[14] In other words, *Māyā* is not as much definable as it is recognizable by and through its ontological and spiritual reduction, or else *Māyā* is known by being dispelled. *Māyā* as appearance has no meaning independently from Reality, which, in *Advaita Vedānta*, is none other than the Supreme Divine Selfhood, or *Ātman*. This is so precisely because "*Māyā* is nullified by knowledge of *Ātman*,"[15] and because this nullification is, in fact, the only way of knowing *Māyā* for what it is. If there is a way to "know" the unknowable, undefinable, inexplicable *Māyā* it is in fact through the realization of *Ātman*. It is this very fact that allows us to consider *Advaita Vedānta* as a set of metaphysical doctrines that lay emphasis on the "nonreal" character of that which is not the Ultimate, notwithstanding the ontologically undecidable and ambiguous nature of *Māyā*. The latter is best described by Shankara in the following passage: "It is not non-existent, because it appears; neither is it existent, because it is nullified."[16] Such terms would seem to contradict our characterization of *Advaita Vedānta* as a perspective emphasizing the "nonreality" of universal relativity since they deny both the "nonexistent" and "existent" aspects of *Māyā*. However, it is quite clear that the negation of the "nonexistent" nature of *Māyā* is methodologically and epistemologically less important than the negation of its "existence." In fact, or in practice, the state of epistemological and spiritual delusion from which the *Advaitin* practitioner is called to awaken is not as much connected to the need to recognize the "non-nonexistence" of *Māyā* as it is to the necessity of discerning its "nonexistence." If it were not so, *Māyā* could not be referred to symbolically by Shankara, for example, as a "harlot" whose "coquetry" allures only those who do not make use of discerning scrutiny (*viveka*).[17] It is clearly the seductively "nonreal" aspect of *Māyā* that serves as a point of reference for the *Advaitin*'s discriminating meditation toward deliverance, especially when considering the ability of *Māyā* to shortchange the human mind in posing as reality.

*Madhyamaka* Buddhism, or the Middle Way initiated by the Indian "Patriarch" of *Mahāyāna*, Nāgārjuna (second and third century AD), is no less adamant than *Advaita* in asserting the "nonessentiality" or "non-self-nature" of what we have been referring to as "metaphysical relativity." The ultimate lack of substance of phenomena is extended by Nāgārjuna to everything, including the Self, in concordance with the Buddhist teaching of *anattā* or no-self. Indeed, it could be argued that Nāgārjuna emphasizes further than *Advaita* the "unreal" character of phenomena in the sense that no absolute Selfhood is posited by him that would lend some reality to the latter. One of the fundamental reasons for this state of affairs lies in that, from a Buddhist point of view, metaphysics is determined by soteriology, and the concern for doctrinal conceptualization or perspective superseded by a focus on method. This means that the spiritual and moral reality of suffering is connected to craving, and craving is itself a function of an ignorance of the status of reality. The whole issue revolves, therefore, around an erroneous notion of the "substantiality" or "essence" of phenomena and the self. The basic intent of Nāgārjuna is to deny the "own being" (*svabhāva*)[18] of the latter, thereby freeing consciousness from its attachment to the sources of delusion (*moha*) and suffering. The Nāgārjunian rejection of "self-existence," "own being," or "inherent essence" is not to be equated, however, with an utter negation of the reality or existence of phenomena. It simply means, as we will discuss further, that there is no such thing, for Nāgārjuna, as an inherent, essential, timeless nature of phenomena that would define them as discrete entities.

What has just been specified indicates that the most proper way to characterize the ontological status of phenomena consists in denying both that they are "existent" and that they are "nonexistent," hence the characterization of *Madhyamaka* as Middle Way. This Middle Way is defined in contradistinction with two metaphysical pitfalls, which are often referred to, in Buddhist

commentaries, as "eternalism" and "nihilism." Eternalism refers to the status of
"essences" as independent from time and change, whereas nihilism is simply
the negation of any existence whatsoever:

> "Exists" implies grasping after eternalism. "Does not exist" implies
> the philosophy of annihilation. Therefore, a discerning person should
> not rely upon either existence or non-existence.[19]

According to Candrakīrti, a major seventh-century disciple and commentator
of Nāgārjuna, a lack of insightful and contemplative intelligence may result
in either of two errors with respect to the doctrine of emptiness: The first is a
confusion between emptiness and nothingness, or *śūnyatā* and *abhāva*. This is
the basis for the common Western misinterpretations of Buddhism as a form
of pessimism, or else nihilism. The second erroneous interpretation of *śūnyatā*
consists, in Guy Bugault's terms, in "hypostasizing" it, misleading one thereby
into a mental fixation that obstructs one's recognition of emptiness.[20] Let us
note, in this connection, that the characterization of phenomena as neither
"existent" nor "nonexistent" appears as analogous, but not identical, to the
*Advaitin* status of *Māyā* as neither "real" nor "unreal." A closer examination
shows that the matter is both ontological and epistemological in *Madhyamaka*
and *Advaita* alike, but with a definitely different emphasis in each case. Here
is a passage from Nāgārjuna that epitomizes the *Madhyamaka* outlook and will
help us bring it into sharp contrast with *Advaita*:

> When something is not related to anything, how then can that thing
> exist? For example, when it is not related to "long," how can "short" exist?
> When there is existence there is non-existence, as there is short when
> there is long. Since there is existence when there is non-existence,
> each of the two does not exist.[21]

As it appears plainly in the previous passage, the refutation of both "existence"
and "non-existence" is entirely connected to relationality, relativity, and the
duality and multiplicity they entail. Without relation, there is no existence
because existence is empirically and ontologically relational, and always implies
nonexistence, the same holding true in return for nonexistence in regard to
existence. For Nāgārjuna, the refutation of existence and nonexistence is therefore
founded both on ontological relationality and epistemological and linguistic
relativity. There is nothing that lies outside the range of this relativity, and
therefore everything is "empty," neither existent nor nonexistent.[22]

The originality of Nāgārjuna's perspective lies in his connecting *nirvāna*
to an existential recognition of the emptiness of all phenomena, without

which the "blowing out" of bound, deluded, and alienated consciousness would be impossible.[23] In this view, the origin and cessation of suffering that lie at the very core of the Buddhist intuition of reality are accounted for in terms of emptiness, which is none other than "dependent co-origination" or "relative conditioning," *pratītyasamutpāda*.[24] Accordingly, the direct methodical implication of *pratītyasamutpāda* appears on an existential level when referred to the central focus of Buddhism, to wit, suffering. As is well known, the latter is conceived as the result of a chain of conditioning that begins with ignorance and ends with birth and the manifold limitations and frustrations it entails:

> And what is dependent co-arising? From ignorance as a requisite condition come fabrications. From fabrications as a requisite condition comes consciousness. From consciousness as a requisite condition comes name-and-form. From name-and-form as a requisite condition come the six sense media. From the six sense media as a requisite condition comes contact. From contact as a requisite condition comes feeling. From feeling as a requisite condition comes craving. From craving as a requisite condition comes clinging/sustenance. From clinging/sustenance as a requisite condition comes becoming. From becoming as a requisite condition comes birth. From birth as a requisite condition, aging and death, sorrow, lamentation, pain, distress, and despair come into play. Such is the origination of this entire mass of stress and suffering.[25]

The end of ignorance, first link of this chain, is none other than the cessation of the delusion of ontological causality or arising that makes "substances" out of objects of experience. This cessation is the realization that there is in reality no arising and no ceasing. The doctrine of dependent co-origination is therefore intimately bound to the practical goal of the Buddha's teachings, which is the eradication of suffering. In other words, *pratītyasamutpāda* teaches that the above chain should not be understood as a sequence of causal links, since its doctrine reveals, through meditative intuition, the nonsubstantiality and emptiness of the various links themselves, and in fact of the whole chain of phenomena. Realizing *nirvāna* means realizing the truth of *pratītyasamutpāda*. This realization amounts to a recognition of the nonsubstantiality of suffering itself, without which recognition there would not be any way out of the latter into *nirvāna*.[26]

To sum up our previous reflections, *Pratītyasamutpāda* could be succinctly outlined as follows. Everything whatsoever is relational, and therefore relative and contingent, that is neither ontologically independent nor metaphysically necessary. Nothing, therefore, can be legitimately substantialized, objectified, reified, nor even quite adequately verbalized. Nothing is a self-existent substance ontologically separated from other existents, nothing is an object independent of a subject, nothing is a "thing" if by "thing" is meant a reality defined by a substance and circumscribed by it.

### Paradoxes of Reality and Non-Reality: Appearance and Emptiness

The preceding remarks are indicative of a sharp contrast between *Madhyamaka* emptiness and the relativity of the Advaitic *Māyā* which is, as we have seen, revealed by That which is not relative, or *Ātman*. In fact, *Māyā* is not real because it is not *Ātman,* but it is—in a sense—not unreal because there is only *Ātman*, and *Ātman* is Reality as such. It is important to note, in this connection, the way in which the "not-real" aspect of "other-than-the-Ultimate" is qualified in Shankara's *Advaita*. This is illustrated by the onto-cosmological dimensions of Shankara's doctrine of *Māyā*, and more specifically the doctrine of the *gunas*, upon which we touched earlier. The *gunas* are the three cosmo-logical principles known as *tamas, rajas,* and *sattva.* Now, it is quite clear that as cosmological principles these three *gunas* belong to *Māyā* since the cosmos pertains to the latter. However, it appears that the principles of inertia and passion respectively epitomized by *tamas* and *rajas* are not to be placed on the same ontological level as the ascending quality of *sattva,* which is luminous, pure, and Reality-centered. Therefore, *sattva* is like a seed or a trace of the Real in the "nonreal," and it is as such "not unreal." Shankara writes:

> The property of *tamas* is to cover, as scattering is the property of *rajas.* It makes things appear to be what they are not, and that is the cause of bondage, and even of decentralization [projec-tion]. . . . Pure *sattva* is blissfulness, realization of Self, supreme peace of attainment, cheerfulness, and an abiding quality in the Self, by which one becomes ever blissful.[27]

The preceding quotes make it plain that one can distinguish, within relativity, levels of reality that could be approximately referred to as "higher *Māyā*" and "lower *Māyā*." The "higher *Māyā*," as epitomized by the *guna sattva* provides us with a picture of relativity in which the perspective of *Māyā* as "not real" is largely counterbalanced by the point of view of *Māyā* "not being unreal." This means that *Māyā* is in a certain sense a "manifestation" of *Ātman*, although the term *manifestation* would normally not be satisfactorily applicable in the context of *Advaita* inasmuch as the main *Advaitin* emphasis lies upon

*Māyā* as an epistemological obstacle to metaphysical recognition, rather than as a positive projection of *Ātman*.

In contradistinction with *Advaita*, the perspective of *Madhyamaka* is less prone to acknowledge this secondary "not unreal" dimension of relativity and more inclined to emphasize more exclusively its "not real" aspect by ignoring qualitative distinctions within the context of *pratītyasamutpāda*. There are three ways, however, in which one must qualify this statement. First, as we have mentioned, phenomena are no less "nonexistent" than "existent." Secondly, *Madhyamaka* Buddhism makes use of a concept of reality, or *tattva*, which, without being the equivalent of the concept of Self, or *Ātman*, is nevertheless denotative of truth or "things as they are." In this context, *Madhyamaka* draws a very clear distinction between *svabhāva*, which is an ontological notion, and *tattva*, which pertains primarily to epistemology. The latter refers to reality as it is, in its truth, but this reality is not to be identified with existence as commonly understood, nor with nonexistence either: its status transcends the duality of existence and nonexistence. *Tattva* is the "object of a cognition without an object,"[28] in the sense that it is a recognition of the emptiness of all objects, and of the subject itself as dependent upon an object. Nonduality is here radicalized to the point of abolishing not only the duality of subject and object, as in *Advaita*, but even the very terms of the duality. This "consciousness-without-an-object," to make use of Franklin Merrell-Wolff's expression, or nondual wisdom, *Advayajñāna*, coincides with the recognition of *tattva*.

The recognition of *tattva* is none other than the goal of Buddhism: it points to the end of the Buddhist wayfaring as leading from suffering, *dukkha*, to a state of "blowing out" of the causes of suffering, *nirvāna*. But at the same time, in its ultimate truth, it has been deemed, at least as a perplexing metaphysical riddle, to deny the essential reality of the path and its goal. This is the supreme spiritual paradox of *Madhyamaka* that introduces us to the third qualification of our argument concerning the *Madhyamaka* nonrecognition of the "not unreal" aspect of phenomena. This paradox is most directly expressed by Nāgārjuna in his *Mūlamadhyamakakārikā*:

> The Buddha did not teach the appeasement of all objects, the appeasement of obsession, and the auspicious as some thing to some one at some place.[29]

The meaning of this prima facie perplexing statement makes full sense when referred to the fundamental distinction between two kinds of truth; this is the doctrine of *satyadvayavibhāga*. Nāgārjuna articulates the distinction between conventional truth (*sammuti-sacca* or *vohāra-sacca*) and ultimate truth (*paramattha-sacca*) as follows:

The teaching of the doctrine by the Buddhas is based upon two
truths: truth relating to worldly conventions and truth in terms
of ultimate fruit.

Those who do not understand the distinction between these
two truths do not understand the profound truth embodied in the
Buddha's message. Without relying upon convention, the ultimate
fruit is not taught. Without understanding the ultimate fruit,
freedom is not attained.[30]

The truth, in an ultimate sense, is none other than emptiness or codependent origination. However, the teachings of the Buddhas need to make use
of conventional truth in order to lead mankind toward the ultimate truth. In
that sense, conventional truth is none other than the *upāya*, or the "expedient
mean" par excellence, through which people may be brought toward ultimate
reality. The paramount distinction between "teaching" and "ultimate fruit"
is akin to that between doctrine and method, or that between intellectual
cognition and spiritual recognition. Conventional truth is both a necessity in
terms of teaching and a potential impediment in terms of recognition.[31] The
latter aspect appears in the fact that conventional truth unknowingly relies on
linguistic phenomena that pertain to what the *Madhyamaka* tradition refers to
as *prajñaptir upādāya*, which is understood by most commentators as "dependent designations." A radical interpretation of this concept, in the wake of
Candrakīrti, sees all designations as not related in any essential way to objects,
but as constituting, rather, a conventional network of metaphorical modes of
cognitive perception that are ultimately illusory. This view implies that emptiness itself as a concept is necessarily a dependent and provisional designation
and therefore itself empty. Such an understanding allows for a maximal, and
indeed radical, differentiation between emptiness as such and the doctrine of
emptiness, the latter being subsumed under the realm of conventional truth,
the former denoting ultimate truth. When other commentators and translators
have resisted such an understanding of the concept of codependent origination
as pure "dependent designation" they have done so on account of its effectiveness in leading to spiritual recognition, an effectiveness that seems incompatible
with pure emptiness and utter lack of referentiality.[32] Douglas Berger has thus
argued, against the emptiness of all uses of language as implying "being," in
favor of a distinction between two kinds of linguistic practices, one assuming
being and the other not. The latter is the language of *upāya*, which makes it
possible to refer to the emptiness of reality through its own referential transpar-
ence, as it were, that is, without falling into a kind of self-substantalization.
In this sense, the most effective *upāya* is the one that invites us not to treat
it as an independent substance. Regardless of whether one universalizes the

view that designations are codependently arisen and empty or one leaves room for a conventional language adequate to convey the truth of emptiness, epistemological truth needs to be equated with that which produces positive outcomes or recognition.[33]

As the previous pages have intimated, emptiness is not the essence of realities in the sense in which a transcendent source, or a transcendent paradigm of their being would be, but it is so if we understand by essence the basic "structure" of reality: "We state that whatever is dependent arising, that is emptiness."[34] This explanation, for Buddhists, is not the recognition of a Supreme Object, because no object can be supreme in the sense of being independent of reciprocal conditioning in its being. It is not the recognition of a Substantial Subject either, since no subject is without being relational to an object upon which it depends to be a subject. For Nāgārjuna, the position of a Subject or Self as *Ātman* necessarily gives, or lends, some substantial existence to all phenomena. This is so because the position of an *Ātman* that would be independent, as it were, from universal codependent origination, is incompatible with the latter and therefore implies the self-substantiality of everything else. To postulate a Self is to substantialize not only the Self but also, by the same token, everything else, since the substantiality of the Self is mirrored in the countless substances to which it is immanent. In that sense, Nāgārjuna goes a step farther than *Advaitin* metaphysics in stressing the "nonreality" of phenomena. By excluding the consideration of a reality that would be exempt from *pratītyasamutpāda*, Nāgārjuna asserts an utter and fundamental emphasis on the conditioned nonsubstantiality of everything to which the mind could cling.

The all-encompassing validity of *pratītyasamutpāda* must lead us to ponder its meaning with respect to the ontological status of *nirvāna* itself; it must be considered, in particular, whether *pratītyasamutpāda* does not deprive *nirvāna* of any ultimate reality and meaning, thereby betraying a radical incompatibility with the ultimate goal of Buddhism itself, as some of Nāgārjuna's opponents have argued. Early Buddhist teachings from the *Abhidharma* canon[35] point to a nirvānic mode of being from the vantage point of which the relatively conditioned can be perceived as such, without being itself relatively conditioned, but on the contrary literally unconditioned. This is expressed by one of the most famous canonical Pali passages:

> There exists, monks, that which is unborn, that which is unbecome, that which is uncreated, that which is unconditioned. For if there were not, monks, that which is uncreated, that which is unconditioned, there would not be made known here the escape from that which is born, from that which is become, from that which is created, from that which is conditioned. Yet since there exists,

monks, that which is unborn, that which is unbecome, that which
is uncreated, that which is unconditioned, there is therefore made
known the escape from that which is born, from that which is
become, from that which is created, from that which is conditioned.[36]

Thus, there is a sense in which the "not unreal," the "unbecome," the "unborn,"
which is transcendent to the "unreal," the "become," and the "born" is also
mysteriously immanent to them, without which the validity and effectiveness of
the path itself would be called into question. *Mahāyāna* Buddhism has drawn
the ultimate conclusions from this principle in the paradoxical recognition
that "*nirvāna* is *samsāra* and *samsāra* is *nirvāna*," or that the "unbecome is the
become and the become is the unbecome," or else, transcendence is immanence
and immanence is transcendence. In this perspective, however, the transcendent
is neither apprehended as a supreme Object (God) nor as an ultimate Subject
(*Ātman*). It is neither Object nor Substance: Neither an ob-ject, that is, an
element of a cognitive duality, nor a sub-stance, that is, a reality that would
be independent of codependent relationality by being, as it were, "sub-jacent"
to it. In Nāgārjuna's thought, transcendence is envisaged as immanent in that
the "object" of recognition or "ultimate truth" is the very "structure" of an
experienced reality. The empirical problem, for Buddhists, is a "subjective"
problem, or how to stop the mental process that inherently objectifies and
substantializes, and is, thereby, a source of craving and suffering. Although not
being the only Buddhist position on the matter—as testified, for example, by
the definitely and ultimately affirmative bent of influential streams of Chinese
Buddhism—the *Madhyamaka* response is that deconditioning is only possible
through "negation," or rather through the "negation of negation"—since conditioned consciousness is a negation of the unconditioned, which opens access
to an adequate perception of reality.[37]

## The Unity of Reality

By contrast with the previously examined metaphysical accounts of relativity,
we would like to review and analyze, in the second section of this chapter,
the ways in which some major and influential forms of mystical theology are
characterized by an emphasis on the "not unreal" dimension of that which is
not the Ultimate Reality. In doing so, our objective will not merely be to draw
a contrast with the *Advaita* and *Madhyamaka* perspectives, but also to look
into some of the theoretical and spiritual implications of this contrast. In order
to do so, we will focus on the Śaivite perspective of Abhinavagupta (ca AD
950–1020) and some other authoritative figures and texts of the nondualistic

Tantric tradition on the one hand and, on the other hand, on the doctrine of the "Unity of Being" (*wahdat al-wujūd*) exemplified by Sufi masters of gnosis such as Ibn al-'Arabī (1167–1240) and 'Abd al-Karīm al-Jīlī (1366–1424). It is important to recognize, as a starting point, that both perspectives are focused, a priori, on the Divine Reality as it is envisaged respectively by the Hindu Śaivite and Islamic traditions. In this context, Śiva and *Allāh*—notwithstanding the profound contextual differences that shape their reality—are considered on the level of the Personal Divinity referred to in Hindu and Islamic scriptures as well as in devotional practices, but also on the level of the Divine Essence as such, which both traditions understand to lie beyond all determinations, qualities, and actions, including the personal dimension of Divinity.[38] Mystical metaphysicians hailing from these traditions, such as Abhinavagupta and Ibn al-'Arabī, have in fact no difficulty whatsoever envisaging Śiva and *Allāh* on these two distinct ontological levels.[39] Hence, Śaivism considers Śiva as *Paramaśiva*, or Ultimate Reality, and as such, "It is non-relational consciousness."[40] At the same time, each and every Śaivite treatise begins with words of dedication and worship to Śiva, and the latter has been the focus of devotional adoration on the part of those Hindus who made him the more and more exclusive object of religious fervor.[41] Similarly, *Allāh* is both the Personal Deity who speaks in and through the *Qur'ān*, and the super-ontological Essence (*dhāt*) that is both boundless and unknowable. Jīlī clearly characterizes the latter as follows:

> Know that the Essence [*adh-dhāt*] signifies the Absolute Being in its state of being stripped of all connection, relation, assignation and aspect. . . . This is the pure Essence in which are manifested neither Names nor Attributes nor relations nor connections nor anything else.[42]

This passage marks without any ambiguity the distinction between the Divine Essence and the Personal God as comprised of aspects and involved in relationships. Two general conclusions may be drawn from the preceding remarks: first, Śaivism and Sufism present us with perspectives that are centered a priori on the objective Reality of the Divine rather than being primarily focused on the subjective need for deliverance or freedom from suffering—in other words, they begin with God's fullness rather than man's lack; secondly, their capacity to envisage the Divine both as unconditionally absolute and personally "engaged" allows them to recognize the Divine Presence both in its ontological immanence and creativity as flowing from its own infinite Essence and in its revelatory and devotional relationality. Now, both dimensions ascribe a significant coefficient of reality to the relative realm since relationality and creativity presuppose a degree of ontological reality on the part of the latter.

Furthermore, let us note that the aforestated regard for immanence is symbolically and suggestively marked by the fact that both perspectives make a
significant use of the image of the relationship between the ocean and its
waves—notwithstanding the general consonance of this symbol with mystical
expression in general and its occurrences outside of these two universes of
meaning—as a representation of the relationship between the Ultimate and
the non-Ultimate, or the Absolute and the relative.[43] In Abhinavagupta's metaphysical account, the Supreme Self is equated to the ocean of consciousness
(*sindhu, ambhonidhi, samudra*), the waves (*ūrmi*) of which are the vibrations
(*spanda*) of consciousness that constitute finite reality. Describing the latter,
Abhinavagupta writes:

> For that vibration, which is a slight motion of a special kind, a
> unique vibrating light, is the wave of the ocean of consciousness,
> without which there is no consciousness at all. For the character of
> the ocean is that it is sometimes filled with waves and sometimes
> waveless. This consciousness is the essence of all.[44]

The ocean is a direct symbol of the infinite consciousness, which is none
other than Śiva. As intimated above, the symbol is, moreover, apt to connote
the dimension of energy, motion, and vibration that characterizes consciousness
in Śaivism. Similarly, the symbol of the ocean is used in Sufism as a suggestive
pointer to the Divine Essence in its limitlessness. Thus, Ibn al-'Arabī's prayer,
"Enter me, O Lord, into the deep of the Ocean of Thine Infinite Oneness!" is,
as Martin Lings has indicated, one among many instances of a reference to the
ocean which is "mentioned again and again" in the treatises of the Sufis.[45] For
Ibn al-'Arabī, the knowledge of God, like the knowledge of self with which it
is intimately connected, is understood as "an ocean without shore" since "there
is no end to the knowledge of God" who is infinite reality.[46] As for Rūmī, in
conformity with his approach of the Divine as Love, he identifies the latter
with "an ocean whose depths cannot be plumbed."[47] It is quite clear that the
choice of this symbol is already indicative of perspectives that are particularly
attuned to a focus on the boundless and creative infinity of the Ultimate on
the one hand, and on the "participation" of the waves into this divine ocean
on the other hand, thereby suggesting the "not unreal" aspect of the former.

## Reality as Creative Freedom

It has been repeatedly asserted by scholars that Kashmiri Śaivite metaphysics
and mysticism, by contrast with *Advaita Vedānta*, are primarily focused on the

dynamic and active dimensions of Absolute Consciousness, namely, Will, or *icchā*, and Action, or *kriyā*. These attributes of the Absolute derive from Śiva's primary understanding as utter freedom. The *Śiva Sūtras* identify absolute freedom as the nature of Śiva par excellence:

> Though Highest Śiva has infinite number of other attributes, such as eternity, all-pervasiveness, formlessness etc., yet because eternity etc. are possible elsewhere also, here it is intended to show the predominance of absolute freedom which is not possible in any other being.[48]

In other words, the Supreme Liberty of the Absolute Consciousness is the essence of this Consciousness.[49] In this metaphysical context, freedom involves two main aspects, which are a lack of constraint on the one hand, and an infinite creativity on the other. The first character implies that there is nothing external to Śiva that could either limit, compel, or contain Him in any way, which ultimately means that everything is Śiva.[50] This is the doctrine known in India as *ābhāsavāda,* or the thesis of "limited manifestation," following which limited entities themselves are delimitations of the limitless consciousness of Śiva. The second aspect, which is in fact intimately connected to the first, points to the dynamic and productive nature of the Absolute that Śaivism always envisages as ever flowing in an unending multiplicity of new forms. This is the doctrine of *svātantryavāda*, the thesis of self-dependency, according to which the intrinsic power of the Ultimate is the utterly free energy of conscious manifestation.[51] Manifestation is in the nature of Supreme Consciousness, and this principle, when fully understood, silences any question as to the why of existence and its myriad of forms and contents.[52] This is so because the realm of finite reality is, in essence, none other than Śiva himself, the Supreme Consciousness, that both manifests and binds itself through its Śaktic vibration and projections. In the Śaivite perspective, everything is pure Consciousness or *Cit*. There is not an ounce of existence, on whatever level of being, which is not Śiva's consciousness. Everything is consciousness, and therefore everything *is*. Relative beings *are,* and they are *as* limitations of the Supreme Consciousness. In this sense, Śiva is both absolute and relative, and He, in fact, transcends the two categories of absoluteness and relativity. It is clear that the Śaivite emphasis lies on the "not unreal" dimension of the relative realm inasmuch as it is none other than the unbound, infinite domain of Consciousness and, as such, gives potential access to the latter.

This dynamic and creative process through which the Absolute Consciousness outpours into multiplicity is highlighted in the central teaching of the intrinsic union of Śiva and Śakti. While Śiva is pure Consciousness (*citi*) and

Light (*prakāśa*), Śakti can be characterized as the intrinsic and efficient power of Self-revelation of Śiva through which he manifests, supports, and reabsorbs the realm of manifestation. In this sense, Śakti is none other than *Svātantrya*, or the intrinsic energy of Śiva.[53] By contrast with any dualistic understanding of Śakti, such as in the *Nyāya*, Śaivism emphasizes the intrinsic unity of being and its power, the relationship between the two being akin to the indissociable unity between fire and its power to burn.[54] As such Śakti is the inner, dynamic reality of Śiva, and their intimate unity is more powerfully asserted as we consider the essence of the Ultimate, while their latent duality, although more and more perceptible as we descend the stages of the limitations of Consciousness by and through manifestation, is nevertheless ever transcended by Śiva's sovereign Infinity and unending ability to affirm Himself in and through the negations of Himself. As Paul Eduardo Muller-Ortega puts it, "[Śiva] is always the 'third' element that transcends, undercuts, and in the end, unifies all possible oppositions."[55] To this could be added that He is the third because He is the first and because He is essentially none other than the second. Śiva always reconciles all oppositions because He is, with and through Śakti, the very productive source from which they emerge and into which they flow.

In Kashmiri Śaivism, Śakti is the principle of universal relativity, since it is through Her that everything is brought into existence. By contrast with the *Advaitin Māyā*, Śakti is not ontologically ambiguous nor deficient—although She manifests in a variety of degrees—but rather powerfully and creatively productive. As such, she is less a negation of Śiva, as *Māyā* would be one of *Ātman*, than like an inner dimension of Śiva that actualizes and exteriorizes His freedom to be all that He can be, that is, everything. This being said, while Śakti is eminently affirmative and dynamic, there is also a vantage point from which she could be considered as a kind of "negation" of Śiva. This somewhat negative aspect of Śakti appears inasmuch as Śiva being infinite and undivided Reality, she cannot but appear in some respects and on some levels as the principle that brings out the finite and discrete realities that delimit and "divide" the Śivaic plenitude. In that sense, Śakti is within Śiva the seed of the principle of negation, limitation, and division that allows for the unfolding or outpouring of Śiva's infinite nature on the level of finite realities. However, Śaivism is not intent on attributing this negativity to Śakti herself, but rather to the lower ranges of the process she triggers. Thus, Śakti is first and foremost the principle through which the nature of Śiva as infinite reality and sovereign power is affirmed. In fact, when Śiva is approached as Emptiness, Śakti will be deemed to express Divine Fullness.[56] On that account, Śiva being characterized as *śūnyatā*, like an empty sky in which the colors of the dawn are shimmering, Śakti will be the fullness of these colors:

The [dawn] sky, though one, appears radiant white, red and blue, and the clouds accordingly seem various; so pure, free consciousness shines brilliantly with its countless forms, though they are nothing at all.[57]

Here, Emptiness is like the reverse side of Fullness, if one may say so, or the silvering void of the mirror in which Fullness manifests its wealth of reality: it is the metaphysical "ambiance" of universal exteriorization. It stands "under" Fullness as an infinite Sub-stance that ever transcends the flow of delimitations.

As the principle of projection and manifestation, Śakti needs to be considered on a plurality of levels. Indeed, as we will further suggest, the capacity to consider the projection of Consciousness on a multiplicity of degrees can be deemed to be one of the hallmarks of metaphysical perspectives that emphasize the "not unreal" character of relative phenomena, among which Śaivism and the Sufi doctrine of Unity rank eminently. Thus, Abhinavagupta's foremost disciple, Ksemarāja, distinguishes three levels of Śakti, which are Parāśakti, Parāparāśakti, and Aparāśakti, or Supreme, Intermediate, and Inferior Śakti. These three levels subsume no less than thirty-four degrees of projection of Consciousness, or tattvas, from Śiva Himself as pure "I" to prthivī, or earth, the utmost limit of condensation and materialization of consciousness.

The Supreme Śakti, Parāśakti, while pertaining to abheda or "non-difference," also refers to the level of Pure Consciousness that is already the seed of the process of production; it is, among other possible characterizations, the level of vimarśa. Jaideva Singh notes that the term vimarśa implies through its root the meaning of "touching," and through its prefix a reference to the mind, probably through the implications of negation, discrimination, but also intensification.[58] It is the free and conscious self-determination of Absolute Consciousness. Vimarśa refers to the emergence of a state of Self-Awareness within the Absolute Consciousness Itself.[59] It is in fact none other than svātantrya, or utter freedom of manifestation, and this freedom manifests itself through a sort of "doubling" awareness of oneself that is at the same time source of differentiation and manifestation. This emergence of vimarśa is described by Abhinavagupta as having four stages, which could be symbolized by the numbers 1, 2, 3, and 0.[60] There is, first, an intrinsic move to differentiate the other from within the self, secondly a reaffirmation of the self in contradistinction with the other, then a unification of the two, and a final reabsorption of their union within the Infinite Self. The selfsame Consciousness is therefore affirmed in and through negation, and reaffirmed further in and through the transcending of the unity of affirmation and negation. This parāśakti is identified by Abhinavagupta to the pronoun I because it is the one and only

supreme Self-Consciousness that affirms Itself through the myriad of productions, transformations, and reintegrations through which It proceeds. As such,
*parāśakti* is that which makes everything real, or not unreal. The centrality of
*parāśakti* means that Śaivism is always inclined to approach phenomena as "not
unreal," precisely because they are produced by her ontological energy, which is
none other than Śiva's. Hence, *Parāśakti* is in fact identified by Abhinavagupta
with the couple Śiva-Śakti which is, in this case, considered as an intrinsic
bi-unity of I-consciousness, and not as a duality. As a linguistic expansion of
this principle, Abhinavagupta considers the Śiva-Śakti Supreme Consciousness
as being comprised of I-ness—or *Aham*, an expansion of I-ness—or *A-ha-m*,
in the sense that it contains the first Sanskrit letter, A, symbolizing Śiva, the
last letter, H, symbolizing Śakti, and their "passion" expressed by the totality
of the alphabet that joins them together.[61]

At a second stage, that of *parāparāśakti*, we enter the realm of that which
could be most satisfactorily referred to as relativity, both in the sense of a field
that takes us away from absolute and pure Consciousness, and more specifically
in that the relationship between subject and object, unity and diversity, is most
emphatically present therein; this is the domain of *bhedābheda*, or "identity
and difference." It is on this level that the Unity of Consciousness and the
multiplicity of its productions are as it were meeting in the confrontation of
Consciousness and its objects, the latter still being endowed, however, with the
Light of the former. In this connection, Abhinavagupta associates the realm of
*parāparāśakti* with the pronoun *thou* and with Śakti (inasmuch as she can be
distinguished from Śiva) because it is the domain of correlates, as well as the
field of cross-relations between subject and object, unity and diversity, pure
consciousness and its productions. The Śaivite sage also associates this intermediary level with the first, second, and third degrees of consciousness below the
Supreme bi-unity of Śiva and Śakti, that is *Sadāśiva* (the revealer, by contrast with
*Maheśvara*, i.e., the Supreme who conceals), *Īśvara* (the creator who introduces a
slight gap in non-difference), and *Śuddhavidyā* (pure knowledge of equilibrium).
This ontological zone of contact, junction, and relative equilibrium is also, by
the same token, one of ambiguity, and therefore a site of potential bifurcation.
What Mark Dyczkowski calls the middle level of "unity-in-difference" is the
critical parting point between the recognition of the one pure Consciousness in
and through the diversity of its manifestations, and the deadly submission to
their binding limitations. At this stage, the polarity I-thou reveals ontological
division without for that ever essentially severing the unity and integrity of
Śiva's Supreme Consciousness. *Parāparā* means both identity and difference in
the sense of *bheda* (difference) and *abedha* (non-difference) being in equilibrium,
or one and diverse at the same time. It is therefore at this intermediary point
of junction—and separation—that contact with the Supreme Consciousness

from the vantage point of multiplicity can be established, or, conversely, it may be the channel through which unity may be overwhelmed by diversity. In other words, it is at this juncture that the potentiality of liberation and that of alienation and perdition are both most affirmed.[62] Therein lies a "precarious balance" between the subject and the object—or rather the other subject, thou—inwardness and outwardness, the number two referring in this case to a relatedness that provides one with the possibility of experiencing both terms within the context of an underlying unity of consciousness. In the "thou" of *parāparāśakti* the I of Supreme Consciousness is still at hand, as it were, since Śakti can be recognized as the other "side" of the same subject, a side that also shares in the same consciousness.

On the third level of projection of Śakti, or *aparāśakti,* we move forward or downward from the realm of duality in unity to that of a multiplicity increasingly abstracted from unity. It is the realm of difference and distinction, or *bheda*. It ranges over twenty-nine *tattva*s or degrees of Śaktic projection, the highest source of which is *Māyā*, or more exactly *Mahāmāyā*. With the latter, we enter the domain of *bheda* or difference, or at least its emergence (the latter being associated with *Mahāmāyā* and the former with *Māyā*). This is the level of maximal objectification and thereby diversified exteriorization, of Śakti. It is the realm of multiplicity, fragmentation, and knots where the underlying unity of Consciousness has become most difficult to perceive and realize. The relative balance between I and thou is broken as the scales are tilted on the side of objectification. Abhinavagupta relates this level of Śakti to *nara*, that is, empirical and phenomenal reality, and to the third personal pronoun *he*. Here the emphasis is on the multiplicity of empirical experience, the focus of consciousness being brought down from unity into diversity and multiplicity. *Aparāśakti* takes us down from the recognition of the "I" in the "thou" to a lower degree at which consciousness is not recognized in alterity but simply apprehended and treated as a mere object. It is important and instructive to note that Kashmiri Śaivism generally makes use of the concept of *māyā* to refer primarily to a lower dimension of Śakti, at the degree of *bheda* or difference, where the pole object has taken precedence over the pole subject, or the domain of the "insensible" that lies on the outer edges of Consciousness has obfuscated, as it were, the Light of Consciousness. This teaching is made explicit in Abhinavagupta's *Parātrīśikā-Vivarana*, a source in which the sixth and seventh *tattva*s are associated with *Māyā*.[63] This is a way to suggest a distinction between Śakti as such and *Māyā*, thereby emphasizing the positive function of the former. Along seemingly diverging lines, the *Śiva Sūtra* considers *Māyā* in three different aspects or levels, which are *Māyā Śakti, Māyā Tattva,* and *Māyā Granthi*: the first is the freedom of consciousness that manifests Śiva's nature, the second is the objective limitation and the fragmentation that is

inherent to the process of this manifestation, while the third is the coming
into contact of the two in and through which *Māyā* functions as a principle
of bondage by "confusing" the two levels of the free Supreme Consciousness
and objective fragmentation. However close this latter "confusion" comes to
the *Advaitin* concept of superimposition upon *Ātman,* it is most significant to
note that the *Śiva Sūtra* considers that *Māyā* can and in fact must be "purified"
by the knowledge of Śiva consciousness: in other words, the matter is not so
much to dispel *Māyā* as to cleanse it by reintegrating into its highest aspect
as Śakti. At any rate, whether *Māyā* is identified with the lowest degrees of
Śaktic projection and its *bheda* aspect as if to preserve the positive function
of Śakti, or it is conceived as being susceptible to be purified through a sort
of reintegration into its Śaktic roots, it is clear in either way that Kashmiri
Śaivism is intent on emphasizing the "not unreal" aspect of Śaktic projections
and productions.

     While the previous pages have outlined the various degrees on which
Śakti manifests, fragments, limits, and reabsorbs consciousness, it must be
added that these various Śaktic ontological levels, although delineating in one
sense a decrease in consciousness, as illustrated by the series of descending
*tattvas,* need be integrated in order to account for the full spectrum of the
unfolding of Śiva-Śakti, and therefore the whole range of reality. It must be
so since there is ultimately and essentially, indeed *really,* not any gap in the
unity of Consciousness that is Śiva. Śakti does not lessen the plenitude of Śiva,
she manifests it, and therefore entails the paradox of its self-negation. Accordingly, the three planes of Śakti that we have sketched above, namely, supreme,
intermediary, and lower, encompass and express the integrality of Śiva's nature.
This ontological totality is moreover mirrored in realizational perfection, in the
sense that the supreme spiritual maturity and utmost inner deliverance lies in
the recognition of the essential unity of all the moments of the unfolding of
Śakti within Śiva's underlying consciousness. As Mark Dyczkowski puts it:

> The harmonious union [*sāmarasya*] of these three planes are Bhairava's
> [Śiva] Supreme glory, the radiance of the fullness of His power
> (*pūrnaśakti*) which fills the entire universe.[64]

The vertical projection of Śakti is also the key to the reintegration of delimited
consciousness into the One.

     Aside from these vertical degrees of manifestation, projection, contrac-
tion, fragmentation, and limitation, Śakti must also be considered in its various
modes, among which most important ones the tradition mentions *caitanya,*
*sphurattā, spanda, mahāsattā,* and *parāvāk.*[65] In itself, the absolute Consciousness
is apprehended as Light (*prakāśa*) in the sense of being the substratum and

the condition of possibility of everything. Without *prakāśa* there would not be a metaphysical "context" for reality, if one may say so. Absolute Consciousness keeps reality alighted at every new instant through its Śaktic energy by the power of *citi* or *caitanya*.[66] The way in which Supreme Consciousness is understood to project her power in unfolding the manifold existence is sometimes compared to reflections on a screen or a mirror. In the second *sūtra* of Ksemarāja's *Pratyabhijñāhṛidayam* we read:

> By the power of her own will [alone], she [*citi*] unfolds the universe upon her own screen [i.e., in herself as the basis of the universe].[67]

The commentary of the same *sūtra* indicates that *citi* unfolds the universe "like a city in a mirror, which though non-different from it appears as different." *Citi* is the very reality, the very being that underlies all manifestation, and from within which all manifestation springs forth. As for *mahāsattā*, which is none other than *citi* in its aspect of infinite wealth of being, it has been translated as "absolute possibility of being," or literally "great possibility of being."[68] It is the metaphysical equivalent of the Supreme Freedom of Śiva, or the All-Possibility that is his infinite nature. Closer to the extrinsic effects of this nature, *sphurattā* is the radiance of the world-producing energy of Śakti. Jaideva Singh translates this term as "throb-like gleam of the absolute Freedom of the Divine bringing about the world-process."[69] It refers to the radiating projection of Śakti as manifested in objective forms and subjective senses, like the innumerable rays of the Sun of Being. As such, *sphurattā* refers to a sort of oscillation or quivering of light, an "immovable movement" in and by which the light of consciousness is propagated from the conscious Subject to its objectifications.[70] Notwithstanding the importance of the three aforementioned characterizations of the I-Consciousness, the two most representative aspects, or modes of manifestation, of Śakti in Tantric Śaivism are no doubt *spanda* and *parāvāk*, pulsation or vibration and "Supreme Word" or "Speech." It belongs to *spanda* and *parāvāk* to differentiate most clearly the Śaivite perspective from other Hindu perspectives such as *Advaita*. These two concepts bring to the fore the centrality of the rhythmic, pulsating, and vibrating energy of reality and consciousness in Śaivism, as well as the parallel Śaivite emphasis on the sound-centered, linguistic, and "mantric" dimension of Śakti. The concepts of pulsation and vibration (*spanda*) express a sense of continuity in discontinuity, a kind of rhythmic alternation that is the very life of the Absolute. The Infinite and finite realities are linked in a series of expansions and contractions the essential continuity of which is to be grasped through and in its apparent discontinuity. The Tantric emphasis is on succession as alternation of manifestation and reabsorption. In its origin, the vibration of the Absolute is none other than the disturbance of an equilibrium that results in opposite motions toward manifestation and reintegration.[71] In a sense, relativity is the very pulsation of the Absolute: it is not only the exteriorization, fragmentation, and ultimately objectification of Consciousness, it is also the very motion through which Consciousness is realized both in a centrifugal and centripetal way.

Relativity is dynamic motion, and the latter is like the rhythm of the Absolute: hence, Śaivism's thrust in celebrating the totality of the cycle of expansion and contraction. By contrast with *Advaita* and *Madhyamaka,* there is a strong emphasis on levels of succession and propagation, degrees of projection and continuity. If relativity is primarily considered as "not unreal" it is because the contraction is no less real than the expansion, the manifestation no less important than the reintegration. The dynamic nature of relativity stems from its being the result of a disequilibrium inherent to the nature of the Absolute. However, this disequilibrium is not as much a lack—which it is also, relatively speaking, in its results—as it is a fullness—in its principle: it is an intrinsic motion toward radiation and vibration, a tendency to be one and other, unity and diversity.[72] If equilibrium is conceived as a static unity without productive energy, then the Absolute Consciousness can be described as ontological disequilibrium. To speak of disequilibrium amounts here to perceive the root of diversity within unity as self-consciousness. It goes without saying that the disequilibrium in question is in fact, from another point of view, part of a greater equilibrium that has to do with the ebb and flow or the pulsation of reality at large. In another sense, one could also refer to this creative fullness as to a delicate, ever mobile equilibrium between subjective consciousness and its objectification. The importance and centrality of the *parāvāk,* or Supreme Word or Speech, in Śaivism, pertains to this inherent exteriorization and objectification, which is none other than the very freedom of the Absolute:

> Consciousness has as its essential nature reflective awareness [*pratya-vamarśa*]; it is the supreme Word [*parāvāk*] that arises freely. It is freedom in the absolute sense, the sovereignty [*aiśvaryam*] of the supreme Self.[73]

Divine Speech is both internal and external: the latter is obvious since the Word is manifested outwardly, but the former is also a central tenet of Kashmiri *Śaivism* precisely because there is no consciousness that is not a priori language. The articulation of Divine Speech is already present *ab initio* in the Supreme Consciousness but it is so in a "compressed" way (*saṁhṛtarūpa*).[74] The Absolute Consciousness is never in a state of nonawareness of itself and therefore in a sense never in a state of non-utterance, albeit non-articulated. Relativity as utterance and projection is already present in Absolute Consciousness, hence its not "nonreal" ontological status since nonbeing cannot be part of Being. The Supreme is both Consciousness and Speech, *parāvāk,* in its most essential, intrinsic ipseity.[75] Once exteriorized, fragmented, and objectified into signifiers and signified, Speech becomes, or reveals itself as, the "ontological alphabet" of universal reality. This is the concept of *mātrkā,* the divine matrix of all phonemic manifestations, but also, and by the same token, of all onto-logical emanations.[76] The projection or emanation of the energies of *parāvāk* into letters and sounds is closely dependent upon its triadic division into Will, Knowledge, and Action, or *icchā, jñāna,* and *kriyā.* These three aspects are respectively connected with Śakti, Sadāśiva, and Īśvara who are, as we may recall, the three levels stemming from the bi-unity of Śiva-Śakti and preceding the level of *Māyā.*[77] Below the level of the distinction without separation char-acteristic of this Triad, the manifestation and objectification of Consciousness appears like a garland of letters and sounds that constitute the emanation of the worlds. These energies of emanation and manifestation are at the same time energies of reintegration in the form of the *mantra.* The highest source of these energies of Consciousness is none other than the supreme *mantra, parāvāk* itself. Hence, any *mantra* is ultimately the manifestation of *parāvāk,* or in Lyne Bansat-Boudon's words, "the *mantra* is not a simple formula for ritual usage, but represents ultimate reality itself."[78] It represents reality in the strong sense of making it present because it "contains" it. The *mantra* is like the central energetic substance that flows from the Self or the I-Consciousness.[79] It is the world as reality, or the reality of the world, which amounts to saying that it is a most direct Śaktic manifestation, or indeed Śakti herself. Hence, its capacity of projection and its power of reintegration are substantially one.

The *mantra* is none other than the focal vibration of Consciousness and, as such, the source and the end of the cycle of manifestation, and likewise the origin and the goal of the spiritual path. As Consciousness unfolds its Self-Awareness, the bi-unity of signifier and signified, or manifesting subject and manifested object, tends to be cut asunder and open wider and wider, thus entailing a greater and greater objectification, without, however, altering in the least the essential unity of Śiva's I-Consciousness. On the level of linguistic awareness, the dichotomy between words and things is the final product of this emanation. In the *mantra,* however, the synthetic unity of signifier and signified is reaffirmed in such a way as to give access to the unicity of pure Consciousness. As Mark Dyczkowski puts it, the language of *mantras* "is not concerned with external objects" and it is "directed inward, deriving its energy from the supreme power of consciousness into which it ultimately involutes."[80] As a foremost means of spiritual realization, the *mantra* allows Śaivite practitio-ners to be reabsorbed, together with the world that surrounds them, into the pure Subject, in a nondualistic and nonobjectified state of being. This being so, the *mantra* is like the symbol, as well as the ontological and soteriological evidence, of the "not unreal" nature of the non-Ultimate. Indeed, its liberating, realizational, power is based on this "non-unreality," without which "mantric exteriorization" would be powerless to achieve the reintegrative goal of the path, the end of the *sādhanā*. Such are the means and the goal of Śaivism: to "realize" the world of appearances—in the sense of giving it back its full reality as modification of Supreme Consciousness—whereas, by contrast, *Madhyamaka* Buddhism "de-realizes" the world of phenomena by undoing the perception of the latter as a set of self-existent substances. Similarly, while *Advaita* emphasizes discrimination, or separation and discontinuity, as a way to free oneself from the lures of *māyā* as superimposition upon Reality, the strong Śaivite emphasis on the power of the *mantra* as the productive and reintegrative vibration of Śiva-Śakti is in keeping with its concentration on the creative and dynamic unity of Consciousness.

## No Reality but The Reality

The Sufi doctrine of the "Unity of Being" (*wahdat al-wujūd*) presents a number of central commonalities with Kashmiri Śaivism, the most evident of which are perhaps no better suggested than by a single quote and commentary of Ibn al-'Arabī unexpectedly gleaned in a note from David Dubois's edition of Utpaladeva's *Īśvarapratyabhijñākārikā*:

> There is only one Essence and one Reality." This reality appears as *Ilāh* (God) in a certain respect and as *'abd* (servant) and *khalq* (creature) in another respect.[81]

The unicity and diversification of Absolute Consciousness that lies at the heart of both perspectives could not be more plainly affirmed. However, this selfsame affirmation unfolds in contexts and with emphases that are significantly different. While Śaivism emphasizes Freedom as the chief characterization of the Absolute, and considers the manifestation of this Freedom within and through the bounds of limitations, Sufism stresses the Necessity of the Absolute, or the intrinsic unity of its Essence and its Being, and envisages the non-Ultimate by contrast in terms of mere ontological "possibilities." Moreover, by contrast with Śaivism, the main matter in Sufism is not as much the manifestation of the productive energy of the I-Consciousness into and through the manifold as it is the relationship between Divine Unity and the world of multiplicity and creation. The world of Islam is entirely dominated by the metaphysical and spiritual imperative of Divine Unity. It is also, and this is less often stressed, a world in which the importance of the multiplicity of creatures and phenomena is paramount. Such a diversity ranges, in the *Qur'ān*, from the multiple "signs," or *āyāt*, on the horizon of the cosmos and the soul, but also in the many verses that form the texture of the Book, to the enumerations and pairs that characterize its content, including the Names of God and the alternations of the masculine and the feminine. It could be said that doctrinally and spiritually Sufism is a way to account for and realize Unity within multiplicity. This also means that, on the basis of the principle of essential Unity that has been mentioned above, there could not be an absolute chasm between the One and the many. In other terms, the "not unreal" nature of the many, or the relative realm, pertains to its being indissociably connected with the Real. The way this connection occurs will be described in the following pages.

However, before proceeding with our analyses of this connection, we must readily acknowledge that Sufism is a diverse set of phenomena, be it doctrinally or spiritually. Some forms of Sufism, and some particular statements within others, tend to lay emphasis on a way of perceiving and realizing the Real that strikes more harmonic chords with Shankarian *Advaita* than the teachings upon which we have focused in this essay.[82] It is enough to consider the following passage from Ibn al-'Arabī to realize to what extent the discriminative perspective of *Advaita* and its focus on the pure Subject can find a striking echo in some expressions of Sufism:

> Naught is except the Essence, which is Elevated in Itself, its elevation being unrelated to any other. . . . Thus, in a certain sense, it may be said that He is not He and you are not you.[83]

Be that as it may, it is important to remember, in order to understand the foundations of the *wahdat al-wujūd*, that the central formulation of Islam is the testimony of faith, the *shahādah*, and particularly its first half that states "*lā ilāha ill'Allāh*" or "no divinity if not the Divinity." This formula is, first of all, the expression of the Muslim creed, and a most direct affirmation of its monotheistic emphasis. Beyond this first and evident meaning of the *shahādah*, however, there have developed since the start of Islam modes of understanding of this formulation that reach the most consistent and significant metaphysical meaning of the doctrine of Unity, in a way that transcends, without abolishing it, the ordinary understanding of *tawhīd* as enunciating the reality of one God as opposed to many. It needs be stressed that this ultimate metaphysical meaning of the *shahādah* is not the mere theoretical production of speculative reason, but that it is above all the doctrinal outcome of the spiritual assimilation of the principles of the *Qur'ān*. To put it differently, the fact that the tenets of the *wahdat al-wujūd* may be unfathomable, or even anathema, to most Muslims, does not mean that they should be considered as external borrowings a priori foreign to Islam. Quite to the contrary, they constitute the doctrinal crystallizations of an interiorization of Islam in the most metaphysically profound and consistent way.

These interpretations of the *shahādah,* most often associated with Sufism, present us with a metaphysical account of the relationship between the Absolute and the relative that is strewn with metaphysical paradox. The crux of this metaphysical understanding of the *shahādah* lies in the definition of *Allāh* as the Reality, or the Real—*al-Haqq.* This means that the word *God* does not only refer to the Supreme Divinity but also, and consequently, to the Real as such, *Wujūd.* As a consequence, Sufism has tended to derive two conclusions from its consistent consideration of God as the Real: first, Reality cannot be predicated of anything besides God, and secondly; everything that *is* participates in one degree or another, in one mode or another, in God's only Reality. The term *wujūd,* which is most often translated by *being* or *existence,* is akin to the Arabic root WJD which denotes "finding" and "knowing about." *Wujūd* as that which may be found and known about can refer to at least three different realities: It may first refer to the Divine Reality whose Essence is Being; it may secondly refer to any *mawjūd,* any entity that is "made to be," and it may finally denote the reality that underlies all existents in a single unity, or *wahdat al-wujūd.* The *shahādah* implies both the first and third of these meanings. According to the first acceptation it is metaphysically exclusive, while it is inclusive according to the third. It exalts the Divine as that which lies above everything while being the essence of all things; it posits God both in His transcendence and immanence. By virtue of transcendence it affirms the nothingness of all else, while following its inclusive immanence it affirms the "non-unreality" of creation. The originality of Islam, however, is that the exclusive and inclusive aspects of Unity, as real as both are in their own respective rights, are not situated on the same "credal" level, as it were. While the exclusiveness, transcendence, and incomparability of God as *the* Real, in Arabic *tanzīh,* directly pertains to the immediate, plain, binding, religious meaning of the Revelation—a meaning that is theoretically understood and accepted by all, the full meaning of the immanence, analogy, and inclusiveness, or *tashbīh,* of the Real as One without a second can only be alluded to esoterically as a subtle, delicate, and perplexing truth that presupposes a measure of metaphysical and spiritual intuition without which it could be misunderstood, and either rejected or accepted on the basis of erroneous assumptions. This being said, it is also true that, from the point of view of Sufi gnosis, the recognition of God's immanence through his "signs" (*āyāt*) is more accessible to believers at large than is the pure transcendence of the One, which remains for most an abstraction rather than being, as in the highest forms of Sufi gnosis, a matter of inner realization. Now, one of the keys for understanding *wahdat al-wujūd* lies precisely in the metaphysical tension between exclusive transcendence and inclusive immanence. Ibn al-'Arabī expresses the paradox of this tension in the following way:

> The Elevated is one of God's Beautiful Names; but above whom or what, since only He exists? . . . In relation to existence He is the very essence of existing beings. Thus, in a certain sense, relative beings are elevated in themselves, since (in truth) they are none other than He and His elevation is absolute and not relative. This is because the (eternal) essences are immutable unmanifest, knowing nothing of manifested existence, and they remain in that state, despite all the multiplicity of manifested forms. The Essence is Unique of the whole in the whole.[84]

Although the immanence of the Real cannot be artificially severed from its transcendence without distorting Ibn al-'Arabī's doctrine by making it into a pantheistic confusion, it is also true that this immanence refers to the essential nature of the Real since it follows from the very affirmation of transcendence as predicated upon otherness. Hence the question: "The Elevated is one of God's Beautiful Names; but above whom or what, since only He exists?"

The interplay between transcendence and immanence, or exclusive Unicity and inclusive Unity, is no better expressed than in Ibn al-'Arabī's doctrine of the "permanent essences" or "permanent entities," *a'yān thābita*. According to this doctrine, everything that exists is a priori a "possible entity" in God's pre-eternity. It is only through God's existentiation that possible entities come to be actualized in the world of creation. In God, or in God's knowledge, entities are both metaphysically "real" and inexistent. In creation, by contrast, entities are existent but ultimately "unreal." By "reality" is meant here identity with or participation into Reality, by "existence" is suggested *ek-sistere*, that is, "standing out" from the Source of Being and being projected into the world of creation. The paradoxical ontological status of "existents" between "essential nonexistence" and "nonreal existence" is referred to in another suggestive way when saying that "the possible thing is that reality whose relationship to existence and non-existence is equal."[85] According to Ibn al-'Arabī, to say that a possible entity is existent without qualifying this existence by inexistence is like mistaking it for the Real, that is to say, God Himself, while to affirm that it is inexistent without qualifying it with existence amounts to making it impossible. Entities have, therefore, two sides, each of which is like a sort of negation of the other, while they are of course one and the same in the last analysis. Their existence in the cosmos is their "nonbeing" in God, and

their "being" in God is their nonexistence. With respect to the former, it is
not that an existent in this world ceases to be a possibility in God when it
is existentiated, since this would absurdly make a possible impossible, but it
means that its existence is pure "nothingness" in relation to the act of God
which "has clothed it in the robe of existence through Himself," or in relation
to the Divine Name which has brought it into existence. As for the latter, it
means that there is no room in God for other than God, and therefore no
existence of entities. The nonexistence of entities is their reality in God since
it *is* God, whereas their existence in the world is not real in and of itself since
it is none other than the manifestation of the very Being and Qualities of
God "through" and "in" them.[86] In this connection Ibn al-ʿArabī refers to the
phenomena of the world as "places of manifestation," *mazhar*, of the Divine
Being and Qualities. A *mazhar* is a place where God appears by making it
appear through His existentiating act. In a way, there is a sort of reciprocity
between God and the *mazhar*. The latter is actualized by God's creative act from
its state of mere possibility, while the Divine Being is made manifest through
its receptable, or place, of manifestation. A ponderous consequence of this is
that the ontological status and salvific virtue of the phenomena of the world
depends on whether they are considered, and one may even say experienced,
as "places of manifestation" of God or as mere phenomena as such. In his
*Niche of Light*, the *Mishkat al-Anwār*, Ghazālī—whose perspective includes in
his most esoteric treatises very penetrating insights into the *tawhīdic* concept
of relativity—refers to these two aspects of creatures as follows:

> "Everything is perishing except His face" [28:88]: It is not that
> each thing is perishing at one time or at other times, but that it is
> perishing from eternity without beginning to eternity without end.
> It can only be so conceived since, when the essence of anything
> other than He is considered in respect of its own essence, it is
> sheer nonexistence. But when it is viewed in respect of the "face"
> to which existence flows forth from the First, the Real, then it is
> seen as existing not in itself but through the face adjacent to its
> Giver of Existence. Hence, the only existent is the Face of God.
> Each thing has two faces: a face toward itself, and a face toward
> its Lord. Viewed in terms of the face of itself, it is nonexistent;
> but viewed in terms of the Face of God, it exists. Hence nothing
> exists but God and His Face.[87]

As emphasized by Ghazālī, the phenomenon "considered in respect of its own
essence . . . is sheer nonexistence." However, it is existent as "facing" its Source
or as a "place of manifestation" of the radiance, *tajallī*, of Divine Being.

The Islamic rejection of any "second" to God leads, paradoxically, to stressing the "not unreal" aspect of what we have called relativity. This "non-unreality" of the non-Ultimate has already appeared in three ways. First of all, relativity is not "not real" inasmuch as it is possible as *a'yān thābita* in God. In fact, it follows from the doctrine of the *a'yān thābita* that, according to Ibn al-'Arabī, relative beings are elevated in themselves inasmuch as they are "included" in the Real as "immutable essences," or inasmuch as they *are* the Real. To put it in a somewhat elliptical manner: "other-than-God" is *in* God, *is* God, and thereby *not* unreal. Secondly, each relative reality is a site of Self-disclosure of the Real, to make use of the English lexicon proposed by William Chittick. The "not unreal" nature of the world of creation as "theophany" or *tajallī* is therefore clearly asserted, as each unit of reality in creation is none other than the revelatory appearance of Reality Itself. The qualities, determinations, and properties of the receptacles of the Real cannot be unreal: if they were, they could not function as sites of manifestation of Being. Another aspect of the same point is that each instance of receptivity to the One Being is "unified," that is, "made one" by the One. Whereas the situation of the "possible entities" in God's knowledge pertains to the One as *al-Ahad*, and can be mathematically symbolized by the multiplication of unity ($1 \times 1 \times 1 \ldots$) that bars any existential plurality, the reality of the "existent entities" relates to the One as *al-Wāhid*, that "unifies" and "constitutes" each and every entity in differential oneness in the form of the addition $1+1+1+1 \ldots$[88] The theophany of Unity in and through "unities" is at the same time the very principle of the Unity of the Real in each and every of the occurrences of unity, as well as through the whole spectrum of multiple existence: hence, the expression *wahdat al-wujūd*. Interestingly, the Śaivite notion of *kula*, or "group," refers to a similar principle of unity in which "because of the presence of Śiva within each of these units, each part in some sense contains all the other parts."[89] Thirdly, the "not unreal" nature of the non-Ultimate appears in the very existentiation of the entities by the act of Being. "*Kun fa yakūn*," God says "Be! And it is" (36:82). This means that the immanence of the Divine Being to the various theophanies through His Act makes it impossible for one to consider them as "nonbeing." This threefold "not unreal" aspect of the non-Ultimate amounts to a recognition of the relative necessity, if one may say so, of creation in relation to God. The *Amīr* 'Abd al-Qādir al-Jazā'irī encapsulates this paradox of the necessity of the contingent in the following lines:

Without God the creatures would not be existentiated (*khalqun bi-lā haqqin lā yūjad*) and without the creature, God would not be manifested (*haqqun bi-lā khalqin lā yazhar*)[90]

The Islamic notion of theophany is thereby central to the articulation of the One and the many. The latter are as many unveilings or disclosures of the limitless Real. Sufism highlights the central function of these theophanic disclosures both from an ontological and a soteriological or spiritual point of view. From the latter perspective, the doctrine of theophany teaches that there is no other way of knowing and "seeing" God than through His theophanic manifestations, or through His Aspects and Qualities as they are manifested in the world of creation. This is clearly asserted by Ibn al-'Arabī when he writes that "contemplation of the Reality without formal support is not possible, since God, in His Essence, is far beyond all need of the Cosmos."[91] This is a very significant point in Sufi doctrine as it emphasizes the centrality of the recognition of immanence in the Way. It follows that there is no contemplative path without a full recognition of the "not unreal" aspect of the world of relativity.[92] Now, it must be added that this perspective does not exhaust the cognitive possibilities envisaged by the *wahdat al-wujūd*. For there is in fact a way in which the Essence is known "by Itself" through or within the heart of the gnostic, independently from external theophanic mediations, and it cannot be otherwise, since the Essence is ultimately all that is. It behooves the commentator to distinguish, therefore, between an analytical, theophanic knowledge of the Essence through the Names, and a synthetic Self-Knowledge of the Essence beyond all theophanies. Although our thesis lays emphasis on the former, which we deem to be more representative of Islamic spirituality at large, the significance of the latter in some major sectors of Sufi metaphysics cannot be disregarded.

It flows from the previous considerations that, when discussing the non-Ultimate, or relativity, in Sufism, it is important to differentiate between the two concepts of *mā siwā Allāh*, or "other-than-God," which underscores the "inclusive exclusiveness" of the Principle, and Divine Names or Qualities, *Asmā'* or *Sifāt*, which tend to accentuate its theophanic inclusiveness. The *mā siwā Allāh* is not, precisely because only *Allāh* is in a true sense. To grant reality to *mā siwā Allāh* would amount to severing the non-Ultimate from the Divine, and setting it into an illusory otherness. By contrast, as we have already suggested, if one were to look for "non-unreality" in the relative realm one would have to consider, rather, the nature and function of the Divine Names. The Names (*Asmā'*) do not only refer, here, to linguistic designations, be they divinely revealed, but to the actual Qualities (*Sifāt*) or Aspects of the Divine Itself.[93] In fact, every existent being is a name of God,[94] and when we capitalize the substantive we are more specifically referring to a Name as Divine Quality, or Aspect, such as the Compassionate (*ar-Rahmān*) or the Beautiful (*al-Jamīl*). Be that as it may, the consideration of the ontological reality of the Names must be related to their two aspects. On the one hand, the Names are none other than the Essence inasmuch as they "face" the Essence. This also means, as indicated by Ibn al-'Arabī, that each Name can be qualified by all other Names by virtue of its and their *being* the Essence.[95] On the other hand, the Names are "relational" and therefore "relative" to creation. Names are relationships, they are not existing substances. For any of them to become distinct from the others it needs to be brought into the created realm through and in its relationship to its effects. The *Amīr* 'Abd al-Qādir refers to this process of distinction and manifestation through the analogy of colors, which "were inexistent in the dark," and light, which "was a condition *sine qua non* of their existence."[96] The "darkness" of the Essence does "include" all the Names and all the "possible entities," but it is the Light of the Divine Existentiating Act that makes them manifest in and through the "shadows" of the existents. As such, the Names are principles of "non-unreality" for relativity precisely because they are no different from the Essence that *is,* and given that they have no meaning outside of the entities of creation that they actualize.

The diversity of Names is not the only way in which the Essence and the world of creation are, as it were, connected. Besides the horizontal range of Divine Names and Aspects, the relationship between Unity and multiplicity also appears in the various Sufi versions of the doctrine of the Divine modes of Presence. These Divine Presences (*hadarāt*) highlight the strong "immanentist" bent of Sufi metaphysics in that they express the universal underlying Presence of the Divine, while manifesting this Presence in a hierarchy of levels of being that encompasses the whole ontological scale, from the Divine Essence to the material shell of the universe. Sufi metaphysics differentiates the degrees of Divine Presence in a binary, tertiary or—most often—quinary pattern. The binary model, which stems from Qur'ānic terminology, distinguishes between the "world of mystery" (*'ālam al-ghayb*) and the "world of testimony" (*'ālam ash-shahādah*). The first refers to invisible Divine realities, and the second to manifestation. In his *Mishkāt al-Anwār*, Al-Ghazālī refers to the first as the "world of dominion" (*'ālam al-malakūt*) and to the second as the "world of sensation and visibility" (*'ālam al-hiss wa ash-shahādah*). The vertical descent of Divine Presence that links these two worlds is clearly expressed in the following passage:

> The visible world comes forth from the world of dominion just as the shadow comes forth from the thing that throws it, the fruit comes forth from the tree, and the effect comes forth from the secondary cause. The keys to knowledge of effects are found only in their secondary causes. Hence, the visible world is a similitude of the world of dominion.[97]

The world of sensation is a similitude (*mithāl*) of the world of dominion. This means that it is a reflection of the higher world, thereby testifying (*shahādah*) to the reality of the latter. This binary layout of reality is the most elementary way of expressing the relationship between the Divine and the world of creation. Other descriptions of the levels of Divine Presence differentiate further by distinguishing within the invisible world the domain of "fire" and that of "light," which correspond respectively to the animic and imaginal level, on the one hand, and the spiritual and angelic level on the other hand. This distinction results in a tripartite universe that encompasses, in ascending order, *al-mulk* or *al-nasūt*, *al-malakūt* and *al-jabarūt*.[98] But the most encompassing account of the degrees of Divine Presence is to be found in the doctrine of the five Divine Presences (*hadarāt*). Al-Qāshānī, one of the foremost commentators of Ibn al-'Arabī, enumerates these *hadarāt* as follows: the Essence (*dhāt*),[99] the Divinity as Qualities and Names (*ulūhīyah*), the plane of Divine Acts (*rubūbīyah*), the level of imagination (*khayāl*), and the level of physical and sensory existence (*mushāhadah*).[100]

Other accounts are characterized by a slightly different terminology.[101] It is so that the level of the pure Essence is often referred to as *al-Hāhūt*, from the pronoun *Huwa*, He, that points to the Essential Ipseity. The plane of the Qualities is referred to as *al-Lāhūt*, referring to *Allāh*. The level of the Divine Acts is *al-Jabarūt*, which has to do with God's Power as expressed by His Acts and his Angels, and is akin to the Divine Name *al-Jabbār*, which entails irresistible compelling. The two lowest domains of manifestation of the Divine Presence are that of imagination, *al-Malakūt*, and that of the physical forms, *al-Nāsūt*: that is, the world of invisible animic realities and that of corporeal existence.[102] Whatever might be the specific distinctions and syntheses brought about in the various versions of the metaphysical doctrine of the Divine Presences, what needs to be stressed is that the doctrine itself highlights the "non-unreality" of the relative realm of manifestation by affirming the ways in which the principle of Reality is present and efficient throughout. Instead of emphasizing an exclusive discrimination between the Real and the illusory, these teachings suggest a gradually decreasing but never annulled inherence of the Divine Presence throughout the totality of existence, leaving thereby no entities or phenomena "out of touch" with Reality, as it were. Moreover, notwithstanding the discontinuity between their respective realms, the Divine Presences involve an essential continuity from the Divine Source precisely by virtue of pertaining to Presence, and not to absence or ontological chasm. This teaching is in keeping with the Qur'ānic verses that stress the absence of "rent" or "rift" in the fabric of creation: "He Who created the seven heavens one above another: No want of proportion wilt thou see in the Creation of (*Allāh*) Most Gracious. So turn thy vision again: seest thou any flaw (*futūr*)?"[103]

Moreover, the Sufi emphasis on the immanence of the Divine finds another important correlative manifestation in the significance of the Divine Name both as ontological reality and as spiritual support of inner realization. Jīlī makes this point very emphatically by asserting the ontological identity of God and His Name, on the one hand,[104] and consequently by underscoring, on the other hand, that this Name is the only methodical means of access to the Divine.[105]

As we have noted, the Kashmiri Śaivite and Sufi *wahdat al-wujūd* share a consideration of "theophanic degrees" in the manifestation of the Absolute within and through the fold and garb of relativity. The main thrust of the Śaivite perspective is the need to recognize the Supreme Consciousness of Śiva in all the phenomena that surround us, and to enlarge our awareness, as it were, through this recognition. There is nothing that is not Śiva, although our perception may not be adequate to this supreme truth, which is why we must untie the knots of limitations and contractions through and by our connection to the productive and reintegrative energy of the Śakti, instead of identifying exclusively with particular stases or moments in the unfolding of the Absolute. Similarly, there is nothing in existence but God, or *"Laysa fi'l wujūd ill'Allāh,"* to make use of Ghazālī's expression. The Islamic "sin" of "association" or *shirk* is a result, therefore, of a spiritual inability to recognize the pure Unicity of the Real, a failure to acknowledge the most inclusive and consistent understanding of the first *shahādah*. It follows from their strong emphasis on immanence that the perspectives of Śaivism and Unity of Essence tend to underscore the ontological continuity between the various degrees of reality, thereby pointing to the Supreme Reality by recognizing and actualizing It within and through that which appears to be distinct from It. In other words, the "not unreal" nature of the domain of "other-than-the-Ultimate" must lead to the Ultimate since it is not in the last analysis other than It. This is in sharp methodical contrast with those perspectives that accentuate the need for a "nullification," "subrating," "dissolving," or "emptying" of delimited phenomena and experiences. It is also significant that in such metaphysical accounts of Reality as to be found in Kashmiri Śaivism and the *wahdat al-wujūd*, the lower degrees of existence are, as it were, included in the higher ones. This is eminently true of the Real Itself, which, as Supreme Being and Consciousness, embraces within itself *in potentia* all that is. The Śaivite image of the feathers and egg of the peacock[106] and the Akbarian concept of the "preexistential possibilities" express, in different ways, this metaphysical inclusion of the relative into the Absolute. The common emphasis on the methodical centrality of the *mantra*, or *dhikr* in Sufism, is akin to the aforementioned metaphysical perspectives, since it rests upon an essential identity between the projection and power of the linguistic symbol and its divine matrix. It is by virtue of this identity that relativity as a whole can be, as it were, reabsorbed into its Source.

## Transcendence and Immanence in the Economy of Reality

As we hope to have intimated throughout our essay beneath the surface of our conceptual distinctions and classifications, none of the four metaphysical perspectives that we have sketched can be deemed to be utterly exclusive of the others, if only to the extent that they all tend to caution against any excessive fixation on ideational phenomena. The fact is that none of the four perspectives in question may be deemed to brand the relative realm with unqualified reality, any more than any of them can be considered to deny its reality altogether.

In order to recapitulate the findings of our inquiry, it might be pedagogically useful, as well as epistemologically expedient, to situate the four metaphysical traditions that we have analyzed as ranging from an emphasis on transcendence to one on immanence, notwithstanding the unavoidable simplifications that such a classification might entail. In such a contrasted spectrum of metaphysical vantage points, *Madhyamaka* Buddhism may appear as the doctrinal epitome of what could be called, paradoxically, a "transcendence of transcendence." This elliptical phrase may be understood to mean that, by refusing to affirm a reality that would transcend *pratītyasamutpāda*, *Madhyamaka* Buddhism aims at transcending, as it were, the perspective of transcendence, resulting in a position of the principle of emptiness as a reality immanent to everything that "neither is nor is not." Thus, the backbone of this perspective lies in the negation of the assertion of any Absolute, or any Self, that would transcend the realm of codependent origination and make it henceforth impossible to reach Emptiness. By contrast, *Advaita* may be deemed to highlight a perspective chiefly characterized by a "transcendence of immanence," meaning thereby that *Ātman* transcends radically, and therefore annuls, the realm of *Māyā*. This amounts to saying that the ordinary, benighted, state of consciousness fails to recognize that which transcends the realm of immediate and appearing existence.

However, lest this *Advaitin* standpoint be taken for a one-sided "transcendentalist" perspective, it bears remembering that this annulment results in its turn in the highest affirmation of the universal immanence of the Self, since there is nothing but *Ātman*. At any rate, in both *Advaita* and *Madhyamaka*, one is confronted with a clear-cut need to free oneself, through transcendence, from the conditioning relativity of binding phenomena and states of consciousness. In contradistinction with those perspectives, both Śaivism and Sufism are by and large characterized by an attention to the theophanic and soteriological sheaves of immanence. They perceive the latter as manifestations of the Ultimate, and tend to make a maximal methodical and spiritual use of them. Considering the Sufi perspective of *wahdat al-wujūd*, we would be tempted to refer to it as expressing, by and large, the point of view of the "immanence of the transcendent." Starting as it does from the Islamic premise of an exclusive Divine Unity, abstraction, and incomparability, or *tanzīh,* the doctrine of *waḥdat al-wujūd* cannot but affirm the Divine Immanence that this exclusive Unity implies as its metaphysical counterpart and corollary. "No god but God" or *lā ilāha ill'Allāh* signifies both the exclusive transcendence of *Allāh* and His immanence as *az-Zāhir,* the Manifest or the Outward.

Finally, it would not be inaccurate to refer to Kashmiri Śaivism as to a metaphysical and mystical perspective that focuses upon the dynamic, liberating, and universal "immanence of the Immanent," if one may say so without apparent redundancy. This means that Śaivism is intent on recognizing and "freeing" the Divine Consciousness and Energy that pervades everything within and without, which amounts in fact to teaching that this selfsame Consciousness frees us from its delimitations through the very same delimitations that It has assumed. Here again, however, it needs to be kept in mind that this awareness of the immanence of Śiva is ultimately realized and actualized into its full meaning in and through a realization of his transcendence as pure Freedom.[107] The preceding lines must, therefore, lead us to underscore *in fine,* lest our classification be overstated or unduly isolated from its overall context, that the distinction between immanence and transcendence is both provisional and relative. In Reality Itself, or for Consciousness Itself, as well as in the heights of spiritual realization in which It manifests most gloriously, there is neither transcendence nor immanence, these notions presupposing otherness, hence provisional duality.

## Paradoxes of Metaphysical and Mystical Discourse

The quasi-totality of the considerations that precede are theoretical, and the reader might be entitled to raise the question of the practical, spiritual, implications of these metaphysical notions, given that contemplative mysticism is primarily a matter of realized knowledge. Whatever might be the important differences in emphasis among the various contemplative traditions, it cannot escape us that the centrality of the doctrine of universal metaphysical relativity in contemplative teachings stems from a radical difference of accent in the way religion at large and mysticism as a distinct current within religious traditions envisage the relationship between the human and the Ultimate. Religions, and theology inasmuch as it is the rational and apologetic mouthpiece of religion, deal primarily with the moral and social conformity and alignment of the human with the Ultimate, both individually and collectively. In other words, they aim at ordering, coordinating, and balancing the various aspects of human existence on this earth in conformity with, or in view of, the ultimate end of Reality. Religious teachings are therefore primarily "symbolic," in the sense of fostering a human approximation of the Above that might be conducive to a life according to transcendent principles. Paradoxically, and perhaps unexpectedly given its affinities with symbolic expressions and its usual distance from formalism and literalism, mysticism is more literal than religion in the sense that it takes the highest teachings of religion at face value by lending them the most powerfully consistent meaning and impact. This is why it asserts the exclusive Reality of the Ultimate and the utter transcendence of this Reality vis-à-vis any relationship that would essentially limit It or confine It within human mental coagulations. Consequently, contemplative metaphysics refrains from considering any existent aside from its utter dependence upon the Supreme, thereby intimating its paradoxical, ambiguous, status as "neither real nor unreal": Not real because only the Real is real, but not unreal because everything *is* the Real.

As an initial response to the question raised at the beginning of these concluding remarks, it could be proposed that the metaphysical rigor of mystical discourse cannot but translate into an exacting awareness of the Ultimate, thereby informing the totality of the spiritual and moral components of the spiritual path. In this respect, the contemplative emphasis on the shimmering dimension of reality needs is understood once again in contradistinction with the ordinary religious perspective. As we have indicated above, the latter could be defined as a system of beliefs and practices destined to orient mankind toward the Ultimate Reality of the creed. This is the primary aspect of religious laws, codes, and disciplines, without which religion has no effectiveness in relation to the needs and limitations of the individual as such, as well as to those of the collectivity. Such orientation presupposes a conventional density and quasi-absoluteness of the means, in a way that is not without opening the way to the possibility of a confusion between the finger and the moon. By contrast, mystical teachings on relativity tend to go well beyond such structuring and facilitating goals, while parrying any danger of the aforementioned confusion of means and end, inasmuch as they aim at a radical modification of one's perception of reality. A reassessment of reality and its criteria of definition and perception requires the acquisition of a mode of consciousness that fundamentally alters and upsets the largely delusory balance of one's mental habits and existential comfort.

Thus, the methodological focus on the ontological paradoxes of the non-Ultimate may be, on the part of sapiential and mystical teachings, a function of the operative imperatives of the metaphysical path as a way of life and an awakening of consciousness. Even though the teachings concerning relativity are obviously every bit as conceptual as the affirmative doctrine of the Real as such, they converge on a conversion of outlook that is the very hallmark of contemplative teachings. Arguably, such an operative priority comes more obviously to the fore in *Madhyamaka* than it does elsewhere, the general economy of the Buddhist tradition being the most reticent of all vis-à-vis any conceptualization of the Ultimate. Nāgārjuna underlines the principle in question when specifying, in conclusion to his *Vigrahavyāvartanī* that "(dependent origination) is to be understood by each one by himself according to this instruction" and "only some of it can be taught verbally."[108] This statement, which is echoed in various degrees and diverse modes in all metaphysical and mystical teachings, highlights two core principles that may provide us with a suggestive coda. First of all, the understanding of the teachings is to be effected "by each one by himself." On this point, the Sufi *tahqīq* as inward verification or realization of *tawhīd* provides a striking parallel to Nāgārjuna's injunction inasmuch as it implies a spiritual actualization of enlightened consciousness through a breaking of the shell of outward conceptual language.[109] Secondly, and concurrently, this call for inner and transformative understanding presupposes a gap between theoretical knowledge and operative recognition. It is in this gap that lies one of the most perplexing questions of metaphysical and contemplative expression, for "only some of it can be taught verbally." The shimmering ambiguity of existence or the non-Ultimate invites the question of the puzzling status of any discourse giving access to it. The notion of *upāya* remains a key symbol in this respect, one that allows us to account for the plurality of perspectives and degrees of spiritual fruitfulness, as it embraces both epistemological power and ontological emptiness in the shimmering language of contemplative metaphysics.

# 2

## Christian and Buddhist Insights into a Metaphysics of Salvation

This chapter is an attempt at exploring parallel and contrastive avenues in the respective outlooks of Christian and Buddhist teachings with regard to what will be referred to, throughout the following pages, as metaphysical or ontological relativity, in contradistinction with the concept of the Absolute. What is meant herein by "relativity" and "Absolute"? In order to answer this question, it is suitable to begin with the etymological and conceptual assumption that the Absolute is literally *absolutum,* which literally means utter freedom from any determination and limitation, as also from any trace of nonbeing, hence from any contingency or "non-necessity." The Latin past participle *absolutum* is derived from the infinitive verbal form *absolvere* that denotes the action of setting free from bounds, and therefore separating. The Absolute as such is the only Reality that is radically free and "separate" or radically "other" from a metaphysical point of view. Such an absoluteness is not only inherently exclusive of any contingency and dependence, it is also transcendent vis-à-vis any relationship. This is a central dimension of the idea of the Absolute as it has been conceptualized by a number of metaphysicians throughout the ages and across traditions, and as it is understood and illustrated in this essay. In such views, the Absolute is pure necessity and pure freedom: it cannot but be, and cannot but be what it is. Now, it may be deemed that relations involve, by definition, a limitation of necessity and one of freedom. The limitation of necessity stems from the principle that a relation implies the contingency or codependence of two realities in relation to each other. Even when it entails the anteriority or primacy of one term in relation to another, there is a sense in which any reality involved in a relationship cannot but be in some way defined in terms of this relationship. Thus, for instance, God the Creator cannot be understood outside of his relationship with creation. Analogically, the absoluteness of any given reality—besides the Absolute as such—could refer to its substantial identity, or its essence, inasmuch as it is envisaged as different and independent from other substances. The absoluteness of a reality is therefore denied to the extent that its relationship with other-than-itself is considered as constitutive of its very being. This is why no reality but the Absolute can be considered as absolute *stricto sensu*. Given what precedes, one of the main questions to elucidate amounts to knowing whether the relations predicated of a given reality are essential or accidental to its being.

Aside from its limitation of necessity, the relationship appears to involve a limitation of freedom because it cannot but go without a measure of determination, whether active or passive, by another. There is, therefore, in the metaphysical concept of the pure Absolute, an intrinsic transcendence of relation qua relativity. Although not all instances of relativity are relational in the highest sense of a full reciprocity, all relationships may be considered to carry a measure of relativity that seems to be incompatible, *stricto sensu*, with the notion of a *purum absolutum*. Needless to say, such "absolutist" consider-ations have been at times received with qualifications, if not objections, and have stirred controversies and debates. One of the aims of this chapter is to consider critically the implications of some of these discussions.

If one were to look for direct expressions of such a concept of the Absolute in world wisdom traditions it may be suggested that the Hindu and Islamic worlds would likely be the most fertile grounds for inquiry. Not only do these traditions provide us with unambiguous notions of an Ultimate Reality as pure Necessity and pure Freedom, but they also lay out, in some of their schools of thought, a rigorous delineation of the degrees of this Reality that, without calling into question its essential Unity, or rather its Nonduality, envisage various levels of its metaphysical unfolding, as it were. In the Hindu world, for example, both schools of *Advaita* Vedānta and Tantric Śaivism assert the nonduality of the Absolute in the most clearly affirmative way. For a Shankara, the Absolute Reality of *Brahman,* referred to as *Ātman* when envisaged as universal and divine Selfhood, is the Ultimate Undifferentiated or Non-Qualified Reality, *Nirguna Brahman,* that can nonetheless be approached through its dimensions of Being, Consciousness, and Bliss, or *Sat, Cit,* and *Ānanda.* In such a view, there is prima facie only the notion of the Absolute, on the one hand, and that which is not the Absolute, the relative, on the other hand, hence the need to discriminate between the two, a discrimination that cannot be perfected but by the recognition that only the Absolute *is* in a real sense. Similarly, Śaivism considers the Supreme Śiva Principle, Paramaśiva, as absolute Consciousness and absolute Freedom.[1] While the whole metaphysi-cal emphasis of both traditions lies in the Absolute Reality of the Supreme, as previously characterized, it is also considered on a lower degree of Reality, which, while absolute in its own right and rigorously unseverable from the pure Unqualified Ultimate, highlights a differentiation or a qualification that is understood as the prelude and principle of manifestation as such. Thus, *Advaitin* metaphysics distinguishes between *Nirguna Brahman* and *Saguna Brahman,* the latter being the qualified and therefore in a certain way "relative" dimension of the Absolute. Similarly, Śaivism presents a distinction between the level of absoluteness in which the Supreme Śiva is undifferentiated and the level of the principial differentiation between Śiva and Śakti. This seed of differentiation is sometimes compared to the eye of the peacock feather, the unmanifest principle of the universal unfolding of Śiva-Śakti. Hence, it can be seen that, in such teachings, the Absolute is inclusive of degrees of absoluteness, if one may say so, that "articulate" the latter with the relative field without affecting its necessity and freedom.

Although it does so with definitely different emphases, and in a religious language that takes more stock of Divine Qualities from the point of view of their creaturely, if not anthropomorphic, symbolism, Islam as a whole is no less adamant than the highest Hindu metaphysics in asserting the absoluteness, transcendence, and unknowableness of the Divine Essence as such. Indeed, the surah *al-ikhlās* contains one of the most expressive and comprehensive enunciations of this pure monotheism: "Say: He (*Huwa*) is *Allāh*, the One and Only (*Ahad*); *Allāh*, the Eternal, Absolute (*As-Samad*); He begetteth not, nor is He begotten; And there is none comparable unto Him" (Yusuf Ali). Although the transcendence and indivisibility of the Essence are unambiguously stated in Islam, the Divine Names are conceived, particularly in Sufism, both as one with the Essence and involving an effusive diversification within the Absolute in view of, and in relation to, the field of manifestation. This is why Qualities are normally understood in Sufi metaphysics as relational, hence in a sense "relative." Thus, the Sufi 'Abd al-Karīm Al-Jīlī distinguishes three "degrees" of the Essence: the Essence as Unknowable Darkness (*al-'Amā*), which is the Absolute for and in Itself, the Essence as Unity (*al-Ahadiyyah*), which is the Absolute as Pure Affirmation of Itself, and the Essence as Unicity (*al-Wāhidiyyah*), which is the revelation of the Essence as Qualities and Qualities as Essence. This triplicity pertains to the Absolute and suggests the unfolding of Relativity within the Absolute through degrees of Reality. It could be said, schematically no doubt but nonetheless effectively, that, in such metaphysical teachings, the Absolute is not confused nor conflated with the relative, nor is it essentially distinguished from It, this paradoxical tension being accounted for in terms of a recognition of degrees of Relativity within the Absolute Itself.

It is important to note, within the context of our argument, the striking independence of these metaphysical teachings, on a purely doctrinal level, from any spiritual or religious soteriology. To put it differently, the doctrine of the nondual *Brahman,* like that of the Unicity of Existence (*wahdat al-wujūd*), stands on its own as a metaphysical mapping out of Reality, as it were, that provides intellectual supports of meditation for ascetic and contemplative practices and may be enriched, deepened, or sharpened as a result, but is not determined a priori by any methodical intent pertaining to the latter. Granted, the traditions within which these metaphysical teachings flourished are also eminently soteriological, and the doctrine itself imperatively points to the spiritual realization of its content, but it would not be an oversimplification to state that their soteriology is determined by their metaphysics, rather than the other way round. Thus, it is the metaphysical truth that saves or awakens, inasmuch at least as it is realized or actualized through religious and spiritual means. The Shankarian metaphysical discrimination between Reality and appearance, as the human alignment with the Islamic doctrine of *tawhīd*, provides the only sine qua non for realization.

## Introduction of the Argument

Our contention, in this essay, is that the Christian and Buddhist universes of meaning present us, in their respective intellectual economies, with analogous, yet profoundly different, and indeed somehow reverse, ways of envisioning metaphysics from the vantage point of their sui generis soteriology. In other terms, our argument is that Christian and Buddhist conceptual elaborations are essentially informed by the tenets and components of their spiritual way, whether redemptive or emancipative. This often means, in point of fact, a rejection of metaphysics as such on account of the spiritual primacy of modes of consciousness that challenge the tendency of metaphysical teachings to become all too easily fixed into doctrinal abstractions and their insufficiency in terms of spiritual awakening.

Furthermore, we suggest that the soteriological thrust that questions metaphysics and largely undermines "absolutist" discourses manifests chiefly in the respective tendencies to an "absolutization of the relative," on the one hand, and a "relativization of the absolute," on the other. As will be further elaborated in this chapter, the first formula refers, more specifically, to major trends in Christian Trinitarian theology, and the second to the Buddhist soteriological ontology of emptiness. These two expressions are more than convenient ways of encapsulating intellectual developments that are, of necessity and in fact, much more complicated than mere formulas. They seem to us to provide a theoretical framework that both suggests a major driving force of the internal coherence of each of the two traditions and the diversity of the ways in which this thrust has been understood and transformed within the tradition itself. It is not claimed, therefore, that the whole of Christianity can be summarized as a religious absolutization of the relative, no more than it is argued that the totality of Buddhism amounts to relativizing all absoluteness. However, it is suggested that Christianity as a whole can be better understood in all of its diversity by considering the ways in which its major dogmatic orientations have amounted to a conflation of the Absolute and the Relative, the Divine Essence and the *relating* Divine Persons, thereby arguably calling into question a strictly metaphysical concept of the Absolute. In fact, however, this theological tendency to absolutize the Relative has not prevented the unfolding of a wide spectrum of Trinitarian accounts, some of which are arguably more conducive to a consideration of stricter concepts of the Absolute than a general assessment of the tradition would grant. Analogously, the relativization of all absoluteness that characterizes the psychological and spiritual teachings of the Buddha, such as they unfold in the *Abhidharma Pitaka,* has been crystallized in a variety of doctrinal formulations and resulted in a very diverse array of schools. Scholars have sometimes identified no fewer than eighteen schools (*ācariyavāda*) of early Buddhism, although classifications vary themselves to a significant extent. Notwithstanding this diversity, contemporary scholarship has tended to focus more attentively on the *Madhyamaka* perspective of the *Śunyavāda* persuasion, particularly such as it was expounded by its main exponent, the second- and third-century Nāgārjuna, whose rigorous argument in favor of codependent origination, *pratītya-samutpāda,* or emptiness, *śunyata,* has come to be raised by many to the status of a quasi-archetypical and normative expression of Buddhist thought, not unlike the way in which Shankara's *Advaita* has nearly become synonymous with Hindu metaphysics. We cannot fail, therefore, to treat this perspective as exemplarily representative of a metaphysical exposition informed by a powerful relativizing purport. The unfolding of Buddhist intellectuality, and particularly its Mahāyāna modalities, already with the schools of Yogācāra—and most evidently at a later stage in the development of the *Ālayavijñana* ("storehouse-consciousness") and *Tathāgatagharba* ("Buddha Matrix") in the context of Chinese readings of the Buddha-nature, was to be characterized by tendencies to bring the Absolute back to the center stage in a way that may be deemed to supersede the overall anti-absolutist orientation of the early teachings. It can be argued, however, that even this absolutist inflection of Mahāyāna remains largely determined by the methodical and negative premises of the Buddhist emphasis on emptiness and interdependent arising. Thus, it will be suggested that the relativistic bent of Christian and Buddhist teachings does not necessarily result in formulations fully representative of an "absolutization of the relative" or a "relativization of the absolute." We will, therefore, point out the limits of relativizing leanings in the discussion of significant developments of Christian and Buddhist thought, even though these qualifying instances may be deemed arguably marginal in the overall self-definition of the respective traditions. At any rate, these qualifications indicate that the use of the aforementioned formulae "absolutization of the relative" and "relativization of the absolute" is to be understood as primarily heuristic, and should not be construed as the principle of an all-encompassing and systematic classification.

Finally, it must be acknowledged that the following considerations involve a measure of generalization that may not satisfy all analytical needs and all academic scruples. On the one hand, it seems possible to write about Christianity and Buddhism in terms that presuppose, for each of these traditions, a certain unity of religious vision—unless one prefers to drop the very terms *Buddhism* and *Christianity* in the way Cantwell Smith proposed to drop the very term *religion*.[2] Recent scholarship has recognized the need to bear with the tension that historical contextualization and normative Buddhist discourses entail.[3] This means that meeting the challenge of a dialectical approach is indeed possible without losing sight of the extreme diversity of outlooks and schools characterizing each of these traditions. On the other hand, the following pages bear witness to an intention to pay the meaningful diversity of Christian and Buddhist perspectives its due. Without being able to claim, needless to say, an all-encompassing consideration of the Buddhist and Christian scopes, it is hoped that the reader recognizes the extent to which some of the most representative, complementary, and sometimes divergent views within each of the two traditions have been incorporated and addressed. It will appear clearly enough that our choices, although obviously exclusive of some currents that arguably could have been included in our analyses, have been primarily motivated by the importance and influence of the selected schools and authors, as well as the significance of the differences and complementarities among them. The first half of the chapter will be devoted to an extensive study of our focal concepts in seminal segments of Christian theological literature, while the second half will be focused on analyzing some of the implications of our thesis in a representative array of traditional and contemporary Buddhist doctrinal positions.

## Seeds of Trinitarian Discourse

The Christian outlook could be generally characterized, in its central theological streams, by a tendency toward an absolutization of the relative, if by relative is meant the relational and, more specifically, the relational "in God," that is the interpersonal life of the Holy Trinity. As was indicated earlier, this supereminence of the relational within the very Essence of the Divinity raises the difficult question of its compatibility with a view of the Absolute as radically *absolved* from any relation.[4] Thus, as a result, the doctrine of the Trinity, which essentially consists in the view of intrinsic and necessary relations among the Divine Persons, tends to place the latter in a position of ultimate metaphysical eminence. The idea of a "beyond" the Trinity, although occasionally expressed in some threads of Christian mysticism, most often probably with a more spiritual than theological intent, remains profoundly ill-sounding to a Christian theological sensibility. In most of Christian theology, the idea of the divine Essence transcending the Persons would seem to radically undercut the main theological tenets of the Christian faith. As will be elaborated farther on, even if the fundamental unity of the Essence and the Hypostases were to be preserved by being understood as referring to degrees of the Essence, this would remain unacceptable to most Christian theologians. In their eyes, such vertical understanding would simply jeopardize the Divine Unity. Indeed, a "subordinationist" view of the Persons that would entail both a purely monotheistic affirmation of the Unity of the Essence and a vertical ternary of hypostatic degrees implying a gradual "relativization" of the Absolute Essence from the Father to the Son and the Holy Spirit—while leaving utterly unrelativized the unconditioned and absolutely absolute Essence per se, identified from the highest point of view with the Father—would be deemed by most as falling short of the theological need for preserving a Unity that is also, intrinsically and on the same metaphysical level, a differentiated Trinity, thus a Tri-Unity. Conversely, a view of the Hypostases that would understand them as undifferentiated realities contained within the absolute Essence of God would not do justice, from most Christian theological points of view, to the distinction of the Persons that is necessary to make sense of their relationships, hence of the Trinity as diversity and principle of Divine Life. To put it in a slightly different light, such a view of the Trinity as being comprised of "possible dimensions" contained within the One Essence would not satisfy the Christian yearning for a full recognition of the differentiation that is called for to account for the generation, procession, and spiration that constitute the Divine Life. To sum it up, a Trinity as comprised of degrees of the Essence is unacceptable to most Christian theologians because it appears to them to deny the Divine Unity of the Persons—thereby verging on unitarian Arianism, while a Trinity conceived as internal, undifferentiated, dimensions of the Divine Essence is also flawed for most Christian theologians because it does not seem to make room for any distinctions among the Hypostases, therefore amounting to a sort of Sabellian modalism; hence, the adamant and "unjustifiable" identification of the Absolute and the Relative in God, an identification that can be read as an "absolutization of the Relative."

It must be emphasized that the doctrine of the Trinity, in its normative formulation as encased in the Nicene Creed, was elaborated to a large extent as a response to the liturgical and spiritual needs of the faithful, and as a way of clarifying the nature of the three Divine Persons involved in the Gospel's economy of salvation. The questions "To Whom does or should a Christian pray?" and "What are the relationships between these Divine interlocutors or objects of devotion?"—questions that arose out of decades and centuries of lived faith and early institution—were, therefore, central to the efforts of Christian theologians to develop a coherent doctrine of the relationship between the three Persons within a monotheistic context. The adage *lex orandi lex credendi* is thus crucial as a key to what could be called the spiritual intentionality of the Trinity. Thus, this priority of the experience of faith vis-à-vis metaphysical teachings as such may be deemed to be one of the hallmarks of the specific crystallizations of Trinitarian theology. Such theological crystallizations are, moreover, and quite evidently, intrinsically connected to the Incarnation and the Sacrifice of the Father's only Son as the central elements in the universal economy of Redemption. The metaphysical and historical unicity of the *Redemptor,* His begetting by the Father, and procession of the Holy Spirit called for a clear conceptualization of the Divine Unity that would account for the personal and functional realities of the Father, the Son, and the Holy Ghost. Needless to say, the onto-historical "miracles" of the Incarnation and Redemption made it virtually impossible to envisage and define the Divine independently from the relationships that they entail. The soteriology of the economic Trinity of Redemption could not but lead to a theology of the immanent Trinity in God Himself. If the Son is the only direct redeeming manifestation of God, then the Divine cannot be understood outside of, or aside from, this manifestation. The uniqueness of the Incarnation implies the plurality of the Persons or Hypostases in God, and the relational plurality of the Persons, being a necessary dimension of the Christian God, cannot be envisaged otherwise than as indissociable from the Essence lest it give metaphysical precedence to one of the Persons, namely, the Father, thereby altering the integrity of the monotheistic faith itself. To put it in a different way, the faith-based immediacy of the "economic Trinity," that is, the three persons involved in the economy of the historical Redemption, cannot but have spiritual precedence over the understanding of the "immanent Trinity" as a theological Mystery; and indeed, the latter flows, at least theologically, from the former. On the basis of the doctrinal needs inherent to the unfolding of the economical Trinity, the theological crystallization of the immanent relativity of the Divinity may be deemed to amount, therefore, to an "absolutization of the relative," relational relativity being taken up into the fold of the Ultimate Reality itself, or, rather, identified with it *tale quale*.

## Two Fundamental Intents

As was hinted at in the previous pages, the main concern of Christian theologians has been to preserve the unity, distinction, and equality of the Persons of the Trinity by avoiding any monotheistic and polytheistic reductions. In this respect, the Judaic and Hellenic traditions functioned, stereotypically, as representative of two pitfalls from which Christian Trinitarianism intended to keep itself. In such a light, these errors could even be schematically coined as religious absolutism and religious relativism. The first seven ecumenical councils of the Church, from Nicaea in 325 to the Third Council of Constantinople in 681, were primarily centered on enunciating and repudiating theological positions pertaining to the nature of the Trinity and the divine and human nature and will of Christ. They elaborated a dogmatic theology of the Trinity. The point here is obviously not to provide an extensive survey, nor even a summary, of these complex and acutely disputed theological elaborations, but rather to articulate a few introductory reminders deemed to be most relevant to the current thesis.

The basic intellectual tools used to elaborate a Trinitarian theology consistent with the monotheistic outlook while emphasizing the full divinity of both the Son and the Holy Spirit were forged by theologians of the earlier centuries of the Church, and came to a kind of theological maturity with the Cappadocian Fathers of the fourth century. The main contribution of those Fathers, Saint Basil of Caeserea, Saint Gregory of Nyssa, and Saint Gregory of Nazianzus, was to articulate the distinction within the Divine Unity between the *ousia* (οὐσία) and the *hypostasis* (ὑπόστᾰσις), or the Divine "substance" common to the three and each of the three distinct realities themselves. One of the analogies favored by the Fathers was, in this respect, that of the relationship between the one "human nature" common to three human beings and their distinctive traits as individuals. This distinction allows one to preserve the Divine simplicity of the Essence while fully acknowledging the diversity of Persons. Obviously, the delicate question, then, has remained that of determining the relationship between Essence and Hypostases, *ousia* and *hypostaseis,* and it is on the answer given to this question that hinge many of the difficulties and tensions inherent to later Trinitarian developments.

In this regard, two main intents and tendencies seem to us worthy of analysis here in the theological developments of the centuries following the fixation of one of the major fundamentals of Trinitarian dogmatics at the Council of Nicea, that being the divinity of the Son and His consubstantiality with the Father. These developments can be traced among several of the early Fathers, among whom Saint Dionysius the Areopagite and Saint Maximus Confessor will be highlighted, two immensely influential theologians whose works have been widely venerated and commented upon in both Eastern and Western Christianity.

Our first point is that early Christian theology, particularly in its mystical and Neoplatonic forms, tended to extol the supereminence of the Trinity in such a way as to blur, in quite a paradox, everything that would make it rationally and humanly recognizable, and indeed cognoscible, as a determinate ternary. This tendency is eminently at work in the mystical theology of Dionysius the Areopagite. The name of Dionysius, whose identity as author of the corpus that bears his name is quite uncertain but irrelevant to our current focus, is connected to writings dating back to the early sixth century. In his celebrated *Mystical Theology* the distinctions of Persons and Relations are as if overwhelmed by the supereminent Light of the Godhead that contains them in a seemingly undifferentiated mode. Dionysius presents us with a concept of the Trinity that places It at the metaphysical pinnacle of Reality, and identifies it squarely with the highest possible concept of the Absolute: "Trinity! Higher than any being, any divinity, any goodness!"[5] But this absoluteness is blinding one to diversity as it blinds one to unity. God "transcends the unity which is in beings"[6] and He is "indivisible multiplicity," thereby transcending multiplicity as it is known here below, since the latter is intrinsically divisible. Multiplicity is present within Unity in a way that transcends any distinction between the two. Indeed, the ultimate words of Dionysius's *Mystical Theology* resounds with a purely and emphatically apophatic approach to the Ultimate that denies any affirmations concerning It, including those of its being One, Oneness, Father or Son: "(The Cause of all) is not a substance, nor is it eternity or time. It cannot be grasped by the understanding since it is neither knowledge nor truth. It is not kingship. It is not wisdom. It is neither one nor oneness, divinity nor goodness. Nor is it a spirit in the sense in which we understand that term. It is not sonship or fatherhood and it is nothing known to us or to an other being."[7] All this implies that, on the one hand, no attribution—including those indicative of personal distinctions in the Trinity—is adequate to the Divine Essence and, on the other hand, that the various attributes and qualities that have been denied are at the same time present in the Ultimate in a superessential manner.

This leads us to the second characteristic of Dionysian Trinitarian theology, one that cannot be severed from the first, and could be envisaged as the horizontal complement to the vertical apophatic way that has just been sketched. This second point lies in the assertion that while Unity is higher than the differentiations that it envelops upstream of their differentiation, so to speak, a no less important claim is that each and every one of the differentiated Realities contains the whole of Unity within Itself without any division. The first assertion, pertaining to "undifferentiated unity," is characterized by Dionysius as "the abiding and foundation of the divine persons who are the source of oneness as a unity which is totally undifferentiated and transcendent."[8] The second point, which is obviously designed to safeguard an "absolute" equality among the Persons at the risk of jeopardizing the very principle of their distinction, is also expressed by Dionysius—when he states that "the entire (divine) wholeness is participated in by each of those who participate in it (and) none participates in only a part"[9]—and given full rein, in some representative passages of Maximus Confessor (c. 580–662), a most prominent theologian and monk who was keenly engaged in the theological debates of the time, and whose positions were ultimately upheld by the Sixth Ecumenical Council.

What is most striking with Maximus is not only the way he emphasizes the equality of the Persons of the Trinity in their common unity with the Essence, but also the seeming obliteration of any kind of affirmative distinctions among them: "For the whole Father is entirely in the whole Son and Holy Spirit; and the whole Holy Spirit is entirely in the whole Father and Son. This is why there is only one God, Father, Son, and Holy Spirit. For there is one and the same essence, power, and act of the Father and Son and Holy Spirit, and no one of them can exist or be conceived without the others."[10] So, in a bewildering paradox, the extreme emphasis on the maximal reality of each Person, that is, its coextensiveness with the Essence, may be deemed to result in the absorption of any personal differentiation within the Unity. It is as if the absolutization of the relative resulted in its quasi-disappearance qua relative, so that consubstantiality may appear to end into unitive undifferentiation, both ontologically and conceptually.

This essential undifferentiation seems to extend in fact to the level of nonduality when Maximus asserts that God can never conceive nor be conceived.[11] To conceive, here, means to be a subject in relation to an object that is conceived. To be conceived means to be an object dependent upon a subject to be conceived. Now, God lies beyond this relation of conception or lies beyond the very relation, or polarity, between a subject and an object. This development is quite remarkable in that it seems to reject any kind of objectification within God, and therefore, it would seem, any relation that would entail polarization and opposition. Stating that God cannot conceive nor be conceived amounts to saying that He is a Subject without an object, or pure Subject independent from any object, so that the term *subject* is here purely provisional to refer to a Selfhood that excludes any objectification, and therefore the relative limitations of the very term *subject* itself in contradistinction with an object. This would appear to exclude any understanding of the relationship between the Persons in terms of God's Self-knowledge. In the same way as the Divine Unity makes it impossible for any person to be characterized by something that would be its own independently from this Unity, the Divine Selfhood makes it impossible for anything to be situated within the polarity or duality of separative knowledge. The fundamental nonduality of the Ultimate does not exclude plurality, but this plurality cannot but be undifferentiated or purely principial.

Does this supereminent undifferentiation "contain" more or less Trinity, if one may speak in such a symbolically quantitative manner? More and less, it could be claimed, depending on whether one considers the matter from the vantage point of absoluteness or that of relativity. To the question of knowing whether there is more or less distinction in the supreme Unity as comprised of undifferentiated plurality than in the differentiated distinction itself qua distinction, a first answer could be that the relation, and therefore distinction, is more real in the Essence than anywhere else, simply because of the supereminence of every positive quality and mode in the Essence. The exaltation of personal reality is therefore a function, in this case, of the exaltation of its metaphysical root. But to the same question could be given a very different answer should one focus on relation, and distinction, as an extrinsic reality that presupposes a distance, or a separation, from the Essence. In this case, it is this separation that is precisely proportional to the reality of the distinction, and therefore relation. In this junction can be perceived the meaning of the paradox of Dionysius's exalted statement about the Trinity "higher than being" and higher than "divinity." Metaphysically, both unity and diversity are to be found, at their highest degree of reality, in That which surpasses any determination, including being and divinity. Unity refers here to the principle of exclusive absoluteness, and plurality, including trinity, to that of inclusive infinity. From a different point of view, it could be added that distinction can be envisaged positively and negatively. Positively, it is a principle of identity, while negatively, it is a principle of limitation and privation. When considered positively, distinction reflects the absoluteness of the Ultimate, which it "reproduces" in a relative mode. However, the distinctive principle cannot be considered, in the Ultimate, as privative, since what it excludes is either nothing or the Ultimate itself. What is meant herein is that, in nondual metaphysics such as Hindu *Advaita*, the absoluteness of *Nirguna Brahman* is, on the one hand, discriminated from the non-Ultimate, *Māyā*, which is in a way pure appearance, and on the other hand, inasmuch as it *is*, affirmed as none other than *Brahman*.

Returning to the "supereminentist" and "egalitarian" concerns of the two Church Fathers with respect to the Trinity, it appears that both intents can be read as forms of an absolutization of the relative. Dionysius's identification of the Trinity with the Ultimate obviously lends itself to such an interpretation, as has been clearly demonstrated, among other sources, by Vladimir Lossky's reading of Dionysius's work as *absolutely* Trinitarian, if one may put it so. Similarly, Maximus's emphasis on the perfect equality of all three Persons undoubtedly amounts to a sort of absolutization of each and every one of them, and of their relations.

It could be suggested, though, that another reading of such theological tendencies could be proposed that does not, or would not, entail an absolutization of the relative but rather an undifferentiated prefiguration of the relative within the Absolute. This would correspond to a metaphysical *situs* from which the distinctions of Persons would be envisaged exclusively in their dimension of being and identity, not in their aspect of separativeness and privation. As noted above, this is a reading that is, by and large, rejected by Christian theology because it does not do justice, from an economic and therefore immanent point of view, to the intrinsically relational nature of God, therefore to the distinctions this nature implies.

Finally, it is not without importance to note that Dionysius's "supereminentist" and apophatic bent is primarily epistemological in intent, whereas the "egalitarian" thrust may be evaluated as being more ontological in emphasis. Thus, with Dionysius, the focus is on the ascension of the human faculties of spiritual knowledge toward the Ultimate Mystery. This is clearly indicated by the form of the assertion: "Again, as we climb higher we *say* this."[12] The matter is one of thinking and one of saying, and in this respect, the mind must be divested of any conceptual determinations, including those that pertain to the Persons and their relations. This point will be maximally exploited and developed by Eastern Orthodox Trinitarianism, as discussed further below. The other bent is clearly ontological in that it aims at highlighting both the flawless unity and simplicity of the Godhead and the equality among the Persons. The three Persons are mentioned separately but they cannot be disassociated in any possible way, so that they form an absolute Unity in which each of them is totally, perfectly, and *absolutely* God. Such an envisioning of the Trinity may take one in two very different directions, depending on whether the Trinity is conceived as being *latent,* as it were, in the Unity or, on the contrary, the Unity of the absolute Essence is identified with each of the Hypostases to the point of absolutizing It without any reservation.

## Relation as Absolute and Relative

The Western theological approach of the Trinity has tended to take the "eminentist" road opened by Dionysius's mystical Trinitarianism while somewhat downplaying its "apophatic" dimension. It has considered the matter from the point of view of Unity as the inclusive principle of plurality, on the basis of a complex theological elaboration of the notion of relation in God. Moreover, it has been, by and large, dominated by an attempt at working out the meaning of the Triune God within the confines of a rational account of its main dimensions without claiming to exhaust the Mystery of Divine Life. This is no doubt why the notion of relation has occupied such a central position among scholastics, first among whom Aquinas, probably because of a sense that this notion, by contrast with that of person, which had been a priori associated with the Father as the Person par excellence, provided a more direct and comprehensive entry into the domain of Divine "plurality" as such. In other words, Thomistic Trinitarian theology is intent on demonstrating that God *is* relation, and to draw from this equation an ontological basis from which to unfold the theological account of the internal and interpersonal life of the Divinity.

What does it mean to say that God is relation? It is important, from the outset, to understand that, for Aquinas, all perfections to be found in creation are present a priori in its Cause. Thus, Aquinas approaches the question of relation in the terms of a metaphysics of Unity that postulates the supereminent presence of all creaturely modalities in the Unity of their Principle, or in God. Relation, like any other modes of being, must be found a priori in God, but it is so in a manner that must be, in part, distinguished from the way of creatures. To grasp this point one must realize that, for Aquinas, relation is apprehended as a perfection that is both similar to and different from other modes of being. This is so because, in creatures, relation is an accident that does not enter the substance itself but is merely a modification of it: the relation "happens to" the substance, but is not the substance. In fact, relation is a unique accident in this respect, by contrast with, say, quality or quantity, which enter the substantial entity. However, the matter is different in God, in whom and with whom there is no accident, and in whom, therefore, relation can neither be conceived as a modification of the "Divine Substance" nor indeed as separable from it. This allows one to understand why and how relation in God is conceived by Aquinas as *subsisting* relation.[13] In fact, Divine Persons are none other than subsisting relations, as will appear more explicitly further on. This is an important point for Aquinas to emphasize in order to shield the Divine Essence from any "relativization" through relations. This means that, for him, relation in God can, and must, be fully relation without in the least modifying God's Essence. To sum it up, in God relation is not accidental since there is no accident in Him, nor does it, therefore, modify the Essence, from which it is metaphysically no different.

The above characterization of relation is connected to another cardinal distinction. This second distinction pertains to the difference between a real relation, that is to say, a relation as it exists between two "relatives"—meaning here two beings that are in relation—and on the other hand a purely rational, or notional, relation, such as can be envisaged theoretically, for instance, between something that exists and something that does not. The consideration of these two types of relation is particularly pertinent to the question of relations in God by allowing Aquinas to distinguish between three types of relations: first, those which are integrally real, second, those that are exclusively notional, and third, those which involve both ontological reality and conceptual reality, but do so on different sides of the relation. The relation between God and creatures ranks among the latter, whereas the relations *in divinis* are representative of the first type. The point made by Aquinas, one most relevant to our inquiry, is that in the relation between God and creatures, God's relation to creatures is only notional, whereas the reverse relation, say between mankind and God, is real. This means that God's relation to a creature does not in the least alter His Essence, nor does it add anything *real* to It, nor is He in any way dependent on it. This is, clearly, the measure of His absoluteness. By contrast, the relation linking mankind to God is real, and not merely notional, in that it is intrinsically inscribed in the essence and existence of mankind. In other terms, the essence of mankind includes its relation to God; without it there is no mankind. As for the relations between the Persons of the Trinity, by contrast, they are real from all sides in the sense that they are intrinsically necessary to, and in fact constitutive of, each of the Hypostases, since, as already mentioned, each Person is a subsisting relation. Now, it remains to examine the status of this *reality* of the relations within the Trinity with respect to the Essence.

In order to do so, one must consider that the relation in God can, and indeed must, be envisaged in two different ways. These are the real, or entitative, point of view, and the logical, or formal, point of view. Thus, the core distinction in Aquinas's concept of relation is the one between relation *as pure being* and relation *as referring to another*. The first aspect of relation is its "absolute" aspect or, put differently, "a real relation . . . cannot exist . . . without a reality which itself does not belong to the order of relativity."[14] On the Divine plane, this reality pertains to the Essence, and is indeed no different from the Essence. This amounts to saying that relation, as being, is absolute in God, that it is in God *eminenter,* and that it is indeed none other than God as the Absolute.

However, relation can also be understood from the vantage point of its connection to the external relative or *ad extra,* hence notionally or *formaliter.* Insofar as relation does not concern the substance itself, but rather its extrinsic respect, it can be applied to God *tale quale,* and not merely by way of eminence, without altering His Essence. As such, for instance, it does not constrain the freedom and necessity of God. Relation as being is the divine Essence itself, but it cannot be the Essence as regards another: formally, it is not with respect to the Essence but in relation to otherness, or to the opposite. This amounts to saying that relation in God can be considered both *eminenter* as the Essence—or as the unqualified Absolute, and *formaliter,* as extrinsic to It, or as only relationally Absolute, as it were, and in this sense not notionally different from created relation.

It is clear that, for Aquinas, these two aspects, as stated in the *Summa,* differ only "in our way of thinking;"[15] and so there is evidently a conflation of the Absolute and the Relative in God, since nothing *real* distinguishes the

Essence from the Hypostases. Aquinas acknowledges that this unity is difficult to grasp for our usual way of thinking since in our experience personal essence is really distinct from relation. Thus, a radical gap is introduced between the terrestrial experience of substance and relation and their reality *in divinis*. In the field of creation, relation inheres in beings as modification: a substance is a subject of relations, but not the relation itself. Thus, the total identification of relation and God in being pertains to the domain of the humanly incomprehensible. The relation, or relativity, as well as the "relatives" in Saint Thomas's sense of the term, are literally absolutized in a way that challenges intelligibility. Thus, an emphasis on the humanly unthinkable nature of relations in God is preferred to the possibility of any recognition of a vertical differentiation within the Divine Reality, a differentiation that would be deemed to both alter the Divine Unity and relativize the Trinity.

Nonetheless, it may be considered that the aforementioned distinction between an absolute and a relative respect of the relation in God could have opened the way to a recognition of degrees of reality within the Divine itself. Thus, one might have envisaged, in a mode analogous to the Hindu distinction between the unqualified and the qualified Absolute, an undifferentiated degree of the Essence, one including relation in a supereminent way, and a differentiated degree that would entail distinction through the Hypostases. The latter may correspond to what is referred to by the Western tradition as "relation of opposition with respect to origin." This signifies that Persons are the "products" of relations that "oppose" them—in the neutral sense of a mere polarity—in terms of their origin, such as paternity, filiation, and procession. It is quite instructive to note that this relation of opposition is conceived by the Scholastic tradition as the smallest possible relativity to be introduced in God, in a way that appears to concede, not insignificantly, that plurality could affect Unity.

The theological principle not to draw the above possible metaphysical conclusions from the distinction between absoluteness and relativity in God, together with a blurring of rational intelligibility, bears its most strikingly provocative implications in Eastern apophaticism. In Thomistic Trinitarianism, by contrast, the limits of this choice of the humanly unintelligible over any hint at vertical subordination are met with the principle that no relation with reference to another is without a subject in which it either inheres or *is*. This means no "relativity" without "absoluteness," really and not only notionally, which is tantamount to arguing that if the relations are indeed real among the three Hypostases it is only because they are *not* real in the Essence. As already intimated, the distinction taken as such could have given rise to the recognition of a demarcation between a degree of pure absoluteness and one of divine relativity. Such an interpretation, clearly at odds with the main theologi-

Christian and Buddhist Insights into a Metaphysics of Salvation    63

cal currents of Christianity, would mean that the Relative can solely be in the Absolute in a purely undifferentiated way, and can only become differentiated as *real* relation with respect to another on the plane of a relative absoluteness, if the expression may be allowed.[16] Some contemporary theologians have argued that Meister Eckhart's mysticism of the Essence stands for such a metaphysical orientation in suggesting the apophatic and impersonal transcendence of the Essence beyond the Hypostases.[17]

It could be argued, moreover, that the Thomistic *via eminentiae* omits to be applied to the distinction between God and the creation, or the Absolute and the relative, a distinction that is indeed *real* within the latter. Like any other mode of relation, this distinction should be transposed into the Absolute itself as a reality, and not simply as a notion. If so, however, it cannot be qua Absolute but qua distinction, or rather both as being absolute and as distinction, since the distinction between two relative beings is not more real than is the distinction between the relative and the Absolute itself, indeed quite the contrary. This would mean distinguishing absoluteness and relativity in the Divine Reality without affecting its Unity. To put it differently, this distinction must be *in* the Absolute, or even *be* the Absolute, but without being the Absolute *as such*; or else the Absolute qua Absolute cannot be absolute and nonabsolute at the same time on the same level of reality. If one objects to this on the grounds that the relation between God and creation is only notional, then it still remains that the relation between creation and God is indeed real. Hence, it begs the question of why this real relation is not present supereminently in God since there is no positive mode or aspect in creation that cannot be transposed eminently in the Divine without denying Its perfection.

Whether one understands the distinction between absolute relation and relation with respect to another in a merely notional sense, as the Western tradition does, or in an ontological sense likely to be rejected as subordinationist or anti-Trinitarian, it remains that the very distinction itself has appeared to most Eastern theologians as too much of a concession to the strictures of "rational Unity," and indeed something like a "relativization of the relation," if one may say so, therefore a "relativization of the Persons."[18] By contrast, the Eastern emphasis is akin to the early theological concerns that paved the way for a theological construction of the Trinitarian concepts. It is less centered on the intellectual, and even less rational, coherence of the latter than on its relevance to the spiritual life of the Christian soul. In fact, the typical reproach leveled by Eastern theologians at Thomistic elaborations, for instance, is that of rational abstraction. In such a perspective, an initial focus on the principle of Divine Unity may appear too tied up with pre-Christian philosophical speculations of a Neoplatonic bent, and deemed not to take sufficient account of the Divinity as a principle of transformative and theurgic grace. Thus, the

Trinitarian flavor of Eastern Orthodox theological thought tends to flow from a mystical recognition of the irreducibility of the Divine Persons as agents in the process of deification of mankind. The instance of the liturgical preeminence, in the Eastern Orthodox churches, of the Holy Trinity over Christ is a clear indication of this emphasis. Hence, the Eastern rejection not only of unitarism and modalism, but also of Jesuanism understood as an excessively Christocentric perspective. Orthodox theologians are prone to emphasize, often in a somewhat polemical way in relation to the West, the centrality of the Trinity as relational paradigm, and as the informing current of love of the Christian life, both liturgically and spiritually. Thus, John McGuckin warns, in quite a representative way, that "without the prior understanding . . . that the Trinity is first and foremost our focus of praise in the liturgy, and our call to have compassion on the other, then it is doomed to scholastic sterility."[19]

The Eastern metaphysical equation might be simply stated in affirming that "Three is One" and "One is Three," without attempting in the least to relativize this irreducible paradox. In fact, this is so much so that Eastern theologians have been keen on debunking any hint at any "supremacy" of the Essence over the Persons.[20] Consequently, antinomism and apophaticism lie at the core of such an "absolutist" way of envisaging the Trinity. On the whole, Eastern theologians, far from trying to reduce or explain away the contradiction between identity and difference in God, take it as foundational of the Christian outlook on the Divinity, and the very process of participation in Divine Grace that opens onto deification. This apophaticism implies both the static supra-rational contemplation of an arresting awe, and the dynamic power of an unending noetic motion. One of the most suggestive and provocative expressions of this point of view is to be found in Lossky's statement that "(our thought) must swing ceaselessly between the two poles of the antinomy, in order to attain to the contemplation of the sovereign repose of this threefold monad."[21]

As one of the most authoritative and influential earlier statements in this line of thought, St. John of Damascus's definition of the Trinity encapsulates most effectively all the major elements of its Orthodox understanding: "One essence, one divinity, one power, one will, one energy, one beginning, one authority, one dominion, one sovereignty, made known in three perfect subsistences adored with one adoration, believed in and ministered to by all rational creation, united without confusion and divided without separation (which indeed transcends thought)."[22] Six major interconnected points may be highlighted: the emphatic declaration of the Unity of the Essence, the association of the Hypostases with the process of communication and acquisition of spiritual knowledge, the oneness of worship, the cosmic dimension of the Trinitarian reality, the conjunction of unity and distinction, and the supra-rational and apophatic horizon of the Mystery. First, it is to be noted that the distinction between Essence and Hypostases is related, by implication, to the possibility of the knowledge of God. In this regard, there is in the Eastern tradition a strong emphasis on the unknowableness of the Essence, and no less strong a stress on the Trinity as the dimension of the Divine that makes the latter known both to mankind and the entire cosmos. Furthermore, this association of the Trinity with the process of knowledge does not entail any sense of dispersion in worship. In other words, the Trinity makes the Divinity known but this knowledge does not result in any sense of disjunction within It. Finally, the unambiguous and combined affirmation of union and distinction, by contrast with confusion and separation, takes one into a realm that transcends the capacity of reason and resonates with antinomy, opening onto apophatism. This means conjunct absolutization of unity and difference in the Divine, without any sense of hierarchization between the two. However, it is important to note that the distinction between Essence and Hypostases is primarily understood in terms of the human knowledge of the Divine, hence in relation to the creaturely realm. The Hypostases are this dimension of the Divine that is clearly *relative* to creation, whereas the Essence is not.

This raises the complex question of the relationship between the Hypostases and what Eastern theology has theorized, in the wake of Saint Gregory Palamas, as the Energies, in Greek *energeia*. The theological development of the Divine Energies was directly connected to a need to account for the central soteriological point of the Eastern Church, and *mutatis mutandis* of the universal Church, that is, the spiritual perfection, and ultimate human goal, of deification or *theōsis*. Given the oneness of the immanent Trinity with the Essence, one lingering question has been that of the economic dimension of the divine Persons at work in salvation without introducing any duality between the latter and the former. In a sense, the energy of salvation and deification is to be equated with the Holy Spirit, at least when the latter is understood in its economic aspect rather than in its hypostatic one.

Be that as it may, what relates the Mystery of the Trinity and the Mystery of the Communication of the Uncommunicable at stake in the Energies is their antinomic character. In the way, says Saint Gregory of Thessalonica, that one must hold on to the unity and distinction of the Hypostases, in the same way one must hold on to the inaccessibility and accessibility of God, in other words, to his transcendence and immanence. Analogically, just as distinction is no less real than unity in God, accessibility is no less real than inaccessibility. There is, in other words, an absolute relativity in God, and that is the Trinity, as there is also a relative absoluteness in creation, in the form of deification as the coincidence of transcendence and immanence. The latter is undoubtedly divine, therefore absolute in its substance, and still undeniably relative inasmuch as it concerns human, hence relative, beings. Now it matters to grasp that the antinomic characters of both realities are related in that the first is, as it were, mirrored in the second, while the second is made possible by the first. To say that the Trinity is mirrored in deification means that the latter reflects, *mutatis mutandis,* a coincidence of opposites in which identity and difference meet. To say that deification is made possible by the Trinity means it is in the Trinity that what, in creation, is actualized as union, namely, the antinomy of unity in difference, begins. But there is a clear difference: while the Trinity and the Hypostases are absolute, the deified human soul is never so. It is precisely because the Trinity is the Absolute, or the Essence, and the soul cannot be so, that the distinction between Essence and Energies is needed to account for the possibility, indeed the reality of deification. Humans cannot be one with the Essence, nor with any of the Hypostases: that would mean that they are a Hypostasis, and it is why they can only participate in the Divine through Its Energies. These Energies, essentially unseverable from the Essence, are the extrinsic modes of relationality, therefore relativity, of the Divine. This distinction goes back, according to Lossky, to the early Fathers as illustrated by the Dionysian concepts of "unions," *enôseis,* and "distinctions," *diakriseis,* the first being intrinsic and pertaining to the unfathomable, the second being extrinsic and making God knowable, as *proodoi* or processions. The distinctions do not affect the Unity of the Divine, as Saint Gregory Palamas illustrates it through the symbolic analogy of the sun and its rays. Whereas the rays can be distinguished from each other, the sun is entirely in each of them, which amounts to saying that it is indivisible.[23] On the other hand, Palamas highlights that "Essence and energy are not totally identical in God" in the same way that the sun cannot be reduced to the ray.

In a sense, the Energies are the theological complement of the nonrelativization of the Trinity. This amounts to saying that the absolutization of the relative in God, or the absolutization of the Hypostases, makes it necessary to consider a domain within the Absolute that would be extrinsically and actively relative with regard to other-than-God, and situated on a lower degree than the absolute absoluteness of the Essence. This is because the Essence and Hypostases are inaccessible, and therefore in a sense unrelatable, outside the Divinity. Thus is opened the realm of the Energies that make the inaccessible accessible, in an irreducibly antinomic but necessary way. Lest they be confused with the Hypostases, it bears stressing that these Energies are the divine powers and acts of the *entire* Trinity as Essence. In fact, the distinction between Energies and Essence makes it clear that the extrinsic operations of God such as creation, revelation, and deification are fundamentally different from the intrinsic operations, that is, generation and processions within God. On the other hand, it appears undeniable that the latter can be considered as the transcendent sources and, in a way, "relational paradigms" of the former. This is so because the economic Trinity can be distinguished from the immanent Trinity only operatively, but not essentially. Indeed, Lossky sees the Energies as bridging the respective domains of the immanent Trinity and the economic Trinity.[24] The latter pertains to God's acts and operations whereas the former relates to the internal life of the Essence. Thus, the relation between Essence and Energies is one of distinction, without, however, implying an ontological scission between the two. This raises the question of the meaning of distinction without difference. In Hindu metaphysics, particularly in Qualified Nondualism (*Visistādvaita*) the concept of *bhedābheda* is referred to when pointing to such a subtle distinction within Unity without difference. *Bhedābheda* is a synthesis of identity and plurality.[25] It is relevant to the devotional outlook of the way of love, *bhakti,* in that it affirms conjointly the Unity of the Principle and the irreducibility of the difference between the human devotee and the Divine Lord. This is functionally analogous to the status of the Energies as mediating, as it were, between the Essence and creation. In radical Hindu Nondualism, such as *Advaita Vedānta,* the concept of a qualified Absolute, *Saguna Brahman,* is also found, thereby introducing a distinction within *Brahman,* hence reserving pure and unqualified absoluteness to *Nirguna Brahman,* the Ultimate without qualities nor forms.[26] Thus, Shankara characterizes *Brahman* as one, but he also specifies that it may be considered either with limiting attributes or as free from them. The interesting point is that this distinction, typical of the contrast between *Saguna* and *Nirguna Brahman,* is envisaged by him as connected to two modes of knowledge of the Absolute. In the first case, the matter is *Brahman* as "conceptually meditated upon," whereas in the second it is a question of *Brahman* as "known." Thus, the first characterization of *Brahman* is connected to the need for mental relations, while the second pertains to immediate recognition, or knowledge by identification, which is the ultimate epistemological aim of *Advaita.* Notwithstanding, the "God with qualities," Īśvara, is not merely a conceptual reality. If *Saguna Brahman* refers, as Comans puts it, to Īśvara as "further characterized by a series of further qualities for the purpose of meditation or worship,"[27] it would seem that relationship implies a reality that is more than merely conceptual, otherwise meditation and worship would be related exclusively to figments of the mind. In actuality, it is clear that the *Brahman* that is worshipped or thought is not different from the *Brahman* that is realized. The crux of the matter lies in the various perspectives concerning Reality. Indeed, from the point of view of *Nirguna* everything *other-than-Self* is conceptual in the sense that there are no real ontological differences, since nothing is but the nondual Reality and since this Reality is universal Consciousness. Differences presuppose a dual or dualistic point of view, and are therefore in a sense relatable to conceptual distinctions, which derive from relationships between subjects and objects.

Notwithstanding this distinction between Essence—including the Hypostases—and Energies, including those involved in the economy of salvation, the
Son and the Holy Spirit seem to be, at times, difficult to differentiate from
the Energies. Some Patristic formulations[28] characterize the Son as image or
manifestation of the Father, and the Holy Spirit as image or manifestation of
the Son. Such expressions would appear to be an invitation to understand the
second and third Persons of the Trinity as hypostatic Energies. As seen throughout
what precedes, the distinction between Essence and Energies, as that among
the Persons, pertains to what the Eastern Church approaches as an antinomy.
The same types of relationship are also considered as entailing apophaticism.
The antinomy refers to the rationally unresolvable coincidence of unity and
distinction, oneness and multiplicity, identity and alterity. It lies at the heart
of any "absolutization of the relative." It is, as it were, a negative affirmation.
It therefore constitutes the test of the limits of human knowledge and Divine
comprehensibility that opens the way to true apophaticism. It is by negating,
apophatically, the very terms of the antinomy, through a "neither . . . nor"
that one may receive intimations of the Unknowable that is the Ultimate.

One important question to be raised, in this connection, refers to apophaticism as relatable to the Essence, *ousia* or to the Persons, *hypostaseis,* or to
both. The second position has been proposed by Vladimir Lossky, for whom
the apophatic nature of the Hypostases is paramount in the very process of
Christian spiritual transformation. It is through the doors of apophaticism in
relation to the Hypostases that the domain of deifying presence is reached.
By contrast, some other theologians have contended that only the Essence is
known apophatically. A contemporary theologian such as John Zizioulas considers that Christian knowledge of the Trinity does not pertain to apophaticism,
but flows, rather, from sacramental encounter. Thus, Zizioulas emphasizes the
need to distinguish the "what is" and the "how it is." The Hypostases are the
way of being of God, the "how it is," and this "how" is known existentially,
or sacramentally. Only the *ousia* is unknowable as "what is" and remains,
therefore, within the realm of the apophatic.[29]

By contrast, for Lossky, apophaticism relates primarily to the nature of
God as Trinity. This apophatic emphasis is founded on a need to hold on to
an irreducible and unfathomable conjunction of Triplicity and Unity, but at
the same time, it can be interpreted, at least virtually, as referring to an undifferentiated Reality of the Three, or an undifferentiated unity of the One and
the Three. This paradox explains why some analysts have highlighted a tension,
in Lossky and other apophaticist theologians, between apophaticism and the
positive content of a theology of the Person, the latter running the risk of
being dissolved, as it were, in the unknowable recess of the Divine Darkness.
Thus, quite paradoxically, that which was highlighted as shielding the Trinity

from any rational and philosophical reduction may result, in its turn, in a reduction of the spiritual import of the Trinity. Apophaticism, by shrouding the distinctness of the Persons in the Mystery, may result in their paradoxical and unintended relativization. In other words, the apophatic reality of the Divine Trinity becomes absolutized, and potentially obstructs one's participation into the actual Life of the Hypostases. The concern for parrying any rational abstraction ends up by producing its own kind of abstraction. In a sense, the reproach that Lossky is leveling at the Western mysticism of the Essence, of which he finds the clearest example in Eckhart, could be applied to his own apophaticism inasmuch as the latter may appear to forbid any knowledge of the Persons as such in their distinctiveness. This is, incidentally, a critique that has been occasionally directed at the Eastern Orthodox theological tradition from the side of Evangelical personalism.

As suggested above, the theological "absolutization of the relative" in God is as if pulled between two poles. On the one hand, Aquinas presents his reader with an intellectual delineation of the Divine Reality that intends to provide an understanding of the Tri-Unity of God without sacrificing either His Essential Oneness or the distinction of Relations and Persons. This aims at preserving the absoluteness of the Absolute and Its Relativity without compromising Its Unity. On the other hand, such a theological orientation leads to what seems like a recognition, at least conceptually, of degrees of the Divine Essence. By contrast, in the East, Lossky's theological synthesis of Orthodox Trinitarianism highlights a radical, and fully claimed, absolutization of the relative through antinomic and apophatic coincidence that may paradoxically lead to a blurring of personal distinctions into a Superessential Undifferentiation. Although both ideas of degrees and undifferentiated dimensions of the Essence are explicitly rejected by most Christian theologians as contrary to the very core of the Christian perspective on the Trinity, they nevertheless appear as two possible theological consequences to be drawn from the main theological concepts of the Western and Eastern churches, the rejection of which is motivated, both historically and psychologically, by a need to shield the doctrine from any seemingly Arian and Sabellian understandings of the Trinity.

The Western orientation highlights, to the extent that it is possible in a matter that touches upon a Mystery of faith, the intellectual coherence of Trinitarian theology. The emphasis on relation, and the distinction between the real and the notional in terms of understanding the metaphysical layout of essence and relation is, at it were, the limit of the absolutization of the relative. Some of its Eastern critiques charge these tendencies with a dangerous relativization of the Persons. Against such perceived rational relativization, Eastern Trinitarian theology tends to extol the supra-rational dimension of the Trinity. This is, in a sense, a mystical "subversion" of the intellectual setting of Trinitarian theology. However, it can be deemed that this antinomic stress tends to reassert the absoluteness of the Absolute through its apophatic emphasis, as if against the grain of its own theological impulse. The Absolute is the Unknowable, and this principle is also, in its own way, a limit t the absolutization of the relative, since the latter would seem to imply the possibility of distinction in love and knowledge. Although the West comes closer to admitting a degree of relativity within the Absolute, through its distinction between "real" and "notional" relation, or absoluteness and "respect to other"—by contrast with the Eastern reveling in antinomy—the East recognizes a relativity within the Absolute in the Energies, whereas the West denies it by rejecting the latter.[30]

## The Buddhist Predicament

The general economy of Buddhism proceeds along a metaphysical way that is, in a sense, the analogous reverse of the Christian theological development. Whereas the theological bent of Christianity consists in absolutizing the relative as the very nature and essence of the Divinity, the prime bent of the Buddhist spiritual path lies in its relativizing any absoluteness, at least provisionally, in order to clear the ground for the realization of nirvānic awakening. It is important to note, from the outset, that this "relativization" aims, first and foremost, at the ascetic goal of a radical modification of one's mode of consciousness. It is, therefore, less metaphysical in the objective sense of a *Weltanschauung* than spiritual in the subjective sense of a perception of reality. Accordingly, the fact that the starting point of Buddhism is experiential relativizes a priori any metaphysical teaching about the nature of reality since it subordinates it to the realization of the experience of awakening. This significant consideration is brought to the fore with the central notion of *upāya*, or skillful means. Metaphysics, Buddhist metaphysics, can only be an *upāya*, a teaching means, which amounts to saying that it is only one among other means, and also that it is less a doctrinal foundation than a methodical path of access to an ultimate mode of intellectual and spiritual awareness. Masao Abe has characterized Buddhism as a religious system "that defines *dharma* in terms of *dharmas*."[31] This means that the Buddhist perspective envisages the Ultimate in terms of the multiplicity of outlooks on phenomena and, therefore, in the mode of a relativization of the Absolute. In this regard, the plurality and instrumentality of schools are, in the Buddhist tradition as a whole, a direct evidence of the significance of the relativistic emphasis that serves as our heuristic principle.

In reaction to the absolutization of the Self that is inherent to the non-dualistic Hindu Brahmanic way of knowledge, such as the *Advaitin Ātman*, the Buddha's teachings pronounce and proclaim the relativity of everything, including that which would be traditionally considered as the Absolute per se, that is, God and the Self. Once again, however, these pronouncements appear to be taken as methodical signposts on the path rather than as metaphysical doctrine as such. This is the way one of the most authoritative contemporary Theravādin thinkers, Walpula Rahula, spells out the meaning of "conditioned genesis" (*pratītya-samutpāda* or *paticca-samuppāda*) as the "synthetical method"— by contrast with the analytical decomposition of the aggregates—according to which "nothing in the world is absolute." Thus, Walpula Rahula refers to the Buddhist "theory of relativity," according to which "everything is conditioned, relative, and interdependent," and therefore empty.[32] In Theravāda, however, the emptiness implied by interdependent arising tends to be considered solely from a phenomenological and spiritual point of view. This is all the more so that *pratītya-samutpāda* is conceived as a response to what early Buddhism considers to be the substantialist or eternalist error inherent in the Hindu metaphysics of *svabhāva* or self-nature. So, in this context, emptiness is not so much a metaphysical notion designed to counter other metaphysical views as it is in itself a repudiation of metaphysics as being inherently substantialist. Its pragmatic intent is to dispel any view that would attribute a separate and independent substantiality to realities, and therefore give hold to attachment and craving. In what follows, however, the focus will be on the ways in which this spiritual therapy gives rise to discourses that become unavoidably tied up with specific strands of ontology. Hence, it is recognized that once the methodical concerns of early Buddhist teachings come to be theorized within a philosophical framework, they typically result in such classical expressions as are to be found in Nāgārjuna's foundational tetralemma included in the intro-duction of his *Mūlamadhyamakakārikā*: "No existents whatsoever are evident anywhere that are arisen from themselves, from another, from both, or from a non-cause" (I.1). While the first point is a direct rejection of the notion of *causa sui* or Absolute as such, all other rejections, based on expressions used by the Buddha himself, are also denials of any sense of self-nature, and pave the way for the idea of an interdependent arising of everything whatsoever, thereby parrying any purely mental sense of priority that could function as a trace of absoluteness; hence, Nāgārjuna's tetralemma is a prime example of the kind of intellectual tools that are brought to bear in "relativizing the absolute." When applied specifically to the Ultimate, such dismissal of any attempt at substantialization and reification may indeed not qualify as an exclusive char-acteristic of Buddhist teachings since it is also at work, in different modes, in other non-Buddhist, metaphysical frameworks. In fact, mystical theology as a whole, whether in Semitic or Indic contexts, tends to resist any "ontification" of the ontological, if one may put it that way, that is, a treatment of Being as a mere being, or rather as an existent. However, what is particularly striking in Nāgārjuna's and kin Buddhist outlooks is the radical nature of their treatment of the very notion of an independent and ultimate selfhood of any sort, which lies in stark contrast with, for example, the metaphysical thrust of Hindu *Advaita* or Islamic theology. This does not necessarily mean that the heuristic concept of a "relativization of the absolute" as applied to Buddhist teachings needs always be understood as amounting to an utter *negation* of the Absolute. In fact, this principle may be read in at least two different ways, which have been sometimes conceived as the two sides of the same reality. On the one hand, it amounts to a clear relativization of all realities that could be apprehended in absolute terms, including the concepts of God and the Self. On the other hand, if and when the Absolute is approached, or simply implied, it is—as we will see—through the epistemological prism of the "universal relativity" of codependent conditioning, whether the latter is understood as ultimate or propaedeutic.

It can be argued, therefore, that the central concern of the Buddhist *dharma* is analogous to that of Christian theology insofar as a spiritual reality, or a spiritual event, for instance, awakening and the end of suffering as crystallized in the Buddha's *nirvāna*, unfolds as a set of teachings that have to account for it while providing a scriptural and doctrinal basis for its duplication. It bears stressing, in this connection, that the Buddha's teachings, as expressed in the *Sūtra Pitaka*, can be characterized by their ametaphysical, if not antimetaphysical, bent inasmuch as they constitute a spiritually centered response to Upanishadic formulations and speculations. That which is true is that which is empirically effective, or bears cognitive and moral fruits (*attha sahita*). Thus, the methodical teachings of the Buddha are summarized in the Four Noble Truths, which are all of an existential and spiritual nature, and particularly in the first and last ones, suffering and awakening or liberation. As a result, spiritual awakening, or *nirvāna*, lies at the core of any Buddhist doctrinal pronouncement, while being at the same time its finality. From the Buddha's point of view, the most urgent and indeed only question to be answered is that of the cause of suffering and, correlatively, that of the impediments to awakening. The answer to this question is none other than the second noble truth: craving, *dukkha samudaya,* is the root of suffering. But it is with the third noble truth, *nirodha,* or the cessation of craving and therefore suffering, that one truly enters the sphere of salvation and the view—if it is considered at all a view[33]—that conditions it.

On an immediate level, the reality of craving is expressed in terms of psycho-moral conditioning, such as is taught in the doctrine of the twelve-link chain. This teaching makes explicit the connection between a series of causes and effects that ranges from ignorance to rebirth, and highlights the central nexus between craving (*tanhā*), clinging (*upādāna*), and karmic becoming.

This foundational teaching of the Buddha's *dharma* is developed in the *Kaccāyanagotta-Sutra* where the twelve causal conditions (*nidānas*) are enumerated as dependent upon each other for their arising and their ceasing, beginning with ignorance (*avidyā*) and ending with suffering (*dukkha*). On the level of immediate spiritual pedagogy, this chain appears to express a one-directional causality that describes how a given cause produces a given effect, and so on and so forth. What matters most here is not the beginning point, which varies according to diverse readings of the *nidānas,* but the mere fact of the concatenation, since it is the very principle of the cycle of birth and suffering. This is the basic Theravāda understanding of the pragmatic validity, or truth, of *pratītya-samutpāda.* However, later insights, in Māhāyana, provide a view of the twelve *nidānas* which, going beyond the unidirectional pragmatic teaching on the concatenation of causes and effects, involves a wider, bidirectional, interdependent conditioning, which moves us from the conventional teachings of the path to the ultimate teachings of the structure of reality, the latter allowing one to envisage the former not only in its instrumental nature, but also and above all in its inherent vacuity. Thus, a mindful examination of this causal chain leads, through the insight of codependent origination, or emptiness, to the undoing of its links, pragmatically, and to the revelation of its own emptiness, so that it realizes that itself *was* never in any ultimate sense. Hence, on a first level, codependent origination refers to a purely practical concern for dispelling ignorance and craving. The principle of *pratītya-samutpāda,* inherent to samsāric reality, is in that sense set in contradistinction with the reality of *nirvāna.* But the very nature of Buddhist teaching as *upāya kaulasya,* or skillful means, predisposed it to adapt to the most diverse modes of receptivity. This meant, in the Indian context of its early development, the need to extract from its pragmatic vision of Awakening the doctrinal gist that could serve to refute competing views, primarily Vedāntic formulations. Now, the very foundation of such theoretical elaborations was available in and through the very teaching of the *nidānas,* or rather *pratītya-samutpāda.* The paradox of Buddhist doctrinal development is, in this way, that the primacy of causality leads to the very undoing of causality. Nāgārjuna's previously quoted negation of causes through his tetralemma (*catuskoti*) constitutes the classical formulation of this *emptying* insight: "No existents whatsoever are evident anywhere that are arisen from themselves, from another, from both, or from a non-cause" (I.1). By recognizing the interdependence of all phenomena one also realizes that the bondage of causality is actually empty of substance, and this is, soteriologically, the key to the liberation from ignorance and suffering.

The question remains, however, whether and how the very principle of codependent origination applies to codependent origination itself. To put it

differently, one must consider whether codependent origination holds as a
"right view" that somehow transcends the realm of interdependent phenomena,
or it needs itself to be undone in order to give way to true liberation from a
belief in substances. The second of these options needs to preserve the pragmatic effectiveness of emptiness without turning it into an absolute truth.[34]
Either way, the spiritually pragmatic nature of the Buddha's teachings was not
to be without doctrinal implications which, deriving as they did from the
development of the notion of emptiness, have been increasingly identified, in
contemporary scholarship, with the most fundamental Buddhist tenet, namely,
emptiness. Now it is quite clear that the epistemological focal point of this
tenet lies in revealing the deluded character of substantiality as a source of
craving and suffering. There are no substances, there are no "absolutes," and
this truth is the key to enlightenment.[35] The term *substantiality* connotes,
here, a variety of conditions that come down to a notion of absoluteness as
entailing ontological necessity, independence, freedom, and permanence. The
term *svabhāva*, often translated as "self-nature" or "own essence," is the most
adequate to refer to that which Buddhist epistemology aims at debunking
as insubstantial and unfounded. The sense of impermanence, so strikingly
representative of the Buddhist spiritual ethos, is particularly central in this
respect, as it conveys a path of liberation from the unenlightened belief in
the reality of phenomena. The inner emancipation from the epistemological
lure of *svabhāva* amounts to, or results from—conventionally at least—the
realization of universal emptiness, or so-called co-dependent arising or origination, *pratītya-samutpāda*. This teaching exposes the nonsubstantiality of all
phenomenal existence in contradistinction with the two erroneous views of
"eternalism" and "nihilism." The first position, *śāśvatavāda*, which was attributed
by early Buddhism to such Hindu schools of thought as nondual *Vedānta*,
could also be referred to as "essentialism" in the sense that it postulates the
self-subsistent existence of things as discrete and definable essences. Thus, the
main currents of Buddhism stand in sharp contrast with the Neoplatonic thrust
of most schools of Western and Islamic mysticism in their negation, or at
least lack of consideration, of any equivalent of Platonic "forms" or archetypes.
This radical anti-essentialism should not be understood, however, as an utter
denial of the reality of things, or as an affirmation of ultimate nothingness.
The latter position—referred to as "annihilationism" (*ucchedavāda*)—radically
denies any reality to phenomenal existence, and is at times mistakenly confused for the doctrine of emptiness, from which it needs to be emphatically
distinguished. Epitomized, at the Buddha's time, by the concepts attributed to
the ascetic Kesakambalī, *ucchedavāda* is moreover characterized by the negation of any continuum of existence after death, thereby amounting, from a
Buddhist point of view, to the invalidation of the relevance of any spiritual

path; hence, the Buddha stressed its incompatibility with any sense of karmic continuity, and highlighted its defying the very purpose of the *Dharma*.[36] In rejecting both "eternalism" and "annihilationism," the doctrine of emptiness lies as a middle path between these two erroneous positions. Against the first, it argues for the reality of change and transformation that *śāśvatavāda* makes arguably impossible, while stressing, against the second, the permanence of a conditioned chain of being. Thus, by contrast with these two extremes, *pratītya-samutpāda* teaches the reality of a universal network of interdependent realities that accounts for both continuity and discontinuity, therefore for the possibility of transformation, while avoiding the twin pitfalls of substantialization and nihilism. Emptiness is, therefore, emphatically not inexistence, since the latter is in a sense impossible, and indeed unthinkable within the context of codependent arising. From this point of view, it could be argued that the position of inexistence is in its own manner as "absolutist" as that of eternal substance. At any rate, the process of "absolutization" that erects phenomena as independent and permanent is the very source of all attachments and, therefore, of all suffering. The key to a dispelling of ignorance lies, therefore, in a radical relativization of any trace of "absoluteness" that would give way to an alienating belief in the reality of phenomena. At the same time, this relativization must be compatible with asserting the reality of the nirvānic mode of consciousness that constitutes the primary goal of the teachings. It is clear that the term *absoluteness* is extended, in this case, beyond its strict definition as presented in the introductory paragraphs of our essay. Thus, the terms *absoluteness* and *absolute* can be taken, in the context of Buddhist teachings, both in the sense of the Ultimate, Unconditioned Reality, and in the relative sense of a substance or a selfhood denoting an ontological delimitation and independence. As will become increasingly apparent, this raises the central question of evaluating the extent to which we should conflate the two meanings when considering the Buddhist epistemological process of relativization. In other words, it must be determined whether the unconditioned can be considered as a "reality," if not a "substance," and therefore understood as free from codependent origination. This is all the more necessary when presented with scriptural evidence that the ontology of emptiness is independent from Buddhahood, and can therefore be understood "ontologically" aside from any subjective experience of it.[37]

So it might be legitimate to suggest that while there appears to be an objective ontological reality, or state of affairs, which remains in principle independent from experience, this "necessary condition of existence" is indissociable, at least from a human point of view, from its recognition or realization. It would seem that insisting upon the former would amount to opening the way to some sort of "re-absolutization" of *nirvāna*, whereas, by contrast, an emphasis on the latter would evidence the most irreducibly anti-absolutist bent of Buddhist teachings.

Whatever might be the emphasis of the answer given to the above question, it remains nevertheless true that the relativization that is at stake does not amount to nothingness in the privative sense of the term. In other words, a Buddhist way needs to be able to reveal the lack of substantial texture of the world by highlighting the universal relativity of everything, but this relativity must not be mistaken for nothingness lest it lead to the exclusion of a mode of consciousness from which this very relativity might be contemplated. The doctrine of codependent origination accounts for such a possibility by asserting both the conditioned and the unconditioned that is inherent to the recognition of the former: "There exists, monks, that which is unborn, that which is unbecome, that which is uncreated, that which is unconditioned. For if there were not, monks, that which is uncreated, that which is unconditioned, there would not be made known here the escape from that which is born, from that which is become, from that which is created, from that which is conditioned. Yet since there exists, monks, that which is unborn, that which is unbecome, that which is uncreated, that which is unconditioned, there is therefore made known the escape from that which is born, from that which is become, from that which is created, from that which is conditioned."[38] Now, it must be acknowledged that while this passage is no doubt the one most often called for by the proponents of an "absolutist" leaning of the Buddha's teaching, it can be understood, and has indeed been understood, in less absolutist ways. Thus, some translations and commentaries of this and kindred passages limit themselves to stressing the spiritual and psychological character of this "unborn" and "unbecome" by associating it with the "calm" and "sorrowlessness" that it entails.[39]

Be that as it may, such passages leave us, in effect, with the critical task of pondering the status of the mode of consciousness that realizes an awareness of emptiness, or a consummate mindfulness of universal interdependence. Cannot this unconditioned be taken as an "absolute," since it corresponds to "Ultimate Truth," *paramārtha,* and could constitute thereby the limit of the "relativization of the absolute" that has been highlighted? Or, on the contrary, is this state itself codependent with the conditioned, while remaining unconditioned? Thus, it appears that two divergent roads are opened, or—to put it in a less exclusive manner—two poles highlighted: one may emphasize the universality of codependent arising, in which *nirvāna* itself must be situated within the realm of Emptiness, hence the fundamental recognition that *nirvāna* is *samsāra* and *samsāra* is *nirvāna*; or, on the contrary, one may emphasize the unconditioned reality of *nirvāna* to the point of identifying with the unveiling of an absolute Nature of things, whether it be approached as *Tathāgatagarbha,* the "Buddha-nature," or in the way of the Vajrayāna's

*Ādi-Buddha,* the "Buddha-principle," supreme divinity and origin of all Buddhas who can even be represented in human form.[40] Or else, to put this question in the most schematic way, is the unconditioned absolute, relative, both, or neither? Buddhist history presents us, in truth, with a spectrum of answers to this question, highlighting once more the diversity of the intellectual traditions that it shelters, since all four possible responses may be deemed plausible from various doctrinal points of view, notwithstanding that, in recent Buddhist studies, the hermeneutic center of gravity has lain by and large on the side of a barely qualified universalization of relativity.

It is at this critical juncture that, as implied by our prior remark about the interdependent and unconditioned imperatives of nirvānic consciousness, a delicate distinction between the unconditioned and that which is not codependently originated may emerge. In other words, *nirvāna* may—or may not—be, and has—and has not—been, considered as both and at the same time *asamskrta* and not *apratītyasamutpanna,* or as both and jointly unconditioned *and* not codependently originated. In the context of this subtle distinction, unconditioned is a synonym of absolute qua exclusive of any relative conditioning, while the status of being codependently originated amounts, by contrast, to that of being intrinsically interdependent with other phenomena or realities, and therefore in some way relative. In point of fact, Nāgārjuna refers to the interdependence of *samskrta* and *asamskrta,* the conditioned and the unconditioned, as one of the eighteen instances of emptiness, or codependent arising.[41] However useful the above distinction might be in order to preserve both the epistemological coherence and the soteriological effectiveness of the Buddhist outlook, it bears stressing that it has not been universally admitted. For example, first among the schools of early Buddhism, the Sarvāstivādins (*sarvam asti,* "everything is") actually equated the two concepts in a way that clearly opens the path to an ontological understanding of the unconditioned. By contrast, *Madhyamaka* Buddhism gives rise to a differentiation between the two concepts, one that emphasizes the codependent dimension of the unconditioned. It is so that, as pointed out by David Kalupahana, Nāgārjuna wants to avoid even an understanding of conditional arising that would be understood metaphysically, or as another kind of substance to which one may cling.[42] It is in this context that the correlative and necessary distinction between the "made" (*krta*) and the "arisen" (*utpannā*) can be considered, which leads Kalupahana to translate *samskrta* as "dispositionally conditioned." This is based on the fact that *samskrta* is akin to *samskāra* (condition as way of "making") and therefore related to acquired dispositions. Thus, the term can be understood, at least in some contexts, as being more practical and spiritual than ontological. At any rate, it is clear that, in such a perspective, the Buddha's teachings imply that "all dispositionally conditioned phenomena are dependent, but not all dependent phenomena are dispositionally conditioned."[43] The preservation of this distinction highlights the universal dependency of everything, which includes conditions but is not limited to them; hence, the unconditioned also can be said, paradoxically and on the brink of logical collapse, to be dependent upon the conditioned.

## The Relativizing Scope of Emptiness

The aforementioned distinct positions on conditioning and dependence signal, therefore, the need to consider the ways, and the various extents, to which a Buddhist "relativism" excludes a recognition of the Absolute but also, paradoxically, how it may allow for a different understanding of what the absoluteness of the Ultimate may mean. We have so far highlighted different modes and degrees of relativization. First of all, the most encompassing sense of universal emptiness as extending to emptiness itself rejects the suggestion that emptiness may be considered at all as a "view." A lesser degree of relativization sees emptiness as retaining a merely pragmatic value as a "right view," while avoiding the impulse to impute any metaphysical ultimateness to it. The dual understanding of *samskrta* as "unconditioned" and "not dispositionally acquired" reveals another meaningful distinction between the latter's "relativist" bent and the arguably more "absolutist" view of the unconditioned. Thus, at the most "relativistic" pole of Buddhist interpretations, it is held not only that emptiness is the universal truth of the *whole* of reality, but also that it is not even a view. Any ontological and epistemological absolutization is therefore cut off at its very root. This position is akin to a form of radical apophatism that rejects forging anything of spiritual and soteriological import from the concept of codependent origination, thereby informing the whole of the doctrine with the sine qua non of the spiritual method. As such, it is not without analogy with Eastern Orthodox apophatic Trinitarianism, *mutatis mutandis,* in its relentlessly consistent focus on the "relative" as an indispensable spiritual key. This "relativistic" outlook is indeed highlighted in Nāgārjuna's *Mūlamadhyamakakārikā,* "The Philosophy of the Middle Way," which is held to be the prime classical exposition of the doctrine of emptiness, and in *Vigrahavyāvartanī,* or "The Dispeller of Disputes," in which the doctrine reaches its logical pinnacle in arguing for the emptiness of the very teachings of emptiness. In the latter text, Nāgārjuna explicitly states that his teachings on emptiness are themselves empty, and therefore do not fall under the objection of contradicting emptiness by falling back into a convenient substantialism: "since my speech is dependently originated it is not established substantially."[44] Therefore, Nāgārjuna's "speech" cannot even be understood as a "view" or "thesis" (*pratijñā*). When charged by opponents with the objection that such a negation of any thesis is the very negation of the validity of the doctrine of emptiness, Nāgārjuna responds that this would be true were that negation itself a thesis claiming "substantiality," *quod absit.* His point amounts to arguing that the emptiness of his statement is basically analogous to the emptiness or lack of substance of anything and everything else. In other words, in the same way as the emptiness or lack of substance of a chariot or a pot does not prevent these objects from fulfilling their instrumental function, the emptiness of the statement of emptiness does not prevent it from validating what it expresses, to wit, emptiness. There is an ontological truth and a functional truth, as it were. Emptiness encompasses the first, while the second operates within the field of causes and conditions. Thus, codependent origination is evidently a universal reality, but it must not be confused with inexistence and, therefore, does not affect the functioning validity of phenomena.

As has been evident in the previous pages, much of Buddhist thought takes the road of a radical de-substantialization of everything whatsoever, at times not even excluding *nirvāna.* This radical, relentless, relativization of any trace of absoluteness is tantamount to the Mahāyāna principle that *nirvāna* is *samsāra* and *samsāra nirvāna*[45] since any static differentiation could be thought as introducing some sort of substantialization in one form or another. To affirm *nirvāna* in contradistinction to *samsāra,* or to distinguish form from emptiness, would mean relativizing emptiness by excluding *something* from its fold. Abiding in *nirvāna* would signify giving *nirvāna* a substantiality that would sever it from the field of *samsāra,* making it thereby contrary to the very nature of *nirvāna* as predicated on the awareness of universal emptiness. Similarly, a form that would not be empty would be a denial of the principle of emptiness, and an emptiness that is not form would contradictorily escape the universal validity of its own principle. It could be proposed, therefore, that the relativization of the absolute that is at work in the ultimate doctrine of emptiness brings the methodical and spiritual intent of Buddhist teachings to the fore by denying their very reality, at least in an ultimate sense, since their functional reality as *upāya* is never in question.

However, it must be noted that Nāgārjuna's inclusion of his own doctrine of emptiness within universal emptiness could be distinguished, at least theoretically, from the mode of consciousness that it presupposes, or the realization of which it intends to foster. In other words, one may argue for the relativity of the words of teaching, referred to above as "my speech," without for that excluding the unconditioned mode of consciousness that these words intimate. To put it differently, such a position would presuppose an implicit distinction between epistemological emptiness and ontological emptiness. The former would refer to *teachings about the way things are,* while the latter would actually coincide with *the way things are.* Furthermore, this distinction would amount to a subordination of the methodical intent, in the form of an epistemological "relativism," to the ontological realization, in the way of a nirvānic "absolutism." Nāgārjuna does not embrace this distinction, however, and this is clearly evidenced by the way in which he approaches the question of the "ultimacy" of emptiness. This ultimateness is never considered by him as an object of apprehension, whether spiritual or epistemological. In fact, the attempt at reaching or "grasping" emptiness is deemed by him to be the most serious, indeed incurable, spiritual malady.[46] This is so inasmuch as emptiness is not something that could be attained, be it through a form of enlightenment, since it is literally no-thing. If there is "something" to awaken to, it is not emptiness itself.

## The Absolute as Buddha-nature

It is against the background of such a relativistic bent that one must consider the paradoxically "absolutist" shift that can result from some of the implications of the doctrine of emptiness. This deflection is already quite apparent in Indian Mahāyāna texts from the early centuries of the Common Era such as the *The Lion's Roar of Śri-Mālā,* the *Ratnagotravibhāga Sūtra,* and the *Lankāvatāra Sūtra,*[47] as well as in the great Mahāyāna classic *The Awakening of Faith (Mahāyāna-Śraddhotpāda-Śastra),* a text that was until recently attributed to the second-century AD Aśvagosha but which most scholars consider now to be a later Chinese source. Indeed, probably the most explicit and extensive occurrences of these orientations arose primarily in the civilizational context of China, foremost among which the *Hua-yen* school studied by Peter N. Gregory.

In these sources, a preeminent significance is given to such essentialist notions as *Dharmakāya, Dharmadhātu, Bhūtatathatā, Tathāgatagarbha,* and *Ālayavijñāna,* which provide Mahāyāna teachings with various modes of conceptualization of emptiness and absolute Suchness. The first notion refers to the "Absolute Body" of the Buddha, the highest of the three *trikāya,* which is the nonmanifest nature of Buddhahood that can be conceived as a "body" in reference to the essential "core" of the nirvānic reality. The *Dharmadhātu,* for its part, designates the encompassing dimension of Buddhahood, its essential "space," as it were. The third concept, *Bhūtatathatā,* or "Suchness of existents," pertains to the actual Nature of Suchness beyond ignorance and illusion. These three terms ultimately converge in pointing to the essential Nature of that which is experienced in *nirvāna,* but in a way that is strikingly affirmative and absolutist. As for the *Tathāgatagarbha,* it designates literally the "womb or embryo of the One Who Has Thus Gone," a way to refer to the genetic and teleological dimension of Buddhahood, the matrix of Enlightenment. The fifth concept refers to the "storehouse consciousness," that is, the repository of karmic seeds that ultimately unfold in reaching toward the Awakening that lies dormant within each sentient being. What all of these concepts—identifiable as one in their ultimate reality—have in common is an affirmative concept of the ontological reality that dwells at the foundation of the subjective experience of *nirvāna,* and correlatively an understanding of *śunyata,* or emptiness, that is significantly different from the Śunyavādin account.[48]

The *Tathāgatagarbha* can be characterized as the ontological matrix of Buddhahood. What is remarkable, in the context of this inquiry, is that the *Tathāgatagarbha* provides a metaphysical ground for the whole chain of sensory affects, emotional experiences, and volitions that characterize the cycle of suffering as well as the path of aspiration toward release. While all the segments, elements, and agencies at work in the unfolding of suffering and liberation are recognized to be transient and empty of self-reality, it is also deduced that they cannot be the ultimate "subject" that experiences them. This subject is therefore explicitly referred to as transcending the conditioned, *samskrta.* This means that the relativity of the means and ways of existential experience betrays, in both senses of the word, the reality of an absolute subject.[49] Now the nonidentification of this subject with any sense of selfhood or personhood remains in principle preserved, but it appears that this restriction applies only to the extent that self and personality are deemed to entail conditioned being. In fact the *Lankāvatāra*'s comparison of the *Tathāgatagarbha* with an "actor (who) takes on a variety of forms and (in itself) is devoid of an ego-soul"[50] unveils the extent to which the concept of a "selfless subject" remains problematic, and may give rise to suspicions of reintroducing an *ātman* into Buddhist teachings. Besides the ontologically leaning concept of *Tathāgatagarbha,* the concept of *Ālayavijñāna,* originating from Yogācāra idealism, and which has been most often translated as "storehouse of consciousness," played a parallel role in giving rise to Buddhist teachings akin to a "subjective absolutism." Thus, the *Ālayavijñāna* may be referred to as the deepest support of consciousness from which all other modes proceed. It is not reducible to sensory, mental, and intellectual modalities of consciousness but contains the "seeds," or *bījas,* from which all others flow. Although originally called for in the context of spiritual psychology and providing the source of continuity in the various modes of individual consciousness, it came to be equated, notably in the *Lankāvatāra Sūtra,* with the *Tathāgatagarbha* itself, taking on a universal and ontological significance beyond its consideration as the basic principle of the karmic flux. However, it is this latter aspect of change, and both the active and passive modifications that it entails, that distinguishes it, from the point of view of its proponents, from the *Advaitin Ātman.* The *Lankāvatāra*'s symbolic analogy of the *Ālayavijñāna* and a "great ocean in which the waves roll on permanently but the deeps remain unmoved" accounts in its own suggestive way for the inclusion of becoming into the fold of the Absolute. While the *Tathāgatagarbha* is transcendent, at least in the sense that it cannot be identified with the transient percepts, it is also immanent, lest no path be left toward the unconditioned freedom of *nirvāna*. It is the synthetic and essential Suchness, or the Absolute reality, that is presupposed by existential relativity, and thereby invites the latter to the realization of its own true nature. The *Ālayavijñāna*, by contrast, following its psychological and methodical roots, orients one from the particularity of the karmic storehouse of a given subject to the universal foundation that ultimately contains the seeds of its becoming. It is immanent, in the sense that it is one with the percepts, oneness in the absence of which no room would be left for any karmic continuity, and therefore for any gradual access to *nirvāna*. At any rate, the identification of the *Tathāgatagarbha* and the *Ālayavijñāna* highlighted in the *Lankāvatāra Sūtra* stems from the principle that only Ultimate Suchness as ground of Being or Buddha-nature can be the source, the development and the finality of *samsāra*, whether one considers it as the ontological support or the seminal principle of all becoming as oriented toward Awakening.

The relationship between the absolute Suchness and the principle of Emptiness could not but be one of the major issues at stake in the context of such a discussion. One of the most authoritative and influential treatments of the matter is to be found in *The Awakening of Faith*. This text provides a clear exposition of the way in which Ultimate Suchness (*bhūtatathatā*), to the extent that it can be conceptualized, is to be thought as both *śūnyatā* and *aśūnyatā*. As *śūnyatā*, Suchness can be understood, through negation, as radically different from all conditioned beings, from that which is not truly real. In this perspective, no relative consciousness can fathom or embrace the Absolute, which is therefore pure Emptiness. It is in this respect that the utter independence of Suchness from existential and conditioned defilements is affirmed. As *aśūnyatā*, by contrast, Suchness is envisaged as the matrix of seeds of Awakening, and therefore as the substantial principle of all reality. This second dimension of Suchness arises directly out of the first in the sense that "[as soon as we understand] that subjectivity is empty and unreal, we perceive the pure soul manifesting itself as eternal, permanent, immutable and completely comprising all things that are pure."[51] Thus, Suchness is both negation and affirmation, it is the true Middle Path of the *Mahāyāna*—not in the sense of a school but as pointing to the ontological "vehicle" of all Buddhas. Emptiness means that "neither that which is negated [viz., the external world] nor that which negates [viz., the mind] is an independent entity."[52] The text also states, however, that there is no particularizing affirmation in Suchness itself since it is situated beyond any conditioned selfhood. This means that the affirmative aspect of the perception of Suchness does not reintroduce any misleading belief in selfhood, at least not in the terms of a substantialization of any subject that would be distinct from the objective field. In that sense, *aśūnyatā* could be couched as an "affirmation without affirmation." Thus, *The Awakening of Faith* refers to the *Mahāyāna* as Suchness (*bhūtatatathatā*) or heart and kernel of everything, but also, as a way of consequence, as samsāric unfolding. In other words, the Ultimate is both nirvānic and samsāric, but this interdependence of the two, far from relativizing the former in the universal fold of emptiness, "absolutizes" the relative field of all things in the sense of situating it within the very "space" of Suchness. Hence the *Awakening's* pronouncement, "Therefore Buddha teaches that all beings are from all eternity ever abiding in Nirvāna."[53]

In order to reach a deeper insight into the absolutist readings that have just been touched upon, it is important to be aware of the way they understand their own status in the unfolding of the Dharma. Thus, Peter Gregory has shown that the *Tathāgatagarbha* teachings,[54] as they were typically elaborated and crystallized in Chinese schools such as the *Hua-yen,* highlight a differentiation between a "hidden intent"—which they attribute to Śunyavādin teachings, and a "direct intent," which characterizes the *Tathāgatagarbha.* The first refers to a nonsubstantialist "relativism," while the second opens onto the "absolutist ontology" of the Buddha-nature. This means that even though the Śunyavādin point of view has come to be deemed normative in many contemporary Buddhist studies, important streams of Māhayāna, have, by contrast, taken maximal metaphysical stock of the unconditioned nature of *nirvāna.* In this more affirmative view, to state that *nirvāna* is the unconditioned from which one may escape the conditioned, must mean that it is free from that which constitutes codependent origination, given that the latter is understood, in this perspective, as coextensive with conditioned existence. This positive and absolutist approach is particularly prominent in the Chinese *Tathāgatagarbha* schools, in which the understanding of the Buddha-nature, subject of enlightenment, as a universal and in a sense absolute reality, is explicitly asserted. As indicated above, the *Hua-yen* school minimizes, as it were, the scope of codependent origination by distinguishing, among Buddhist teachings, those which are of "hidden intent" and those of "revealing intent." The first type is akin to the anti-substantialist teachings of emptiness, which are only indirectly pointing to Reality by destroying the attachment to the realm of conditioning. For the ninth-century *Hua-yen* Patriarch Tsung-mi, such teachings are tantamount to spiritual propaedeutics that should not be elevated to the status of an ultimate doctrine. It is only with the teachings of Buddha-nature that Reality is directly revealed. While the Buddha-nature is universal enlightenment or ultimate awareness—an awareness that cannot be equated, however, with mere mind consciousness, emptiness is only a gateway to the universal nature as such.[55]

In point of fact, Tsung-mi's critique of the "relativization of the absolute" goes so far as to target the limits of Śunyavādin "relativism" by highlighting the absoluteness of the mode of awareness that transcends relativity. In other terms, if everything is relative, then what is it that knows that everything is relative?[56] The matter herein is obviously ontological and epistemological, and not merely pedagogical or linguistic.

In this vein, Tsung-mi recognizes more specifically three levels of teachings that range from the most indirect to the most direct.[57] The first two types are indirect, or of "hidden intent" (Gregory's translation of the Chinese *mi-i*), while only the last one manifests the truth in a direct fashion (*hsien-shih*). The first level corresponds to the teachings that are based on phenomenal appearances. These pertain to the Buddha's teachings based on conventional views. They are indirect inasmuch as they do not reveal reality as it actually is, but only make use of ordinary appearances as a pointer to it. They take mankind where it ordinarily stands, as it were, and rely on the *upāya* as a fully valid way of access to reality. They are insufficient, though, inasmuch as they fail to eradicate the belief in the reality of phenomena as a basis for clinging to them. This is the reason why the second degree of teachings addresses this deluded tendency by calling into question the very substantiality of phenomena. This second level corresponds, by and large, to the teachings on emptiness. Thus, according to Tsung-mi, "the Buddha provisionally negated everything"[58] to free people from clinging to phenomena. However, this is still an indirect way of revealing reality since it does not characterize the real *as it is* but rather *as it must not be conceived* in order to free oneself from suffering. It is not an ultimate truth, nor is it either a conventional one, in the sense in which Nāgārjuna would understand these concepts. It is, at any rate, a provisional view, since it does not directly reveal the true nature of reality. Only this third teaching is ultimate which reveals the Buddha Nature: "Because [this category of teaching] directly points to the fact that one's very own mind is the true nature, neither revealing it in terms of the appearances of phenomena nor revealing in terms of the refutation of phenomenal appearances (*p'o-hsiang*), it has 'is the nature' [in its name]. Because its intent is not hidden by expedients, it is said to 'reveal it directly.' "[59] It is particularly meaningful to note that in order to reveal the limitations of the "relativistic" outlook of the "Teaching of Hidden Intent That Refutes Phenomenal Appearances in Order to Reveal the Nature," Tsung-mi teaches that it is precisely because the misleading thoughts that are concomitant to craving and delusion are in reality empty that their negation, which is thereby codependently originated, cannot be ultimate. Even though Nāgārjuna argued that emptiness is the middle ground between nonexistence and existence, Tsung-mi tends to equate emptiness (*k'ung*) and nonexistence inasmuch as he understands the former negatively as the reverse side, as it were, of the "tranquility" (*chi*) of the true Buddha-nature.[60] Whereas emptiness is understood by Śunyavādins as the very reality of codependent origination, thus the very "name" of universal relativity, Tsung-mi character-izes it as the external "face" of the Buddha-nature, the "no" that presupposes a "yes."[61] It should not come as a surprise, therefore, that he would make use of symbols that Hindu and Sufi mystical schools have typically included in their metaphysical lexicon, namely, the ocean and the mirror: "If there were no water whose wet nature were unchanging, how could there be the waves of illusory, provisional phenomenal appearances? If there were no mirror whose pure brightness were unchanging, how could there be the reflections of a variety of unreal phenomena?"[62] Far from being its negation, relativity is, in other words, the very "proof" and indeed the very "stuff" of the Absolute. The latter is the metaphysical sine qua non for the unfolding of the universe, the formal manifestation of the formless. This is confirmed by the fact that *Hua-yen* understands the concept of *pratītya-samutpāda* in a way that greatly differs from Madhyamaka interpretations, as it highlights the harmony and unitive participation that it denotes as "perfect interfusion" (*yuanrong*) rather than its denotations of illusoriness.[63] Let us note in passing that Shin Bud-dhism, with its emphasis on the saving power of the formal *upāya* of the *nembutsu*, is particularly attuned to this interpretation of emptiness as the very space of the countless forms, the colorless light that sustains the rainbow of phenomenal existence.[64] Thus, not being a substance amounts for the absolute/emptiness to being the source and heart of all substances. Therein are to be found, to wit, the limits of the Buddhist "relativization of the absolute," since the metaphysical foil of the mirror precludes, according to such views, any ultimate negativity and relativity.

## *Soku*: The Relative as Absolute

When considering such positive or affirmative interpretations of the Buddha's teachings, in contradistinction with the "relativistic" stream of the Buddhist negation of any absolute, the question of the relationship between the Real and the illusory, the Ultimate and the provisional, may lead us into further perplexity, for, to use Tsung-mi's symbolic language, are not the waves one with the water, and the reflections one with the mirror? In other words, is not the very distinction between an absolute and a relative realm tainted with a misguided "substantialization"? The major implications of this question came to the fore in the twentieth-century philosophical elaborations of the Kyoto School, as a result of the engagement of Japanese Buddhist scholars with the Western philosophical tradition, its Aristotelian understanding of substance

and its exclusionary logic. Thus, the nondual articulation of "absolute" emptiness and phenomena lies no doubt at the foundation of the paradoxical bent,
among eminent contemporary Buddhist scholars such as Masao Abe, to resist
any substantialization of the Buddha-nature while conferring a kind of present
absoluteness upon phenomena.[65] Accordingly, a relentless anti-absolutism tends
to give rise to a paradoxical *coincidentality* with a manner of pan-absolutism.
This paradox may be apparent only, though, when one considers that the
word absolute may be given, on each side of the discussion, an arguably
different meaning.

What is rejected by Abe and contemporary kindred-minded Buddhist
scholars is a view of the Buddha-nature that would turn it into a supreme
substance, of which the manifold phenomena would be modifications. In
other words, such a view would delimit the Absolute as Being by its own
and on its own, while understanding phenomena as so many accidents of
this Being. On such accounts, the Ultimate could be accordingly characterized as both transcendent and immanent. Now, Abe emphatically rejects the
idea that the Buddha-nature may be either of the latter or both. This is so
because the Buddha-nature is neither "above" phenomenal reality nor "within"
it. In Abe's reading of Buddhism, the Buddha-nature is neither transcendent
nor immanent insofar as both concepts introduce and presuppose a sense of
duality that wrongly substantializes that which is fundamentally empty or
intrinsically interdependent. Transcendence implies an ontological separation of
sorts between that which transcends and that which is transcended, therefore a
suspension of the principle of codependent origination. Similarly, the notion of
immanence is based on the presence of something into something else, thereby
surreptitiously reintroducing a sense of duality. In such a context, therefore,
the only absoluteness that may be recognized amounts to the immediate and
present emergence of phenomena *as* the Buddha-nature. The Buddha-nature is
present immediacy indistinguishable from phenomena, and each of the latter
is a *presentation* of the whole Buddha-nature in the current occurrence of its
single actuality. Such is, for Abe, the ultimate meaning of the provocatively
enigmatic Zen response to the question, "What is the Buddha-nature?" which
is, "the cypress in the courtyard!"

Echoing Abe's point, Toshihiko Izutsu has explicitly referred, in this very
connection, to the fact that "Zen 'absolutizes' the Phenomenal itself."[66] However,
such an "absolutization" cannot be rational or conceptual since it is radically
incompatible with the separative function of discrimination and any sort of
mediation; it is, therefore, in a sense, the opposite of the absolutization targeted
by the doctrine of emptiness. In keeping with the non-transcendentalist and
non-immanentist view of Reality highlighted by Abe[67] it can even be said that
the relative phenomenon *is* the Absolute, whereas denying this equation would

either divide the Absolute, or else exclude it from the here and now. Moreover, this position must be emphatically distinguished from pantheism inasmuch as the latter "lacks a clear realization of the *negation* of subject and object."[68] It is precisely because it fails to reach beyond the polarity of subject and object into their basic negation that pantheism cannot but remain a "confusing" affirmation. If any transcendence may be referred to, it is that which reaches beyond the dualistic polarity of a subject and an object as well as beyond the sequence of past, present, and future that is its conventional existential horizon, but this transcendence does not lie somewhere or sometime beyond.[69] To sum up, between the negation and relativization of every possible absolute in light of codependent origination and the direct revelation of the Buddha Nature as the ultimately positive and absolute content of the aforementioned relativization, the metaphysical and spiritual "logic" of Buddhism must involve a *recognition* of the relative *as* absolute through the emergence of the latter *as* the former.

We must note that the term *recognition* points to a primary consideration of the subjective mode of awareness of phenomena. Buddhist thought is, from its inception, centered on the training of a subjective adequateness to things as they are. However, the term *subjective* is only provisionally valid, since the immediacy of the realization of the Buddha-nature also amounts to reaching beyond the very polarity of subject and object. The latter is ordinarily substantialized and absolutized as a basis for conventional perceptions. It presupposes an illusory familiarity with the self and its objects of perception and cognition, a familiarity that needs be dispelled through a sudden grasp of the interdependent relativity of the two terms, thereby negating their conventional appearance as discrete substances. The subjective process of transcending the polarity of subject and object is typically couched in the oft-quoted Zen commentary on the three stages of perception of "mountains" and "rivers:" "In the beginning the mountains are mountains, and the rivers rivers," then, "the mountains are not mountains and the rivers are not rivers," and finally, "the mountains are mountains and the rivers are rivers." These three stages correspond to three modes of metaphysical perception that could be termed "conventionally affirmative," "ecstatically (or nihilistically) negative," and "ultimately affirmative." Considering the stage of "mountains are mountains, rivers are rivers," Masao Abe has made use of the three words differentiation, identification, and objectification to refer to this elementary mode of awareness. The concept of "absolutization" could also be added to these three. At this stage, phenomena are exclusively self-identified and differentiated from each other, this differentiation being fundamentally predicated on a scission between subject and object. This stage is characterized by a flat and static application of the law of identity that keeps to the horizon of phenomenal evidence as purely phenomenal. It could be referred to as daily "absolutism" in the sense that it is conventionally

functional while erecting phenomena into "absolute substances." Keiji Nishitani
has encapsulated this perspective by a symbolic reference to 90-degree angles,
which indicate polarity and duality, such as heaven and earth and earth and
heaven.[70] Angularity is here a symbol of fragmentation, and even opposition.

As a response to this tension of ordinary consciousness, the second stage
introduces an epistemological chasm that relativizes the ontological density of
things, and steeps them, as it were, into pure emptiness or "nothingness." This is
Nishitani's 180 degrees, the stage of emptiness that collapses differentiations and
stable identities. This stage is characterized by "total openness," indifferentiation,
loss of identity, although it still entails a small measure of objectification. Phenomena lose their absoluteness: they are relativized but, as pointed out by Abe,
this relativization is still an object for a subject, if only faintly. Abe compares
this situation to that of a transparent wall: the opacity of the wall of separation
of the first stage has disappeared, but there remains a sense of two sides of the
wall. This is, in a sense, abiding into *nirvāna*. Abe surprisingly alludes to the
"nihilistic" bent of this stage, probably on account of the fact that in it emptiness might be confused with mere inexistence. A third stage finally arises that
is characterized by a deeper articulation of negation and affirmation.[71] This is
an absolutization of the relativized, if one may put it so, in which phenomena
are endowed with full reality *as* Reality. Abe does not hesitate to refer to it as
"affirmation in the absolute sense."[72] Nishitani's 360 degrees epitomizes this
emptying of emptiness, this *soku* that equates form *and* emptiness.[73]

It must be noted that, according to Toshihiko Izutsu, the second and
third stages are intrinsically simultaneous, and their conjunction provides an
actual key to understanding the Buddhist approach to what has been coined
"Absolute nothingness." In Izutsu's words, "At the last stage 'A is A' is but an
abbreviated expression standing for 'A is non-A; therefore it is A.'"[74] In other
words, Izutsu, by contrast with Abe, does not seem to consider the possibility
of the second stage independently from the third stage: the emptying of emptiness is simultaneous with the realization of emptiness. If stage two is to be
what *it is* "then," stage three "establishes itself at the same time." The second
and third stages are coincidental, and their sequencing can only be logical, and
not existential. They are the two faces of a same perception of reality. For his
part, Abe insists on the discontinuity between the three stages, each of them
involving a leap into a radically different mode of awareness, which could be
referred to respectively as non-emptying, emptying of being and emptying of
emptiness.[75] The emptying of being, including the Absolute, is none other
than Emptiness, and it is akin to a process of universal relativization. But the
emptying of Emptiness means Wondrous and Absolute Being (*myō-u*), a process
that cannot but be characterized as "absolutization." In other words, there is
an emptiness that is but the static opposite of being, and a being that is but

the counterpart of emptiness, but Ultimate Emptiness is not the opposite of anything, and certainly not of Being, nor is Ultimate Being the opposite of Emptiness. Without the emptying of Being, there is no insight into the basic relativity of phenomena, but without the emptying of Emptiness there is no awareness of their reality qua Emptiness. Short of an emptying of Emptiness what is left is a conceptual reification of emptiness that is not the realization of its full meaning, but confines one to a kind of nihilism without a positive horizon.[76] One must therefore distinguish between absolute negativity—which is also absolute positivity—and dualistically determined negativity. In this respect, Abe comments upon the two Japanese Buddhist concepts of *u* and *mu,* or being and nonbeing, as being "impossible without the other" on some relative level;[77] to which must be added that the *mu* that is ultimate is not only "impossible without the other," that is, the *u,* but it *is* also and *indeed* the other.

Herein lies what could be referred to as an "absolute relativity," which includes both the relative, or the negation, and the absolute, or the affirmation. In this way, the process of relativization of the absolute opens onto an absolute relativity, a pure negation of the negation that is affirmation of the affirmation. As Abe has clearly demonstrated in his commentary on Nāgārjuna, this negation is ultimate or absolute, which is to say, not susceptible to other negations ad infinitum, precisely because it is not merely the negation of a negation but the negation of "two mutually negating items, that is A and non-A."[78]

Now, we need to return *in fine* to the difference of interpretation between Abe and Izutsu with respect to the relationship between the "mountains are not mountains" and the "mountains are mountains again." Let us note, first, that stage two does not seem to be a stable stand in and of itself, since, with it, there lies a fundamental contradiction that does not allow for any resolution. This is, no doubt, what Abe designates as "nihilism," and why he argues that, in this state, "there is no positive ground for one's life and activity."[79] It is likely that this position is only mental or "intellectual" in the negative sense of the term, for if it were to entail an existential totality it could not but open onto a renewed realization of the third moment as "mountains are mountains." Therefore, a radical and consistent negation must involve a negation of negation in its wake, or rather within its very fold. In this connection, it is important to note that Abe acknowledges the inadequacy of the term *stage* to refer to the third moment in the odyssey of spiritual awareness. Since this last mode of awareness involves an absolute present and "presence" of phenomena, it evidently rises above any sequential understanding of a process.[80] It is therefore quite clear that the first and second stages are indeed included and recapitulated, as it were, in the third one, without which the very realization of absoluteness qua relativity and relativity qua absoluteness would be simply impossible. While the discontinuity between the stages is undeniable from the point of view of the lower stages, it is not so from the point of view of the third stage, which includes, as it were, the two previous ones, in the way in which Nishitani's 360 degrees may deem to embrace both 180 degrees and 90 degrees.

It must be stressed finally that the emptying of emptiness and the correlative nonduality of being and nonbeing are not to be conceived in terms of a pantheistic oneness of a static kind, but rather as an endless activity, as a pure act of emptying. Abe encapsulates this process in pointing out the fact that "true emptiness is *pure activity of emptying* which empties everything including itself."[81] Failing this continuous actualization, emptiness is turned into a stasis that does not stem from the ground of reality. Thus, the dynamic reality of the "absolute emptiness" envisaged by Zen bears witness to a constant sustaining of awareness in the present: "Ultimate reality is realized in the dynamic realization of emptying. However, as soon as the pure activity of emptying loses its function of self-negation, that is, the negation of negation, it turns into 'emptiness' in noun form and the Ultimate Reality will be lost. Incessant self-emptying is essential to the realization of true emptiness."[82] This is an echo of Nāgārjuna's account of the activity of the *bodhisattva* "whose arrows are continuously held aloft, so none are allowed to fall back down into *nirvāna*."[83] The "falling back down into *nirvāna*" would be none other than the absolutization of *nirvāna* into a substance.

Let us note that such a negation of negation may be understood in a way that is less metaphysical than mystical, less objective than subjective, since it is a priori centered on a modification of consciousness. This is, in a sense, a subjective account of metaphysics, and also, quite evidently, a spiritual and methodical one. This spiritual and existential focus is not without resonance with the Christian spiritual ethos of perpetual denial and gift of self. Significantly, much of the highest speculations of Buddhist-Christian theological dialogue have revolved around the affinities between the "emptiness of emptiness" and the *kenōsis,* the human path of emptying that reflects, and responds to, the divine self-emptying of the Persons of the Trinity in their reciprocal relationships.[84] Inasmuch as it shuns any substantialization of the interpersonal relationships, the Thomistic doctrine of the "subsisting relations" ("a substance is never a relation"), which was analyzed in the first section of this chapter, is not without analogy, in a similar sense, with Buddhist emptiness, both placing and emphasizing dynamic relationality at the very center of their metaphysical teachings.

## Concluding Remarks

In Christianity, "absolutizing the relative" means that the relative in God is identified with the Absolute. By way of consequence, the relative "outside of

God" is also absolutized in that the "manifestation of God in history" and the economy of Redemption tend to be conflated with the Absolute, and become as if inseparable from it. Therefore, it could also be said, as the reverse side of the same reality, that the Divine Absolute is relativized, as if brought down into the relative order. The absolutization of the Relative amounts to a relativization of the Absolute, which might be deemed to be thereby bereft of its independent Necessity. The extreme reticence of many early, and even more contemporary, Christian theologians vis-à-vis metaphysics, which they tend to understand as heterogeneous to theology and suspect of abstraction, is a direct illustration of this principle. Thus, Peter Phan powerfully crystallizes a representative Christian outlook in the following lines: "The effort to reconcile unity and plurality in God is not a matter of solving a mathematical conundrum or a metaphysical puzzle of how one is three and three is one. Rather, early Christians are compelled to account for the three distinct ways in which the one God is experienced as present and active in their lives and in the history of salvation."[85] Hence, the possibility—not in the normative theological traditions of East and West but perhaps in large sectors of contemporary Christianity—of a humanization of the Divine realm that may be conducive, arguably, to an unconscious metaphysical debasement.

It is plain that the Buddhist relativization of the absolute means a priori the rejection of any absolute selfhood as independent substance from the field of existence. This is the critique of *svabhāva* and eternalism. By extension this relativization refers to God as the Absolute and the absolute Self. This comes to a relativization of the absolute in two senses. The first is a universalization of the principle of codependent origination or emptiness, the limits of which have been alluded to in our treatment of the *Tathāgatagarbha* doctrine. The second sense amounts to the affirmation that the Absolute *is* the relative: "What is the Buddha? The cypress in the courtyard!" Therefore, the Buddhist relativization of the absolute comes down to an absolutization of the relative, in the sense that the latter is experienced as an "occurrence" of the former within which the Absolute is entirely and simply "given," without any consideration of a "something beyond," inasmuch as a "beyond" would introduce a duality in a mode of perception that is radically nondual. As encapsulated by Toshihiko Izutsu: "Seeing the cypress tree in the courtyard as an actualization of the Field does not mean seeing 'something,' say, the transcendental Absolute, beyond the concrete thing."[86] Two points need to be stressed in this respect. Firstly, the "transcendental Absolute" is tellingly equated, in this passage, to a "something" among other "somethings." Now, such an understanding reveals that the Absolute that Zen Buddhism intends to debunk or deny cannot be the Absolute as it is understood in *Advaita Vedānta* or Sufi metaphysics, for instance, because the Absolute that the latter envisage can in no way be defined as a "something."

The Supreme *Nirguna Brahman* is emphatically not a "something" that could be defined and objectified as "Absolute"; in fact, it lies beyond any determination inherent to "things," while being also the unobjectifiable universal Self. Secondly, this point makes it plain that what Zen rejects is not as much the Absolute as such as any possible sort of reification of the Absolute. In other words, Izutsu's passage implies that the Absolute that is rejected by Zen lies "beyond" the phenomenal world, and could be "seen" as such. But it is quite clear, in the Sufi teachings of the *wahdat al-wujūd* for example, that the only way the Absolute can be "seen" is not "beyond" but "within" theophanic manifestations, although it can also be said to be realized subjectively in a way that can in no wise be objectified, and therefore not "seen." Once again, it appears that most Buddhist thinkers do not negate transcendence as such but rather the objectification of transcendence as a reality that could be "viewed" or "seen" or "reached," if one may say so. This is why their relativization of *any* absolute leads to the absolutization of *any* relative as pure *presentation* of Reality. That such an "absolutization of the relative" may be turned, through ignorance or undue secularization, into a "spiritual materialism" or a psychological pragmatism without metaphysical horizon is another story.

It must be noted that the best approximation of the concepts of absolute and relative in Buddhism would likely be the distinct notions of ultimate Truth, *paramārtha,* and conventional Truth, *samvrti.* The Buddhist Absolute is a matter of awareness, or cognitive perspective, rather than ontology, to the extent that a distinction between the two is possible. The Absolute is, as it were, "subjectivized" in conformity with a vantage point centered on subjective recognition or awakening. If one were to translate these notions in monotheistic terms one could write that Buddhism is concentrated on subjective God-consciousness rather than on the objective being of God, or on absolute consciousness rather than on the consciousness of the Absolute. This being said, the nirvānic perception as absolute truth can be interpreted as being inseparable from an ontology, since it amounts to a recognition of emptiness, or, in more positive terms, Buddha Nature. In other words, there is a way of seeing things as they are because there is a way things are, although the latter is ultimately indissociable from the former. However, this does not mean that there is anything that could be thought as absolute or relative in itself. As suggested in a number of passages from the above, everything is both absolute and relative from the ultimate point of view, or from the vantage point of the Absolute. This is so inasmuch as the ultimate point of view recognizes everything as dependently originated and at the same time as the very locus of manifestation of the absolute Buddhahood. By contrast, the relativization of the absolute at the core of Buddhist teachings is only representative of the literal, initial, and conventional Truth.

Buddhism and Christianity are, in a sense, the most nonconceptual religions. They are also, as it were, the most antiphilosophical and nonmetaphysical ones. This is illustrated by the Buddhist skepticism vis-à-vis conceptualization and verbalization, the symbolic epitome of which is the Buddha's Sermon of the Flower. It is also highlighted by the Paulinian rejection of the "wisdom according to the flesh" and the general spiritual animosity of early Fathers toward Platonism. In a way, this nonconceptual emphasis is closely related to the respective Buddhist and Christian treatments of the Absolute, inasmuch as they may appear to be less concerned with the strict metaphysical coherence of the teachings than with what could be termed their spiritual coherence and effectiveness. The truth that saves, or the saving truth, is all that matters, and the rest is merely a matter of *metaphysics,* the latter term being not uncommonly connoted with intellectual sterility or illusions; hence, no doubt, the lack of emphasis on the metaphysical integrity of the concept of the Absolute.

What might be referred to, more suggestively than literally, as the "anti-absolutist" dimension of the two traditions accounts for a situation in which the very discrimination or distinction between an absolute and a relative realm is transcended. The antinomic and paradoxical turn of many Buddhist and Christian accounts of the relationship between absoluteness and relativity reveals a clear affinity with modes of metaphysical and theological exposition intent on producing a sense of intellectual perplexity. The mental puzzlement that stems from the coincidence of opposites and calls into question the superficially discursive differentiation between the two very notions of absoluteness and relativity is, in itself, the very evidence of the pertinence of our approach. It is also an indication of the location of the existential center of gravity of the Buddhist and Christian psyche, one that coincides with shattering mental crystallizations through spiritual realization: *credo quia absurdum est.*[87] Even though it is quite evidently impossible to subsume the whole Christian and Buddhist traditions, and their challenging intellectual and spiritual diversity, under the strict boundaries of such general concepts, the proposed framework has made it possible to highlight what may be deemed to be a significant structure of the Christian and Buddhist worldviews, and one that definitely set them apart, as a whole, from other major religious traditions.

This being said, although both the Buddhist and Christian outlooks involve paradoxical or antinomic articulations of the Absolute and the relative, it is clear that there is no exact equivalence between the two. The Buddhist perspective is more epistemological and existential than ontological, whereas the affirmation of the Trinity as ultimate is quite evidently a statement about Divine Being. However, it is no less clear that the two traditions are, by and large, moving away from a strict concept of the Absolute as a result of a direct or indirect absolutization of the relational and the relative, or a concomitant relativization of ultimate absoluteness. They cannot do so, however, without opening the door to metaphysical qualifications, or even at times negations, of their relativizing bent.

While Christianity and Buddhism have provided their faithful and prac- titioners with an adequate and, ultimately or virtually, nondual metaphysics of Unity, they have, overall, done so in ways that are intimately tied up with their respective soteriological systems, and indeed in the very terms of the latter. This is not without having affected their ability to provide a balanced, stratified, and justifiably hierarchized vision of the Ultimate. This appears, for instance, in the puzzling equality in difference of the Persons of the Trinity and the Buddhist negation, or at least lack of consideration, of archetypes or essences. By contrast, the metaphysical and mystical nondualistic systems of Hinduism and Islam make it possible to distinguish degrees of reality within the Principle (Non-Qualified and Qualified *Brahman*, *Allāh*'s Essence and Qualities) without jeopardizing its Unity. It is not suggested that this is an unconditional superiority on the part of the latter over the former, nor the reverse, since the matter lies, at least practically, in the fundamental moti- vating factor of the respective religious systems, whether it be for some the spiritual immediacy and effectiveness of the soteriological principle, or—for others—the unambiguous intellectual clarity of the metaphysical doctrine. When led to recognize that Christianity and Buddhism are less "logical" in their concept of the Ultimate than are Hinduism and Islam, it must also be acknowledged that the potentially derogatory implications of such recognition cannot but be moot within the context of their own soteriological systems, if only because discursive logic is not the highest intellectual faculty—as both Hindu and Muslim metaphysicians would readily admit too, but also and above all since reason cannot fathom the Mystery of the Christian Ultimate nor the supra-mental reality of nirvānic consciousness. In point of fact, logic appears to be, in both cases, an impediment. What can be granted to this point of view, without espousing its anti-intellectualist bias, is an acknowledg- ment that an overly rigid concept of the Unity of the Absolute can easily give rise, as it does so in some sectors of Islamic "rational" theology, for instance, to what Henry Corbin has referred to quite audaciously and paradoxically as the most dangerous form of idolatry. For most Hindu and Islamic schools of thought, *buddhi* and *'aql* are, respectively, reflections of Divine Intelligence and enlightening light-streams from the Self, whereas for much of Buddhism and Christianity *ratio* or mind, although being ultimately connected to the Real, is bent on inducing a sense of illusory completeness, as dualistic mind or "wisdom according to the flesh," which cannot but venture to obstruct the saving rays of the redemptive and awakening Light.

These parallels and differences are not only significant in their own right; they also foster a deeper understanding of the ways various religious and contemplative schools recognize Reality. In addition, the reverse analogy that they suggest is not without significance in providing avenues of dialogue between Buddhists and Christians. It points to some spiritual affinities between the two traditions, affinities that may serve as areas of focalization in any attempts at mutual understanding and cross-fertilization. The "nonabsolutist" direction of their teachings and interpretations might be eminently fruitful in this respect since it lends to their spiritual perspectives a common specific bent or style. But the main hermeneutic lesson to be drawn from those comparative considerations might have to do, more generally, with the specific status and function of metaphysical and theological formulations in contemplative and soteriological traditions. It may invite the analyst to be particularly sensitive to contemplative ways of conceiving metaphysics that both the Buddhist and Christian contexts bring to the fore. In other words, it calls for a treatment of conceptual and textual matters not only on the level of their discursive coherence in mapping out reality but also, and above all, from the point of view of their power of transformative and emancipative assimilation. In this soteriological emphasis lies a possible—but not exclusive—way to open a wider space for a hermeneutics of aspects and vantage points, as well as for warding off any overly rigid conceptual crystallizations through a deeper recognition of the interplay between principled intellectual unity and the manifold of human existence.

3

_____

# On the Good beyond Good and Evil

Evil is conventionally considered in our times both as one of the most challenging problems from a philosophical and religious point of view and as a
concept and principle whose reality remains largely elusive and uncertain.
Indeed, contemporary mankind tends to see evil as an objection to the reality of
God while not quite believing in the existence of evil itself. On the one hand,
there is something deeply disconcerting to modern minds and sensibilities in
the idea that God could let evil be while still being God. On the other hand,
the overall relativist and constructionist mood does not quite know what to
make of evil, which it would rather consider as an outcome of various types
of external conditionings, starting with sociopolitical ones, than as an ontological principle. In a sense, contemplative metaphysics stands on positions that
are antithetic to such contemporary views. Mystics and contemplatives do
recognize and address the existence of evil, but they tend to see this existence
as inessential and ultimately unreal. A statement by Simone Weil may serve
as a suggestive introduction in this respect: "The word good has not the same
meaning when it is a term of the correlation good-evil as when it describes
the very being of God."[1]

As suggested by the title of this chapter and the previous sentence, the
term *good* can be understood on different levels of reality, and may, therefore,
imply various approaches to the concept of evil. There is no doubt that, in
distinguishing a dualistically defined good from one that transcends any duality, Simone Weil was echoing mystical and metaphysical considerations of the
Ultimate Reality such as are to be found in the Neoplatonic tradition. What
characterized this tradition and kindred metaphysics in the most general way
is their placing of Absolute Reality at the center of the metaphysical universe,
as well as identifying it with the supreme Good and the supreme Consciousness or Subjectivity. Henceforth, the relationship between human consciousness
and Supreme Consciousness is, from a metaphysical point of view, the most
determining factor in human experience, being both foundational and final.

97

In the prevalent modern *Weltanschauung*, the principles of which are informed by the postmedieval scientific outlook, physical reality—in whatever scientific framework it may be understood—comes first, and consciousness, in all of its forms, is but an epiphenomenon, albeit a sophisticated one, thereof.

Although religious perspectives, in sharp contrast with modern science, do place a supra-physical reality as the principle of the universe, they also tend to emphasize the gap between the Supreme and creation or the exclusive transcendence of the Source of reality vis-à-vis the relative realm. In contradistinction with these common religious representations of reality, contemplative doctrines, although often founded on meditations of scriptures that entail a clear sense of transcendence, invite us to perceive the universe as flowing, in a kind of paradoxically discontinuous continuum, from the Supreme Reality itself. In this regard, mystical metaphysics and theology tend to favor an account of relativity, or other-than-the-Supreme, whereby the latter is understood as a determination, modification, projection, and fragmentation of the Supreme Reality. Whereas exoteric and rational theological perspectives are for the most part concerned with situating the Supreme beyond and only beyond the created or manifested order—as in the concept of creation ex nihilo—mystical and theosophical outlooks frequently teach, or at least suggest, an essentially nondualistic apprehension of reality as a whole. Such an apprehension has profound implications with regard to the notion of evil.

While kindred metaphysical outlooks are all too often hastily labeled as pantheistic—in the philosophical sense highlighted by Spinoza with his formula *Deus sive Natura*—on account of their stressing the immanence of the Ultimate, it bears emphasizing that they, in fact, do not negate transcendence in the name of immanence but point, rather, to a *coincidentia oppositorum* at which the two terms are divested of their rational exclusiveness. Neither the teachings of Shankara, nor those of Abhinavagupta, Ibn al-'Arabī, or Chuang-tzu can therefore be properly characterized as pantheistic, in the sense that none of them could be reduced to a statement of equivalence between the Divine and creation. Indeed, all the aforementioned teachings recognize some form of immanence of the Divine to creation but they also point to a transcendence of the Principle in relation to the manifestation. Nonduality, or essential Unity, is therefore not exclusive of duality or multiplicity from the standpoint of lower levels of reality, and it is therefore in no way equivalent to the "night in which all cows are black," to make use of Hegel's critical assessment of Schelling's thought in his *Phenomenology of the Spirit*. Notwithstanding these metaphysical qualifications and distinctions, a contradiction or scandal is all too often deemed to result, when envisaging these doctrines from the outside, from a consideration of evil as a production or outcome originating in the unmixed Good. It is this seeming contradiction that we will investigate further by looking into the ways in which some major, metaphysically diverse, contemplative traditions have articulated the problem of evil. To this effect, we have chosen to delve into traditions that belong to both the Semitic and Indic religious families while keeping in mind the function of intellectual and spiritual bridge that has been sometimes attributed to Islam. Thus, our inquiry will focus on the traditions of Jewish Kabbalah and Kashmiri Śaivism as well as Christian mysticism, with the figure of Meister Eckhart, and the Sufi school of Ibn al-'Arabī.

Inasmuch as the world is experientially marked by the presence of evil, whether the latter is understood in cosmological or moral terms, or both, the specifically mystical understanding of this presence reveals nondualistic inclinations that considerably affect its ontological status. Thus, on the one hand, these doctrines entail a tendency to trace the sources of evil in the Ultimate Reality itself, while denoting, on the other hand, a definite relativization of evil that borders on, if not amounts to, its negation. Accordingly, in an apparent paradox, mystical theologies perceive the seeds of evil in the ontological Origin itself, whence rational theology and common religious belief would exclude it, while denying its reality on the relative plane where conventional awareness affirms and experiences its unavoidable presence.

Jewish mysticism is arguably, among all forms of contemplative metaphysics, the one that has been most concerned with the reality of evil. Its treatment of it has been informed by the seemingly contradictory double postulation that God is the unmixed Good and that He is in a mysterious way the source of evil. This double postulation is founded on Biblical statements such as Isaiah 45:7, "I form the light, and create darkness; I make peace, and create evil; I, the LORD, do all these things," on the one hand, and the narrative of the human transgression in Eden, on the other hand.[2] Consequently, Kabbalists have by and large envisaged evil in two distinct ways, either as a necessary result of the process of separation from the One, or as a transgressive experience grafted onto this process. Along the first line, Kabbalists have variously situated the source of evil on four different levels of Divine Reality. This point requires that we touch upon the doctrine of the Infinite, *Ein Sof*, the unfathomable Divine Essence, and the ten *sefiroth* or divine channels of light that proceed therefrom. These *sefiroth* are situated on the two levels of the Great Face (*Arikh Anpin*), with *Kether,* the Crown, *Hochmah,* Wisdom, and *Binah,* Intelligence, and the Lower Face (*Zeir Anpin*) of the six creative *sefiroth* together with *Malkuth,* the *sefirah* that transmits the Divine Light to creation.

Some Kabbalistic schools, preeminent among which is Isaac Luria's, account for the reality of evil by reference to the Infinite *Ein Sof* itself. In the words of the thirteenth-century scholar Moses Nahmanides, "Before the creation of the world, *Ein Sof* withdrew itself into its essence, from itself to itself within itself. It left an empty space with its essence, in which it could emanate and create."[3] Further elaborations on this withdrawal process known as *tsimtsum* specify that it resulted both in a thickening opacity, through God's contraction and withdrawal of Himself as it were, and a flow of light through His emanation and manifestation. It results from this twofold process that creation emerged as a mixture of light and darkness.

If the ultimate metaphysical raison d'être of evil is therefore to be found in the contraction of *Ein Sof* onto itself, it is only as we come down the degrees of the tree of the *sefiroth* that the source of evil becomes readily apparent and determining in and through the quality of Judgment. First, in the realm of the Great Face—or the three supreme *sefiroth*—the third *sefirah, Binah,* or discriminating Divine intelligence, delimits the qualities of entities in God's knowledge, thereby prefacing to their cosmic contrasts and oppositions. On this level, though exclusive severity cannot be yet separated from inclusive mercy and one cannot quite speak of Judgment per se, a point alluded by Moses Cordovero when he writes that "*Binah* consists of Mercy" even though "Judgment arises from it."[4] It is only on the degree of the Lower Face, with *Din* or *Gevurah,* the highest *sefirah* of the left arm of God, that Divine Judgment, and the ground of ontological separateness, is affirmed. By introducing a sort of bifurcation in the Divine, this *sefirah* presides over the exclusive limitations of everything in creation. It is in this quality of separateness that the prime locus of evil lies, since the otherness it introduces in God, through the distinction between the Self that is Named and the Other that Names It,[5] is the principle of any further division and negation downstream within universal existence. Accordingly, some Kabbalists have taught that rigorous Judgment is akin to the determinative Naming of the Divine Essence by itself and the source of all creation. As such, the Name is aptly referred to in a Kabbalistic text as "some little bit of manifestation,"[6] as it prefigures any and every further existentiation. In this foundational sense, the otherness of Judgment is the origin of evil.

Finally, evil can be considered as being fully actuated in *Malkuth,* the Divine Kingdom of immanence that transmits the divine influx to existence. This realm is symbolically connected to the Female, the *Shekhinah,* the Divine Presence connecting everything to the highest realms, but whose separation from the male *Yesod* can also break the flow of unity and, in asserting an illusory independence, create evil. This is particularly emphasized in Kabbalistic commentaries that understand the separation of Eve from Adam as cutting off *Malkuth* from higher levels of Divine Reality. At this point, where the duality inherent to the relationship self-other gives rise to a distorting claim of ontological independence, there does evil flow.[7] In a sense, this lowest instance of emergence of Judgment within the sphere of the Divine is a key to understanding human responsibility vis-à-vis evil, since it constitutes, so to speak, its metaphysical archetype.

Indeed, while evil finds its source in divine separations and metaphysical "curtains," it is also the prerogative of mankind in the exercise of its freedom. Thus, some Kabbalists distinguish between judgment as it stems from the economy of the Divine production, and that misguiding aspect of it, actualized by mankind, that implies not only a distancing and cutting off from the ontological source but also a subversive mingling of domains.[8] This is expressed through the dual symbolism of the serpent. In the divine order, the latter is the principle through which the cosmos is brought out. It is considered to be a good servant of the Lord as long as it remains outside the divine precinct while facilitating the Divine emanation and, beyond, the overarching scheme of universal existence from God to God. The tree of the knowledge of good and evil symbolizes, in this sense, the orderly separation between the divine and cosmic domains. Its fruit can be read as the symbolic crystallization of the positive outcomes and spiritual benefits of the divine plan. However, the irruption of the serpent within the holy precincts and the premature and transgressive eating of the fruit that ensues, appears to treat the centrifugal phase of the divine plan as if it were an end in itself, or as if it were the centripetal completion of existence, thereby subverting the order of creation and erroneously confusing the domains of reality. Indeed, it amounts to treating the relative production of the world as an absolute, which is the essence of all further transgressions. In this scenario, it is not so much the ontological unfolding of the world down the divine degrees that accounts for evil, but rather the misused human ability to relate to it and make use of it through its free will.

In sharp contrast to Kabbalah, Kashmiri Śaivism is, arguably, the school of metaphysical mysticism that places the least emphasis on evil. In fact, as Kamalakar Mishra has indicated, "In the texts of the system one does not find explicit reference to the question, much less a discussion of the subject."[9] As we will see, this is mostly due to the centrality of the Śaivite principle of immanence of Śiva to the whole of existence. In Kashmir Śaivism, the aspects and productions of the Absolute derive from Śiva's primary understanding as utter freedom (*svātantrya*). This freedom is expressed in Śiva's constant creativeness in the ever-flowing multiplicity of new forms. This creative process through which the Absolute Consciousness outpours into multiplicity originates in the union of Śiva and Śakti. Śakti can be characterized as the efficient power of Self-revelation of Śiva through which he manifests and reabsorbs the realm of manifestation. Śakti refers, therefore, to the level of Pure Consciousness that is the seed of the process of production; it is, among other possible characterizations, the level of *vimarśa,* the emergence of Self-Awareness within the Absolute Consciousness Itself. Thus, Divine freedom manifests itself through a sort of "doubling" awareness of self that is the source of further differentiation and manifestation. However, Śiva always reconciles all oppositions because

He is, with and through Śakti, the very productive source from which they emerge and into which they flow. It could be said, therefore, that *Śiva* makes it impossible for evil to have any reality of its own.

On the other hand, while being eminently creative and positive, there is a vantage point from which Śakti could be considered as a negation of Śiva. This negativity may appear when considering that, on the one hand, Śiva is infinite and undivided Reality, Śakti, on the other hand, brings out the finite and discrete realities that delimit and divide the Śivaic plenitude through disseminating its power. However, Śaivism is not intent on attributing this negativity to Śakti herself, but rather to the lower ranges of the process she triggers. This appears quite clearly in the extremely differentiated range of *tattvas* or degrees of ontological reality—that is, no less than thirty-six degrees of projection of Consciousness, from pure Śiva I-Consciousness to *prthivī*, earth, or the outermost reach of materialization of consciousness. In this perspective, evil is nothing but the outcome of the human ignorance of the all-encompassing reality of Absolute Consciousness. Outside of it, one may speak of limitations or imperfections but not of evil properly so called, since limitations and imperfections are not in themselves "severed" from Reality, and therefore are essentially participant in it. Evil is not positively defined in any way, being no more than a shadow in relation to light. In fact, even though ignorance and impurity can be deemed to be principles of human evil, they are no less consequences of the metaphysical principle of freedom, therefore foundationally good. Hence, if evil is to be envisaged at all, it must be from the extrinsic point of view of spiritual realization rather than from that of metaphysical reality. In this regard, the Śaivite notion of *mala*, or dross, refers to impurities that are the spiritual roots of any kind of human evil. Manifestations of *mala* are three in kind, and pertain respectively to the domains of action, thought, and being. The impurity of action or *kārma* is connected to the feeling of pleasure and pain, and the deluded sense of duality it entails. The second type of impurity is *māyīya mala*, based on the experience of *bhinnavedyaprathā*, or the ignorant sense of difference between I and the other. As for the last impurity, *ānavamala*, it is defined as the feeling of being incomplete, therefore the failure to recognize the all-encompassing fullness of Śiva.

The primarily epistemological dimension of evil is quite apparent in the symbolism of the snake, or the power of the Kundalini Śakti, that is central to the spiritual economy of Śivaite practice. The latter has been defined as the "revealing and concealing energy of Lord Śiva."[10] It is a latent energy that ranges from the very heart of Śiva, in its universal, infinite power, to the life essence, *prāna*, the vital breath which is the fuel of Tantric meditation. This energy in itself has no evil connotation, but it is potentially destructive as long as it remains unconscious.[11] Once actualized, however, it rises to the level of consciousness and unleashes its divinely transforming power. While energy is intrinsically connected with the Absolute that is pure being and pure consciousness, it must be known for what it *is* in order not to become a source of benighted evil. Awakening means that consciousness becomes aware of itself as Śiva's I-Consciousness, instead of being confused with the limitations of individual consciousness. All human evils derive from a lack of awareness of being-consciousness, and from a misuse of the energy inherent in it. Evil is unreal inasmuch as it results from a misperception of reality: when the latter is acknowledged and realized, evil dissipates like a morning mist in the sun.[12] Evil flows from the nonrecognition of the light of Śiva as the immanent principle and reality of everything. Abhinavagupta defines the impure as that which has not been perceived as resting in the Heart.[13] It is not that evil needs be discarded, or opposed; it is, rather, that pure consciousness needs be recognized as being what it is.[14]

As already highlighted, nondualistic Śaivism is based on the utterly free power of creation and reabsorption of the absolute I-Consciousness of Śiva, the Supreme. Considering evil as a mere byproduct of ignorance, this school of thought does not place morality, in the ordinary sense of the term, at center stage. Indeed, the mythological figure of Śiva is himself apprehended as transmoral, defying as he does the norms of social ethics. The god appears in the form of a disconcerting blend of asceticism and eroticism, and his terrestrial career is that of a wandering outcast who does not shun association with conventionally "evil" phenomena. While Śiva is also worshiped as a destroyer of evil, it is so inasmuch as he dissipates darkness in light of pure Consciousness. Anything "evil" is ultimately connected to a separation from that Light. While Śaivism does not consider evil as a substance in any way, it considers impurities, as states "of seeming separation from consciousness,"[15] as obstacles to the recognition of Supreme Consciousness. What is needed, therefore, is a discipline of union that reabsorbs the separated elements into the unity of Consciousness.[16]

The previous considerations should not lead one to think that evil is not a concrete presence in Tantric Śaivism. Even though it is metaphysically nothing, evil is an operative force to reckon with in the domain of spiritual and daily life. However, the reality of hostile forces is never disconnected from an awareness of the obstacles to recognition. The originality of Śaivism is that the latter tend to be envisaged as doubts, inner irresolution, and dilemmas that stem from the pressure of conventional consciousness. The asocial and amoral features of the god Śiva symbolize this fight against the socially constructed mental contents that hinder the full manifestation of the freedom of Consciousness.[17] Thus, the slayer of evil is also the destroyer of the psychosocial limitations covering the Self. Paradoxically, the conventional notions of the good and evil can thereby function as sources of ignorance and therefore evil. Some of the most disconcerting forms of Śaivism are precisely intent on addressing these limitations, and on shattering their nefarious effects. So-called lefthanded Śaivism, or rather Śāktism, which makes ritual use of the three transgressive Ms—meat or *māmsa*, wine or *madirā*, and sexual intercourse, *maithuna*—is characteristic of this perspective. Inherent to this path is an alchemy through which the yogi is freed from the paralyzing and constricting dualities that define ordinary consciousness, and which are particularly absolutized by moral codes and taboos. The transcending of the polarity of ordinary, socioethical, good and evil is in such cases the very means of freeing oneself from spiritual evil.[18] It clearly points to a metaphysical degree of reality at which the relative notions of good and evil do not apply any longer.

The complexities of the relationship between the relative dimension of good and evil and the position of the Absolute beyond all polarities and dualities also appear, albeit with very different theological emphases, in the highest nondualistic reaches of Christian mysticism. Thus, in his *Commentary on the Gospel of Saint-John*, Meister Eckhart meditates the sentences of the prologue, "All things were made through the Word," and, "Without him was made nothing," following Augustine, as intimations of the "nonexistence" of evil. He writes: "Sin and evil in general are not things that exist, so they are not made through him but without him."[19] This typical, and in a sense elliptical, expression is founded, as it is by and large in the whole Neoplatonic tradition, on the equation of being with the good. Now, of course, the negation of the "existence" of evil must not be understood as a pure and simple negation of evil. It is simply a somewhat hyperbolic way to highlight the fundamental "nonbeing" of evil as a mere privation of the good, therefore of being. The past participle "made," in Latin *factum*, is equivocal. The "making" of being, or the good, is the work of the Word, simply because it is the Good itself, and from the Good can only result goods. By contrast, the "making" of evil cannot be the Word's work, it can only be "made" as "nothing," therefore by other than the Word. This corresponds to the subsequent distinction, put forward by Eckhart between "effects" and "defects," the former being the work of the Word, whereas the latter are not. Now, Eckhart specifies the meaning of his assertion when adding that "everything that is made by any agent whatever is nothing without him."[20] This amounts, as in numerous mystical texts throughout a variety of traditions, to what could be referred to as an ultimate negation of secondary causes. Eckhart does not absolutely deny the production of effects through secondary causes, but he insists upon the metaphysical principle that "every being" from nature or being is "immediately from God alone."[21]

Now, it is apparent that this cannot apply to evil things, thoughts, or actions. In other words, the "defects" that Eckhart has in mind must proceed from mankind, or perhaps from another relative being. The idea that created realities flow *immediately* from God cannot apply to those realities that are "defective." In the general economy of the Fall, "defects" cannot but refer to sin, which was introduced into creation by the transgressive autonomy of humankind—leaving aside the further question of the "demiurgic" dimension of evil within the very "texture" of creation, as epitomized by the presence of the snake in the garden. So it is plausible that the *immediacy* of God's creation of "effects" may be altered through the negative *mediation* of the human will, thereby removing the reality of things from the realm of *immediate* Divine Will. It follows that Eckhart's insistence on the Neoplatonic equation of being and good and his emphasis on the immediacy of God's creation results, paradoxically, given the de facto reality of evil, in a sort of metaphysical independence of mankind as source of evil. The sinful will, or the ego, could be interpreted as being a human layer that covers the divine work of creation, and corrupts the good that it "makes."

The paradox is that, in sharp contrast with the aforementioned reflections, Eckhart definitely places human evils under the scope of the Divine Will, and therefore existentiation, appearing thereby to contradict his statements about the "nothingness" of evil and about its not flowing immediately from God. This is plain in some of the passages of his work that have been condemned in the Bull *In agro dominico* (1329), such as the statements that even in an evil work "God's glory is revealed and shines forth in equal fashion," and "the more gravely he (a person) sins, the more he praises God."[22] This statement was defended by Eckhart on the grounds that God's permitting this evil glorifies his patience and mercy. In a sense, this is nothing but a particular instance of the principle according to which evil is demanded by the overarching perfection of the universe. This is also illustrated by Eckhart's reflection that one should never regret having performed an evil action if one is now in a state of grace.

Thus, in essence, Eckhart's meditation on evil takes two ways. The first, typically Neoplatonic and Augustinian, consists in asserting that since evil has no substance and is merely privative, it cannot possibly have been "made" by God. In this case, God functions as a conjunction of material, formal, and efficient cause in relation to creation. He is exclusive of evil because His goodness, being the cause of the universe, cannot possibly be made "responsible" for bad effects. On the other hand, however, God cannot but be the "author" of evil since the latter has a meaning and a function in the providential economy of the whole. To state that He simply "allows" it amounts to saying the same thing in a different way, since this "allowance" cannot be understood otherwise than as a kind of will, and therefore a "responsibility" in the defects of creation. On this level, however, God appears in the mode of a universal final cause. He is implicitly equated with the All-Possibility, which encompasses everything, good and bad, within the universal economy of Being. Here, God is not the good, but That which is beyond good as being: "God is not being or goodness. Goodness adheres to being and does not go beyond it. . . . God is not 'good,' or 'better' or 'best.'"[23] This Universal Possibility lies even beyond Being, since as Essence set beyond all determinations, it even transcends good and evil.

It could be argued that the ambiguities and contradictions resulting from these seemingly contradictory statements on the part of Eckhart stem from a confusion of two different dimensions of the Divine Reality. At times, Eckhart seems to equate the Good with Being inasmuch as it is the "opposite" of non-being, while at other times he appears to envisage the Good as the Ultimate that encompasses the universal range of possibilities, referred to relatively as good and bad, within an overarching context that transcends the very duality implied by these notions.

In a sense, analogous questions can be raised with respect to Sufi conceptions of evil, most likely due the co-presence in both the Christian and Islamic traditions of a Platonic affinity, or source of inspiration, and a personalist, not to say anthropomorphic, theological language. Thus, Sufi views of evil vary greatly depending on whether they are framed within a religious and spiritual context or a more strictly metaphysical one. To put it in a nutshell, evil is considered within the range of meditations that span from the doctrine of Divine Unity (*tawhīd*) to the primacy of the Divine Law (*sharī'ah*). Our current analyses focus on Ibn al-'Arabī's writings on evil, not only on account of their preeminence and influence in the Islamic mystical tradition, but also because they arguably offer the most encompassing and intriguing perspective on the matter.

In order to understand Ibn al-'Arabī's conceptions of evil, one must first of all delve into his metaphysical and cosmological account of the production of universal existence. This is because one cannot understand evil, to the extent it can be understood, without understanding Reality and being. In this respect, Sufi metaphysics, like Eckhart's, parallels the Neoplatonic principle of the metaphysical nonreality of evil. As Ibn al-'Arabī puts it in his *al-Futūhāt al-Makkiyya*: "Evil is only the non-existence of good."[24] It has no reality or being as an entity in itself. In this regard Ibn al-'Arabī meditates most specifically on the Prophetic supplication, "The good, all of it, is in Thy hands, while evil does not go back to Thee." This traditional statement implies that evil cannot pertain to God because nothingness cannot relate to Being. The impossibility of evil being assigned to God results in the metaphysical pronouncement that "all of existence is good," as well as in the recognition of the nonexistence of evil. It is at this stage that we need to analyze further the concept of nonexistence. In Ibn al-'Arabī's metaphysics, the concept of nonexistence cannot be separated from a complex meditation on the notion of possibility.

It bears stressing, first of all, that creatures can be considered on two different levels, namely, their immutable essence and their existential manifestation. Everything is, first of all, a possible and permanent entity *('ayn thābita)* in God's knowledge. As such, it is nonexistent in creation. Obviously, though, permanent entities also exist in creation as existents, following the Qur'ānic *kun* or "let it be." Existents are therefore good inasmuch as they are brought into existence by the Good, but they are, or may be, evil to the extent that they "tasted" of nonexistence as merely possible realities.[25] This is why Ibn al-'Arabī can describe at times existentiation as a passage from evil to good. It goes without saying, however, that creation can also be viewed as a transition from good to evil, that is as a passage from God's unitive being and knowledge to multiplicity and composition, the latter entailing oppositions, and therefore evil. From the first point of view, the principle of the goodness of creatures is God as the Good, whereas the source of their evil lies in God's knowledge of them without being identifiable with God qua Good. This is just another way of saying that "possible entities" are not necessary, but precisely only possible, God only being Necessary Being without any trace of nonexistence. There is, therefore, in existents a possible disjunction between essence and existence that clearly differentiates creatures from God, in whom Essence is none other than Necessity. This distinction makes it possible for existents not to be fully themselves by failing to align with, and participate in, the Good that projected them into existence. Moreover, evil appears as the consequence of diversity and composition that necessarily produces differences, conflicts, and corruption. There is, in summary, a gradation of reality that may be sketched as follows. As permanent entities in God's knowledge, entities are fully real and are indeed identifiable with the Real, *al-Haqq*. When considered from the point of view of their nonexistence in creation, they take on, as it were, a relative aspect from within God's knowledge itself. In other words, they stand for relativity in absoluteness, and are seeds of evil, as it were. Considered as existentiated entities they are direct manifestations of the Goodness of the Real, since they flow from it. Finally, still considered as existentiated entities they are in a certain sense nonexistent in God, and this is, precisely, their aspect of pure accidence and evil. The limit of this accidence is impossibility or nothingness, a limit that can never be reached but that takes one in the direction of a contradictory pure "accidence" and an impossible pure evil.

We have so far described the metaphysics of evil. But what is the share of human responsibility in the appearance of moral evil? In order to answer this question, one has to distinguish between two levels of the Divine Will. The first is the existentiating act identified as the source of Good, which Ibn al-'Arabī refers to as *al-amr al-taqwīnī*, or the "order to be." Within the context of the creation resulting from this existentiating order there appears a second command, which is the "legal order" (*al-amr al-taklīfī*). This legal order aims at coordinating and harmonizing the human will in conformity with the Good as goal of existence. It stems from divine wisdom as a guidance to mankind. In relation to it, human evil appears as free disobedience to the Law: "Nothing determines opposition except the prescription of the Law."[26] Metaphysically, and without negating the immediate exercise of free will, disobedience and evil are predetermined by God in the Name of Misguidance or Humiliation (*al-Mudhill*). *Al-Mudhill* is the centrifugal and distracting dimension of the existentiating order that causes humans to go astray. It must be added, however, that this attribute of rigor participates essentially in Mercy, since it ultimately aims at a return to the One; it is nothing other in this sense than a kind of detour toward felicity. Evil cannot but exist in the world but it can be overcome by placing oneself under the shield of the Good, the most radical way of which is to recognize its exclusive and inclusive sole Reality in and through the realization of *tawhīd*.

It is only to the extent that human beings do not fall under this existentiating act of misguidance that they do not succumb to evil. This is why it is important to keep in mind that Ibn al-ʿArabī does not say that there is no evil in existence. All he claims is that existence is good, therefore contrary to, and exclusive of, evil qua existence. In order to account for the presence of evil in existence, Ibn al-ʿArabī refers to it not as a substance but as an accident, *ʿarad*, an Arabic term that connotes appearance or show, lack of necessity, and temporariness. It is because phenomenal existence does not entail necessity in its essence, by contrast with God, that the possibility of nonexistence, therefore evil, enters accidentally into its economy. This possibility is all the more actively asserted by mankind that humans have the capacity to exercise free will by choosing "not to be" what they actually are. Ibn al-ʿArabī defines this evil potentiality of humans as a "failure to reach one's individual desire (*gharad*) and what is agreeable (*mulāʾim*) to one's nature." The term *gharad* refers to design, purpose, and destination, and evil could be fittingly defined, in this respect, as missing the mark of human and creaturely finality.

The participation of mankind in the manifestation of evil is envisaged from another vantage point in the chapter on the "Word of Muhammad," from the *Bezels of Wisdom*. In it, Ibn al-ʿArabī draws a symbolic distinction between the "root" of realities and their "smell."[27] The smell relates to the spiritual influence or ambience, but it is also and above all an indication of that which issues from a given being and is, therefore, perceived as effect of this being. In this sense, there is no evil at the "root" of phenomena, since the root is the Divine, but there may be evil in the effects or perceptions of phenomena. Hence, Ibn al-ʿArabī's statement, "It is not the thing itself that is to be detested, but only that which issues from it."[28] Thus, the Prophet is reported to have said that he disliked the smell of garlic but, as Ibn al-'Arabī emphasizes it, he did not say that he disliked garlic itself. We can infer from this example that evil is never situated in beings themselves as beings, but only perceived by a given subject who determines it as evil. Ibn al-'Arabī does not teach a sort of moral and aesthetic relativism, but he acknowledges that the very notion of evil presupposes a set of relative circumstances that allow one to perceive it as such. In other words, evil presupposes that one considers phenomena from a standpoint that is other than that of pure being. Consequently, evil is defined "relatively" as that which is detested: "Such an aversion may be a question of custom, natural antipathy, law, deficiency, or something else."[29] As soon as we enter the realm of relative reality and perception, the distinction between a good and a bad becomes relevant and indeed necessary. In fact, the perception of this distinction enters into the very definition of any given being, hence the Qur'ānic verse about vile men and vile women. The entire universe is made up of dualities and contrasts that are inherent to it.

Moreover, this relative reality of evil does not only exist in the cosmos: it is, in fact, present in the Divine Itself. This may come as a surprise when considering Ibn al-'Arabī's teaching that evil has no substance and therefore no reality. In the context of a discussion of whether there exists in existence something that can see only the good, and not the bad, Ibn al-'Arabī does not hesitate to write: "We would say that there is not, since in the very source from which the Cosmos is manifested, which is the Real, we find aversion and love, the bad being that which is loathed, while the good is that which is loved."[30] The very source from which the Cosmos is manifested cannot but be the delimited Real, without which the Real would bear no relationship with the world of delimitations. As delimited, this dimension of the Real is Being, which excludes nonbeing and therefore evil. The Supreme Delimitation is therefore the source of the distinction between good and evil. However, if one were to envisage the Real in its purely nondelimited Essence, it would be impossible to assign to It the function of being the source of a distinction between good and evil.

The nondelimited Real cannot be referred to in terms of distinctions and dualities, and from its point of view everything is good inasmuch as it is divine at root. We are therefore led to distinguish, with respect to evil, the Divine Essence as such and the Lord as first Delimitation and source of all multiplicity. The former is to be essentially identified with the Divine Mercy, which is none other than the intrinsic nature of the Divinity. This Essential Mercy lies beyond the distinction of good and evil and encompasses everything. In Ibn al-'Arabī's own words, "The Mercy of God inheres in both the good and the bad," and, "From its own standpoint the bad is good and the good bad."[31] The first statement means that *Allāh* is the only Reality in *wujūd*, or that He is *wujūd* as such. The second statement suggests that, from the vantage point of the Essence, "the bad is good" because, as existentiated reality, it proceeds from the Breath of the Compassionate and is none other than the Essence since there is none but it. As for the good, it is "bad" because it constitutes a delimitation that lies below the "infinite good" of the Supreme Nondelimitation. This dual relativization of good and evil has numerous spiritual and moral implications in the world of operative Sufism. First, the recognition of God's Mercy in good and bad is the foundation of the virtue of *tawakkul,* or general and unconditional trust in God. Second, the recognition of the "good" of the "bad" refers more specifically to *ridā* or the contentment with, or acceptance of, the rigorous decrees of destiny. Thirdly, the perception of the "bad" of the "good" amounts to a sense of transcendence of the absolute Good and a constant negation of delimitations as potential object of *shirk* or ontological "association."

This latter dimension is developed in a most illuminating and challenging way by one of the foremost spiritual and intellectual heirs of Ibn al-'Arabī, the nineteenth-century Algerian gnostic *Amīr* 'Abd al-Qādir. In one of his *Mawāqif* (*Spiritual Pauses*), the *Amīr* comments upon a *hadīth* in which the Prophet addresses the question of the ways one should respond to evil. The *hadīth* enumerates three ways in which this should be done, first by "one's hand," second by one's words, and thirdly by one's thoughts, or in a purely internal manner.[32] While these recommendations are generally thought to apply to three different levels of "censuring evil" that may regard each and every believer, depending upon the scope of his power and the gravity of the evil encountered, the *Amīr* begins by delineating the different responses by referring them to three different categories of Muslims: the rulers, the doctors of the Law, and the ordinary believers. The first are empowered to oppose evil actions by force, the second are authorized to decree religiously against them, and the third are commanded to exercise moral judgment by censuring in their hearts that which must be disapproved. However, the main argument of the *Amīr* does not relate to these three categories, but rather to a fourth one that, in an enigmatic manner, does not belong to any of these three groups, and which the *Amīr* describes as "one who (in every act) contemplates the unique true Agent."[33] To this one, writes the *Amīr,* there is no obligation to oppose evil. First of all, it must of course be specified that such a one does necessarily belong to the third category in one sense, that is, that of the believers belonging to the community of the faithful, and that he may even belong to the first and the second one, since his sociopolitical status may very well involve political or religious authority. It may be, therefore, that the same individual must oppose evil by his words— for example, as a doctor of the Law—while not opposing it from the point of view of his degree of metaphysical knowledge. This explains why the *Amīr* adds: "But the fact of not opposing evil in one's heart does not in itself result in the ruin of any of the pillars of the Sacred Law nor does it have the effect of making licit what is illicit."[34] What is meant, essentially, is that one must be able to consider evil both from the point of view of its existence and from that of its naught in relation to the Essence. The *Amīr* quotes a Sufi saying: "He who looks at sinners with the eye of the Law, hates them; he who looks at sinners with the eye of essential Truth, excuses them." This distinction allows one to understand how the Sufi understanding of evil avoids the two pitfalls of denying it and absolutizing it. It does not deny it on the level upon which it is morally and legally a reality, no more than it would claim that sickness is not sickness or that it is health, but it does not assign to it a metaphysical reality that it does not actually hold. Hence, the difficult and subtle perfection of apprehending evil from two perspectives depending on the needs of the situation and the moment: "The gnostic who possesses the sense of spiritual discrimination knows how to distinguish the places and the circumstances and what each of them imposes as an obligation."[35]

We would like to emphasize that the mystical doctrines that we have sketched are, for their proponents, no more than provisional symbolic frameworks, and not philosophies or dogmatic doctrines. They are supports of meditation for the mind in view of assimilating realities that lie beyond mind. In this sense, the concepts of evil propounded by mystical theologies are less theoretical statements than they are existential and spiritual riddles designed to transcend rational polarities and antinomies. What we have gathered in terms of these supports of meditation can be summarized by the four following conclusions: The Ultimate Reality lies beyond the polarity of good and evil as the Unconditioned Good. Secondly, it contains, in an unmanifested way, the source of separation in the form of a seed, or a self-determinative Name or intrinsic Creative Energy, which although essentially one and undividable from the Good is also a distant source of evil. Thirdly, the projection, emanation, manifestation, or creation that ensues from this prime determination unfolds into separation, fragmentation, and composition, hence potential or actual evil.[36] Finally, mankind is free to neutralize and redeem evil, or else actualize and increase it through its modes of consciousness and actions. This contemplative schema excludes the relativization of evil, by grounding it in the ontological reality and cosmological process, as well as the absolutization of evil that results from dualistic theological orientations, whether in theory or in practice. From an existential point of view, there is no doubt that evil does exist. However, mystical theology teaches that, metaphysically or ultimately, evil *is* not. In fact, for contemplative metaphysicians, to negate the metaphysical inexistence of evil amounts to failing to comprehend the nature of the absolutely Real and its relationship with relativity. It also deprives one, as a way of existential consequence, from the only actual means to overcome evil, that is, placing our will under the protection of the Real, and more fundamentally identifying with the unconditioned Good through our transpersonal intelligence.

# 4

## On Hindu *Bhedābheda* and Sufi *Barzakh*

In *The Bow and the Lyre*, Octavio Paz writes: "Western history can be seen as the history of an error, a going astray. . . . The Western world is the world of 'this or that'; the Eastern, of 'this and that' and even 'this is that.'"[1] This "going astray" suggests a "right path" from which Western consciousness has strayed, a primordial state of being that has been lost along the way. This original mode of perception is equated with an Eastern polysemy (this and that) that culminates in coincidence (this is that). There is little doubt that in highlighting this contrast, Paz has in view a distinction between an exclusionary logic, not only in the domain of rational investigation, but in all matters of human endeavor in which Western "dualism" is clearly traceable, and an inclusionary intuition that has remained attuned to the anthropocosmic unity of the universe. The Cartesian "clear and distinct" ideas are perhaps not as much at stake here as the dualism of mind and matter, subject and object, and other such pairs of opposites. It could be added, in fact, that the "Eastern world," or whatever we may understand by these words, has even tended to lead farther beyond the "this is that" by opening onto a "this that" without copula and, ultimately, fusing into That, in the sense of the Upanishadic *Tat tvam asi*, That Thou Art: from analogy to coincidence to nonduality. By contrast with this nondual tropism, the "Western mind" has valued distinction as a principle of individual identity and rational intelligibility. The law of the excluded middle, Descartes's *idées claires et distinctes,* and the Kantian bifurcation of the phenomenal and the noumenal, are emblematic of this way of approaching intelligence and reality. The Western mind, particularly in the wake of the Renaissance, has leaned toward highlighting that which defines and separates, thereby entailing dualities. By contrast, the "Eastern perspective" can be deemed to begin with the Unity, or the Nonduality, of the Ultimate and only consider differences and distinctions as secondary aspects of reality that have to be resolved, metaphysically or contemplatively, into That which is their principle. Between the "this" and the "that" lie the "this is that" of correspondences and the "this that" of Unity-in-difference. Poetry, as Paz reminds us, has been by and large a language founded on "this is that"; it has grown on and from analogies, similitudes, and correspondences. By evoking these analogies, poetry suggests both the meaning and the mystery of the universe. It evokes an underlying order or harmony that makes sense, and at the same time the human inability to fathom and express this sense within the strictures of its terrestrial limitations and merely rational understanding. What it points to, in fact, is a unity within multiplicity, a unity that does not cancel or exclude diversity, but on the contrary, unveils its deepest meaning. This is the "this that" of identity-in-difference, this mysterious coincidence of opposites that mysticism and metaphysics have situated at the very core of their concern for reality.

What follows is an attempt at exploring the ways in which unity and multiplicity have been articulated, in two very different worlds of meaning— those of Indian metaphysics and Islamic mysticism, through the complex notions of *bhedābheda,* which is rendered literally by "difference-non-difference" or more aptly by "identity-in-difference," and *barzakh,* an Arabic term that can be translated by "barrier," or better, by "isthmus." In doing so, we will proceed from the textual, beginning with the scriptural occurrences that lie at the foundations of these notions, to the contextual, by which we mean the metaphysical and religious framework in which they must be understood. We will attempt, thereby, at characterizing the content of these notions with a view to highlight, *in fine,* synthetic conclusions concerning the problem of the articulation between the metaphysical pull of Unity, or Nonduality, and the existential and phenomenal evidence of multiplicity and difference.

In terms of texts, the concept of *bhedābheda,* which is understood in a number of different ways in the Hindu intellectual traditions, is basically a response to hermeneutic issues resulting from two seemingly contradictory kinds of statements found in the *Vedas,* and particularly in the *Upanishads.* The term refers to more than two hundred texts ranging probably from the sixth century of the Common Era into the first millennium at least. These texts are considered part of the *Vedas* or divinely revealed scriptures, *Śruti.* Without entering the complex and disputed question of the early meaning and commentarial development of the *Upanishads,* it is important to note, for our current purpose, that some of those early texts include archetypical *mahāvākyāni,* or Great Pronouncements, that have functioned as the intellectual and spiritual axioms of Hindu metaphysics. Among those sacred statements, the main ones unambiguously equate the Divine Reality, the Absolute *Brahman,* which is also referred to, when considered from the point of view of its Selfhood or Divine and Universal "I" as *Atman,* or *Paramātman,* with the individual self or soul referred to as *jīva.* Probably the two *mahāvākyāni* most often referred to are

*Aham Brahmāsmi*[2] (I am *Brahman*) and *Tat tvam asi* (That thou art). They express the point of view of nonduality, *Advaita,* or nondifference, *abheda.* On the other hand, some other scriptural statements imply duality, and difference. Such as this passage from the *Maitri Upanishad*: "There is indeed another, different soul, called 'the elemental soul' (*bhūtātman*)—he who, being overcome by the bright or the dark fruits of action, enters a good or an evil womb, so that his course is downward or upward and he wanders around, overcome by the pairs of opposites" (3:1).[3]

Now, in terms of intellectual context, the various philosophic and theosophic systems of Hinduism, and India in general, have provided a wealth of different interpretations of this tension, or contradiction. Looking at it in a most synthetic way, we have fundamentally three kinds of understanding of this tension: the nondual (*Advaita*) that postulates nondifference (*abheda*) between *Paramātman* and the *jīva,* foremost represented by Shankaracharya; the dualist (*dvaita*), represented first and foremost by Mādhva (1199–1278), which teaches difference (*bheda*), the plurality of selves, and the reality of the world, and is connected to *bhakti* or devotional yoga; and *bhedābheda* schools that teach "difference-non-difference" or "identity-in-difference," with various understandings of what this term means.

It is important to keep in mind that the reason why this question is crucial in India dwells in the principle that these schools are essentially soteriological: they aim at the realization of *Brahman* or union with *Brahman.* The intellectual and the spiritual are intrinsically connected, in a way that too many contemporary scholars may understate, or even fail to take into account. Therefore, the way one understands the relationship between *Brahman* and the *jīva* has significant consequences upon the way of achieving this realization, which amounts to a deliverance from all conditioning fetters, or *moksha.* In particular, this question hinges upon the contrast between ways of knowledge, which tend to reduce appearance to Reality, and ways of loving devotion, which maximize the reality of the relationship between the devotee and the Divinity, and therefore also both terms of the relationship.

Now, as a transition, and before we move into a deeper exploration of the meanings and implications of *bhedābheda,* it is important to understand that this concept denotes a relation, and not a *relatum,* that is to say not a related or relating term or phenomenon. As we are going to see, by contrast, the Islamic *barzakh* is a relating *relatum,* albeit a very particular and puzzling one.

Textually speaking, the term *barzakh* is used three times in the *Qurʾān.* Two of these references appear in the context of a partition between two seas, a third one refers to a separation between the current life and the thereafter, a separation that prevents damned souls from fulfilling their desire to revert to the herebelow to perform good deeds and be saved thereafter. Our focus will be mostly on the first kind, primarily because it has more direct implications for the understanding of the relationship between God, mankind, and the world.

One of the two main Quranic occurrences of the *barzakh* reads as follows: "*Maraja al-bahrayn yaltaqiyāni baynahumā barzakhun lā yabghiyān* [He spread two meeting seas between the two of them a *barzakh* they do not transgress]" (55:19–20). The second occurrence, from *Surāh Al-Furqān*, runs as follows: "*Wa huwa alladhi maraja al-bahrayni hādhā ʿadhbun furātun wa hādhā milhun ujājun wa jaʿala baynahumā barzakhan wa hijran mahjuran* [He is the One who has spread two seas, one palatable and sweet, and the other salty and bitter, and he has made between them a *barzakh* and a partition (*hijr*) forbidden (*mahjuran*]" (25:53). In the latest passage, one notes that the term *barzakh* is used together with *hijr*, which is reinforced by *mahjuran*, a term that is exclusively separative, and implies, interestingly, interdiction in a legal sense.

The most immediate aspect of the *barzakh* is that it has two functions: to separate and to connect. By and large, exoteric commentaries emphasize the aspect of separation, while esoteric commentaries, particularly in the school of Ibn al-ʿArabī, stress the aspect of *third entity* of the *barzakh* as site of contact, and therefore communication and union, between two separate domains. This should not come as a surprise since the sciences of the "exterior" (*zāhir*) have to do with legal distinctions, while the sciences of the inner (*bātin*) relate to ways of union.

Aside from these scriptural sources, one must also attend to the more central contextual and intellectual framework of the doctrine of Divine Unity or Oneness, or *tawhīd*. Now, for Muslim theologians, and also mystical metaphysicians, this Unity is not only unique it is also unifying. In other words, it implies both transcendent incomparability, by highlighting the "singularity" of God, and immanent analogy, thereby making it possible to relate, and come closer, to Him. In other words, Oneness means being one, and being the only one, while Unity means not being multiple, and bringing multiplicity into Unity. By and large, this is the difference that can be drawn, among the Names of God in Islam, between *al-Ahad* and *al-Wāhid*. The first cannot be associated with anybody or anything and denotes self-subsistence, absoluteness, and incomparability, whereas the second reduces or embraces everything into His Unity. By using the two verbs *to reduce* and *to embrace*, what is suggested is their being the two contrastive aspects of the same reality. The Name *al-Wāhid* is used nineteen times in the *Qurʾān*. *Al-Wāhid* is typically used in conjunction with *ilāhun*, divinity, or in conjunction with the Name *al-Qahhār*, the One who compels, overcomes, and subjugates. In fact, all of the six uses of *al-Qahhār* in the *Qurʾān* occur in conjunction with *al-Wāhid*. So it is obvious that *al-Wāhid* has a strong relational denotation, and evokes a reduction of multiplicity to Unity. All the "divinities" are reduced to the One Divinity.

However, this exclusive aspect is not the only one. In fact, Unity is also all-embracing as Mercy. The Divine *Rahmah* encompasses everything, as indicated in the verse: "*'adhābī usību bi-hi man ashā'u wa rahmatī wasi'at kulla shayin* [With My punishment I visit whom I will; but My mercy extendeth to all things]" (7:156). Thus, the *Qur'ān* suggests that the rigor of punishment is particular—*man ashā'u,* being a manifestation of God's will in relation to specific phenomena, whereas mercy is universal—*kulla shayin,* being the substance of reality. We propose to show, in what follows, that the *barzakh* both articulates and synthetizes these two dimensions.

The notion of *barzakh* intrinsically entails two domains—or three, with the *barzakh* itself—but to speak of duality in Islam is paradoxical, and can only happen when focusing exclusively on the aspect of transcendent uniqueness: the transcendent and that which is transcended or, on the rigorous side of the unifying dimension, the compelling and that which is compelled. But metaphysical dualism, on the other hand, appears contradictory in Islam since everything other than God is vain and vanishes, and therefore cannot be turned into an eternal substance in the sense in which God is one. In this sense, any duality is ultimately resolved into Unity, but it must also retain some degree of reality to justify the need for an affirmation of Unity. It is at the very juncture of this tension between the metaphysical "logic" of Unity and the religious need for duality, and multiplicity, that the *barzakh* lies in its enigmatic but necessary reality.

## Identity and Difference

To put it quite elementarily, *bhedābheda* characterizes any teaching that holds onto both identity and difference, without reducing the second to the first. Hence, the two questions: Why is there need for *bhedābheda*? and How is *bhedābheda* conceptualized? Answering the first question is arguably simpler than addressing the second.

The notion of *bhedābheda* is needed by those Indian metaphysicians who oppose both the dualism of Mādhva and the radical nondualism of Shankara's *Advaita*. To express it concisely, what differentiates, epistemologically, the thirteenth-century dualist from the seventh-eighth-century *Advaitin* nondualist is their respective concepts of the knowing subject and the known object. For Mādhva, knowledge presupposes the full reality of both the knower and the known.[4] Knowledge is dualistic by definition. To use the terminology coined by the Shankarian contemporary American philosopher Franklin Merrell-Wolff, the position of Mādhva amounts to asserting that all consciousness is a "subject-object-consciousness." By contrast, although he does not deny that most modes of knowledge involve, and certainly presuppose, a distinction between subject and object, Shankara teaches that the supreme knowledge, which is also the essence of all knowledge, is in the mode of "consciousness-without-an-object." In liberated knowledge, or *Moksha*, the scission between subject and object collapses, and we are left with pure consciousness: nothing is objectified and everything is within the subject, *is* the subject. This means that the ordinary field of objectivity, or subject-object-consciousness, is not truly real, but only appearance, or *Māyā*, including the Divine as it relates to creation, or manifestation. Liberation is the perception of appearance for what it is, that is, naught, and the realization that only the Self is. By contrast with both Mādhva and Shankara, *bhedābheda,* in its various forms, flows from a concern for maintaining both identity and difference, unity and duality. In other words, the typically *bhedābheda* view postulates that without identity, or unity, there does not appear to be any way toward true liberation, while without duality, or difference, the very notion of a liberation or union seems meaningless, since from what is there need to be freed?

The ways in which *bhedābheda* is conceptualized in various Indian systems of thought is extremely diverse. We will draw distinctions between three kinds: those which make use of *bhedābheda* in some dimensions of their teachings but which ultimately keep to *bheda,* or difference, as irreducible on some level; those which are truly and ultimately *bhedābhedavādin,* at least in intent if not actually; and those which are only partially so in the sense that their "identity-in-difference" is ultimately reabsorbed, in a way, into nonduality or nondifference. What follows is an attempt at summarizing the role played by *bhedābheda* in each of these kinds of teachings, while acknowledging that this might not go without a measure of schematization, given both the complexity and the diversity of those schools.

In the first category, one must mention the dualistic *darśana* of *Sāmkhya* and, in a very different way, Rāmānuja's *Viśistādvaita,* or qualified nondualism. The second category includes a number of properly-so-called *bhedābhedavādin* metaphysicians such as the ninth-century Bhāskara and the sixteenth-century Vijñānabhiksu. The third category refers broadly to the schools of Śaktism, and particularly Kashmiri Śaivism, an important metaphysical current that arose and spread from the eighth to the twelfth century. What most of these views have in common is that they all postulate that the effect, or the world, is contained potentially within the cause, the Absolute, *Brahman.* This is called *satkāryavāda,* literally the position of preexistence. Thus, the *bhedābheda* view is to be understood in terms of a preexistence of the effect in the cause, and as implying, consequently, a transformation of the cause in and through the effect.

*Sāmkhya* is one of the six orthodox *darśanas,* or points of view, in classical Hinduism. The name of the school, which flourished in the first centuries of the Christian Era, connotes the notion of enumeration, and this is no doubt connected to its doctrine of the twenty-five *tattvas,* or ontological elements. In *Sāmkhya, satkāryavāda* is conceived as the manifestation (*vyakta*) of the unmanifest (*avyakta*) from and through the modifications of the Universal Substance, *Prakriti,* which is both unmanifest and manifest. This manifestation is actualized by the process of three constituents, the *gunas: sattva, rajas,* and *tamas,* that correspond to what Gerald James Larson refers to, objectively and subjectively, as spontaneous activity or desiring (*rajas*), rational ordering and reflective discrimination (*sattva*), and determinate objectivation or awareness of an opaque and enveloping world (*tamas*).[5] It is important to realize that this flow of manifestation, which is none other than the modification of *Prakriti* as substance, is both subjective and objective, meaning a holistic ontological experience without any radical metaphysical scission between subject and object. The twenty-five elements of being—*tattvas*—that unfold cosmogonic manifestation span the entire range of the subject-object field. However, it is noteworthy that among these *tattvas,* which could be characterized as multifarious modifications of *Prakriti,* the highest ones are internal and more subjective while the lowest ones are more external and objective. Thus, the first three *tattvas* are intellect, egoity, and mind, whereas the last five are gross elements like ether, wind, fire, water, and earth. In between, we find senses (such as hearing or smell), action capacities (speaking and procreating) and subtle elements (sound and smell). There is, therefore, a primal substratum that remains essentially identical in and through its process of transformative manifestation and which manifests itself as mind and feelings, as well as matter and physical or animal realities.

Beside *Prakriti, Sāmkhya* introduces a second principle, which is *Purusha,* Spirit or consciousness. It is independent, not involved in, and different from, the modes of awareness that are at work in the highest modifications of *Prakriti.* The mode of influence of *Purusha* upon *Prakriti* has been compared, *mutatis mutandis,* to the action of Aristotle's God upon the world as Prime Mover. This analogy is warranted to the extent that the latter is understood as "detached" from the sublunar world while exercising a "finalizing" function upon it. In that respect, Aristotle's God constitutes the universal entelechy of the universe by serving as a transcendent end that "draws" all beings to their perfection of being.

Not unlike the God of Aristotle, *Purusha* functions as a kind of magnet that affects the inner cosmological balance of *Prakriti* and brings about its modifications, the former influencing the latter in view of the production of its modifications. As a result, *Prakriti* and its transformations, through the "pull" of *Purusha,* are both different and nondifferent. The *bhedābheda* dimension of *Sāmkhya* stems, in a sense, from the unicity of the material cause on the one hand, and its association with a manner of final and formal cause, on the other hand. Hence, the identity inherent to *Prakriti* and the difference "introduced" by the impact of *Purusha*. However, it is clear that there is no ultimate reduction of this difference to unity, given an unyielding focus on the principial polarity of Substance and Consciousness. As Radhakrishnan puts it, "The *Sāmkhya* regards the knower as *purusha* and the known as *prakriti*,"[6] and there lies an irreducible distinction between knower and known. This typically *Sāmkhya* polarity is further expressed, in a most suggestive way, in Īśvarakrishna's *Sāmkhya-kārikā*—fifth century AD: "As a dancer desists from dancing, having exhibited herself to the audience, so does Nature desist, having exhibited herself to the Spirit."[7]

In addition to being the static mover of *Prakriti*, *Purusha* accounts for the purposefulness of the substantial modifications without being involved in them: it is simply implied by it as a spectator is implied by a spectacle. As Larson puts it, *Purusha* "is that for which primordial materiality functions."[8] It is like the "actively passive" overseer, the recipient or beneficiary, but it is also, soteriologically, the guarantee of the possibility of liberation. Without the reality of *Purusha* there would be no way to disengage consciousness from material substance. In sharp contrast with the nondualism of *Advaita* that recognizes *moksha* as the realization of *abheda*, *Sāmkhya*'s liberation presupposes *bheda*, which is another way of stating that it requires that *Purusha* be different from *Prakriti*. It must be added, however, that while *Prakriti* is a single Substance with a myriad of modifications, *Purusha* can only be perceived plurally, because in itself it is without content: its "perceptibility" is contingent upon its "determination" through its "combination" with *Prakriti*. It is important to note, however, that this plurality of *Purusha* is empirical and not essential, the unity of *Purusha* as "final cause" being incontestable and, in fact, postulated as a condition for the very possibility of liberation.[9] Conversely, and as suggested above, the difference inherent in the "combination" of *Purusha* and *Prakriti* is the very foundation, epistemologically speaking, of the need for liberation. According to a *Sāmkhya* text, the *Yuktidīpikā*, an eighth-century commentary of the *Sāmkhya-kārikā*, "This realization of the presence of consciousness emerges as an awareness of the difference between the tripartite process and consciousness."[10]

We must remember, here, that this "tripartite process" corresponds to the transformation of the three cosmological constituents: *sattva, rajas,* and *tamas*. The very use of the English terms *awareness* and *consciousness* must alert us to the fact that the former always implies an immanent difference resulting from the polarity of Substance and Spirit or Consciousness, whereas the second remains in principle, that is, ontologically if not "perceptually," independent from this polarity. In other words, for *Sāmkhya*, awareness is not consciousness, but the epistemological trace or evidence of the reality of the latter. The dualism of *Sāmkhya* implies that there is never any engagement of

*Purusha tale quale* with *Prakriti*. *Purusha* as consciousness is simply a principle of awareness in and through its plural manifestations, or—from another point of view—through its "influence" on *Prakriti*. There is no way here leading to nonduality. As for *bhedābheda,* it simply means that the differences manifested in and through the modifications of the one Substance—thus, principle of "nondifference"—result from the fundamental difference between Substance and Selfhood, *Prakriti* and *Purusha*. Let us note in passing that the traditional association of *Sāmkhya* and *Yoga,* among the six orthodox *darśanas,* highlights the ways in which a sort of methodical focus on the "material substratum" of existence, the psychophysical complex in Yoga, situates the discipline of liberation in a "technically" dualistic context.

Although *Vedānta* all too often tends to be elliptically and expeditiously associated, among *darśanas,* with nondualism, due to the historical influence and intellectual prestige of Shankara, *Viśiṣṭādvaita,* or so-called qualified nondualism, is one of the most interesting to analyze in terms of the significance and function of *bhedābheda.* As will appear clearly enough in what follows, it can be deemed that the very term *qualified nondualism* is, in a sense, a misnomer. Historically, it is recognized that the main exponent of this perspective is the eleventhtwelfth-century *bhakta* Rāmānuja. As with *Sāmkhya,* Rāmānuja's perspective situates duality at the very heart of knowledge, or, as Radakrishnan put it quite cogently, for him "knowledge involves the perception of difference."[11] Whereas the *Advaitin* perspective equates Consciousness with the Divine Subject as "Subject-without-an-object," it is clear that, for Rāmānuja, consciousness is not exclusively subject. In fact there is no consciousness without an object.[12] Such a consciousness is for him altogether unreal, imaginary. Rāmānuja sees a proof of the subject-object imperative of consciousness in the fact that the consciousness of one can be an object for another.

Needless to say, this argument would remain inconclusive for *Advaitin* thinkers since, for them, consciousness as such cannot be an object, and that which appears as "objective" in our relationship with God and other conscious beings is not consciousness itself, but only limited and externalized manifestations of it. For Rāmānuja, in sharp contradistinction, consciousness is fundamentally relational. This is quite evidently connected to the *bhaktic,* or devotional, emphasis characteristic of his spiritual path.[13] It could be said that, overall, Rāmānuja favors connection over identity. Or else, the same principle could be expressed by saying that identity is, for him, diverse and organic. The expression *qualified,* when applied to Rāmānuja's teachings, can only mean that "qualities" amount to "determinations" that are in the very essence of the Divine Reality. This is why Rāmānuja rejects the *Advaitin* notion of *Nirguna Brahman,* or nonqualified Absolute. For Rāmānuja, "the real cannot be a bare identity. It is a determinate whole, which maintains its identity in and through the differences."[14] The very term *viśista* signifies the presence of qualities, or *viśesa*. These qualities are essentially recognized to be of three kinds: *gunas,* or positive attributes; *vigraha,* which denotes expansion in imaginal forms and therefore also divine personality; and *vibhūti,* denoting power, glory, and therefore also nonillusory reality as manifestations of *Brahman.*[15]

These three types of attributes characterize that which in the Absolute Reality makes it an object of meditation and worship by asserting its reality, positivity, and relatability. An extremely important implication of this emphasis on attributes is that the principle of Unity, for Rāmānuja, is therefore not undifferentiated identity as such, as it is in *Advaita,* but a differentiated inseparability involving an intrinsic relational duality. This intrinsic relationality is both ontological and epistemological, in the sense that to be a *jīva,* a self, means ipso facto to worship or know the Lord. Although relationality does not entail a codependency of the kind that is inherent in the Buddhist concept of *pratītya-samutpāda,* one that would level down all the terms involved by unveiling their a-substantial emptiness, there is still a sense in which a sort of interdependency is maintained, even though the relationship between its terms do not amount to a pure "equalization." For Rāmānuja, *Viśistādvaita* "connotes that one of the two entities related is dependent upon the other in the sense that it cannot exist without the other also existing, and that it cannot be rightly known without the other also being known at the same time."[16] Thus, the soul and the world are inseparable from God, they are indeed His bodies, but they are not identical with Him.

The soul is an indispensable "accessory" to God rather than a modification of Him.[17] This inseparability takes the form of three types of relationships. They are called *ādhāra* and *ādheya, niyāmaka* and *niyamya,* and *śesin* and *śesa.* The first relationship is one of metaphysical dependence, the second is one of control, and the third one characterizes the relationship between Lord and servant, while pointing to a normative finality for the soul and the world. The *ādheya* nature of the soul and the world refer to their contingency, in the sense that they need to be "supported" into being. *Ādhāra* and *ādheya* refer to the container and the contained, like the womb and the germ, or the residence and the resident. In addition, *niyāmaka* entails an element of rulership, but also one of direction. The term refers initially to a charioteer or a sailor, and in logic to a "limiting condition." So it implies the power of the Lord over the self, but also the providential goodness of His overseeing its destiny. As for *śesin* and *śesa,* they refer to the "main matter" and that "which is left."[18] The terms also entail the meaning of part and whole. Rāmānuja sees the nature of the *śesa* as unfulfilled in the absence of its perfecting relationship with the *śesin.* In other words, the nature of the soul is to worship the Lord, thereby fulfilling its nature by bringing its ontological nature to completion in and through its "whole."

The three components of the relationship between the Lord and the human worshiper can therefore be summarized as ontological support, directing control, and teleological meaning. These three relational characters make it clear that there is a fundamental reality in the relation, and therefore duality, between the Lord and the soul. But it is also clear that the *pariṇāma* aspect of *Brahman* points in the direction of identity. This allows one to argue for the fundamentally *bhedābheda* nature of Rāmānuja's *Vedānta*, even though he actually criticizes *bhedābheda* in terms of the relationship between the universal and the particular, arguing strongly in favor of a radical and irreducible difference between the two. It must be noted, however, that this criticism seems to be primarily, if not exclusively, confined to the level of empirical perception, in which he sees no way to identify the particular and the universal. For him, the empirical assertion "this is a cow" necessarily implies a recognition of the difference between the particular and the universal by distinguishing imperatively the former from the latter.[19]

If we consider the matter on the level of ontology, and not empirical judgment, we can see that Rāmānuja's views can be definitely characterized as *bhedābhedavādin*. P.T. Raju has cogently argued that even liberation can be considered, for him, as a "process from one form of identity in difference to another."[20] By comparison with *Sāṃkhya*, the type of *bhedābheda* involved in Rāmānuja's perspective takes us one step farther on the way to *abheda*, or a step away from *bheda*, in that the differences inherent to the threefold relationship between God, soul, and world do not result from the reality of a principial polarity, but are simply intrinsically constitutive of the One Reality.[21] This is why it is possible to refer to this form of *Vedānta* as to a kind of nondualism in a relative sense but, it must be admitted, in an inadequate way.

The nonduality refers to the essence of the Divinity rather than to the relationship between the Divine, the soul, and the world. As Hiriyanna puts it, the relationship between "these three elements is a synthetized unity of differences but only that *Brahman* as embodied in or inspiring the souls and matter is one."[22] Or else: "It is the qualified or the embodied that is one, while the factors qualifying or embodying it are quite distinct, though inseparable from it."[23] This qualified nondualism is typically conveyed through the simile of the relationship between soul and body in the human being: the very unity of the human being is predicated upon the duality of two constitutive elements without altering it qua unity of a person. Thus, for Rāmānuja, the Lord has transformed into the world through *līlā*, or divine play, but He remains distinct from it.

The soul and the world *must* be real, without which the devotional relationship that lies at the core of the path of liberation would be unintelligible. In this context, *bhedābheda* means a unity that intrinsically entails differentiation. As it already appears through the analogy with the human psychophysical compound, the reality of this perplexing coincidence between identity and difference is more easily conveyed through images and similes than conceived through notional speculations. In this respect, Rāmānuja takes the *Śvetāśvatara Upanishad* as a reference for illustrating the principle of identity-in-difference. More specifically, the physical analogy that is used is that of the blend of milk and ghee. When the two substances are mixed they form a unity in which no difference is perceptible, and it is only following the churning of the milk and the heating of the resulting butter that ghee appears as distinctly different from the milk. So it is clear, from this example, that *Viśiṣṭādvaita* lays emphasis on the function of time in its understanding of the modifications of the Divine Reality. In the beginning, and also in the end, which is truly none other than the beginning, only the *Brahman* is, and it contains in a nonmanifested way both conscious reality (*cit*) and unconscious reality (*acit*). The differentiation between the two, in the form of individual self and world, only appears subsequent to creation.[24] This importance given to time is evidently related to a perspective in which the prime mode of realization is through the relationship between the soul and the Lord. Taking the devoted soul as the necessary point of departure of the way of liberation, Rāmānuja cannot but take into central account that which is integral to the existence of individuality, that is, the temporal condition.

Even when considering the highest level of spiritual realization, the most transcendent experience is one in which the distinction between God and the soul remains. The core of this experience is self-surrender to God, *prapatti*. In essence, *prapatti* is none other than the spiritual and moral recognition of one's intrinsic, essential, dependence upon the Lord. It is therefore the highest mode of knowledge of the differentiated nature of Ultimate Reality; it is recognizing oneself as one element in the Lord's *līlā*. By contrast with *Advaitin moksha*, which entails a realization of the fact that *Māyā*, or the principle of dualistic ignorance, is mere appearance, the highest *Viśiṣṭādvaita* mode of realization is one of essential relationality. The emphasis lies, therefore, less on a metaphysical recognition and its existential consequences than on an ethico-spiritual liberation that entails an ontology. In *Viśiṣṭādvaitin* spiritual liberation, "the finite remains, but the fetters of finitude and individualism are removed."[25]

While *Advaita moksha* is fundamentally a reintegration of the *jīva* into the only Self or *Ātman*, *Viśiṣṭādvaita* postulates that the *jīva* retains an essential distinction from God while losing the limitative aspects ordinarily entailed by this distinction. In other words, the self remains a self in its own right, but it moves from a mode of experiencing selfhood as ontologically independent from one of recognizing it as inherently dependent. Another dimension of this important difference is the shift from liberation in this life to liberation after death (*Videha-mukti*).[26] This has been suggestively encapsulated in a contrastive definition of the ideal of the *Advaita jīvan-mukta* and the Rāmānujan *Videha-Mukti* as follows: "Release is not freedom in embodiment but freedom from embodiment."[27] As long as the living body remains, there cannot be full release, precisely because embodiment prevents the self from reaching what P. N. Srinivasachari calls a "coalescence of content without the abolition of existence."[28] The same scholar argues that in Rāmānuja's thought, "the self is Brahmanized" without losing its sense of existence, but while losing its sense of separateness.

In the properly so-called *bhedābheda* systems such as those of Bhartrip-rapañca, Bhāskara, and Vijñanabhiksu, we see complex attempts at situating nondifference and difference on an equal footing. The typical *bhedābheda* view is *Brahma-parināma-vāda*. It postulates a transformation of *Brahman* that accounts for both identity and difference between the Cause and the effects. The difficulty, therefore, is that *parināma* must be compatible with both differ-ence and nondifference without jeopardizing either. It must neither take down the Absolute Cause into relativity nor reduce relativity to mere appearance. In other words, it must place transcendence and immanence on an equal footing.

Bhartriprapañca was a pre-Shankarian *bhedābhedavādin* who taught that *Brahman* is the material and efficient cause of everything, the cause of the universe of the living souls as well as formal and nonformal material realities. Those cover eight modes, from *antaryāmin,* the inner self, to *pinda,* the body. Bhartriprapañca teaches the reality of both *Brahman,* or the cause, which he symbolically compares, in a typically *bhedābhedavādin* way, to clay or the ocean, and the reality of the effects, to which he refers symbolically as various pots or waves. Similarly, Bhāskara makes use of the analogy of sparks and fire to illustrate the reality of *parināma*. What Bhāskara proposes, in a sense, is a *Sāmkhya* point of view in which *Brahman* would take the place of *Prakriti* as the material cause, and in which the duality between Substance and Spirit would be canceled, since *Brahman* "is" both. For Bhāskara, *Brahman,* the Principle, is both cause and effect, this is *satkāryavāda*. As effect, *Brahman* is both the objective universe, which is *acit* and the subjective *jīva,* which is *cit,* or consciousness. *Bhedābheda* is involved in both the relationship between *Brahman* and the world, and that between *Brahman* and the *jīva*. However, difference and nondifference characterize the first, whereas in the case of the soul nondifference is essential and difference only adventitious. We see, through this example, a recognition of the relativity of difference, as it were, and a move toward essential *abheda*. However, the knowledge of identity is only accessible after death, before which a sense of difference and separation always subsists.

It is clear that, for both Bhartriprapañca and Bhāskara, ocean and waves, or fire and sparks, are situated on the same level of reality, even though one is cause and the other effect. This care for preserving the reality of both *Brahman* and non-*Brahman* stems from a rejection of the *Advaitin* reduction of the latter to the former. In this sense, the *bhedābhedavādin* concern echoes Rāmānuja's. It manifests itself, for example, in Bhāskara's criticism of the *Advaitin* notions of *Nirguṇa Brahman* and *Māyā*. The notion of unqualified Brahman is rejected on the grounds that it would introduce a sort of pluralization or multiplication of *Brahman*. As for the rejection of the *Advaitin Māyā*, it is suggestively illustrated by the image of the effect, or difference, or relativity as sparks rather than grass. The fire of *Brahman* is modified into multiplicity, in the form of the sparks, rather than burning it as grass into ashes. This is because the *Advaitin* concept of *Māyā* is seen as affecting *Brahman* retroactively, as it were, through its defective dimension of obscuration. In other words, the ignorance and delusion inherent to *Māyā* must be inferred to be present in the first Cause, *quod absit*. This means, for *bhedābhedavādins*, that *Māyā*, or rather the transformation of *Brahman* that *Advaitins* conceive as *Māyā*, must be real, and not mere appearance, although it is perforce limited by conditions. As Radhakrishnan has shown, the *bhedābhedavādin upādhis* are principles of limitation, but not ignorance.[29]

Typically, the difficulties that such *bhedābhedavādin* views raise are of three kinds. First, the postulation of an equal reality of cause and effect presents a logical challenge since it is quite clear that while the cause, namely, *Brahman*, remains independent from its effects, the reverse cannot be true. This means the need to recognize an ontological subordination of the latter to the former, whereby the cause is a necessary condition of the effect, but not conversely so, challenging thereby the very position according to which the two would be equally real in the same sense. Secondly, whereas the effect can be considered a part of the cause, the reverse is not true, because the whole obviously cannot be part of the part; hence, a second challenge that fosters the view of a reduction of the effect to the cause. Finally, the typical *pariṇāma* point of view presupposes change and transformation on the part of *Brahman,* which runs contrary to the Upanishadic teachings concerning *Brahman*'s transcendence and immutability.

A late *bhedābhedavādin* such as Vijñanabhiksu recognized these last difficulties and worked to provide theoretical responses to them, as has been recently detailed by Andrew J. Nicholson. In essence, Vijñanabhiksu proposes that scriptural statements implying nondifference (*abheda*) be understood to mean "nonseparation," that is, according to Nicholson, "a state in which two entities are perceptually indistinguishable from one another, while nonetheless not having the relationship of identity."[30] For Vijñanabhiksu, therefore, the first way in which *bhedābheda* can be, and must be, satisfactorily understood is through the distinction between nondifference as identity (*tādātmya*) and nondifference as nonseparation (*avibhāga*). The *Brahman* and the soul are not separate, but not identical, and this "inseparability" is, moreover, subject to time. It is metaphorically comparable to the mix of milk and sugar or that of water and salt. In a way, the matter is moved from ontology to epistemology, from being to perception. But if the nondifference qua nonseparation can only be defined perceptually, then it appears that an ultimate ontological dualism does remain even though it may be couched in terms of a kind of nondifference.

Another dimension of Vijñanabhiksu's *bhedābheda* is the distinction between part (*amśa*) and whole (*amśin*) to refer to the relationship between Brahman and the soul. The main problem, in this respect, is to avoid a division of the whole, meaning a division of the *Brahman* among the *jīvas,* given the simplicity and non-dividableness of the Supreme. Vijñanabhiksu responds to the difficulty by asserting that souls are parts of *Brahman,* but not the reverse. Difference works only one way. This is illustrated by the statement of the *Viṣṇu Purāṇa*: "There is nothing different from it, yet it is different from everything" (1.16.78). Here again, we can perceive an intimation of the distinction between nondifference and difference in terms of the former being intrinsically "absolute" and not susceptible of degrees.

Thirdly, the tension between the principle of immutability of *Brahman* and the view of its modifications is addressed through a distinction between unchanging cause (*avikārikakārana*) and changing seed-cause (*vikārikārana*), the second only being modified by the effects, whereas the first remains unaffected by these modifications. The unchanging cause is referred to by Vijñanabhiksu as either matricial, supporting cause (*mūlakārana*) or as material seed-cause (*adhisthānakārana*). Metaphorically speaking, this is, for example, the distinction between a particular soil—the matricial cause—and a given seed—the material cause, the second only being modified by the bursting forth of the sprout, even though the first, albeit not modified by the sprouting, is the necessary milieu for the modification.

What this means, metaphysically, is that the supporting cause remains in a way transcendent to the immanent process of transformation in which the seed-cause is involved. But what is, then, the relationship between the two causes, and are we not brought back to a dualism not without analogies with *Sāmkhya,* and whereby difference is more primordial—in the way of the distinction of two causes, than nondifference? As an answer to this possible objection, it is asserted by Vijñanabhiksu that the supporting cause is not separate from the changing cause and its effects, but does not inhere in them. It is, however, necessary for the changing cause to be modified, as the effect results from the presence of the supporting cause, and not from any modification nor even action on its part.[31] This is a way to distinguish a transcendent from an immanent dimension in the cause by relating this distinction not to a matter of degree but to one of imperceptibility. Nicholson acknowledges both the potential confusion and the flexibility implied by the distinction between supporting cause and material cause. However, the flexibility introduced by the notion of a nonseparability of the two causes is not without raising radical metaphysical issues as to the nature of what is meant by nondifference. Although the inherence of the material cause in the effect undoubtedly refers to a dimension of *abheda,* it seems as clear that the distinction between supporting cause and material cause, albeit "imperceptible," cannot but subordinate *abheda* to a foundational *bheda.* The fact remains, however, that nondifference or identity cannot be essentially absolute without, by definition, losing its ultimate meaning, whereas difference, by contrast, may indeed have a relative meaning. This means, among other things, that while there can be, and in fact must be, degrees of difference, there cannot be degrees of nondifference; and it is most likely on this point that *bhedābheda,* in its typical formulations, may be deemed to come against a stumbling block.

As a conclusion on these considerations, it must be noted that Potter has an interesting point[32] when he notices that among the Indian teachings that make central use of *bhedābheda,* such as *Sāmkhya,* Rāmānuja's *Viśiṣṭādvaita,* and *Bhedābhedavādins* of the kind of Bhartriprapañca, there is a "progression . . . when . . . we consider the number of times identity-in-difference is used," that is, respectively, once, twice, and several times. This may tend to indicate that with each system we come closer to nonduality or nondifference without ever reaching it, precisely because the dualistic imperatives of those systems do prevent it, to various degrees. This gradual and asymptotic motion toward a nonduality that can never be reached might be summarized as follows. In *Sāmkhya,* the two is ultimate, even though the Substance or *Prakriti* goes through difference in nondifference through *Purusha's* informing "contemplation" of her modifications. In Rāmānujan *Viśiṣṭādvaita,* the two could be said to be inherent to the one, in the sense that it is the nature of Brahman to be Lord and to manifest His nature through a play in which He is both the worshiper and the worshiped. The "qualification" of nondualism cannot but result in its ultimate metaphysical "eviction." As we have seen, even though *Bhedābhedavādins* may be deemed to come the closest to recognizing the primordiality of nondifference, they cannot but reintroduce difference in the principle in a way that jeopardizes the full import of this intended recognition. In all cases, duality and difference remain the ransom of a theoretical refusal to let go of a sort of ontological "absolutization" of the reality of the world and the soul.

It may be deemed that the resolution of this *bhedābhedavādin* conundrum finds a most satisfactory treatment in Kashmiri Śaivism. In an article published in the 1930s, Mahendranath Sircar summarized quite aptly, although in a language that may considered somewhat obsolete by many today, the manner in which Śaivism relates to the metaphysical systems of *Advaita* and *Viśistādvaita*: "In Vaishnavaism the appearances are co-real with the Absolute, in Saivaism they are not co-real with the Absolute, though they are not quite ideal or illusory as Sankaraism supposes. Saivaism takes a middle path."[33] Thus, in a way that is parallel to Shankarian *Advaita,* but contrary to standard forms of *bhedābheda,* Kashmiri Śaivism affirms both *Atattva* Śiva—Śiva beyond ontological determinations—and its own form of *Māyā,* while making use of the notion of *bhedābheda* within the context of an ultimately nondualistic and *abheda* ontology. Kashmiri Śaivism, or Śaktism, makes room for *bhedābheda,* but only by clearly subordinating it, as it were, to *abheda.* In a sense, Śaivism reproduces the *bhedābhedavādin* view of the modifications of the Principle through degrees of reality, but it does so within a fundamental nondualistic context. Like Bhāskara it rejects the unreality of *Māyā* and affirms its aspect of manifestation of the Cause, Śiva. Its major divergence from ordinary *bhedābheda* lies in that it poses, like *Advaita,* the Ultimate as Nonqualified beyond all ontological elements. The distinction between *Atattva* Śiva and *Tattva* Śiva reproduces, in this context, the *Advaitin* distinction between *Nirguna Brahman* and *Saguna Brahman,* which is precisely rejected by both *Viśistādvaitins* and most *Bhedābhedavādins.*

There are, however, two ways in which this distinction differs from *Advaita.* First, the distinction in question tends to be couched, in Śaivism, in terms of a complementarity between the static and the dynamic, or the principial and the operative. This complementarity is expressed through the union of the God and the Goddess, as it is put, for example, in Abhinavagupta's *Śrī Tantrāloka*: "The Lord remains always united with His Supreme Force known as *Kauliki* as it is She who has expanded His family who otherwise is shorn of all familial relationships."[34] Secondly, and distinctly from *Advaita,* the differentiation between *Attatva* and *Tattva* Śiva does not lead Śaivism to consider *bhedābheda* and *bheda* as mere appearance, but rather as intrinsic and necessary dimensions of *abheda.* The boundlessness of Śiva, which is the essence of nondifference, entails binding, or the very reality of difference. There is the Reality, which is pure *atattva* and pure *abheda,* and degrees of binding of this Reality through *tattvas.* These are the thirty-six degrees of existentiation, from *tattva* Śiva to the earth, *prithivi,* which can be arranged in subsequent groups corresponding to the three general degrees of Śiva, Śakti, and *nara.* Moreover, this hierarchical tripartition runs parallel to the two other corresponding ternaries of *abheda, bhedābheda,* and *bheda,* on the one hand, and I, Thou, and He/She/It, on the other. This difference from *Advaita* appears clearly with respect to the obscuring aspect of *Māyā,* which characterizes the sixth Śaivite *tattva* that initiates the range of *bhedābheda,* precisely, but it does so in the context of the binding of the unboundedness of Śiva, the Real, therefore not in terms of pure appearance, like *Advaita.*

Thus, by contrast with *Viśistādvaita* and mainstream *Bhedābhedavādins,* Kashmiri Śaivism presents us with a very distinct use and account of *Bhedābhedavāda.* In a sense, it integrates the onto-cosmology of *Sāmkhya*— which is characterized by its hierarchical "enumeration" of *tattvas*—with the nondualism of *Advaita.* It is nondualistic, but it does not base its nondualism in the reduction of other-than-*Brahman* to mere appearance.

A more specific analysis of the non-dualistic Śaivite worldview can result from a consideration of two different points of view, one being synchronic and synthetic, while the second is more diachronic and analytic. Synthetically, Śaivism considers one single Principle, the Supreme Śiva, or the Absolute, which, through a kind of self-awareness (*vimarśa*) de-doubled itself as Śiva and Śakti, Śakti being the power of manifestation of Śiva flowing from the infinite freedom of the latter. In some of the presentations of Abhinavagupta, the most illustrious proponent of Kashmiri Śaivism, the Supreme reality is apprehended as a "group" (*kula*) that consists in Śiva, Śakti, and *nara,* the latter being the empirical reality that proceeds from the devolution of Śakti as the universal creative energy of Śiva. *Nara* encompasses everything from the principle of delusion and difference, *māyā,* to the earth (*prithivī*), which is the very limit of the onto-cosmological process of manifestation of Śiva. It is important to keep in mind that this does not amount to pantheism, as illustrated by the reoccurring Śaivite symbol of the mirror. Even though the reflections on the mirror are undoubtedly one with the mirror from a certain point of view, it remains nevertheless true that the latter is indeed independent of, and therefore "transcendent" to the former.[35] The *Pratyabhijñāhṛidayam* describes the unfolding of the universe as being like that of "a city in a mirror, which though non-different from it appears as different."[36] The highest principle of this unity in distinction is to be found in the reality of Śiva Himself understood as *Parāśiva,* and therefore *atattva,* or the Supreme transcendent Śiva as distinct from Śiva as the Principle of Śakti and *nara.*

This principial and synthetic distinction is reflected, moreover, in the Śaivite threefold consideration of Śakti as *Parāśakti, Parāparāśakti,* and *Aparāśakti.* As Supreme, or *Parāśakti,* Śakti is associated, paradoxically, with the metaphysical degree of Śiva (as distinct from Śakti's and *nara*) inasmuch as She is indissociable and indistinguishable from Him. Considering the second of the three aforementioned degrees, that of Śakti herself, it must be placed in correspondence with *Parāparāśakti,* Supreme-Non-Supreme-Śakti; that is, the very unfolding and active power that characterizes Śakti functionally or per se. Finally, *nara* refers clearly to *Aparāśakti,* or the non-Supreme Śakti, in the sense of the productive plurality of the various "goddesses" who control the empirical field of objective reality.

When considering matters from the point of view of the unfolding of the modes of consciousness and experience encapsulated by the three personal pronouns, *Parāśakti* corresponds to Śiva and to the first personal pronoun. This is the primordial and principial "I" of Consciousness that is pure and undifferentiated Reality. By contrast, *Parāparāśakti* corresponds to Śakti and to the second person, inasmuch as it involves a sense of alterity within identity. *Aparāśakti* corresponds to the third person, and to *nara* as the objectified realm. Finally, and consequently, *bhedābheda* is associated with Śakti, distinctly from Śiva (*abheda*) and *nara* (*bheda*). This ontological range is one of ambivalence between the pull toward pure subjectivity, that of the nondual Selfhood of Śiva, and the attraction of dual manifestation, in which the objectifying powers of the Śaktic force are brought to their ultimate outcome.

These correlations are, moreover, particularly fruitful in view of understanding the significant correspondence between *bhedābheda*, Śakti, and the second personal pronoun. While the "I" is evidently identifiable with nondifference or nonduality as the pure and absolute consciousness of I-Śiva, and whereas *nara* corresponds to the third ontological degree, that which is characterized by objectification, entailing, therefore, a gap between subject and object—the objectification of consciousness as he, she, or it—Śakti conjoins both nondifference and difference. She is essentially one with Śiva while initiating, and presiding over, the emergence of other-than-He. She may be conceptualized as the object within the subject, or the seed of objectification within the subject, or as the subject within the object, meaning that which in the object participates in the subject through the creative vibration of the latter. The "thou" or "you" refers to this domain of difference-nondifference in a way that is spiritually most meaningful. Indeed the "thou" presupposes both nondifference and difference since it involves in a way both the first and third persons. It "contains" the difference pertaining to the he/she inasmuch as it is relational and therefore inclusive of two entities, but it also involves nondifference through the recognition of the I in the he/she, without which no use of the second person would be either possible or meaningful. The essence of *bhedābheda* may be deemed to reside, therefore, in the relationship between subjective consciousness and objectified consciousness, the latter remaining "subjective" within its very objectification. Furthermore, it is significant to note that this centrality of the second personal pronoun is also intrinsically associated, in Śaivism, with the feminine dimension that serves as a point of awareness and articulation between the Absolute and the relative. The feminine appears to lie at the ambivalent conjunction of the subject and the object, being thereby a principle of centrifugal exteriorization and centripetal reintegration.

From a more analytic and diachronic point of view, the pair Śiva/Śakti, which engages, as we have seen, a sort of mirroring relationship, is itself, through some vibration or agitation inherent to its very reality, the principle of an unfolding of lower and lower powers and modes of exteriorization down the chain of thirty-six ontological principles or *tattvas*. Ranging across the aforementioned threefold partition, the Śaivite "chain of being" is divided into five *tattvas* within the scope of nondifference, seven in which identity-in-difference predominates, and twenty-four marked by overpowering difference. According to the *Pratyabhijñāhṛidayam*, the five first principles are characterized as *abheda*, without distinction, because there is therein no actual veiling of the One Self. These are Śiva, Śakti, Sadāśiva, Īśvara, and Śuddhavidyā. The latter three encompass the Śaktic power of "supramundane manifestation"[37] that is the seed of manifestation within the Śiva-Śakti principle, which corresponds, as we have seen, to Śiva in Himself.

While Śiva is pure consciousness and Śakti blissful energy, the three following *tattvas* are characterized by a respective preponderance of Will (*icchā*), Knowledge (*jñana*), and Action (*kriyā*). In Sadāśiva, the predominant mode of consciousness is "*Aham idam*" ("I am this"), although "I" and "this"—the universe—are "explicit," they are still in perfect unity. "I-consciousness" continues to predominate and manifest itself to itself as "world," and the association with Will must not be interpreted as an extrinsic production but as an intrinsic freedom from which arises Self-consciousness as universe, "I am this." The next *tattva*, Īśvara, is characterized by a reversal of the previous mode of identity between the "I" and the universe: "*Idam aham*" ("This is I"). This indicates a stronger emergence of the "independent" consciousness of the universe which, although still nondifferent from the "I," or nonexteriorized and nonmanifested, becomes a focus of "knowledge" (*jñana*) on the part of the Self. The fifth *tattva*, *Śuddhavidyâ* or *Sadvidyā*, sees the very first appearance of *bhedābheda* within *abheda* as it were, or something like a distinction (knowledge) without difference (consciousness); it corresponds to "action," *kriyā*, in the mode of "*Aham idam ca*" ("I am I and also this"). The "also" clearly marks a seminal distinction that the seven following *tattvas* unfold as a manner of veiling of the "I."

These seven intermediary *tattvas*, corresponding to *bhedābheda*, range from *Mahamāya* to *Purusha* through the five so-called coverings or limitations of *Māyā* (*kañcukas*). The *tattva* in which the emergence of *bhedha* is first marked, although still in conjunction with *abheda*, is the sixth *tattva*, that is, *Māyā*, the principle of obscuration, which brings out difference and veils the Self, down to the thirty-sixth *tattva*. The limitations inherent to the five following *tattvas* (*Kalā*, *Vidyā*, *Rāga*, *Kāla*, and *Niyati*) consist in as many coverings over the nature of pure Consciousness, with respect to power, knowledge, totality, eternity, and freedom. *Purusha* represents the very limitation of consciousness resulting from those *kañcukas*. The twenty-four following *tattvas*, beginning with *Prakriti* as matricial cause of the objective universe highlight the predominance of *bheda* through individual intelligence, perceptions, and physical elements.

Thus, Kashmiri Śaivism articulates nondualism in the form of a gradation of being that encompasses *abheda*, *bhedābheda*, and *bheda*. In other words, it accounts for the reality of *abheda, bhedābheda,* and *bheda* in the context of a nondualistic view of the Divine and the universe. Śakti and the *tattvas* are *and* are not modifications of Śiva because Śiva is both unbound and bound, his binding Himself being a dimension of His boundlessness. This means that, synthetically or synchronically, Reality is both dual and nondual. In this perspective, the principle of *bhedābheda* is once again explained by Abhinavagupta through a meditation on the symbol of the mirror. In the mirror, that is, in the supreme, universal, Consciousness, the variegated forms are quite distinct from each other while being undifferentiated from the mirror itself.[38] As Jaideva Singh puts it, "The external world is like a reflection in the mirror of consciousness which, though not different from the mirror, appears as different from it."[39] The mirror can, therefore, be said to be both immanent and transcendent to the objects that are reflected in it. The concept of *bhedābheda* is used precisely to affirm the reality of both formless unity and formal diversity.

Pure *abheda* or nondifference would amount to a metaphysical negation of diversity, whereas *bheda* would imply a fundamental, somewhat irreducible, difference. To say, with Śaivism, that nonduality includes, as it were, duality, amounts to saying that nonduality and duality cannot be placed on an equal footing without involving a relativization of nonduality, a relativization with which nonduality is, in fact, incompatible. By contrast, duality can be as it were relativized, in the way of allowing for degrees, and it is precisely what Śaivism does through its teachings on the *tattvas.* The *Advaitin* way of avoiding dualism in the recognition of unity and diversity lies in distinguishing between *Ātman* and *Māyā,* the first being identified with Reality as such and the second with mere appearance. The Śaivite way, by contrast, affirms the infinite freedom of absolute Consciousness as its very boundless ability to manifest in countless forms, which are none other than Its own Reality.

As indicated previously, occurrences of the *barzakh* in the *Qur'ān* refer both to eschatological conditions and onto-cosmological degrees of reality. The following considerations will not be centered on the first aspect, which is not the most immediately relevant in our current context. One thing that needs be mentioned, however, is that the eschatological context is clearly associated with the dividing aspect of the *barzakh.* In fact, this aspect is so much emphasized that it is endowed with a quasi-absolute character. So it is quite evidently in the verse that pertains to the desire of the damned souls to go back to their earthly life to work their salvation by performing good deeds: "In order that I may work righteousness in the things I neglected." "By no means! It is but a word he says. . . . Before them is *barzakh* (a partition) till the Day they are raised up" (23:100). The desire of the damned is vain, since the cosmic door of terrestrial existence has been shut forever. The *barzakh* expresses the irreversibility of time, and also the demarcation between posthumous states of being, which is a measure of the dignity and gravity of human existence. In Islamic eschatology, the *barzakh* also refers to the median domain between physical death and the day of resurrection. It is commonly understood as referring to an intermediary state that cannot be changed and that leads to a definitive crystallization on the day of resurrection. It is therefore understood diachronically. It is plausible that the *barzakh* refers exclusively to a separation when considered from an eschatological point of view, since the latter considers matters from the point of view of the discrete individuals and their degree of proximity to the One, while also contemplating matters diachronically. However, this eschatological quasi-absolutization of the *barzakh* is far from being the only aspect of the question, and it would actually fail, taken in isolation, to account for the implications of the frequent translation of *barzakh* as isthmus. It could even be ventured to say that this dimension of the concept is by far the most exoteric, precisely inasmuch as it is focused on individual conditions of being and extrinsic separation.

Other Qur'ānic uses of the term *barzakh* are much richer in meaning as far as our current metaphysical focus is concerned. We have already mentioned 25:53: "And it is He who has released [simultaneously] the two seas, one fresh and sweet and one salty and bitter, and He placed between them a barrier and prohibiting partition." We note that in this passage the *barzakh* is accompanied by the term *hijran mahjūran,* which highlights and strengthens, once again, the aspect of separation. However, the very fact of this lexical reinforcement could also point to the fact that *barzakh* in itself may not be so exclusively separative on its own, hence the need to intensify it with an unambiguous expression of partition. This is in a sense confirmed by the third occurrence of the term, which is the one that will interest us most: "He has let free the two bodies of flowing water, meeting together: Between them is *barzakh* (a barrier) which they do not transgress" (55:19–20). We see here that two aspects of the *barzakh* are highlighted. There is a meeting point, which is a dividing point. These two aspects are expressed respectively by the verbal expressions *yaltaqiyāni* (meeting) and *lā yabghiyāni* (they do not transgress). It is in this paradox of a "meeting division" or "dividing meeting point" that the most fruitful metaphysical implications of the concept lie.

As a meeting isthmus and a separating zone, the *barzakh* can be understood as articulating what are arguably the two main foundations of Islam, *at-tawhīd,* or the doctrine of Divine Unity, and *al-furqān,* or discrimination, that is, a separation between Reality and vanity, truth and error. These two principles are immediately connected in the obvious sense that recognition of Divine Unity is truth, and nonrecognition or rejection of it is the source of all errors. But they are also, on some level, in a state of perplexing relationship, since discrimination or distinction between Truth and error vanishes in the realization that only Truth *is* in an unconditional way. The *Qur'ān* implies this metaphysical enigma when stating that "truth has come and vanity has perished," or when asserting that "everything perishes except the Face of God." Anything that could be "associated," "added," but also opposed to God is actually naught. On a first level, the *barzakh,* inasmuch as it expresses a radical distinction between domains, is functionally linked to *tawḥīd* as an instrument of prevention of association or *shirk.* It is also, and subsequently, a symbolic marker of the existential and posthumous consequences of the human choice between the two alternatives. But, on the other hand, the *barzakh* crystallizes as well the necessary partition between realities, and therefore the reality of diversity and multiplicity. This differentiating function is, at the highest level, a relative reflection of the Islamic absoluteness and incomparability of the Real.

Every creature is incomparable in its own way by being distinguished, therefore separated, from others. This positive diversity is both vertical and horizontal. By this is meant that it refers to degrees of being on the one hand, and to formal diversity on each degree of being, on the other hand. With respect to the vertical aspect, Titus Burckhardt has suggested that "the two seas can represent two more or less exalted, but always consecutive, degrees in the hierarchy of Being (*wujūd*)."[40] So the *barzakh* may refer, in fact, to the separation, and connection, between a number of hierarchical pairs, such as the Divine Essence or Quiddity and the Qualities, or *Sifāt,* or the world of Mystery (*al-ghayb*) and the world of manifestation (*ash-shahādah*), or the world of souls and that of bodies, and so forth. Horizontally, the *barzakh* as separation, but also as zone of relation, may refer, as intimated above, to anything whatsoever, inasmuch as this "something" is distinct from everything else, but also potentially or actually a connecting element between other realities. These are the universal dimensions of the *barzakh* as the principle of distinction, those without which there would be no universe and therefore, in a certain sense, no "God" either.

In Sufism, however, the *barzakh* tends to be more specifically, if not exclusively, identified with *'alam al-mithāl* or *'alam al-khayāl,* the world of similitudes and imagination; this domain of universal existence that Henry Corbin proposed to call the "imaginal world," in order to distinguish it from the realm of fanciful, idiosyncratic phantasma. This world mediates between the world of physical realities, within forms, and the world of spiritual realities, beyond forms. The world of imagination, which is that of symbols, myths, theophanies, dreams, visions, and the like, does not abolish the separation between the spiritual and physical worlds, but it allows the two to communicate; or to put it more specifically, it allows for the spiritual to become "accessible" or representable from the vantage point of the physical realm. It bridges the gap of incommensurability between the two.

One of the most profoundly significant concomitances of the intermediary status of the *barzakh* qua imaginal world lies in its ambiguous ontological status. According to Ibn al-'Arabī, who provided perhaps the richest and farthest-reaching meditations on the *barzakh,* the latter is neither real nor unreal, and neither denied nor affirmed, "*lā manfy wa lā muthbat.*" The two terms are highly meaningful insofar as they also refer, technically, to the two halves of the first Islamic *shahādah,* the *nafy* or negation, corresponding to the words *lā ilāha,* and the affirmation, or *ithbāt,* referring to the words *ill'Allāh.* Therefore, the *barzakh* is neither denied as *ilāha* is, nor affirmed in the way *Allāh* is. It is not a false "divinity" or *ilāhun,* which means that it cannot be taken as an object of misguided worship, but neither is it the true Divinity, which signifies that it cannot be treated as an object of authentic worship; in other words, *barzakh* cannot refer to God as such, or at least not to God inasmuch as He is in relation with the world.

This does not mean, however, that the two *shahādatain* do not include a *barzakh.* In fact, according to a number of Sufi teachings, the two testimonies of faith contain *barāzikh.* The *barzakh* of the first *shahādah* is the word *illā,* which is a compound of the affirmative *in* and the negative *lā,* and can be translated therefore literally as "if not." The *barzakh* of the second *shahādah* is the word *rasūl,* which means messenger and mediates syntagmatically between the personal name of the Prophet (Muhammad) and the name of God (*Allāh*).

With respect to the first *shahādah,* it is quite apparent that its immediate signification is negative and exclusive, since it obviously sets God out as the only object of worship and, beyond, as the only Reality. This latter interpretation is representative of the Sufi equation of "worshipable status" with "being." Only That which *is* in the fullest sense is worthy of worship. In that sense, only God *is,* and everything else is not. But, from another point of view, which corresponds to a more esoteric interpretation, the first *shahādah* is indeed inclusive when the *illā* that constitutes its *barzakh* is understood literally as "if not." "If not" can be further elaborated as "if God is not posited" or without God. This means that "*ilāhun*" *is,* or is not without reality, when God is affirmed. This is the secret of unitarian "idolatry" as understood by Ibn al-'Arabī, Shabistarī,[41] and others: any reality *is* to the extent that it is founded in and by God. God gives reality and being to everything. It is in that metaphysical sense, and not in a theological one, that any worshiper is a worshiper of God, the One. This means that, as *barzakh, illā* separates the world from God from below, that is, from the perspective of *ilāhun,* while uniting God to everything, from the point of view of *Allāh.* Moreover, the *in-lā* is literally an affirmation followed by a negation, which serves as a mirror for the greater negation and affirmation of the first *shahādah* taken as a whole. This can be summarized as follows: NEGATION (No god) affirmation (if) negation (not) AFFIRMATION (God). Now, the inclusion of the mirroring element within the statement, with the reflection and the inversion that it implies, constitutes a *barzakh* par excellence, since it involves both a separation and a connection between the negation and the affirmation.

The way the *barzakh* functions in the second *shahādah* is quite different. The name *Rasūl,* which serves as a *barzakh* between Muhammad and *Allāh,* is intrinsically connected to the reality of the *risālah,* the latter being none other, in Islam, than the *Qur'ān* itself. The *rasūl* has no meaning without the *risālah.* Now the theological consensus is that the *Qur'ān* is uncreated in its substantial reality. On the other hand, Islam insists on the mere humanity of the Prophet while giving him the privilege of impeccability for not having been touched by the devil at birth. Some *ahādith* indicate, furthermore, that the reality of his function precedes that of creation.[42] While, with respect to the *Qur'ān,* it is theologically the uncreatedness that has precedence over the createdness, in regard to the Prophet it is, by contrast, the createdness that has theological preeminence over the uncreatedness, *haqīqah muhammadiyah,* the metaphysical implications of which are not fully acknowledged. Now, the *rasūl* lies between the created Muhammad and the uncreated *Allāh.* It is both created and uncreated, as implied by a *hadith* such as "I was a Prophet when Adam was between water and clay."[43] While Muhammad is human, *rasūl* lies at the intersection of the two seas by being an isthmus between the uncreated and the created. We will return to this important dimension of the Prophetic *barzakh* and develop its implications further in our coming discussion of the Amīr 'Abd al-Qādir's metaphysics of the Prophet.

The inherent irreducibility of the *barzakh* to either and both of the two terms it relates, which is the very essence of its ability to function as such, translates into an exclusion of opposites rather than into their conjunction. In order to be what it is, namely, an isthmus between A and B, the *barzakh* needs to be neither A nor non-A, neither B nor non-B. According to Ibn al-'Arabī, "The imagination is not existent and not non-existent, it is not known and it is not ignored, it is not negated and not affirmed, like when man considers his image in a mirror he knows for sure that he is considering his image from one point of view and that he is not considering his image from another point of view."[44] When a man considers his image in the mirror, he does so from his own point of view, that is, from the perspective of the origin of the reflection in the mirror, whereas when he does not consider his image it is because he envisages matters from the point of view of the mirror, or as a mere reflection on the mirror. Thus, the point of view is a determining factor when considering the ontological status of the *barzakh.* It appears as a mere partition only from the vantage point of the lower degree of reality, here the mirror as such, whereas seen "from above," or from the perspective of the contemplator *recognizing* his image in the mirror, it appears as that which joins the "two seas."

The lowest point of view is that of duality and diversity, whereas the highest one proceeds from unity. Needless to say, integral unity can only be perceived from the point of view of the One itself, which means that from this perspective the *barzakh* as separation vanishes. In one respect, the *barzakh* is clearly akin to a delimiting barrier, but this delimitation is "imagined" in the sense of being neither utterly real nor utterly unreal. This means that all things other than the Real are neither real nor unreal.[45] They are a *barzakh*. *Barzakh* means relativity. Relativity means mediation between the absoluteness of the Real and the nothingness of unreality. The *barzakh* mediates between that which is "everything"—the Real—and that which is "nothing"—nothingness. Its commensurability with the incommensurable Real qua "everything" is that it is "something." Its commensurability with the unreal qua nothing is that it is nothing independently from the Real. In Chittick's words, everything in creation is "imagination," or *barzakh*, "God and not-God, real and unreal, existent and non-existent, itself and not itself, He/not-He, it/not-it."[46] There is no absolute distinction between things. The "*barzakh* dimension" of creatures means that things have no absolute boundaries, nor utterly separate reality, and that only the Real is. The *barzakh* is the very mark of *tawhīd* within creation.

This function of the mark is epitomized by a particular kind of *barzakh*, which is, in fact, one of a kind and is the prototype of all *barāzikh*. This is the *barzakh* par excellence, the encompassing *barzakh*, *al-barzakh al-jāmiʿ*. Jurjanī calls it the degree of the Presence of Unicity (*hadra wāhidiyya*) and primordial Self-determination (*taʿayyun awwal*), which is the origin of all *barāzikh*.[47] It is the Muhammadan *barzakh*, or the metaphysical reality of the Prophet, which is expressed among others by the *hadīth*, "I was a Prophet when Adam was between water and clay." Now, according to Islamic teachings, there cannot be a full union or mixture between the terrestrial and the celestial, nor between the human and the Divine, nor even between the Prophet and God. In his mystical nocturnal voyage, the Prophet could only come in the proximity of God, to the the lote tree of the limit. He "saw what he saw," without for that entering into a union with God. The nontransgressible lies, arguably, at the center of Muslim consciousness, and the *barzakh* epitomizes this barrier. On the other hand, if *tawhīd* is to be consistently held, it has to be able to account for the multiplication of Unity and the unification of multiplicity. This means that creation presupposes the *barzakh* as does, conversely, the return to God. These two functions of the *barzakh* lie at the meeting point of two incommensurable domains; hence, the paradoxical function of the *barzakh* and the perplexing status of its being.

Another important manifestation of this principle of "discontinuous continuity" appears in the mediating function of the *barzakh* between the manifest and the nonmanifest. This is, in a sense, a mere symbolic transposition of the duality of the above and the below. The *Amīr* 'Abd al-Qādir comments on this principle through a meditation on the relationship between prayer, the alternation of day and night, and the symbolism of the two eyes. Remarking that Muslim night prayers are partly recited aloud while daylight prayers are silent, the *Amīr* reads in this difference a complementarity between manifestation and nonmanifestation, as well as an interconnection between the two. It is in this regard that the *Amīr* sees the human being, and particularly the perfect human being, as a *barzakh* endowed with two eyes, one inner and one outer, through which he can see the world of nonmanifestation and that of manifestation, respectively. The key to the matter is to understand that the equilibrium inherent to the *barzakh* requires that there remain a connection between the two domains so as to ensure that "he should maintain a link with the manifested so that he would not be separated from it in every respect."[48] This means that the human *barzakh* is none other than the *khalifatullāh* or God's vice-regent in creation, whose double vocation for this world and the next is asserted.

One further illuminating meditation on the paradoxes of the *barzakh* is to be found in the *Amīr* 'Abd al-Qādir's reflections of the *barzakh* between the Divine Reality and the totality of creation as expressed by *āyat an-Nūr*, the Verse of Light. This is a verse that evokes the reverberation of the Divine Light, *an-Nūr*—one of the Names of God—in creation. The discussion is closely related to that of Divine Unity or union, and it, therefore, touches upon the very central matter of *tawhīd*, or Unity, in the context of the relationship between multiplicity and Unity. The main point developed by the *Amīr* is that all creatures flow from the one single Light of God, *an-Nūr*, and are analogically comparable to the shadows of the Divine Names projected by this Light upon the "immutable possibilities" in the "presential knowledge" of God. The Light is Divine Being Itself, which "existentiates," and the Names are the Divine Attributes, which "give form," while the "immutable prototypes" are like the plane of reflection of the shadows. This symbolic evocation is partly analogous to Plato's allegory of the Cave, in which the Sun is the Good, the realities outside the cave are the archetypes or forms, and the shadows on the wall of the cave are phenomena. However, whereas Plato referred to a "participation" (*methexis*) of the sensory in the archetypal, the *Amīr* speaks in terms of illumination by the Divine Light through diverse refractions and "formations." In an Islamic context, it is most important to understand that this illumination by the Divine Light operates without entailing some sort of "materialization" or "incarnation" of Its Divine Reality. Hence, the *Amīr*'s admonition:

"This illumination operates without union, mixture or conjunction through the intermediary of the Muhammadan Reality (*al-ḥaqīqa al-muhammadiyya*), which is the first determination (*al-taʿayyun al-awwal*), the 'Isthmus of Isthmuses' (*barzakh al-barāzikh*), the place of the theophany of the Essence and the appearance of the 'Light of Lights.' "[49]

The notion of supreme *barzakh* functions as a means to actualize *tawḥīd* without involving any admixtion that could give rise to suspicions of an "incarnationist" bent. The metaphysical interpretation that ensues results from an esoteric commentary on the verse: "*Allāh* is the Light of the heavens and the earth. The Parable of His Light is as if there were a Niche and within it a Lamp: the Lamp enclosed in Glass: the glass as it were a brilliant star" (24:35). In this view of things, the Light is God, the glass is the Muhammadan *barzakh,* and the niche is the totality of creation. The glass is this transparent reality through which God illuminates the niche of creation. It is not the Light Itself, but it is so transparent to It that it is referred to, in the *Qurʾān,* as a "brilliant star." This symbol accounts both for the continuous diffusion of the Light within immanence and the unmixed transcendence of Its Divine Reality. Thus, it could be said that the function of the Muhammadan *barzakh* is to "unify" God and the creation without "making them One." It preserves both the single identity of the Light as the principle of the vertical projection of light and shadows, and the irreducible difference between the Light and the shadows.[50]

For Ibn al-ʿArabī as well—within whose spiritual lineage the *Amīr* is situated—the Prophetic *barzakh* "reunites the creature and the Creator" while being "the line of separation between the divine degree and the degree of existentiated things, similar to the line which separates the shadow from the sun."[51] From a certain point of view, this line is something, but from another point of view, it is nothing. It is "nothing" as Divine or from a Divine point of view, and "something" as human or from a human point of view. Whereas the Christian Incarnation consecrates a manner of unitive fusion of the Divine and the human, the Islamic *barzakh* suggests a continuity in discontinuity or a discontinuity in continuity; it expresses the mystery of the meeting point of two incommensurable domains.

Another important symbolic account of the Prophet as *barzakh* is to be found in the rich speculative implications of the mirror. The mirror functions as a *barzakh* between the Divinity and mankind. It is akin to what Sufis such as ʿAbd al-Karīm al-Jīlī refer to as *al-Insān al-Kāmil,* the Universal Man. According to a number of Sufi theosophists, God sees or knows Himself in the mirror of the human in the form of a limited theophany, while the latter knows or sees himself in the mirror of the Divine, and as a possibility that conveys the limitlessness of the Divine. But, once again, this relationship is not totally reciprocal. Ibn al-'Arabī likes to quote the metaphysical *hadīth,* "I was a Hidden Treasure (*kanz*) and I wanted to be known, therefore I created the world." It means, among other things, that the world functions as a kind of onto-cosmic mirror in which God contemplates His own Qualities. But the situation is quite different for creatures, including humans. As it was brought to existence through the Divine "Be!" the creature opened its eyes and "the Real made it witness of its own likenesses among the temporally originated things." And even though creatures had come out into existence to witness the Real—longing for this witnessing as they were only possible entities—they did not witness the Real.[52] This is a result of their separation from God through existence, and it is also the measure of their metaphysical exile. Ibn al-'Arabī explains that this exile is to be understood in terms of their "leaving" their nonexistent status as possibilities.

Among all of these creatures in exile, mankind is the one being able to return "home" in an active mode. As long as human beings have not fully recognized God in creation, they remain indeed in exile. So, even though the human being is a mirror in which God knows Himself, the reverse is not true, at least in respect to ordinary human beings. It is only, according to Ibn al-'Arabī, the consummate gnostics who are not in exile and for whom, therefore, God is a mirror in which they know themselves. This mirror may be taken in two senses: one inward, having to do with the inner Witness, and the other outward, having to do with creation. In Ibn al-'Arabī's words, "The perfected gnostics have no exile whatsoever . . . they are entities immutably fixed in their places; they never leave their homeland."[53] It is why "the Real is their mirror" in the sense that their "forms" are reflected in God's mirror without being identical with the mirror. The perfect gnostic is, therefore, the ontological and epistemological *barzakh* par excellence, since he realizes the reciprocal mirroring that is the meaning of existence, and experiences both God and creation as distinct and one at the same time. Islam rejects the inherence of the Divine in the human, which is designated theologically as *hulūl,* a term that denoted descending, taking up residence into the human, or the penetration of one substance into another to the point of union, as in the case of the two human and Divine natures in Christ. By contrast, the notion of *barzakh* does not imply a descent, since the separation between the higher and lower realities remains marked, nor does it involve an indwelling, since the *barzakh* is neither one reality nor the other. The *barzakh* is that which makes multiplicity possible in relation to unity; it is the prime instrument of *tawhīd* on all levels of reality. It serves both as the point of the effulgence of Unity into multiplicity and as a point of reintegration of multiplicity into Unity. It makes everything unreal real, and everything real unreal. Actually, every *barzakh* is both real and unreal. What differentiates the Supreme *Barzakh* from other *barāzikh* is that it is definitely, or one should say functionally, more real than unreal since it brings Reality into the unreal. From another point of view, however, it remains unreal, since only the Essence is real.

Between the Real and the myriad of lower *barāzikh* that inform the world of multiplicity with *tawḥīd*, Sufi theosophy recognizes an ontological chain that modulates Unity through the entire range of existence. Sufi gnosis teaches, in various forms, the doctrine of the Five Divine Presences (*al-haḍrāt al-khams al-ilāhiyyah*), which are conceived as a hierarchical set of degrees of reality, from the Divine Essence to the world of physical manifestation. These five degrees of Reality are the functional equivalent of the Śaivite *tattvas*, albeit in a less analytical way, in the sense that they suggest, through ontological enumeration, the manner in which the Ultimate and Unconditioned Reality becomes gradually conditioned—without however ever being conditioned in Its Essence per se—through a descending ladder of "discontinuous continuity." This ladder involves more and more reality and less and less unreality moving upward, and more and more unreality and less and less reality moving downward. From another point of view, these domains of Reality can be envisaged from the most internal to the most external, in which case the higher levels will correspond to the deepest layers, and the lowest to the outermost strata of reality. Be that as it may, the notion of presence, or *huḍūr*, is claimed by Sufi metaphysicians to be quite distinct from that of *hulūl*—or "incarnation," in the sense that it does not imply a fusion in which two realities would become one, so that what could be said of one could be said of the other. It is not a matter of inherence—relation of an intrinsic, permanent, and inseparable attribute to a subject, as Divinity is to Christ—but rather one of immanence—implying for a reality that it embraces or manifests another reality.

The first mode of Divine Presence is *'ālam al-jism* or *'ālam an-nasūt*. This is the domain of physical existence; it refers to people, or *an-nās*, because the *Qur'ān* teaches that human beings are made out of "earth," *tīn*. This modality corresponds, in the human microcosm, to the physical body. Next, the "igneous" world of the *jinn* corresponds to *'ālam al-malakūt*, the "world of kingdom"; it refers to the domain in which spiritual realities "take form." In the human being, this is the empirical soul with its mental and emotional contents. The following ontological degree is "the realm of power" (*jabarūt*) which is the properly called "spiritual world" that includes angelic and celestial domains. Its microcosmic expression is the created aspect of the spirit or intellect that joins human beings to the Divine Intelligence. As for the fourth degree, it is the "Divine Realm" (*lahūt*), which is the Divine Being Itself as Supreme in relation to the universe. It corresponds to the uncreated root of the Intellect or Spirit. Finally, the highest Divine Presence is the Divine Essence Itself (*hahūt*, akin to *huwa,* "He") beyond all determinations and relationships—it is the

Divine Self of all selves, the innermost Witness. It is not a degree or a level as such, since it lies beyond all relativities.

It follows that among all five Divine Presences the Essence is the only one that cannot in any way be considered a *barzakh*. This classification is needed to account for the clear delineations that exist between the various domains of realities. It must be taken into account, for example, to distinguish the modes of being of men, on the one hand, and that of *jinn*, on the other hand. It is also necessary metaphysically to distinguish the Divine Essence, which is unknowable, from the Qualities, which are relatable and knowable. As we have mentioned, each of these *hadrāt* functions as a *barzakh* between two other domains, with the exception of the highest. It is also true that the "world of bodies" is not a *barzakh* as a whole, since it represents the lowest point of "fall" and gravity in universal existence; however, existents within the *ʿālam al-jism* do function as *barāzikh* as any reality other than the Unconditioned and Nondelimited. Moreover, it must added that since everything in existence is a *barzakh* there have to be realities that function as *barāzikh* between the various realms of Divine Presence. As we have already intimated, Ibn al-ʿArabī's universe is not one of tightly discrete entities and domains but one of "discontinuous continuity." Finally, it must be emphasized that these distinctions are nothing from an essential point of view. As we have noted earlier in reference to the *ʿālam al-hahūt*, the Absolute Essence has no common measure and no relationship with anything, since it *is* in a sense everything. As Ibn al-ʿArabī puts it in his *Bezels of Wisdom*, the notion of rank does not apply to Him as Essence: "*The Elevated* is one of God's Beautiful Names; but above whom or what, since only He exists? More elevated than whom or what, since only He is and He is Elevated in Himself? In relation to existence He is the very essence of existing beings. . . . Naught is except the Essence, which is Elevated in Itself, its elevation being unrelated to any other. Thus, from this standpoint, there is no relative elevation, although in respect of the aspects of existence there is (a certain) differentiation."[54] This sums up the way in which the *barzakh* functions: from the higher point of view, it absorbs what is below into what is above, and therefore annuls differences, but from the lower point of view it actually affirms these differences and defines them.

It has appeared clearly enough that what Akbari Sufism and Kashmiri Śaivism have in common is an ability to make full sense of a differentiated universe of diversity and degrees of reality within the context of a fundamentally nondualistic vision. The Śaivite gradation of the *abheda*, *bhedābheda*, and *bheda* points of view within the matrix of ultimate *abheda* strikes a metaphysical cord with the differentiated and hierarchized universe of *barāzikh* in which the bedrock of esoteric *tawhīd* remains the principle that "there is none but Him." While the *barzakh* as partition between the various degrees of Reality is undoubtedly in consonance with *bheda,* the most "absolute" of which being that which demarcates the servant as such and the Lord as such, that is to say, the Supreme *Barzakh,* the *barzakh* in general functions primarily, in Ibn al-'Arabī's gnosis, as the very locus and instrument of a kind of *bhedābheda.* It joins infinity and finitude, absoluteness and relativity, and unifies everything within and through multiplicity, weaving throughout "identity in difference."

As a conclusion, it is significant to highlight the fact that the concerns that preside over the respective spiritual economies of the two traditions are quite distinct. In Hindu metaphysics, the principal objective of the *bhedābheda* systems is to shield the reality of the *jīva,* as well as that of the world. In Islam, by contrast, we note a central regard for preserving the transcendence of God. These central concerns are intimately connected to spiritual and methodical intentions. Thus, it is quite obvious that some forms of *bhedābheda,* such as *Viśiṣṭādvaita,* are primarily intent on protecting the ontological foundation of their emphasis on *bhakti,* thereby articulating a system that makes room for some sort of ultimacy for the soul itself. By contrast, Śaivite *bhedābheda* is informed by an intuition that the dynamic creativeness of manifestation provides a way of reintegrating Śiva-consciousness; hence, a "differential" nondualism in the way of "identity in difference" that makes way for a recognition of the methodical wherewithal of immanence. The synthetic and "absolutist" dimension of Hindu thought is in need of ways of articulating ontological differentiations so as to account for the multiplicity of ways. In a sense, and to put it very schematically, the Hindu concept of the Absolute lays primary emphasis on nondual Unity, but in such a way as to be able to account for "division" and difference. In sharp contrast with the Hindu set of concerns, Islamic metaphysicians are primarily concerned with situating the differences inherent to the choice of the Truth over vanity, God over the world, servanthood over polytheism in the essential context of a metaphysics of Unity, one that is scripturally characterized by a Divine "Mercy encompassing everything." The divine flow of compassionate Unity that runs through the entire universe presupposes zones of encountering and merging that still do not jeopardize the ontological foundations for discrimination and separation. We have been arguing that such is the essential function of the *barzakh.*

Śaivism and Sufism are not philosophies, even less so ideologies; they are indeed intellectual and practical disciplines of spiritual realization, without which they become reduced to mere mental speculations. What is strikingly analogous in the two traditions is that they both involve, in their methods, an extensive use of linguistic means. We are referring to the importance of the *mantra* and to the Sufi practice of *dhikr,* or remembrance of God. As we will develop it in the last chapter of this book, the *mantra* is both an onto-cosmogonic reality and a spiritual technique. The manifestation of the world out of the infinite freedom of Śiva is akin to the procession of the letters of the Sanskrit alphabet, and the two are actually mystically connected in complex ways. Everything proceeds from the "agitation" or "vibration" inherent to pure Consciousness. The term *vibration* is most appropriate to suggest three characteristics of this process. First, the onto-cosmic process results from a kind of rupture of equilibrium within consciousness. This is like a quasi-imperceptible "tilt" in the direction of manifestation and expansion. Secondly, the initial stir results in a motion that is both centrifugal and centripetal, one that can be taken both as a moving away from pure consciousness *and* a moving back into it. Thirdly, this vibrating motion is suggestive of a metaphysical continuum through dynamic discontinuities. As a consequence, Śaivite spiritual practice could be compared to an interiorization and assimilation of this vibration with a view to returning to its Source. The power of the *mantra* qua sacred vibration is none other than the process of unfolding and folding of Śiva. Vibration is akin to a discontinuous continuity that "transmits" Śiva's energy through quasi-imperceptible cosmico-linguistic differentiations. There is "identity in difference" in the matricial procession of "ontological phonemes." The matter is one of Śaktic power as expression of the unity of consciousness, and the methodical use of this expression. *Bhedābheda* lies at the unstable center of this universal motion inasmuch as it suggests the very point of articulation between the centrifugal and centripetal aspects of Śaktic expansion.

By contrast, the context of Sufism is religious before being metaphysical, which means that it begins with the Islamic injunction of worship of the One. This injunction stems from the human forgetting of the original covenant with God. The main sin in Islam is said to be connected to negligence and forgetfulness, hence the definition of prophecy and revelation as a reminder, or *dhikr.* The very same term is used to refer, in the *Qur'ān*, to everything that expresses human abiding by this reminder in the form of a remembrance of God. In Sufism, the three cognate terms *dhikr* ("remembrance"), *dhākir* ("rememberer"), and *madhkūr* ("remembered object") refer both to God and to mankind. If it is perhaps religiously obvious that, as expressed in the *Qur'ān*, God remembers those who remember him, it is esoterically even more significant that God has remembered mankind from all eternity. Thus, the *Qur'ān* asks: "Was there ever a time when man was not a thing remembered—*madhkūran*?" (76:1). Thus, *dhikr* is a *barzakh* that connects God and mankind, thereby relating the five levels of Divine Presence, from the Divine Essence to the physical literality of the Name of God. It could be said, following a number of Sufi writers, that *dhikr* is the spiritual tool of *tawḥīd* par excellence; with it, everything that is made one, is "made" into the One. Both the *mantra* and the *dhikr* liquefy the separation that is inherent to the cosmos and to concepts. They connect levels of reality, and they transmute concepts into unifying symbols.

As an epilog to the previous reflections it is tempting to transpose, or rather apply, the conclusions of this essay, to the contemporary predicament of religious communities and their tensions between the inclusivist and pluralistic pull of the modern age and the exclusivist tendencies of their traditions. As a starting point, it seems in order to note that the metaphysical nonduality of the kind we have been exploring in our two traditions has never been, and most likely cannot ever be, a dominant point of view, at least collectively speaking. It is a difficult, subtle, type of teaching that can all too easily give rise to mis-understandings or oversimplifications, the most likely and frequent of which is a kind of "pantheistic" or "material" interpretation of the essential Unity of all things. This being said, there is little doubt that metaphysical nondualism can infuse, through its spiritual diffusion in collective religious sensibilities—we are particularly thinking here of the popular mysticism that echoes devotion-ally its doctrinal tenets—a certain collective predisposition to be receptive to religious differences against the background of a largely unarticulated sense of "nondifference." In point of fact, the nondualistic perspectives, whether *abheda* or metaphysical *tawhīd,* correspond, strictly speaking, as we have sug-gested, to the Divine point of view. Obviously, humans can only be partially participants in this point of view, as indicated by concepts such as those of "liberated soul," *jīvan-mukta,* or "knower by God," *'ārif bi-Llāh.* Be that as it may, nonduality cannot but lead to the recognition of essential nondifference on any level upon which it may be humanly relevant or accessible, and it is, in fact, no coincidence that nondualistic outlooks have unflinchingly been the most universalist and inclusive, whether in India, in Islam, or elsewhere. The nondualistic contemplative outlook is in the best possible situation to evalu-ate the rights and demands of exclusive religion in relation to the infinity of the Ultimate. Ibn al-'Arabī has beautifully expressed this point of view in his *Bezels of Wisdom*: "Beware of becoming delimited by a specific knotting and disbelieving in everything else, lest great good escape you. . . . Be in yourself a matter for the forms of all beliefs, for God is wider and more tremendous than that He should be constricted by one knotting rather than another."[55]

This relationship between differential identity and nondualistic inclu-sion is of course acutely at stake in the religious climate of India. Andrew J. Nicholson, in his thought-provoking *Unifying Hinduism*, has made the point that there have been, in Hinduism, two trends, particularly since the medi-eval period and into the contemporary era. On the one hand, Hinduism has defined itself by contrast with, or in opposition to, autochthonous traditions such as Buddhism and Jainism, and even more so, in the most recent phases of its history, in not uncommonly distrustful contradistinction with Islam and Christianity. The very designation *Hinduism* bears witness to this since it is of very recent construction and appropriation and expresses an a posteriori and largely misleading reconstruction. On the other hand, however, there has been a clearly inclusivist bent in Hinduism, in the sense that Hindus have tended to include all religious faiths as the many branches of the tree of the Eternal Law, the *Sanātana Dharma*. This has led a prominent Hindu scholar such as Arvind Sharma to the paradoxical conclusion that "one is most a Hindu when least a Hindu."[56]

Needless to say, such an appropriating inclusivism has been considered with much suspicion in some Muslim and Christian quarters, since, by englobing religious diversity into Hindu unity, it appears to deny any otherness, and therefore may be deemed to exclude any significant meaning for Christian and Islamic identity. In a sense, these two self-definitions of Hinduism correspond, firstly, to an understanding of Hindu identity as difference and, secondly, to a recognition of nondifference, or perhaps better an acknowledgment of difference based on the recognition of nondifference. Now, if the latter is understood along the lines of teachings in which nonduality, as a basis for identity, cannot but include difference qua difference, then it could hardly be received as a negation of distinct identities but, rather, as the deepest foundation for difference.

The situation of Islam is radically different in several respects. In Islam the main concern today is—as it has always been in different ways—the recognition of Divine Unity, and in a more current and pressing way, the communitarian unity that is expected to ensue from this recognition, together with the unsettling reality of de facto religious division within and without. There are three ways this challenge can be addressed. The first view is that unity has to be imposed onto multiplicity by reducing all elements of otherness, or canceling them out, in one way or another. It is the view of a large, probably growing, segment of the *ummah,* whether the reduction of these differences and divisions may be forceful or peaceful. In all cases, diversity is a problem. The second view consists in cultivating diversity independently from Unity. This is the pluralistic creed of the contemporary ethos, which may be applied to any context, including Islamic ones. It has been largely welcome among Western-educated and modernized Muslims, but it remains held in high suspicion in most other Muslim circles. The third approach would amount to affirm both unity and diversity, but on the basis and in the context of Unity itself. Nondifference (identity) would be recognized to include difference, and not erase it. Identitarian difference would be understood as not being *absolutely* exclusive of universality. By contrast, when difference encloses itself into its own exclusive "logic," it absolutizes itself and runs contrary to the very principle of Unity. It substitutes itself to the latter and becomes the most dangerous and most unconscious form of idolatry. This is what Henry Corbin used to call "the paradox of monotheism," which contradicts and denies itself in and through its own formal affirmation.

We have learned from Kashmiri Saivism that nonduality and nondifference include duality and difference. Universal identity includes distinctive
particularity lest it be reduced to inert indifferentiation. From the Sufi *barzakh*
we have learned that separation entails relation, encounter, meeting, and is
therefore not exclusive of essential unity lest it become a second Absolute,
which would amount to metaphysical *shirk*. We could also say that nondual
Unity includes difference, while discriminative separation entails or presupposes
unifying affirmation. It may be that these metaphysical realities provide the
most profound and effective guiding principles to address the pressing challenges of the "nationalization" and "ideologization" of religion.

# 5

## Knowing the Unknowable

### Upāya and Gods of Belief

Contemporary religious consciousness seems to be characterized, by an apparent paradox, either by a rejection of sacred mediations or by an absolutization of them. We mean thereby that there lies in contemporary sensibilities a need for an immediate religious experience of Reality independently from dogmatic and ritual forms. This is particularly evident in the myriad of phenomena pertaining to neospiritualism, and so-called New Age and Next Age forms of spirituality. Truth is herein a matter of individual experience, rather than one of universal principles. Consequently, the modern ethos of individualism and "informality" leads more and more seekers to explore the untrodden paths of individually tailored, often syncretistic, and above all "practically" oriented, ways of self realization. Such emphasis on individual experience is accompanied by an extreme relativization of, or even an utter disregard for—if not total rejection of—sacred mediations, such as scriptures, rites, and ancestral religious institutions, which are at best conceived as mere metaphorical illustrations of inner realities and are not considered, therefore, as sine qua non but rather as backward impediments.

On the other hand, we can also observe occurrences of an "absolutization" of religious mediations, most often in an exclusively literalist and formalistic mode, and in a way that emphasizes exclusive truth claims. By "absolutization" we are referring to a process whereby the scriptural, dogmatic, ritual, and legal forms of a religious tradition are the prime focus of attention while being indissociably merged with the sense of the Ultimate and, in a sense, the Ultimate itself. In one way, this second trend could be considered as a mere intensification of the process that Wilfred Cantwell-Smith characterized as the "reification" of religion;[1] that is, the move from religion as inner faith to religion as an outer "thing." What is new in contemporary religion, however, is that this reification becomes informed by the specificity of a context in which pluralism and secular culture have become prevalent. This means two things. First, *the* only true and effective religion must be defined and presented in such a way as to be immediately *distinguishable* from its secular competing options. This means that outwardly and easily recognizable concepts, signs, and modes of acting will tend to be moved to the forefront in order to "cement" the identity of the religious community within a context that is perceived as adverse, if not hostile. This is obviously not in itself an exclusively contemporary phenomenon, but it can be deemed that it has become intensified and, in a sense, "absolutized" by being endowed with a strong coefficient of divine imperative, and a value of compelling symbol. The second point is that, in the absence of a rich, profound, diverse and sophisticated theological culture and authoritative magisteria, we attend a phenomenon of redefinition of religion within the categories and molds of contemporary secular culture, whether they be technological, mediatic, political, economic, or other. Olivier Roy has suggestively made use of the concept of globalized "formatting," suggesting no doubt the informing influence of the world of information technology, to characterize these new ways of formulating creeds and practices in a simplified, easily consumable, and quickly communicable manner.[2] We can observe these tendencies in a number of so-called fundamentalist movements, referring thereby to religious currents that tend to focus on the absolute imperatives of scriptures, often in the most exclusively literalist sense, and to dismiss theological elaborations, traditional ecclesial institutions, and other such traditional intermediaries in the name of the *immediacy* of God's Word.

The two aforementioned tendencies—stress on individual experience and absolutization of sacred mediations—sometimes coincide, as in some forms of Christian neo-evangelicalism, where the unmediated experience of Christ and the inerrancy of the Bible are asserted concurrently with the same intensity. By way of consequence, between the rejection of mediating forms and their absolutization, contemporary religious consciousness tends to gravitate around the two axes of psychology and ideology. Thus, it is either often lacking in an objective, intellectual, and ritual grounding, or frequently turned into a program of formatted ideas and social actions without much, if any, focus upon spiritual self-transformation, aside from the bare requisites of moral codes and prescribed practices.

Now, although such trends may be deemed to characterize contemporary religious movements particularly, both within the fold of traditional religions and outside of it, the dialectics of personal experience and universally binding forms have always been part and parcel of religious life. Traditionally, however, these two terms were not typically exclusive of each other, nor even less antagonistic, but rather, normatively, if imperfectly, integrated, largely thanks to the mediation of holy human models, sacred institutions, and ritual practices. With respect to the more specific question of creed and belief, it could be said that the traditional universe as a whole, whether in Semitic religions or in other worlds of faith, functioned by and large as a spiritual and intellectual milieu in which individual representations took shape in a way that was normatively consistent with the theological and "mythological" language of a given civilization. Below the level of universally recognized teachings lay a diversity of hermeneutic schools, subschools, and commentarial traditions, not to mention, downstream, the more individualized modes of worship and devotion. Thus, ideally if not always actually, the relationship between individual experience and universal principles was mediated by a hierarchical set of sacred, traditional, and even cultural realities that facilitated an integration of the personal, the collective, the cosmic, and the divine. Now it is precisely such integrating intermediaries that have been largely dismissed or dispensed with by contemporary religious movements in the name of an egalitarian ethos and a distrust of institutions and sacred forms.

Part of the ambiguous fascination exercised by mysticism upon contemporary seekers lies, precisely, in its seeming personal focus and relativization of sacred mediations. To the modern mind, this appears as an antidote to what it conceives as the stiffening and alienating role of so-called organized religions. As we will suggest in the following pages, this attraction may be deemed to involve shortcuts or misapprehensions that do not do justice to the paradoxes and subtleties of the contemplative and mystical dimension.

It must be acknowledged that it is probably in spiritual and mystical schools that the question of the mediation between the personal and the universal, the human and the divine, is the most directly relevant, since mystics have aimed at realizing a mode of being that transcends the individual while being situated a priori in the individual order. In mystical or contemplative experience, the individual modes of knowing, including memory, reason, and imagination, are brought to bear in a process that ultimately opens onto a Reality that transcends their means of apprehension. The spiritual seeker is therefore confronted by the challenge of knowing the Unknowable. It is on this challenge that we would like to dwell in this chapter by analyzing and comparing the ways in which two very distinct, and very diverse, traditions, in Buddhism and Sufism, have understood, conceptualized, and taught the relationship between human limitations and the unlimited Ultimate. This might provide a contrasting way of balancing out the unduly and one-sidedly "relativistic" and "absolutistic" bents of all too many contemporary religious ways.

One of the fundamental metaphysical questions, from a contemplative point of view—that is, one centered on seeking a spiritual recognition of, or proximity to, the Ultimate—is that of the status of human consciousness. Actually, inasmuch as it is focused on this concern, philosophy is also in its own way contemplative and even "mystical," to the extent at least that it tries to elucidate or evaluate the ontological and epistemological reality of consciousness. There is much to learn, in this context, from Descartes's methodological emphasis on thinking consciousness, as expressed in his famous *cogito ergo sum*. Although the question of the *cogito* is most often approached from the standpoint of its deductive and rational implications as a foundation for "clear and certain" knowledge in Descartes's philosophy, it is to be noted that such an understanding of the *cogito* is not unconnected to the emphasis one ordinarily tends to place on the deductive value of the word *ergo*, or "therefore." Although the expression *cogito, ergo sum* is indeed included in the first edition of the *Discours de la méthode* published in The Hague in 1637, another work by Descartes, *The Meditations on First Philosophy* (*Meditationes de Prima Philosophia*), offers an alternative wording that is no doubt richer in connotations for our purpose. We read in Descartes's second meditation, "this proposition: I am, I exist, (*ego sum, ego existo*) whenever it is uttered by me, or conceived in the mind, is necessarily true."[3] A marginal note from his later *Principles of Philosophy* bears witness to the same intuition: "That we cannot doubt of our existence while we doubt (*existamus dum dubitamus*), and that this is the first knowledge we acquire when we philosophize in order."[4] In both cases, the existential concordance of thinking and being is affirmed in a way that asserts the primacy of consciousness. Thinking is herein not only a rational process but an act of consciousness.

Notwithstanding the epistemological merits of the *cogito* as highlighting the primacy of consciousness, it has been argued that its fundamental limitation, or even flaw, stems from its artificially isolating the individual subjectivity from the relationality and the receptivity that are inherent to it. In other words, the individual "I" cannot be separated from that which founds it as an "I," not only in terms of immanent relationships with "non-I," but above all in terms of relationship with God as the very principle of the "I." This emphasis on the relationality, and indeed contingency, of the ego led the nineteenth-century German speculative philosopher Franz von Baader (1765–1841) to develop a critique of Descartes's philosophy along the lines of a substitution of the *cogitor ergo sum* to the Cartesian *cogito ergo sum*: "Instead of saying with Descartes: I think, therefore I am, one ought to say: I am thought, therefore I think, or: I am wanted (loved), therefore I am."[5]

What Baader does criticize in Cartesian philosophy is not the position of "thinking" as primordial, but rather its identification with "doubting" as an inherent and prior dimension of it. Now, for Baader, this primordial "thinking as doubting" is not connatural to human intelligence, since on the contrary the latter is inherently characterized by its recognition of the Divine Principle. The theological position of Baader is that the intuition of God precedes that of the individual self and that of nonself. It is not God who is a priori an object for the self, but the self who is an object for God: "If (after Cartesius) one wishes to begin cognition from the absolutely primitive 'I,' or from a selfless 'not-I,' and one thereby denies the secondary [character] of these two convictions, since both only appear as part of a deeper, primitive and founding conviction of someone else or someone primary, namely, God, for which the I or the selfless not-I is the other, and not to begin with this is already the denial of him."[6] The primary intuition is that of God, or the supreme Being and Consciousness from which the individual *ego* derives. The "primitive and founding conviction of . . . God" is the intellectual and existential bedrock of any kind of human knowledge.

The rational position of God that Descartes puts forward is insufficient in that it serves, methodically, only as a kind of epistemological seal of reliability on our knowledge of the world. For Baader, as for the whole Neoplatonic tradition and the German speculative metaphysical tradition, God is much more than an epistemological component of human knowledge, as it were. He is the very root of the possibility of knowledge, beginning with self-knowledge. The human subject does not truly know itself or anything else "if it does not know itself [as] known by God, which being known actually is the foundation and presupposition of all knowing."[7] While Descartes would take God as the epistemological guarantor that man can trust in the reality of the world and the reliability of his rational intelligence, Baader understands God as the original source of man's being, the ignorance or lack of consideration of which in matters of knowledge, as in any other domain, is nothing else than a negation of His Being. For Baader, a man cannot consider himself as the subject of the *cogito* because his thinking as a subject already presupposes his "being thought" as an object. In other words, the essence of human subjectivity is receptivity or surrender to that which is the principle of its being. We must note that Baader's thought, differently from Eastern metaphysics such as *Advaita Vedānta,* does not express the metaphysical anteriority of God in a way that would abolish the distinction between a subject and an object. For him, the highest realization in the domain of human knowledge coincides with recognizing oneself as being an object for God. In Baader's *cogitor* lies an unerasable duality between the Divine Subject and the human object of the *cogitare.* So, while the philosophical thrust of Baader's critique of Descartes's *cogito* dwells in his highlighting the contingency and limits of the Cartesian *ego,* the limitations of his own perspective may be deemed to reside in an inability to transcend the epistemological regime of the polarity between subject and object.

Independently from Baader's fruitful critique of Descartes's *cogito,* what we can keep from the basic Cartesian intuition is the sense of identity between epistemology and ontology: being and consciousness are the two faces of the same primordial reality. This intuition of the *cogito sum* implies simultaneousness but also, much more profoundly, inherent identity, in the sense that there is no consciousness without being, which is Descartes's obvious argument, but also no being without consciousness since the certainty of being is such only while there is consciousness—and this even though consciousness is colored and limited by doubt, *dum dubitamus.*

We note that Descartes's fundamental philosophical recognition can be considered as independent from any object, and this is a crucial point to highlight for our purpose, since consciousness is taken here in a quasi-absolute sense, in and of itself. However, this is true only *in principio,* and in reference to a search for epistemological foundations, for the bulk of Descartes's philosophy not only involves a clear separation between subject and object, but it is also structured around a whole host of other dualities, such as reason and faith, mind and body, or else *res cogitans* and *res extensa.* In fact, Cartesian dualism could be deemed to be most representative of the overall dualistic bent of Western modern philosophy, and perhaps even of Western philosophy as a whole.

By contrast, even though it includes a number of dualistic and semi-dualistic schools and subschools, Indian metaphysics has remained by and large characterized by a strong nondualistic orientation. Now, it is particularly instructive to observe that one of the most philosophically minded Western interpreters of Indian nondualism, especially in its *Advaita Vedāntin* form, the American philosopher Franklin Merrell-Wolff (1887–1985) provided a presentation of the nondualistic thrust of Hindu metaphysics by making use of concepts that are, arguably, most central in the Western philosophical postmedieval tradition, that is those of subject and object. Taking stock of a spiritual "experience" of recognition that he chronicled in the initial sections of his book *Pathways through to Space,*[8] Merrell-Wolff develops a contrasted phenomenology of what he considers to be, with the whole *Advaitin* tradition, the two fundamental modes of consciousness. The most ordinary one, which is, in fact, the very principle of philosophical phenomenology, is referred to by Merrell-Wolff as "subject-object consciousness." It is the domain of "relative consciousness" in which most human beings live their entire existence. In this field of consciousness, the latter is always definable by the cognitive relationship between a subject and an object, whether the latter is external to the human subject or internal to it. This means that what is most often understood as "self-knowledge" still refers to the plane of "subject-object consciousness." This is certainly true in the domain of modern psychology, in which the contents of consciousness are objects of study and investigation.

What characterizes further this ordinary degree of consciousness is that it is intrinsically limited by its objects, in substance, space, and time, and is, therefore, unable to provide unadulterated satisfaction and happiness. This is, in a very real sense, the field of what Buddhists call *dukkha* or "suffering through craving." It must be noted that craving and suffering, in whatever form or way one may understand them, result intrinsically from the nature of "subject-object consciousness." It is not only so inasmuch as objects are limited, since one could argue that a supreme, perfect Object such as God could "quench" the metaphysical thirst of the human subject, but also insofar as the very limitations of the human subject affect the ways in which the object is apprehended and enjoyed. Moreover, subject-object consciousness is predicated on a dichotomy and a gap between the two terms that define it. Now, such a distance makes it impossible to achieve a full, unalienable, Self-realization inasmuch as it introduces the possibility, and indeed the necessity, of a lack. This realization is only possible, therefore, on the level of what Merrell-Wolff refers to as "consciousness-without-an-object." The latter has also been referred to as "consciousness turned toward its source or the positive pole of consciousness."[9] This means that "consciousness-without-an-object" is pure consciousness, untainted by any limitations of the subject, which cannot be therefore the individual, relative subject that defines the "subject-object consciousness." The distinction between "consciousness-without-an-object" and "subject-object consciousness" corresponds to the *Advaitin* differentiation between *Ātman* and *Māyā,* that is, the transpersonal and divine Selfhood of the entire universe, which is the only Reality, and the domain of dualistic appearance that ranges from "the god Brahma to a blade of grass." This distinction runs parallel to other ones, such the Absolute and the relative, the Unconditioned and the conditioned, or the Vedantic Sanskrit pair *satyam* and *mithyā.*

The major epistemological difficulty arising out of the distinction between the two types of Reality/Consciousness lies in the very possibility, and modalities, of moving from one to the other. In Shankarian *Advaita* this issue is addressed both from the point of view of *Ātman* and that of *Māyā.* From the first vantage point, *Māyā* is a result of a beginningless and connatural superimposition upon the true reality of *Ātman.* This quasi-phenomenological account of the transition from *Ātman* to *Māyā* has traditionally left much room for challenges and controversies since it does not appear to answer the fundamental question of the why of the superimposition in the first place. As a result, *Māyā* is not uncommonly referred to as a kind of unfathomable mystery, an unintelligible metaphysical "blind spot" that has to be corrected, but which remains, so to speak, irreducible in its own terms. In other nondualistic systems such as— for example—that of Kashmiri Śaivism, the passage from the Unconditioned to the conditioned is accounted for, intrinsically, in terms of the binding of Śiva-consciousness that is inherent to its infinite freedom. The merit of such an understanding is that it allows for a view of relativity as being brought about by the absolute Freedom of the Divine, or a view of the finite as flowing from the very nature of the Infinite. On the other hand, the disciplines of liberation (*moksha*) that are taught in the various nondualistic schools of India are as many answers to the question of the ways one may move from "subject-object consciousness" to "consciousness-without-an-object." This realization of *Ātman* from the starting point of *Māyā* points to the question of the "proportion" or "relation" between the two: how is the Unconditioned apprehended and realized from the point of view of the a priori conditioned? This question can-not but be raised by spiritual traditions since it hinges essentially upon their teachings and their methods of recognition, that is, their ways of representing the Unconditioned from within the conditioned, and their paths of spiritual actualization of Unconditioned Consciousness.

In comparing the two concepts of *upāya* and "gods of belief," operative notions that have been developed in two vastly different spiritual traditions of Buddhism and Sufism, our intent is to delve into some of the major implica-tions of the relationship between the two seemingly incommensurable terms of the metaphysical and spiritual equation that lies at the core of doctrines of realization of the Absolute. It bears stressing, first of all, that the respective general economies of the two traditions lead to raising the aforementioned issue in ways that are a priori quite distinct. The spiritual traditions of Buddhism are centered on the realization of a state of consciousness, whereas the various schools of Islamic contemplative mysticism focus on the ways and means of knowledge and love of the transcendent One. The original Buddhist question is a methodical "how?"—that is, how can Unconditioned Consciousness, or *nirvāna,* be realized? The central question of Sufism—at least in the perspective of speculative knowledge, or the metaphysics of *ma'rifah*—is: What is the nature of the Divine Reality? From the answer to this question derive spiritual and moral consequences that inform the practical dimension of Sufism. It follows that Buddhism could be defined as a religion in which the pedagogical aspect of spirituality is paramount.

By contrast, Sufism, as Islamic contemplative spirituality, is a path of "representation," in the sense that it derives from the concept of Divine Unity and the ways in which this concept is grasped, and acted upon, by the believer. It could be said, therefore, that Buddhism focuses on accessing a mode of consciousness, while Sufism concentrates on recognizing, and conforming to, a reality of Being, that is, Divine Unicity and All-Powerfulness. The primary Buddhist concerns are practical and have to do with means of realization, whereas the main Sufi interest lies with belief, or rather with the depth and breadth of belief and its adequacy to its Divine Object. However, whether the matter is methodical or metaphysical, or both, the major question remains one of mediation. How, or by what means, do we realize the Absolute subjectively, starting from the ordinary individual consciousness? How, or by what representations, do we conceive of that which lies beyond limited conceptions?

The term *upāya* has been etymologically related to the verb *upa-i*, which means to approach, or to arrive.[10] This root is to be found in other words frequently referred to in India, such as *upaguru*, which refers to a "proximate" *guru*, in the sense of an existential closeness, whether it be in the way of a person one has encountered, a living or inanimate being, or simply an event in one's life. The term is used in Hindu schools of thought, for example in Śaivism, where it refers to different ways of accessing liberation, or the realization of Śiva-nature, as in the concepts of *anupāya*, which is a privative of *upāya* and is translated as "means without means," or *śaktopāya*, literally, the *upāya* of Śakti. It is important to note, for our purpose, that *anupāya* is considered to be the highest means of liberation in Kashmiri Śaivism. In the second chapter of his *Tantrāloka*, Abhinavagupta explains this preeminence as follows:

> Now I am starting (to write) this second chapter in order to decide which is the best path leading to the understanding of Śiva. What is the use of any instruction at all! It may need only one-time instruction followed by futility of instruction known as *anupāya*. This Reality is such as does not need anything else to bring it home. If anyone questions the validity of this (Śiva's) Reality, we have to tell them that this is like this.[11]

The essential point that we may derive from Abhinavagupta's comments is that the unconditioned Reality cannot be subjected to any methical conditioning. From an absolute point of view, there is, therefore, no way of access to That which is to be accessed. Śiva's absolute Reality cannot be made dependent upon anything else, and therefore the very realization of this Reality cannot be made contingent upon anything other than itself, as it were. This is, in a sense, the very definition of grace. It is said that the grace of *anupāya* is imparted upon the soul by the presence of a *guru*, or even without any perceptible intermediary. This grace is connected, in Trika Śaivism, to the "initiation of knowledge"[12] that "may be compared to the transmission of light from one lamp to the other." Whether from Śiva's "lamp" or from the "lamp" of the outer *guru*, it is the immediate realization of the Self (*ātma-vyāpti*) that transcends all distinctions, and therefore all mediations inasmuch as they presuppose distinctions. In this "way without a way," all the limitations inherent to methods—insofar as methods take account of the preliminary limitations of the empirical consciousness—are canceled out. In the words of Moti Lal Pandit, "It is a path that is not constricted by the flickering perceptions of the mind or by the attachment for the world, and so for the yogi of this path everything is transformed into the glorious worship of the supreme."[13]

The absence of methodical mediations implied by the concept of *anupāya,* and its connection with Śiva's grace, may make one raise the legitimacy of the very term *upāya.* What can be the meaning of such a paradoxical expression, if not an allusion to the very foundation of nondualistic metaphysics, that is, the actual, ever-present, reality of pure Consciousness? It is along the same paradoxical and perplexing lines that some contemporary teachers of nondualism, such as Ramana Maharshi, have insisted on the fact that there is "nothing to realize" since everything is already Real. Now, the very use of the notion of *upāya* presupposes a very different point of view, one that is founded on the current state of ignorance and suffering of the empirical ego, and which—moreover—does not consider, at least a priori, the reality of any kind of grace as being exclusively and decisively operational within the spiritual path. Such a view closely corresponds to the perspective of early Buddhism.

It is largely recognized that the concept and practice of *upāya* is one of the central elements of the Buddhist spiritual economy. In most general terms, it refers to a method, means, technique, or device facilitating Enlightenment. It is often referred to, more specifically, as *upāya-kauśalya,* one of the most frequent translations of which is "skill-in-means," since the Sanskrit word signifies cleverness or skilfulness. According to Michael Pye, however, neither one of the concepts of means, device, or expediency does full justice by itself to the meaning and connotations of *upāya.*[14] Pye makes the important point that such English terms may easily imply, in the mind of contemporary readers, a sense of mere functionality, and even dispensability, that does not convey the spiritual weight of the term in Mahāyāna texts. This is primarily so inasmuch as the *upāya* flows from a Buddha or a Bodhisattva, and is therefore imbued with the "nirvānic substance" of their Enlightenment. Therefore, it would seem that, operatively, the concept of *upāya* fulfills by and large the function of revelation in other religious traditions. This is all the more true if we distance the term of revelation from its connotations of vertical descent, and focus instead on its etymological implication of an "unveiling." *Upāya* is indeed that by which *nirvāna* is unveiled.

It is said that when the god Brahmā pleaded three times with the Buddha so that he would turn the wheel of the *Dharma,* the Buddha saw the various human beings in the form of various lotuses, some immersed in the water, others rising out of the water. It is also said that some had little dust in their eyes while others had much dust.[15] These two images correspond in themselves to symbolic representations of Awakening, which is both a transcending of samsāric consciousness evoked by the water out of which arise, on various levels, some lotuses, and the need for a clarity of the eye of nirvānic consciousness, suggested by the various amounts of dust in the eyes of the recipients of the teachings. It is on account of the realization of those differences that the Buddha understood the need for his preaching not to be universal and uniform, but rather proportioned to the diversity of degrees of understanding. Wisdom lies in the capacity of the Buddha, or the Bodhisattva, to convey the *Dharma* in the language in which it can be effectively understood and realized, and this language is necessarily manifold on account of the diversity of the potential recipients of the teaching. As John Schroeder puts it, the diversity of degrees of understanding can be considered both from the point of view of the Buddha's "sensitiveness" to their demands and from that of their karmic nature: "He (the Buddha) knew that if he wanted to help others he would need to be sensitive to the karmic differences of human beings and mold his teachings to their level."[16] The "sensitiveness" is part and parcel of Enlightenment as it entails compassion, and therefore attunement to the need of sentient beings, on the part of the Buddha. As for the karmic state of beings, it expresses, in a sense, the other dimension of Buddhism, that which is rigorously exclusive, and has to do with the ineluctability of the law of actions and reactions. Whereas the "conditions" that mold the degree of receptivity of beings is a result of the karmic chain that prevents them from being other than what they are, the unconditioned reality of the Buddha "relates" to those conditions by virtue of its universal compassion, as expressed through a consideration of their needs. Therefore, *upāya* can be said to mediate between the domain of compassion and that of existential rigor.

One of the most striking characteristics of *upāya* as the "specific" language of Buddhism lies in that it is both methodical and doctrinal at the same time, or in that, in it, the doctrine is inseparable from the method to the point of being at times reducible to it. This has led scholars such as John Schroeder to call into question the centrality, or even perhaps the very reality, of Buddhist metaphysics. In Schroeder's terms, the Buddhist concern for *upāya* bears witness to the prime importance of "metapraxis" over metaphysics: "As a specific form of metapraxis, *upāya* is not reflecting on the limits of knowledge, the nature of reality or metaphysical assertions, but on the efficacy and justifiability of Buddhist praxis."[17] The Buddhist rejection of "views" stems, no doubt, from this "metapractical" concern, by highlighting the pitfalls of holding metaphysical positions as "reified" truths. Now, does it mean that *upāya* amount to the absence of any kind of intellectual understanding of reality? This may be deemed not to be the case for two reasons. First, the metapractical aspect of the notion does not preclude, but actually entails, a number of assumptions concerning *the way things are*. In other words, even though the focus of most Buddhist schools might be on the pedagogical means of actualizing nirvānic consciousness, these approaches derive from an enlightened perception of reality that does justice to the latter in its own terms, therefore in a way that can be translated, albeit imperfectly and perhaps sometimes misleadingly, into

theoretical representations. One could, therefore, speak of an implicit metaphysics that can be actualized conceptually when the need arises. Therefore,
and it is our second point, metaphysics must also be considered as an *upāya*.
There is no reason to exclude doctrinal teachings from the arsenal of skillful
means, since the latter must address all kinds of human qualifications and all
aspects of reality.

Now, another significant point to bear in mind is that *upāya* can in no
way be understood as an end in itself, since it is precisely only a means. This
signifies that even though Buddhism as a whole may well be considered as an
*upāya*, or as a set of *upāyas*, that which Buddhism treats as ultimate cannot be
considered as *upāya*, being a goal rather than a means. Leaving aside for now
the problematic aspect of the notion of goal from a Buddhist point of view—on
account of the emptiness of all phenomena, and considering that the mental
position or consideration of any goal is none other than a phenomenon—it
must be highlighted that if Buddhism as a set of teachings can be exclusively
referred to as an *upāya*, this is in no way the case for Buddhism as an experience of Awakening, since it is here a matter of realizing rather than teaching,
one of being rather than conveying.

This distinction is called into play by the foremost Japanese Buddhist
scholar, Kōbō Daishi, or Kūkai (774–835), when referring to the distinction
between exoteric and esoteric teachings. His differentiation is based on the
Doctrine of the Three Bodies (*trikāya*), and more particularly on a contrast
between the *Nirmānakāya*, or the body of the historical Buddha as manifested
in space and time, and the *Dharmakāya*, or principial body of Enlightenment
beyond space and time, which is the essence of Buddhahood.[18] In Kūkai's
view, the former are taught by the *Nirmānakāya*, the historical Buddha, and
are intrinsically tied up with *upāya*. The latter, by contrast, are preached by
the *Dharmakāya*, and they are not dependent upon *upāya*, since they are the
Reality itself. They are Enlightenment as such, or the Buddha-nature: "The
doctrine revealed by the Nirmanākāya Buddha (Shakyamuni Buddha) is called
Exoteric; it is apparent, simplified, and adapted to the needs of the time and
to the capacity of the listeners. The doctrine expounded by the Dharmakāya
Buddha (Mahāvairocana) is called Esoteric; it is secret and profound and
contains the final truth."[19] This teaching is also called esoteric because it is
concealed; it is hidden from phenomenal sight, being the inner nature of the
Buddha, the *Dharmakāya*. For Kūkai, however, the term *esoteric* can also be
understood relatively. In this sense, it pertains to various degrees of teaching,
as well as various modes of apprehension. A particular teaching is esoteric in
relation to another, but not necessarily in an absolute and definitive fashion.
Therefore esoteric teaching has an objective and a subjective ground, it is either
a matter of ontological reality or one of human understanding, or both. In the

second sense, esoterism does not exclude *upāya,* quite the contrary, whereas in the first sense it does exclude it, since it is final.

There lies also the meaning of the classical distinction and complementarity, often depicted in Buddhist iconography, between *upāya* and *prajña,* the latter term being often rendered as wisdom. *Prajña,* which is the supreme perfection, or *pāramitā,* in Mahāyāna Buddhism, refers to the end toward which *upāya* is a means. *Prajñapāramitā* cannot be equated in any way with any limitations pertaining to phenomena as such, and therefore to *upāya* inasmuch as *upāya* entails phenomenal reality. In fact, it cannot even be identified with Buddhas, since the latter are only instances of Enlightenment, which are intrinsically connected to *upāya,* if one may say so, to the extent at least that they exercise a function of Awakening.

Now, the question of the relationship between *upāya* and *prajña* is one that deserves further consideration considering its centrality in the symbolic universe of Buddhism. In this respect, sexual symbolism is paramount, as amply demonstrated by Buddhist iconography, particularly in Tantric schools. The union of *upāya* and *prajña* is in fact presented as the perfection of Buddhism. From the particular point of view of sexual symbolism, *upāya* is considered masculine, and *prajña* is depicted as feminine. By contrast with the world of Hindu Śaivism in which the masculine principle is static and the feminine dynamic, it is here the reverse which is true, with the feminine being static, whether as "acquired" content or "reached" goal, while the masculine is dynamic, inasmuch as it refers to the path as spiritual technique. This distinction is all the more interesting, and prima facie surprising, in that *upāya* is clearly connected to compassion, conventionally attributed to the feminine, and *prajña* to wisdom, which is often associated with the masculine side of the polarity. As for the masculine aspect of *upāya,* it has been suggested by scholars such as Masao Ichishima that it is connected *ab initio* to the teaching and missionary aspects of *upāya,* which are, historically and formally at least, a masculine prerogative.[20] It is attested that in early monastic rules, nuns were not allowed to teach men. Among the *garudhammas,* or precepts established by the Buddha in response to Ānanda's request that women may be accepted as *bikkhuni,* we find several that are relative to the dependence of nuns on male *bikkhus* with respect to teaching the *Dharma.*[21] In this regard, it is the intrinsically formal aspect of method that must be considered paramount. It is this character that defines Buddhism as a way. By contrast, *prajña* is a universal mode of consciousness that is not only the goal of the tradition but also its source, and as such the "mother of all Buddhas": "The Saviours of the world who were in the past, and also those that are now in the ten directions, have issued from her, and so will the future ones be. She is the one who reveals reality, she is the genitrix, the mother of all victorious ones."[22] As the essence of reality that reveals the latter for what it is, she is, significantly, considered as the "teacher of teach-ers." As such, she is obviously the source of all *upāyas* even though she herself transcends all *upāyas* as an eternal matrix of all Buddhas.

If we initiate a comparative reflection on the contrast between Śaivism and Mahāyāna Buddhism in terms of sexual symbolism we can understand how the respective functions of the masculine and the feminine find themselves reversed, so to speak, from one tradition to the other. This provides us with further avenues of understanding the specificity of *upāya*. While Śiva is the principle of Śakti, or the masculine, the principle of the feminine in the divine realm is Prajñapāramitā who is the mother of Buddhas and the source of *upāyas*, therefore reversing the order of the relationship between the feminine and the masculine. Now, Śakti is the feminine in its energetic, productive aspect, and as such the principle of dynamic exteriorization of the entire universe. It is also true, however, that this dynamic dimension is, or can be, the means of realization of Śiva, that is, one of reabsorption into His pure Reality. Śakti is spouse or *paredra,* and not mother: she manifests rather than originates. What dominates here is a symbolism of the union of two into one. Although Prajñapāramitā is also productive in a sense, she is not so in an extrinsic, cre-ative, way, but rather in an illuminating manner. This is why she is identified with Reality as such, and not with its productions, as Śakti is. It also bears mentioning that Prajñapāramitā is, for that reason, not "multiplicable," even though she is the spiritual essence of all Buddhas, whereas, by contrast, Śakti is multiplied, as it were, into innumerable śaktic centers, as she manifests on different degrees of reality.

Going back to the symbolism of the union of *upāya* and *prajñā,* we can see clearly that it points to both distinction and union, or to the mystery of two being one. Both notions imply wisdom and compassion, but each of them does so with a different emphasis. It could be proposed that *upāya* is wise compassion while *prajñā* is compassionate wisdom. Some sort of recipro-cal correlation and participation has to be present, since the "substance" of reality is one. Although it has been sometimes argued that *upāya* is simply, in the Tantric understanding of the relationship between the two, a "masculine" manipulation of the "feminine" unfolding of Reality, or *prajñā,* this does not take into account, or belittle, the existential connection between the former and compassion.[23] While there is undoubtedly a central technical dimension to *upāya,* there is also therein a deeper allusion to the Buddhist apprehension of reality. What the notion of *upāya* teaches us on one level is that every means of spiritual realization is relative and, in that sense, provisional. John Schro-eder has argued this point quite convincingly by emphasizing, for example, that Nāgārjuna's teaching of emptiness is not so much a metaphysical teach-ing—although it is one on some level—as a metapractical affirmation of the relativity of all practical means. Hence, the notion of "emptiness of emptiness" points to the relativity of the doctrine of emptiness itself as a support of practical realization.

Schroeder argues that the problem with a number of interpretations of Nāgārjuna is that they assert "not simply that Nāgārjuna does metaphysics, but that he thinks metaphysical reflection is necessary for enlightenment."[24] This assessment has the merit of highlighting the general principle that there is no broader religious and soteriological system that makes—or in a sense can make—"metaphysical reflection" a prerequisite for attaining its goals. It also points to the more specific principle that Buddhism is particularly intent on highlighting the relativity of metaphysical principles and, perhaps to a lesser extent, considering the universal authority of the Four Noble Truths and Eightfold Path, of the contingency of principles in general. However, one may like to qualify the previous points by suggesting that the very notion of *upāya* may be deemed to presuppose at least an implicit metaphysics. In other words, even though metaphysics as a discipline of meditation may not be inherent to Buddhist paths in general, as clearly illustrated by the existence of devotional forms of Buddhism such as *Jōdo Shin* and as implied by the very diversity of *upāyas,* metaphysics lies at the very core of the understanding of *upāya* since it involves the theoretical or actual recognition of a possible distinction between "conventional truth" (*samvrti-satya*) and "ultimate truth" (*paramārtha-satya).* The conventional truth that we experience on a daily basis, as we take objects of perception and various interactions as "real," does not do justice to reality in an ultimate sense, since the latter is either "emptiness" or "Buddha-nature," at any rate a mode of being and consciousness that profoundly differs from the ordinary one precisely because it is adequate to the *metaphysical* status of reality as it is. Inherent to the notion of *upāya* is the sense of a gap between an unsatisfactory and provisional way of being and knowing and another one that is both fully satisfactory and nontransient. *Upāya* is like the methodical evidence of a metaphysics that may not have to be made explicit conceptually, but which underlies any dimension of the Buddhist soteriological system.

The principle according to which *upāya* is an adequate means of spiritual access that is still both limited and provisional points to the very reality of an unutterable metaphysical "content"—the one that conceptual *upāyas* allude to, and which other types of *upāya* convey in various modes and ways, as a myriad of diverse sounds presuppose silence. Moreover, it must be noted that, in the Buddhist understanding of reality, anything whatsoever can be, in principle, considered to be an *upāya.* This is so inasmuch as "form is emptiness," meaning thereby that all forms are devoid of self-being, and therefore ultimately not different from emptiness. We will see farther on that this does not amount, however, to an obliteration of pedagogically qualitative differences among phenomena. Notwithstanding, it could be asserted that the ultimate realization is one in which the upāyic potential of all concepts, forms, and actions is brought into full awareness. This is in keeping with the very universality of compassion, since to deny the upāyic dimension of any phenomena would amount to denying, in a sense, the possibility of the salvation of "all sentient beings." Hence, Nāgārjuna's symbolic characterization of the ideal bodhisattvic mode of consciousness as that of an archer shooting arrow upon arrow so as to prevent any of them from falling back and being fixated, as it were, onto a particular static "reach" of the target, or achievement of the goal. Thus, the *upāyas* are in a way akin to the arrows of the bodhisattvic archer. Each of them is fundamentally effective in "reaching" the sky while being no less fundamentally unable to "hit" it, and even less so, obviously, capable of encompassing its infinity.

It must be observed that the distinction between the conventional truth and the ultimate truth is by definition not ultimate, and therefore also conventional itself. It cannot be ultimate since, quite evidently, only the ultimate truth can be ultimate, and since ultimate truth admits of no essential distinction by virtue of being none other than the doctrine of universal emptiness. Inasmuch as it is fundamentally tied up with the distinction between the two kinds of truth, *upāya* is therefore non-ultimate, albeit functionally necessary within the economy of Buddhist teaching. Even though it has no reality in itself, it is needed as a point of access to reality, or a point of entry into it. It could be asserted, somewhat paradoxically, that *upāya* is ultimate reality within conventional reality, and conventional reality within ultimate reality. Thus, *upāya* responds to the overall definition of religion when considering the absoluteness of the functional imperative of the latter within the relative field, but also the relativity of its ontological status in relation to the Absolute. In other words, religion makes absolute claims while being, in its own terms, fundamentally relative. Buddhism tends to emphasize the second aspect by contrast with other religions, particularly in a monotheistic context, that may be deemed to stress the first.

It is a common understanding that Islam is centered on faith, by contrast with Buddhism, which focuses a priori on rational reflection and existential experience. Hence, the Islamic emphasis cannot possibly be on human teaching—such as may be deemed to be the case with the Buddha's *Dharma*—but rather on Divine Revelation, such as is clearly established by the primacy of the *Qur'ān* as the source of virtually all knowledge. Two problems can be raised, and have been raised, in this respect. One has to do with the unknowability of the Divine Essence in Islam, and the other with the recognition of the legitimacy, and even positive value, of human difference (*ikhtilāf*) when it comes to faith. Both matters are clearly related to the *Qur'ān*, since the latter does provide some elements of knowledge of the Divine on the one hand, while being *one* and invariable in its form and immediate content, on the other hand. What are we to do, therefore, of the principle of unknowability and that of a recognized, if not always legitimized, diversity of paths?

Qur'ānically, the question of God's unknowability is twofold. The Islamic revelation provides the means of understanding *Allāh* through the Divine Names—the epistemological and ontological status of which has been debated in classical Islam—but it also affirms unambiguously the ultimate transcendence of the One beyond any human ken. The Islamic consciousness is therefore situated, as it were, between a pole of accessibility, one that is related to the concept of *shahādah*, which implies both testimony and manifestation, and a pole of inaccessibility, one that is encapsulated in the concept of *ghayb*, or Divine Mystery. An analogous polarity is to be found in the *Qur'ān* with respect to the question of the diversity of human ways to God. As a divine means of reaffirmation, and indeed restoration, of the pristine doctrine of the Unity of God and the incorruptible doctrine of unification—or *tawhid*—the *Qur'ān* emphatically rejects everything that may, or indeed does, adulterate the truth. In fact, the very legitimacy and eschatological need of the religion brought by the Prophet lies in its being a reminder of that which humans have not only forgotten but also distorted. Many of the most polemical passages in the *Qur'ān* refer to such distortions, whereby difference appears in the garb of sectarian betrayals of the truth. The most obvious aspect of multiplicity, particularly on a human level, relates to its breaking down the original unity of the creed, and that of the community. However, difference is not only a curse, it is also a blessing, depending on the nature of the difference, but also depending on the context in which it manifests. Besides the obviously positive meaning of creatures as manifestations of the Divine Wealth of Being and the diversity of the Divine Names, difference can also be considered positively with regard to human representations as well as human endeavors. When considering the issue of the diversity of humankind, including beliefs and actions, the *Qur'ān* is not exclusively negative, but it not uncommonly recognizes the positiveness of a higher purpose, one that is indeed providential, directly connected to the human "striving toward the good." Moreover, the *Qur'ān* repeatedly acknowledges the diversity of capacities among humans. Capacity is to be taken here in the literal sense of a "measure" (*wus'a*) allotted to each soul at creation, and beyond the limits of which it will not be tested (2:286).

There is, therefore, a kind of merciful proportion between God's messages—whether collective and revelatory or individual and pertaining to one's particular destiny, and the very "form" of the human receptacles of these messages. Considering negatively, or privatively, the "portion" of knowledge alloted to each soul falls short of the Divine Reality, and can, therefore, give rise to what Islam calls *shirk,* or a confusion between God and finite objects of worship. By placing the Divine Essence out of reach, so to speak, of human knowledge, Islam forcefully asserts the limitations of mankind and, moreover, makes the latter utterly dependent upon Divine *wahy* or *tanzīl* to access any kind of knowledge of God. Positively, however, human limitations make it necessary for the Divine Reality to disclose Itself in ways that are apprehensible by human recipients. It is in this regard that Islam teaches the principle of the universality of prophecy. In other words, there is no nation that has not received its own prophet, and the Arab prophet, the Prophet Muhammad, did in fact provide the last one in a long series of divine dispensations.

Now, the exoteric understanding of what precedes results, in the general climate of Islam, in two dominant tendencies. The first lies in an emphasis on divine transcendence, the second, correlatively, consisting in a reduction of man's abilities to recognize the truth and obey its demands. The first aspect is quite apparent in the exclusion of visual living representations of the Divine from Islamic iconography. Islamic iconoclasm is a way to affirm the "absolute" transcendence, as it were, of the Divine. The distrust of images is, in this respect, cardinal, and we will see how this rejection of "imagination" when it comes to religious representations reveals some far-reaching paradoxes when approached by some Sufis. The second aspect tends to deny the possibility of any knowledge of God from a human point of view. The obvious qualifications of the latter point pertain to the *Qur'ān* on the one hand, and to the notion of *fitra,* or primordial norm, on the other hand. Now it is important to note that, from the point of view of the general religion, the *Qur'ān* allows Muslims to know or recognize some things about God rather than giving access to knowledge of God as such. In fact, that which is mostly to be known about God amounts, besides His existence, to that which He expects and demands from mankind. Exoterically speaking, knowledge is intrinsically connected with obedience. It could be said, actually, that knowledge means obedience, and obedience means knowledge. This is so inasmuch as knowledge is identifiable with the recognition of the original covenant between God and man. To be human means being aware of God's original summons, *"alasta bi-rabbikum?"* ("Am I not your Lord [who cherishes and sustains you]?" [7:172]), and responding to it positively. Knowing means recognizing one's dependence on God's existentiating act, and therefore obeying this act existentially by conforming oneself to God's will.

It is well known that Sufism is, by and large, an interiorization, a deepening, and often an intensification, of the human response to the Divine Reality, and the will that flows from it. From the point of view of what has just been discussed, it could be said that Sufism has tended to move beyond a concern for knowledge about God to a more internal focus on the knowledge of God. In other words, Muslim contemplatives and mystics have been more interested in unveiling (*kashf*), or disclosure, of Reality, than in information or "report" (*khabar*) about It, to the extent of course that such a distinction makes sense beyond the evident overlap between these two kinds of knowledge. Knowledge, here, tends to move beyond mental representations to denote a more intimate connection with the Divine. The nature of this connection, or even union, has been a source of much debate among Sufi authors and practitioners as well as between *mutasawwifūn* and the doctors of the Law, and those who restrict their Islam to the latter's teaching, *ahl al-zāhir*. To put it in a nutshell, Sufis have been inclined to assert, through spiritual experience, that God may be much more disposed to unveil His nature to mankind than a mere external reading of Islam would concede. Correlatively, Sufis have been much more audaciously assertive than the rest of believers in their understanding of the potential of human knowledge. Moving beyond a merely rational and obedentialist perspective, they have often defended the prerogatives of transrational knowledge, which they most often refer to as being reached through internal organs of knowledge, such as the heart (*qalb*) or the spirit (*rūh*). This more encompassing view of knowledge has not translated, however—at least in their own understanding of it, if not always in that of their zāhirist censors—in any sense of human glorification with respect to matters of knowledge. In fact, the great Sufi spokesmen of the past have adamantly fostered the exclusiveness of Divine privileges when it comes to knowledge. The most eloquent evidence of this assertion lies in the very way in which the Sufi tradition has been referring to its own human perfection. Thus, the Sufi saint, or *walī*, is traditionally characterized as a *'ārif bi-Llāh*, which literally means a "knower by God." This implies that the only true knower is God, and that human spiritual knowledge is nothing else, in its depth, than Divine Self-Knowledge within and through the human agency. In fact, the Divine character of this type of knowledge is all the more affirmed that it pertains to a higher or deeper mode of "God-consciousness." This is most forcefully illustrated by the Sufi understanding of what Louis Massignon referred to as Al-Hallāj's "theopathic statement," the famously disconcerting assertion *"Anā al-Haqq"* ("I am the Truth") that cost the Baghdadī mystic his life.

One of the most significant—and often commented upon—early and paradigmatic Sufi statements about human knowledge of God is Junayd al-Baghdadī's "The content takes the color of the recipient." This formula has been meditated by *mutasawwifūn* through the centuries as a key to one's spiritual understanding of the relationship between the Divine and the human. In a sense, it contains in seeds Ibn al-'Arabī's whole doctrine of the "gods of belief" that we propose to analyze in what follows. The concept of "god of belief," which could be, from a slightly different point of view, characterized as "god of imagination," lies at a central nexus in Ibn al-'Arabī's gnosis. The term has sometimes been rendered as "the God created in dogmas" (*al-Haqq al-makhlūq fi'l-i'tiqādāt*), or "the deity conditioned by dogma" (*al-ilāh al-mu'taqad*).[25] This concept allows Ibn al-'Arabī to account for both the limitations of human knowledge and the unlimited horizon of God-given human gnosis without compromising the transcendence of God's Self-knowledge. Even though this principle obviously holds an epistemological dimension—as indicated by the very terms of belief and dogma—it is actually grounded in ontology. The English *belief* does not translate, here, the Arabic *imān*, which is a universal concept of recognition of the reality of God, His prophets, His angels, the thereafter, and predestination, but it renders the word *i'tiqād*, which is literally akin to the verb *to knot* (*'aqada*) and is derived from the same root as *'aqīdah*, which refers to the dogmatic tenets of the faith. The term is in itself quite suggestive of the implications of the "gods of belief" and "dogmas" since it conveys both fixity and limitation, the first term connoting the positive dimension of belief, and the second its negative one. As we will see, the concept of "god of belief" is connected to that of "imagination," and would have no meaning without it. Ibn al-'Arabī's words for "imagination" are *mithāl* and *khayāl*. While Sufi authors make wide use of another term, *wahm*, usually to refer to the delusive power of human representation, *mithāl* and *khayāl* do not normally entail a pejorative connotation. In fact, the plural *amthāl* is used repeatedly in the *Qur'ān*—and generally translated as "parables" or "similitudes"—to describe the ways in which the Qur'ānic God teaches humans through analogies, as does Jesus in the Gospel. In a sense, whereas *i'tiqād* refers more specifically to the human realm of knowledge, *mithāl* ranges over a broader ontological field that actually encompasses, in its widest acceptation, the whole of universal reality besides God, or the entire domain of other-than-God. Only God is, strictly speaking, beyond imagination.

As already intimated above, the concept of "god of belief" lies at the very nexus of metaphysics and epistemology. It presupposes, as a foundation, an understanding of God as the unconditioned and unlimited Reality. This reality, considered as a transcendent—and therefore inaccessible—Object of human knowledge is mediated through representations that are referred to as *i'tiqād*, and these knots are themselves part of the world of *mithāl*. The empirical subjects of these representations are none other than human beings or other God-conscious beings. Experientially, or epistemologically, therefore, the "gods of belief" are to be equated with the limited representations of the Unlimited, Unrepresentable, Divine Essence. Since the very Essence of God lies beyond any possible human representations, it follows that the latter are but Its relative delimitations. The practical outcome of this limitation is manifested by the human denial of God in forms other than those that conform to one's "god of belief." Ibn al-'Arabī notes, in this respect, that most men "have . . . an individual concept (belief) of their Lord, which they ascribe to Him and in which they seek Him. . . . So long as the Reality is presented to them according to it they recognize Him and affirm Him, whereas if presented in any other form, they deny Him, flee from Him and treat Him improperly, while at the same time imagining that they are acting toward Him fittingly."[26] From this point of view, the particular "god of belief" is nothing other than what we would call a "mental construct."

Such mental constructs are veils on the nature of Reality. They constitute what some Sufis would consider to be the very foundations of inner *shirk,* that is, the substitution of an "idol" to God. Obviously, the idol that is referred to here is not an external object of worship, but rather an inner form identified by the subject with the God Himself. Given its inherent limitations, this form is exclusive of other ones. It might be necessary to specify, here, that the notion of "form" (in Arabic *sūra*) embraces a very wide range of realities, whether conceptual or "imaginative" and "affective." In its most elementary sense, form entails an external recognizability, as it were, that is connected to certain features and delineations. Typically, form would be contrasted, therefore, with "meaning," essence, or "content." These latter terms all point, in different ways, to something that cannot be reduced to that which crystallizes or articulates it. The higher the realities under consideration the more will their formal clothing, so to speak, be inadequate to convey their being. This is the truest, evidently, in the case of God, whose incomparability defies any possibly adequate formalization. The paradox, however, is that God is the Reality that gives way to the widest kinds of forms, these forms being endowed by believers with a subjective absoluteness that lends them a most determining status in their lives. This is why believers "deny" and "flee from" the forms of the Divine that they do not recognize as their own, both in this world, and in the next. There are, therefore, two reasons for this rejection, one objective and one subjective. The objective reason is that one form excludes another. By definition, the concept of form involves the sense of a "contour" or that of "boundaries" that define a given representation and thereby distinguish it from others. Such objective exclusiveness of forms would not necessarily entail the rejection of other forms, though, if it were not intrinsically connected to a subjective identification with form. It is this identification with form, on one level or another, that necessarily, inherently, leads believers to exclusivism. This explains why the rejection of other "gods of belief" stems from a powerful conviction concerning the truth of one's own. There is, therefore, a subjective confusion between the limited and the Unlimited, between the representation and the Reality. By virtue of being a worshipper, a human being is an idolater.

This seemingly contradictory statement implies the paradox that it is both necessary and impossible to worship God. In a sense, every belief is a belief

in God. In that sense, it is not possible not to worship God. Ibn al-'Arabī
derives this principle, at least scripturally, from verse 17:23 of the *Qur'ān*, which
states: "Thy Lord hath decreed that ye worship none but Him." Now it is, of
course, important to note that the "decree" (*amr*) or Divine Will to which Ibn
al-'Arabī is referring here is not to be taken in the usual sense of the term.
William Chittick has very clearly articulated the Akbari distinction between
what he translates as "engendering command" and "prescriptive command."[27]

Most readings of the aforementioned verse refer to the latter. Exoterically,
the verse obviously refers to God's Qur'ānic command that humans worship
Him at the exclusion of other divinities or realities. This is the prescriptive
command that derives from God's law, or from that dimension of Divine Will
that legislates human behavior within the context of earthly existence. But it
appears quite obviously that this Divine Will presupposes an antecedent Will
that actualizes earthly existence, without which the prescriptive Will would
have no purpose. This is analogous to a situation that would see the same
person be the builder and the maintainer of a house. The will involved in the
maintenance is not the same as that which is at work in building. While we
are speaking of the same person, we are considering two levels of this person's
will and action, the second one being posterior and *intrinsically* dependent
upon the first. Now the latter is the creative—*takwīnī*—command, or what
Chittick refers to as "engendering command" by contrast with the "prescriptive
command"—*taklīfī*. The Arabic term *takwīn* flows from the root of the verb
*to be,* and refers most directly to the Qur'ānic teaching according to which
when God wants to existentiate a creature He says "be!" (*Kun!*) and "it is"
(*fa-yakūn*). This amounts to saying that we must consider three levels of the
Divine Will, the last two only pertaining to the realm of "command." God is
first of all Essence and pure, unlimited, Being (*wujūd*), and in that sense, His
Will is none other than His Nature. On this level, Will does not entail any
exteriorizing or existentiating desire, but merely the inexhaustible Possibility
that "contains" the "stable essences" (*al a'yān al-thābita*) of creatures, that is
what creatures "are" in nonexistence, or "in God," before they are sent into
existence by the "creative command." Now, it is on this level of the Divine
Will, if one may put it so, that Ibn al-'Arabī's esoteric exegesis of 17:23 makes
sense. By virtue of the "existentiating command," all creatures are "made to
worship" God in the very form of their existence and, therefore, degree and
mode of consciousness. This fully conforms to Qur'ānic verses in which creatures such as animals—birds, for example—are said to be totally surrendered
to God's Will. This is, it could be said, the degree of universal Islam, in which
the whole of creation is, as it were, suspended to the Divine Reality, Will,
and Act. We could refer to this mode of being as "ontological" Islam, one in
which it is impossible not to worship God, and therefore in which all modes

of being and consciousness are "worship." One consequence of this universal metaphysical statement is that there is no "wrong" *takwīnī* worship, although there are obviously wrong modes of *taklīfī* worship.

Everything that is is *eo ipso* worshipping God. This principle is directly connected to the general teaching of the *wahdat al-wujūd*, or Unity of Being, since it amounts to a recognition that the worshipper and the Worshipped are one on the level of the Divine Essence insofar as the latter contains the eternal possibilities of all creatures, but also inasmuch as the possibilities and their manifestations are essentially no different. Multiplicity is but the existentiation of Unity as an intrinsic infinity of possibilities. It bears stressing, finally, that this is the point of view of similitude in the sense that possibilities, or *a'yān thābita,* are none other than *Wujūd. Wujūd* is their incommensurable common measure, if one may put it that way.

There is another sense, however, in which nothing is a belief in God, according to the perspective of incomparability. This is because, as we have intimated earlier on, the Essence cannot be an object of belief, inasmuch as it infinitely transcends any possible forms of relative cognition and imagination. Does it mean, therefore, that there is no possibility of knowing God "beyond beliefs" in Ibn al-'Arabī's epistemology? Quite the contrary, there is indeed a way to do so, but this way is a "way of no-way" that defies the epistemological categories of discursive knowledge as it challenges those of ordinary religious belief: it is the "station of no-station" (*maqām lā-maqām*). In the Sufi tradition, *maqāmāt* or stations have come to be known as stable modes of realization of virtues, or modes of knowledge of Divine Qualities through them, which result from exertion on the spiritual path. The two main characters of stations are their stability, or their permanent "acquirability," and the fact that they are thought to "result" from human efforts. This is by contrast with *ahwāl,* or states, that are traditionally considered to be bestowed purely by grace, as well as being temporary. Thus, the station is strongly connected to fixity and individual "realization." In Sufi spiritual criteriology, the reaching of "stations" is by and large equated with inner realization and progression as such, and gives rise to diverse, and sometimes complex, spiritual hierarchies. That which is, in a sense, the "privilege" of *maqāmāt,* is from Ibn al-'Arabī's point of view their very limitation. With an emphasis on individual effort and permanence appears the exclusiveness of the boundaries entailed by individuality and time. By contrast, Ibn al-'Arabī's spiritual perfection is characterized, if one may say so without contradicting its very being, by constant openness and fluidity with no sense of individual acquisition or "achievement." It is like a permanent contemplation of the unfolding of divine possibilities into existence.

Human spiritual perfection is therefore neither an achievement nor a fixed goal. It could be, rather, described as a state of perfect receptivity to the

theophanic manifestations of the Real. The human being who is characterized allusively as having reached the *maqām lā-maqām* is emphatically not a
"believer," at least not in the ordinary sense of the word. This person is not
restricted by any belief, in the sense of the Arabic *i'tiqād*. The term *i'tiqād*
refers to belief in the sense of opinion. It stems from the root ʿQD which
refers to "contract" in the sense of being bound, and is also akin to the word
*ʿaqīdah* which refers, in Islam, to the doctrine and creed of the religion, or
its binding dogmas. William Chittick has suggested the English translation
"knotting" to connote the binding limitation of belief. By contrast with this
"bound" condition, by not stopping at any particular "worship," the perfect
human being, the Universal Man, is literally unbinding himself constantly from
the limitation of his own representations.

One must observe, however, that it is only in and through the sequence
of time and the diversity of circumstances that the perfect human being is
unbound, since his or her opening to theophanies is necessarily delimited by
spatiotemporal determinations. In other words, that which is simultaneous
Infinity in God can only be reflected in the sequential extension of existence.
This is why the supreme perfection is described, from another angle, as a
surrender to what could be called "the theophanic instant," in the tradition
of the characterization of the Sufi as "son of the instant," *ibn al-waqt*. The
limitation of the human soul lies, in that sense, in its greatest nobility, which
is to be a reflection of Divine Unity in and through the unity of its essence. It
is because of this oneness that, according to Ibn al-ʿArabī, "it cannot embrace
two incoming thoughts at once."[28] That which is exclusive absoluteness in God
becomes an exclusive limitation in mankind. On the other hand, the soul is
characterized by Ibn al-ʿArabī as "not too narrow for anything at all, except
one thing."[29] This is an allusion to the fact that God taught all the Names to
Adam, which means that the human soul has the capacity of knowing everything
in existence. The exception to this universal knowledge is the Divine Essence,
which lies, as we have seen, beyond any delimitation, therefore any human
knowledge. But this capacity to know everything can be actualized only within
the strictures of human limitations, that is, within the confines of time and
space, and therefore in an "analytic way," as it were, meaning here not a mental
examination, but simply a sequential, discrete, witnessing of the various modes
in which the Divine manifests to human consciousness. Notwithstanding, this
is the way in which may happen what Ibn al-ʿArabī calls the human "share of
'nothing is like Him'" (42:11), that is, the paradoxical share of incomparability. But this share can only take place within the context of comparability
and analogy, since it entails a recognition of all the theophanies within the
context of human existence. Needless to say, this receptive perfection is rarely
actualized, and humans remain, in the immense majority of cases, "prisoners"

of the delimitations with which they identify. And it is exactly at this juncture that the relevance of religious messages becomes apparent.

In actuality, the "belief" is not only an individual reality; it refers to any kind of limited outlook or perception that conveys the Divine Reality in one way or another. This is true of creeds, collective myths, and representations, as well as philosophies and ideologies inasmuch as they entail a "definition" of the Real. This raises quite evidently the question of the adequateness and validity of the various "beliefs." To say that all "beliefs" are determinations of the Absolute Reality would seem to imply their truth, which would appear to ruin the very notion of truth by excluding the very possibility of error. There are, however, three cardinal aspects of the matter that need be introduced to strongly and decisively qualify this point. First, it is quite obvious that delimitations of the Divine Reality vary in scope and comprehensiveness, as well as adequateness to their Object. While all determinations are perfectly equal within the Real, or from the "point of view" of the Real, this is quite emphatically not the case from the point of view of existence, where multiplicity, and therefore differences and inequalities, prevails. In a formally foreign but metaphysically analogous context, Meister Eckhart teaches that there is, in the Divine Essence, no difference between an angel and a gnat, because their "images" in God are equal.[30] Does it mean that human beings should relate to an angel in the same way as they relate to a gnat? This is plainly not the case, since, on the plane of existence, qualitative and quantitative differences cannot be ignored, if it were even possible, without falling into the most destructive confusions. As Meister Eckhart puts it, one must distinguish the "unlike things" from the like "images of things." While the sages recognize Divine determinations and theophanies in all phenomena—and as such, reflections of "alike images" in God—this does not prevent them from discerning among creatures on the level of daily existence, and from making moral, existential, and aesthetic choices on the basis of this discernment.

Our second point is that, among these theophanic limitations that form existence, there is a particular kind that is directly manifested by God's prescriptive command. All phenomena whatsoever are theophanic to the extent that they necessarily proceed from the creative command, but only those phenomena that provide divinely inspired orientation and legislation to mankind directly and explicitly aim, within the universal range of existence, to lead human beings to a kind of life that allows for the realization of their normative being, and thereby approximate or attain human perfection. The approximation of this human entelechy involves happiness for Ibn al-'Arabī as it did for the Platonic and Aristotelian traditions. It is to be noted, however, that the spiritual perfection envisioned by Ibn al-'Arabī appears to entail a kind of transcendent step in relation to what precedes it. This means that human perfection could be interpreted, on the basis of Ibn al-'Arabī's principle, as involving a transcendence of all delimited forms, including religious ones. As far as the latter are concerned, this implies a potentially ambivalent role on their part in terms of their effects upon the soul. In other words, while revealed phenomena are divinely designed to free human beings from that which, in their individual "belief," prevents them from reaching an effectively adequate perception of the Real, thereby barring them from reaching perfection, they are also, as limited forms, principles of restriction and enclosure that may, and in a certain way must, keep most human beings from attaining that perfection. This is so because even the liberating delimitation of the revealed message cannot but become tied up with human delimitations that obstruct the full range of their liberating potential, or even deviate them, from their goal. Revealed limitations are therefore, strictly speaking, more adequately referred to as a lesser evil than as a lesser good. This is so because fixed delimitations can only be "evil" in relation to the Good that they bind and knot. This being said, the Divine guidance provided by revelation gives, in principle, access to an ontological realm that may free human beings from the very limitations that its messages entail. In fact, such a feature is that which differentiates sacred institutions from non-sacred ones. Let us think, for example, of the ways in which the normative or "ideal" Hindu caste system amounts to a formal hierarchy that provides, within its own fold, the ways and means to transcend its own strictures through reaching the status of a renunciate, or *sannyāsa*.

This human ability, although rarely actualized, to transcend the limitations of religious belief from within the very system of belief, is a direct reflection of the infinity of the Real, one that differentiates humans from other creatures. Among all creatures, only humans can transcend the limitations of their "beliefs." The role of religion, in various forms, is to actualize the highest human potential, the "station of no-station" that amounts to a human recognition, and in a sense realization, of the infinitude of the Divine. This capacity for self-transcendence opens onto the unlimitedness of Reality.

It is connected to the third, already implicitly indicated, aspect of human "belief," which is its susceptibility to being modified through time, learning, and experiences. By contrast with animals, plants, and other creatures, humans have an ability to enlarge or restrict their "beliefs." This datum of common experience is particularly significant in terms of "religious knots" since the same "knot" may result in a liberation from all knots, or, on the contrary, a total and exclusive identification with a knot. It must also be remembered that each individual "religious belief" results from a concretion of individual limitations and "mythological" limitations. There is, therefore, with respect to any "religious knotting" a potential for shrinking and one for expanding. In other words, even though the epistemological and soteriological goal of "religious concretions" is to make it possible for individual human beings to "enlarge" their belief and, ultimately, to transcend the "gods" of belief, the limitations of the individual may bring this belief down to a level of narrower delimitation and greater fixity. Through his concept of "god of belief," Ibn al-'Arabī gives us to understand how religion can be both liberating and alienating.

It must be added, however, that Ibn al-'Arabī's presentation of the "gods of belief" led him to emphasize, in a typically Islamic and in a more general sense "religious" manner, the need for the corrective message of revelation rather than the intrinsic possibility of its corruption and deviation. Like the representatives of virtually all traditional universes, Ibn al-'Arabī sees the greatest danger in the unaided individual subjectivity of mankind rather than in the individual adulteration of divine messages. This emphasis can most likely be accounted for in two ways. First, it is evident that the function of "religious knots" as providential means of attainment of happiness and approximation or realization of human perfection, outweighs the possibility of its privative and corrupted manifestations. To fail to see it would amount to the rejection of a masterpiece of art under the reason that it may be misunderstood or that the material of which it is made is corruptible. Secondly, and more circumstantially, it could be argued that Ibn al-'Arabī lived in a relatively homogeneous religious universe in which the protective and inspiring role of religious delimitations was sufficiently and positively determining to relegate its corruptions to marginal consideration.

Be that as it may, the relationship between individual knotting and God-sent religious knotting raises the important question of the relationship between self-knowledge and God-knowledge. For Ibn al-'Arabī meditating upon the oft-quoted *hadīth,* "He who knows himself knows his Lord," the implications of this statement are far-ranging and must be considered on different levels. In this respect, it appears that the relationship between knowledge of self and knowledge of God is envisaged by Ibn al-'Arabī on three epistemological degrees. The first is that of rational and discriminative knowledge, the second that of mystical unveiling, and the third that of the Divine Reality in and of itself.

The point of view of human existence is one in which two fundamental modes of knowledge are available to us. The first is based on mental distinctions, the second on inner God-given intuitions. From the point of view of existence, which is our point of view as human beings, the root, or source, of our knowledge of God is knowledge of self, and not the reverse. This means that we cannot, qua humans, reach a degree of knowledge of God that would be a sufficient foundation for the knowledge of self. Our limited consciousness as self must be, by contrast, the basis upon which our knowledge of God may arise. But this human self can be apprehended either mentally through a chain of distinctions, or through the heart, unitively and intuitively. The first means reveals the knowledge of the incapacity of the human mind for know-ing the self, the cosmos, and God. To know oneself as human means, in that sense, not only knowing one's incapacity to fathom the Divine Essence, but also one's ontological dependence on God as the principle of existentiation of the theophanic manifestations through which one may come to know Him. This is but the very first level of knowledge of self and knowledge of God, however, since it is purely apophatic. It is in that sense a kind of "negative knowledge" that prompts us to learn further, but only so to the extent that we perfect it. Socrates's paradigmatic statement, "All I know is that I do not know" epitomizes the perfection of this type of knowledge. As such, reason in its fullness and maturity is, in principle, the starting point of a never-ending voyage of self-discovery and God-discovery. What limits it is the fixity of the "gods of belief," which makes humans unable and unwilling, both in this world and in the next, to recognize divine manifestations for what they are. In other words, in most cases, human beings are unable to recognize the Real in forms other than their Lord's.

But whether they are able to do so or not, there is no way to achieve self-knowledge or God's knowledge in this manner. This is why the adequate mode of the consummate believer is, in this respect, "bewilderment." Hence, Ibn al-'Arabī's definition of eminent belief as follows: "The perfect human being is he whose bewilderment has intensified and his regret is continuous—he does not reach his goal because of that which is his Object of worship, for he strives to achieve that which cannot possibly be achieved and he threads the path of Him whose path is not known."[31] This is, so to speak, the negative side of the human perfection, whereby the limitations of the individual are keenly recognized, and the incapacity and limitations of the servant acutely experienced. It is also a path of successive stations. On this path, one may, of course, stop at one or another station, thereby missing the totality of the horizon of knowledge. So it is, most particularly, when the knowledge of one's non-knowledge is too weak or fades, and therefore leads one to identify with a particular station at the expense of the possibility of reaching other, higher ones. Such a possibility looms ahead of the ordinary believer because of the separative and analytic nature of reason. This dimension is, therefore, akin to the domain of the "gods of belief," which involves both possibilities of fixity and transformation depending upon the inner and outer determinations and free choices of the soul.

But there is also a more positive side of the matter, which Ibn al-'Arabī characterizes, paradoxically, as "more perfect than the perfect," in which the heart recognizes the Divine in all the beliefs that it encounters. Therein the heart is made capable of perceiving that all beliefs, including privations, devia-tions, and corruptions, amount to self-disclosures of the Divine Reality. Thus, from the point of view of unveiling, by contrast with mere reason, the human being who knows himself truly, the perfect human being—or rather more than perfect, knows himself synthetically as an "ocean without a shore." "Heaven and earth do not contain Me, but the heart of my faithful servant contains Me": it is only through contemplative unveiling that the infinite potential of the self is revealed, a self that reflects the infinite theophanic unfolding of divine Reality. But this holds true only for the perfect human being who has recognized the infinity of the self and God a priori and immediately as it were. Such recognition corresponds to the level of the transcendence of the "gods of belief," and is none other than the "station of no-station." The unending receptivity of the soul to the theophanies coincides with God's increase of the knowledge that He bestows upon man.

Thus, we can understand how Ibn al-'Arabī may refer to the knowledge of God, in the context of unveiling, as to the branch stemming from the root of self-knowledge; and this is so in an epistemological sense, but obviously not from an ontological point of view, since from the latter it is the opposite that is true, the human self being the "creaturely branch" of the Divine root. This is why the knowledge of God cannot be the root of the knowledge of self from the point of the view of the human self steeped in existence. It is the root of the knowledge of the self only in and through the knowledge that God has of Himself. From the point of view of existence, God knows Himself in the form of the cosmic theophanies, and the self knows itself and knows God as a result through the "increase in knowledge" brought about by these theophanies. But from the point of view of God, if one may say so, God knows Himself as Self and as Self of all selves. Such a knowledge of God as the root of knowledge of self is closed to the self qua human self inasmuch as the latter is constrained by the delimitations of existence. A knowledge of the self deriving from a knowledge of God is reserved to God's Self-knowledge, if one may put it this way, and this is so because it coincides with the pre-eternal knowledge of all possibilities or entities within the Real. While God does know Himself in and through the perfect human being, the latter cannot possibly know God in the way God knows Himself and all selves within Himself.

It could be said, therefore, that the statement "He who knows himself knows his Lord" suggests a path that may be characterized as analytic and asymptotic, from the point of view of discriminative reason, or synthetic and mystical, from the point of view of the heart before which God unveils His theophanies. In the second respect, it amounts to a human participation in the Imparticipable, it is an indefinite expansion that reflects within the limits of existence the Infinite Possibility of the Essence.

As for the statement "He who knows His Lord knows himself," it has no real meaning, according to Ibn al-'Arabī, from a human, existential, point of view. Such a knowledge can only be an essential knowledge of the selves and all other creatures within God's knowledge of Himself as Essence. It is not a human reality accessible from existence.

The gap between "God's knowledge through self" and "self-knowledge through God" parallels the distinction between the Lord and the Divine Essence. The knowledge of the self is necessarily connected to the knowledge of the Lord because the two are, in a way, the two sides of the same Reality. By contrast, the Essence is not relational, and cannot be apprehended, therefore, from the point of view of the human creature. This point is very directly expressed in the chapter of the *Bezels of Wisdom* devoted to the Word of Abraham: "The Essence, as being beyond all these relationships (between the Divine Reality, Names, and creatures), is not a divinity. Since all these relationships originate in our eternally unmanifested essences, it is we (in our eternal latency) who make Him a divinity by being that through which He knows Himself as Divine. Thus, He is not known (as 'God') until we are known."[32] The self and God are like the branches that stem from the root of the Essence. When Ibn al-'Arabī criticizes al-Ghazālī for asserting the possibility of knowing God a priori and independently from the cosmos and prior to the self, what he rejects is the idea that the human qua intrinsically relational to God could know the Real qua Real. Human knowledge as such can never begin with the Real as such, but only with this aspect of the Real with which a human being is in relation as his or her Lord. It also means that the Real, the Essence, cannot know Itself as Divine Lord without the self of the servant. But this does not mean that the Real cannot know Itself as Real, including within and through the human self. This latter Divine Self-knowledge has nothing to do with the "gods of belief," since the latter necessarily entail the principle of "otherness" that is imagination.

As we have seen, the world of imagination or *mithāl* is a world of correspondences and analogies that presupposes existential duality and multiplicity. By stating that the Essence is not a "divinity," Ibn al-'Arabī affirms that the Essence cannot possibly be a "god of belief." The Self-knowledge of God in His unfathomable mystery, *al-ghayb*, is not an Object of knowledge or belief, but it is none other than the infinity of modes of preparedness within the Essence. These are the eternal realities that have no existence, and therefore no "God." It is only when the Real as God lifts the veil of the unseen in projecting existence that the heart sees God in the form of its own belief, that is, according to its particular preparedness.[33] As Chittick puts it quite cogently: "Perception and existence are one. Subjectivity and objectivity are the two faces of the same reality."[34] The perceiving subject is but a created crystallization of the Divine command. Therefore, God "creates" Himself in the very act of being man's Creator. And he recreates Himself unceasingly in the various forms that correspond to the constant transformation of the human heart: "His making Himself known to them corresponds to His bestowal of existence upon them. The self-disclosure through knowledge is the same as the self-disclosure through existence."[35]

The permanent realities of things do not change, but the Self-unveiling of the Divine Reality occurs through constant changes, in the myriad of forms of existence. On this level, Ibn al-'Arabī refers to change as a reality that does not change from changing; its fixity lies in changing.[36] This paradox expresses the fact that *'ālam al-mithāl* always remains what it is, that is, imagination, therefore a moving stream of theophanic existents. Its being lies in its nonbeing, and there is no end to the becoming of this nonbeing because there is no end to Being as delimiting itself through nonbeing.

Even though the concept of "god of belief" has obviously an epistemological dimension, as clearly indicated by the very term *belief*, the context in which this concept arises is metaphysical. It pertains to a certain understanding of God as the unconditioned and unlimited Reality. It also relates to an understanding whereby the absolute or nondelimited God delimits Himself through self-manifestations or self-unveilings. This is the meaning of being *mutlaq*, or absoluteness as implying unboundedness, independence from everything else. Since this Reality, which is *the* Reality, is absolutely independent, it cannot be bound or limited by anything or anybody else, which means that any limitations can only be Its own. Śaivism makes a very similar point when it teaches that the infinite freedom of Śiva is the very cause of Śiva's binding Himself in and through relative beings. At the same time, however, the matter is also epistemological, since creatures, and among them human beings in a more diverse way, are defined by their capacity, or *wus'a*. From this point of view the "god of belief" is none other than the form in which the non-delimited Reality is apprehended within the boundaries of a particular receptacle.

As we have seen, the two sides of the equation coincide within the unity of subject and object, a unity that is essential in the Real itself, and existential in the cosmos: God is "consciousness-without-an-object" and the self is all that it knows. For Ibn al-'Arabī the "god of belief" is both contingent and necessary, a nonreality and a reality. It is necessary because *wujūd*, or being, is pure necessity, and there is, therefore, no consciousness without the perception of being: no human being, for example, can be without belief, in whatever mode or on whatever degree the latter may manifest. On the other hand, beliefs are purely contingent, and therefore also in a sense illusory, because the Real as such is "unbelievable," it is why it is said by Ibn al-'Arabī that the "gods of belief" are not-He, and are He. It bears stressing, however, that the "gods of belief" are more He than non-He, because being *is*, while nonbeing is not. This means that given that the "gods of belief" are perforce more or less limited, they "are not" by virtue of their limitations while they "are" by virtue of their being disclosures of the Real. But since the Real is more real than the limitations of the disclosures that delimit It, to the extent that this comparison has a meaning, it cannot but mean that the "gods of belief" are more real than unreal. This is in keeping with the general climate of Sufism, and the overall spiritual economy of Islam, in which the effective continuity between belief and Reality is stressed. In other words, Islam presupposes the adequacy of the beliefs in Divine Unity, and in a sense, of all beliefs inasmuch as they can be deemed to be beliefs adequate to Unity, because it is founded on the two notions of *fitra* and *wahy*—or *nubuwwah* and *risālah,* prophecy and message. *Fitra* is the reliably subjective source of belief, whereas revelation and prophecy are reliably objective sources of belief and faith, the second being the existential averment of the first. In that sense, the "god of imagination" can indeed be considered a manifestation of divine Mercy or *rahmah,* analogously to the way *upāya* is one of Buddhist compassion. This is true on at least three levels.

First, *rahmah* is the very reality of existence, since God "has prescribed Himself Mercy" and since, according to Ibn al-'Arabī and other Sufis, creation occurs through the "Breath of the Compassionate" (*nafas ar-rahmān*), therefore out of a pure expression of Mercy. Secondly, the "gods of belief," crystallized by the Divine knottings of prophecy, are manifestations of Divine Mercy within the very midst of the world of rigor. They are divine ways and means through which God saves human beings from individual knottings that would not lead them to bliss, and keep them prisoners from their limitations when they do not lead them into wandering. Thirdly, each and every "god of belief" is, directly or indirectly, a manifestation of mercy in the sense that it amounts to a Divine "condescension," if one may put it that way. This holds true on the part of God Himself, as well as on the part of God through the Prophet, and by extension through the prophets in general. First, God manifests Himself to the believer in the form in which the believer is predisposed to receive it. Then, the Prophet himself teaches, in a *hadith,* "*hadithu an-nās bi-mā ya'rifūn,*" or "teach people by means of what they know." If the Mercy of God embraces everything and manifests itself everywhere, even in hell, according to Ibn al-'Arabī, it means that all *tajalliyyāt* are as many modes of manifestation of Mercy. God condescends to make Himself known within the confines of the reality to which and in which He reveals Himself. Even though there is undoubtedly an instrumental dimension to these revelations and teachings, it can hardly be said that they are "expedient formulations" in the way of Buddhist *upāyas.* This is so because, it bears stressing it again, they are delimitations of Reality itself. It is not for nothing that the relativity of beliefs, and their contingency, is not recognized, less so emphasized, in Islam, nor even in Sufism, outside of small esoteric circles and subtle metaphysical teachings such as Ibn al-'Arabī's. By contrast, the notion of *upāya* lies in a much more central position in the economy of Buddhism as a whole. This is no doubt because the matter is couched herein in terms of the realization of a mode of consciousness in consonance with "things as they are" rather than in those of a definition of, and relationship with, the Supreme Reality.

Both the Akbari concept of "god of belief" and the Buddhist notion of *upāya* imply a consideration of Truth as fixed and definitive, and one of Truth as mobile and fluid. They are both "absolutist" from a certain point of view, and "relativist" from another one. The relativity implied by these concepts lies quite plainly in the sense that they cannot be equated *tale quale* with the Absolute, or what may be considered as such.

The very question of the Absolute is indeed an easier matter in Islam than it is in Buddhism, since it has been argued, including by some Buddhists, that the Buddha's teachings do not contain a doctrine of the Absolute. In Islam, the Absolute is unambiguously the Divine Reality, which is "the One and Only; *Allāh*, the Eternal, Absolute; He begetteth not, nor is He begotten" (112: 1–3). On the side of Buddhism, the most often quoted scriptural basis for an affirmation of an Absolute beyond change and becoming, among many other instances, is the previously mentioned famous excerpt from the Buddha's predication in *Udāna*: "There is, monks, an unborn, unbecome, unmade, unfabricated. If there were not that unborn . . . there would not be the case that emancipation from the born, become, made, fabricated would be discerned."[37] It is noteworthy that this prime Buddhist reference to what could be referred to as the Absolute, that is, an unborn, unchanging, and eternally subsistent reality, is situated within the context of a *way* of escape from the changeable, the born, and the become. By and large, the Absolute is not apprehended in itself, or for itself, but relative to the possibility of freeing oneself from the consequences of clinging to what is *not* it. While it could be said that fixity appears at the forefront of Islam, and fluidity in its esoteric background, conversely, fluidity lies in the foreground of the Buddhist worldview, whereas fixity is at best approached only apophatically or obliquely.

In Islam, the "fluidity" of the Supreme Reality cannot be a central object of faith, since the cardinal concern of the tradition is to assert, in the clearest, most forceful, and most definitive way, the transcendence of the Reality that reduces every other possible object of worship, and metaphysically every other reality as such, into ashes. The Muslim first testimony of faith is true and effective everywhere and at all times. That which could be considered "fluid" about the Truth lies only in the modes of its manifestations. One of Ibn al-'Arabī's favorite Qur'ānic expressions is, "He is every day upon a task." His esoteric commentary of this statement alludes to the ever-changing flow of God's unveilings or self-disclosures, which the *Qur'ān* illustrates also, in a different way, by the notion of God's "new creation" (*khalq al-jadīd*), the Sufi interpretations of which tend to amount to an occasionalist view of creation's utter contingence, one that translates into a need for its ever-renewed recreation. Even though this radical view is in full spiritual consonance with the overall Islamic focus on the unmitigated All-Powerfulness of God, it must be admitted that its most metaphysically consistent conclusions are not easily compatible with the demands of an exoteric collective mentality, one that has need of more conventionally stable and "absolute" principles upon which to settle its self-preserving certainties.

In Buddhism, the emphasis on the insubstantiality of everything, including our concepts of the Ultimate, seems to "fluidify," as it were, the very reality of the Ultimate itself. The world of most Buddhist schools of thought is one in which impermanence must be grasped as a universal law that rubs on any sense of fixity, hence the "denial" of the very ontological "emblems" of the latter, namely, God and the Self.

Whether in Islam or in Buddhism, Truth as fixity is beyond determination, and beyond objectification, and its fixity is, in that sense, none other than the reverse side of its inner fluidity. The Divine Essence, not unlike *Nirvāna*, cannot be truly apprehended conceptually because it is, as proponents of the Hindu *Advaita* would put it, "non-qualified," or *nirguna*. This is the only dimension of Reality that cannot be put into a perspective, because it defies any sense of relative point of view, and therefore allows for no fluidity in its absolute Identity to Itself. But at the same time, this nonqualification of the Ultimate implies an internal infinitude that includes, as it were, principial difference into its Unity. Nondetermination means both fixity and fluidity, since it refers to an Identity that is not exclusive of anything without contradicting itself as infinite. Moreover, neither the Divine Essence of Sufism nor nirvānic consciousness can be objectified, treated like a mental object, by any human awareness. This is most fundamentally because both exclude any sense of the duality that is necessarily entailed by the relationship between a subject and an object.

By contrast, as soon as it is apprehended humanly, the Ultimate is determined and objectified. Both Ibn al-'Arabi's "god of belief" and the Buddhist *upāya* are grounded in formal determinations while functioning as an object *for* a given subject. The relativity of human conceptions and needs cannot but be taken into account in the spiritual economy of these traditions, and indeed all traditions. Islam is obviously much less inclined to draw conclusions from this objectification and this determination than are most Buddhist schools, even though it cannot but admit to it in theory. The Muslim consciousness could, and does sometimes, understand the familiar principle that "God knows best" as an invitation not to unduly reify and bind the nature of God to its own human limitations, but it generally prefers to remain content with drawing from this paradigmatic formula a sense of the limitations of human knowledge as such, on the one hand, and one of God's all-knowingness and incomprehensibility, on the other. This explains why it is only in its esoteric dimension that Islam does account for the principle of epistemological mobility. The "religion of love" sung by Ibn al-'Arabī is a most consistent outcome of a full recognition of both the infinitude of God's wealth of being and the perfect surrender demanded from the human heart. What is surrender to the will of God as expressed through the decree of destiny on the level of the will, and therefore legal obedience within the context of religious bonds, becomes receptivity to the cosmic messages of theophanic disclosures on the level of knowledge. This explains why the perspective of Ibn al-'Arabī is both legally exacting in terms of the prescriptive command and inwardly unbound in terms of the engendering command. In both cases, but in two very different ways, the matter is to recognize, and abide by, the Divine Presence.

The mobility of the Buddhist outlook does not stem, by contrast, from a consideration of the diversity of theophany, since Buddhist thought includes neither God nor essences. Here, mobility has a more negative, or preventative, connotation, which aims at parrying the possibility of any fixation on substances or essences as principles of deluded identification. Sufi mobility recognizes permanence in change and behind change, essence in form, and the One in and through the many. By contrast, Buddhist mobility does not stop at any form so as not to make it into an essence;[38] it does not pause at any sense of Unity for fear of freezing this unity into duality. The contingency of *upāyas* reflects, in its own way, this nonessentialist view of things, whereby the transitoriness and relativity of realities as means of spiritual access highlight the methodical eviction of any sense of permanent stability and overarching universality within *saṃsāra,* which would lead one to give up the prey for the shadow.

The contingency of *upāyas* and infinite multiplicity of "gods of belief" raises, moreover, the questions of knowing whether all relative phenomena may be enlisted potentially as *upāya,* and whether any representation may function as a "god of belief." Now, it must be recognized, first of all, that the notion of *upāya* appears to presuppose an intent, or more specifically a teaching intent. So the question amounts to determining to what extent every phenomenon can be situated in the light of such an intent, or more generally whether the nature of reality, that which is recognized and experienced in Awakening, bears within itself an intrinsic *intention* of Enlightenment. The first possibility keeps us within the domain of teaching and method, whereas the second reaches an ontological ground. By and large, these two levels of consideration may be deemed to characterize, contradistinctively, the technical outlook that is prevalent in Theravāda and the recognition of a universal Buddha Nature that has come to the fore in many sectors of Mahāyāna, particularly since the time when "Bodhidharma went East." This ontological intent is quite consistent with the view, not uncommonly expressed in some schools of Mahāyāna, that the whole of existence has been from all times in a state of Awakening.[39] If it is recognized that the "substance" of reality is Awakening, it must follow that this substance is both our true nature and the implicit or explicit message of the whole of reality. In this sense the universe is predisposed to be "instrumental-ized," or better, "actualized" as upāya. Indeed, it could even be said that the universe is intrinsically nirvāna and extrinsically upāya.

While the "gods of belief" are ultimately none other than human repre-sentations, they are quite evidently dependent upon phenomena, images, and concepts that are parts of universal existence. As we have seen, Ibn al-ʿArabī makes use of this concept to refer to representations of the Divine, as expressed in the diversity of religious faiths, creeds, and schools of thought. However, even representations that are not specifically religious may be considered as "gods of belief," insofar as they necessarily imply, avowedly or not, aware or unawares, a concept of Reality to which a given particular human subject subscribes. Since, for Ibn al-ʿArabī, the Divine Reality is wujūd or being, any reality on any level of being is a delimitation of Reality. Any mode of being and consciousness is, therefore, a manifestation of the Exterior, az-Zāhir. The denial of God proffered by the atheist is, as all other views of reality, a "god of belief." Human beings are "believing animals" in the sense that they can-not but refer to a "reality" in one way or another, and also relate to it with a degree of consideration and "worship." Worshipping amounts, in this context, to recognizing as real and "surrendering," on whatever level and in any way, to this reality. In this sense, existence is nothing else than a universe of "gods of belief," for everything is a crystallization or delimitation of wujūd, and therefore a mode of worship.

This universality of the "gods of belief" does not exclude, however, the recognition of degrees of reality and consciousness. In Ibn al-ʿArabī's view, some "knottings" of belief are more adequate, more integrated, and more encompassing than others. As we climb the ladder of being, the "views" of Reality grow wider and wider. The "view" of God enjoyed by angels is evidently much wider and deeper than that enjoyed by gnats. Also, we have seen that the "gods of belief" informed by the laws brought out by messengers are more effective in leading mankind to happiness. As we consider the Sufi stations or maqāmāt, we can also see how they range over a hierarchy of virtues and modes of participation in the Divine Qualities. It is only, paradoxically, on the level of the highest station, the "station of no-station," that any sense of superiority or subordina-tion loses its significance since this perspective is characterized not so much by the content of each maqām as by not letting oneself be limited by it. In a sense, the focus of the Perfect Man lies on the Undelimited or the Infinite rather than on the respective qualities of the delimitations. The perspective of the "station of no-station" reflects on the human plane the Infinitude of the Real that reduces finite differences to "nothing."

If we turn to the *upāya* we can see how any hierarchy among them would have to do either with the range of their respective possible human applications or their relative instrumental effectiveness. To speak of qualitative differences can have meaning, therefore, only in pragmatic terms, spiritually or methodically speaking. But given the intrinsically expedient nature of *upāyas,* an emphasis on their range and degrees is, from a spiritual point of view, quite meaningless. The spiritually practical perspective of the general economy of Buddhism has no immediate need of a hierarchization of means. To paraphrase a familiar Buddhist medical metaphor, the matter is not to provide a structured chart of remedies and therapies, but to administer the one that is appropriate for a particular illness.

Granted the very wide range, if not universality, of the notions of *upāya* and "god of belief," and the way in which they seem to accommodate an indefinite number of relative standpoints, one may be tempted to question whether these notions leave any possible room for error. What could be the meaning of error, if any, in contexts in which all possible apprehensions of reality seem to be justified, either ontologically or methodically? One important response to this concern lies with the implicit distinction between the representation, whether epistemological or soteriological, and the Reality that it points to. This distinction, which is either provisional, conventional, or simply and ultimately "naught," makes it possible to define the greatest possible "error" as that consisting in "confusing the moon with the finger pointing at it," to couch the matter in familiar Zen Buddhist symbols. If we approach, first of all, the relationship between the Real and the "gods of belief," we can see how the latter could be considered as "errors" in relation to the one and only Truth. But it could be claimed with as much consistency that the "gods of belief" are as many manifestations of the Truth. Thus, Ibn al-'Arabī's "gnostic" enjoys a perception of existence in which "the Reality is (always) known and not (ever) denied,"[40] thereby reducing "error" to naught. It is here that a consideration of perspectives, or "directions," is in order to suggest the contemplative richness and complexity of existence. For what can be labeled as "error" when considered from the point of view of the individual knotting, or rather from the point of view of the exclusive limitations that it claims for itself, cannot but appear as truth when pondered from the point of view of its existence as self-disclosure of the Divine Reality.

In addition to the aforementioned collapse of Reality and illusion, the second type of error would consist in affirming, by contrast, an essential

difference between the expedient or contingent existent and the Ultimate. It
is at this juncture, of course, that the term *essential* raises questions. It does
so in Islam because it seems to be reserved for the Divine Ipseity, as it does
in Buddhism inasmuch as it appears to be altogether excluded from the Buddha's *Weltanschauung*. So, what can we mean by essential unity, or essential
nondifference?

As we have seen, Ibn al-'Arabī's Sufi metaphysics emphasizes the exclusive
and inclusive Reality of the Divine Ultimate. Taking maximal metaphysical
stock of the Muslim testimony of faith, "no god but God," it affirms that "He
is the very essence of existing beings" and "Naught is except the Essence."[41]
"Error" would, therefore, amount to separating any existent from the Essence.
In this perspective, the "gods of belief" are none other than the Real Itself.
"Essence" refers to metaphysical ultimacy. It points to that Reality that is the
irreducible ground of everything, including Itself.

When considering *upāya*, analogously, it is apparent that there is no
"ultimate" difference between the expedient means as existents and the Awakening to which they point, or toward which they lead. From this vantage point,
introducing a difference would amount to introducing an essence, as conversely
introducing an essence would signify the reality of differences. Whether the
matter is expressed in terms of emptiness or in terms of Buddha-nature it is
apparent that the rejection of dualism is tantamount to a rejection of "essentialism" and vice-versa. "Essentialism" could be defined here, either affirmatively as
that which erects phenomena as independent substances, thereby ignoring their
emptiness, or negatively as that which detaches phenomena from the Buddha
Nature, thereby depriving them of their enlightening quality.

In conclusion, we would like to draw a few lessons from the two notions
that we have explored, in terms of both parallels and divergences. Our first
contention, and probably the most relevant one with respect to the contemporary religious predicament, is that both notions allow us to articulate the
Universal and the individual, the Absolute and the relative, the Ultimate and
the conventional, while avoiding both subjective relativism and formal absolutism, arguably the two pitfalls of contemporary religious consciousness. There
is much to learn, in our contemporary world, from the Buddhist idea of
"expedient means" in terms of the need for an inner hierarchization of means
and end. The notion of *upāya* entails alignment, commitment, and ultimate
contingency. There is something deeply satisfying, from the viewpoint of a
contemporary subject molded by various forms of individualist culture and
wary of institutional and collective truths, in the idea of a spiritual adjustment
between individual needs and ultimate ends. This alignment, or this "harmonic"
resonance between the human subject, the *upāya*, and the universal goal,
synergizes personal commitment and religious instrumentality. There is a sort

of "subjective objectivity" inherent to the *upāya,* one that calls on the subject with an objective power of persuasion and transformation that cannot easily be turned into an "idol," given the strong emphasis placed on its expediency. What Frithjof Schuon has called "the sense of the Absolute"[42] remains exclusively placed on that which cannot even be called absolute, without in the least altering its subjective effectiveness as spiritual means. There is, therefore, a sort of spiritual transparency of the tradition and the path, one that does not easily leave room for the dark powers of appropriation from the side of individual "certitudes" and "righteousness."

By contrast, it could be proposed that the "god of belief" is characterized by an "objective subjectivity." What is meant by this paradoxical expression is that the notion of "god" remains, in a monotheistic climate, the mark of an ideal of objective anchoring, whereas the term *belief* refers quite obviously to an inner, subjective, representation. The notion does not let go of the theologically compelling primacy of the Semitic notion of "God" while opening the way to its harmonic "gradation" in conformity to the diversity of souls. It therefore maximizes the monotheistic recognition of, and emphasis on, the irreducibly individual character of the human self as such.

While both notions show the ways of an individualizing modulation of the universal truth, it must be emphasized that the Buddhist concept is both mainstream and pedagogical, while the Sufi one is definitely marginal in the economy of the Islamic tradition. *Upāya* tends toward a certain relativization of religion as such, precisely to the extent that the religion is equated with a set of *upāyas,* or is understood itself as one. Buddhism is by and large, among all religions, the one that is best equipped to undo itself by its own means, offering thereby fewer opportunities to project its own shadow on its practitioners. By contrast, the Sufi notion of "god of belief" is definitely esoteric within the general economy of Islam. To the extent that it is both epistemological and ontological, the two being—as we have seen—the two faces of the same reality, it tends toward a much lesser relativization of religion in highlighting the hierarchy of beliefs and—most particularly—the role of prophecy. It also draws the limits of its "relativistic" bent from its being ontologically grounded in God Himself. On the other hand, by giving a maximal extent and import to the diversity of the "paths of the sons of Adam," the notion of the "gods of belief" may contribute to move the focus of the tradition from an exclusive consideration of the universal imperatives of the Law to an inclusion of the specific "capacity" of each soul. This principle is indeed Qur'ānic, as expressed in the oft-quoted verse according to which "God imposes on the soul only in proportion to its capacity" (*wus'a*) (2:286).

In summary, the *upāya* is a pedagogical reality, but it implies a particular metaphysics, if only in the sense that it highlights an understanding of Reality as non-conceptualizable and non-objectifiable. The "god of belief" is ontological but it implies a divine pedagogy, if one may put it this way, insofar at least as it entails a measurement of the Divine Reality to the capacity of the "ontological places" (*mazāhir*) in which It manifests itself. The difference that we have just highlighted leads us to note, in conclusion, that *upāyas* are more "unreal" than "real," in the sense that they are purely provisional, at least as long as one's emphasis is on their methodical reality, whereas the "gods of belief" are more "real" than "unreal" inasmuch as they are indeed the very delimitations of the Real. This means, in other words, that contrary to what one may have expected a priori, Buddhism lays more emphasis on "transcendence" while Islam stresses "immanence." By these two terms is meant, on the one hand, a Consciousness that lies beyond the appearance of phenomena, including cognitive ones, and on the other hand a Reality that discloses its Being and Qualities through the cosmos. It goes without saying, however, that this contrast should not be overstated, since the Sermon of the Flower *is* the Buddha Nature, while the "gods of belief" cannot but fall short of the fullness of Reality.

6

## Transmutation, the Sacred Word, and the Feminine

The transmutation of human consciousness is, in traditional paths, a function of the transformative power of the Divine over the terrestrial realm. As such, transmutation is the concomitant effect of a human orientation toward a full existential recognition of the Divine. Thus, transmutation can be conceived as an assimilation of the Infinite by the finite, the Absolute by the relative, the Eternal by the temporal. St. Gregory Nazianzen's definition of humankind as a deifiable animal (θεούμενον; *Epistulae*, 6.3) responds quite aptly to the meaning of transmutation as a passage from a lower, animal state of being to a higher, divine one through a paradoxically discontinuous continuum. Hence, transmutation as a path of return to the Divine responds to creative causation as manifestation from the Divine. Reintegrative transmutation is the reversal of the onto-cosmogonic process of transformation of the Infinite into the finite. Our main proposition in this chapter is that transmutation tends to be actuated, in spiritual traditions, through means that can be symbolically denoted as feminine and linguistic. We will develop this thesis by reference to two spiritual traditions that have specifically emphasized the theurgic and transmutational dimensions of language and femininity, namely, Sufism and Kashmiri Śaivism.

### The Transmutational Plenitude of the One Consciousness in Śaivism

One of the fundamental principles of Kashmiri Śaivism is that the vibration that lies at the core of Absolute Consciousness, Śiva-Consciousness, the first inward motion within the Divine, is none other than the feminine power of Śakti, the free and creative energy of the god. The term often used by Śaivites to refer to this power of self-awareness is *vimarśa*: a word that connotes both "touching" and "mind," hence a sort of reflexive contact. Here, Śiva and Śakti form a syzygy of the two supreme among the *tattvas*—the thirty-six "states of reality" or "states of being," while inherently entailing a sort of doubling of consciousness[1] akin to a swelling seed about to burst. Next, the process of unfolding of the Absolute Consciousness gives rise to the distinction between Subject and Object, a duality that either rests in equilibrium or breaks out in disequilibrium, thereby releasing manifestation. Thus, by contrast with the initial faint vibration of *vimarśa,* the emergence of a polarity between Śiva and Śakti is symbolically signified by the churning of the goddess by Śiva, which coincides with the god's contemplation of Śakti as Object.[2] This can be encapsulated as a passage from "duality in unity" to "duality from unity." The rupture of equilibrium that the latter triggers results in the emission, *visarga,* that sparks manifestation. However, the same energy presiding over emission also prompts withdrawal, or its reabsorption into pure Śiva-Consciousness.

If it is asked for the final cause of this cycle of distinction and polarization, emission and reabsorption, the answer would lie in the process itself inasmuch as it expresses the very life and bliss of Consciousness. The Play is justified by its beauty and the pleasure it provides, as well as by the creativeness of its Author. Abhinavagupta relates this intrinsic finality as follows:

> The power which resides in the Heart of consciousness is freedom itself. The purpose of its creative activity is the "group" (*kula*), the entire range of perceiving subject, perceived object, and process of perception.[3]

Not only is the purpose of creation the ternary of knower, known, and knowledge itself, but the delight derived from this "group" is as purposeful as liberation itself. In other words, it is impossible to sever *Śiva,* as absolute principle of creative freedom, from the "group," as well as from the "Lady of the group," *kaulini,* Śakti. It is impossible to disjoin liberation from enjoyment because true enjoyment is at its core liberation, and true liberation the essence of enjoyment. The Śaktic unfolding is not an illusory epiphenomenon to be dissipated, but it is actually inherent to the overwhelming plenitude of Śiva. This principle is beautifully expressed by the image of the *kimciducchūnatārūpa,* or slightly swollen seed, a symbol of the plenitude of Śiva as it is about to vibrate into a prelude to manifestation.[4] Hence, the bursting forth of Śakti is productive of the rhythmic or cyclical alternation of manifestation and reabsorption. As will become evident, therein lies the very principle of Tantric transmutation.

Kashmiri Śaivism recognizes a variety of methods of spiritual realization, which range from the most centered on human actions (*ānavopāya*) to the method of no-method (*anupāya*), which is purely divine grace, therefore more identifiable to recognition itself than to a path (*upāya*) per se.

In our context, however, the most relevant of methods lies in between these paths of exertion and grace, involving as it does the interiorizing impulse of the principle of production and reintegration, Śakti, that lies at the dynamic juncture, as it were, of the individual and the Universal, *śāmbhavopāya*. Here, the sharp, intense perception of emotional or physical shifts is used as a means of reabsorption into universal Consciousness, *samvid-samvitti*. For instance, the delight experienced in sexual union, or even the intensity of sensory memory, can be isolated, focused upon, and seized as a means of reabsorption into the bliss of *samvid-samvitti*, since "this delight is in reality that of one's own Self."[5] The throb of enjoyment is freed from its limitative context or causation, and recognized as identical with the bliss of *Śiva*. Similarly, the pleasure derived from music and songs gives rise to an expansion of consciousness that can give access to *samvid-samvitti*. Finally, the calming of the mind through a mere swinging of the body is also an experience of *śāktopāya*, or "way of Śakti." All of these means of recognition make use of the energy of the goddess to access the fullness of Consciousness by dispelling the ordinary states of consciousness.

Although the practice of the *mantra* pertains to *āṇavopāya*, or effort, rather than *śāktopāya* or higher *upāyas*, the *mantra* itself is none other than the pure Consciousness of Śiva. In Lyne Bansat-Boudon's words, "For (the) *yogin*, the *mantra* is not a simple formula for ritual usage, but represents ultimate reality itself."[6] Representing means here much more than providing a conceptual replica of reality, since it entails the making-present of the Divinity. As crystallization of pure Consciousness, the *mantra* epitomizes the twofold process of Śaktic projection and reabsorption. The *mantra* is a phonemic symbol of the various moments of I-Consciousness, as well as a means of access to it.

Among the Śaivite *mantras, AHAM* is the most universal and all-embracing. As a whole, it literally refers to "I" as the origin of all manifestation. Analytically, it is comprised of the three letters *A, Ha,* and *M. A* is the first letter of the Sanskrit alphabet, whereas *Ha* is the last: the two letters represent Śiva, or the first principle, and Śakti, or the energy of the total unfolding of manifestation down to the last letter. As for the final *M,* or *bindu,* it "stands at the threshold of both emission and absorption without being involved in either."[7] It is the void and fullness that follows the emission and precedes the absorption, a contented state of rest, but also a coiled power containing the undivided union of Śiva and Śakti. This point has been characterized as "a potential multiplying,"[8] the "place of adamantine intensity,"[9] and even "the very core of Reality."[10]

Most prominent as well in the Śaivite path is the Heart-*mantra, SAUH,* formed of the three phonemes *S, AU,* and *H.* Akin to one, the *S* evokes *sat,* or pure Being, which Śaivite texts equate to pure objectivity, or the "known object": "Just as girdles, earrings, and bracelets, by setting aside their differences, are seen to be gold, so likewise, the universe appears as pure Being when difference is set aside."[11] This is the Self as Being, the ultimate goal of nondualist *Vedānta* as deliverance through identification with the sole Reality, the Supreme Self, *Ātman*. For Śaivites, however, this nondual reality lacks the effervescent fullness of the self-diffusive infinity of Śiva. It is the ultimate Ground of Reality, the Self of all selves, but it does not convey the creative, interiorizing, and transmuting totality of Śiva's nature. This is the function of *AU* and *H*. According to Abhinavagupta, the Self without the three energies of Śakti—Will, Knowledge, and Action, or *icchā, jnana,* and *kriyā*—is about as powerful as a "flower in the sky." *AU* corresponds to this Shaktic, Triadic, energy, the internal power of the free unfolding of Śiva. This is what Abhinavagupta refers to as the "process of knowing," by contrast with the "known."

Finally, *H* corresponds to the "knowing subject." It is the outward emission *within* the Consciousness of Śiva: "This entirety is emitted by the god of gods into himself, the Supreme Lord, the ultimate reality to which has been given the name Śiva."[12] This *H* is comprised of two vertically aligned points, the first being inward and the second outward. These two hint at the universal alternation of emergence of the world with the occultation of Śiva, and Śiva's manifestation and reabsorption of the world.

In the odyssey of Consciousness encapsulated in the *SAUH mantra*, *S* is likened to the root, *AU* to the trident (a symbol of Śiva's triadic energy), and *H* to the emission, while the three letters are one in the nonduality of Śiva's Consciousness as expressed by the whole *mantra*. From a numerical point of view, one corresponds to absolute and Self-sufficient Being, three refers to the dynamic and triadic Self-knowledge, whereas two epitomizes manifestation in a dialectical relation to nonmanifestation.

By contrast with *Advaita Vedānta,* which refers to the Self as *Sat, Cit,* and *Ananda* (Being, Consciousness, and Bliss) without any direct reference to a reintegrative virtue of manifestation as such, the hallmark of Kashmiri Śaivism is to stress the potentially transmuting status of manifestation within Consciousness. While *Advaita* teaches that manifestation qua manifestation dissipates as appearance upon the rise of the Self, Tantric Śaivism emphasizes a reintegration of manifestation within Śiva when perceived and experienced as the unfolding of Śakti. Rather than negating the limited in order to realize the Unlimited, Kashmiri Śaivism perceives the limited *as* the Unlimited. In this perspective, metaphysics and cosmology amount to doctrinal accounts of the transformations of Śiva through Śakti, whereas the spiritual path is but a transmutation of the individual self and of phenomena through the reintegrating power of the selfsame Śakti.

This power is approached both in terms of feminine reality and linguistic or phonemic vibration, the two coinciding in *Parāvākśakti*, the Supreme Power of the Word. Furthermore, the term Śakti refers to a wide range of realities along the axis of onto-cosmic deployment. When referring to Śakti in the singular, we refer to the creative energy immanent to Śiva Himself. When the polarization between Śiva and Śakti comes into play, it becomes the seed of manifestation through the three supreme Śaktic powers of Will, Knowledge, and Action, the six levels of *Māyā's* concealment of Absolute Consciousness under *kancukas* or coverings, the twenty degrees of mental and sensory consciousness, and the five *bhūtas,* or gross elements.

The affirmation, unfolding, and limitation of Śiva through Śakti range, therefore, over thirty-six *tattvas,* or states of reality, from pure Śiva-Consciousness to matter, *prithivī.* All *tattvas,* with the exception of Paramaśiva, participate in Śakti, since they proceed from her energy. In another sense though, each level and aspect of reality constitutes a *śakti* of its own. In a third sense, each and every *śakti* is contained in the Supreme Śakti. Every phenomenon and experience is a *śakti* capable of functioning as a means of realization of Śiva-Consciousness by participation in Śakti.

This is true also, analogically, of Śakti as language, word, or speech. The Supreme *Parāvākśakti* is the eternal sound or word (*vāk*) that is immanent to everything. While *Parāvākśakti* contains within herself the totality of letters and sounds within the Sanskrit alphabet, these particular phonemic entities are themselves *śaktis,* they possess their own energy, and the manifold manifestation and combination of these energies can either be a source of delusion or liberation. The tradition teaches that whereas mental states derive from the nature of Śiva, sounds derive from the nature of Śakti.[13] Thus, the subjective side of manifestation is akin to the Supreme Consciousness of Śiva, whereas the objective side, consisting in vibrations and productions, is akin to Śakti. Ultimately the two are one in a state of nondifferentiation, and the end of phonemic and cosmic productions lies in the restoration of this state beyond separations and differences.

From the point of view of relative consciousness, recovering the nondual origin requires, however, that the impurities, or *malas,* identifiable to the sense of duality, the sense of separation, and the sense of incompleteness, be washed out. However, these impurities can also be defined more positively as modes of restricted knowledge said to be brought out by *mātrikā.*

On a phonemic level, *mātrikā* is the matrix of all letters of the Sanskrit alphabet. Beyond this most immediate function, *mātrikā* is the universal source of language, *Parāvākśakti,* and by ontological analogy, the mother of the entire universe, from whom manifestation originates. The word *mātrikā* has been translated by Jaideva Singh as "the little unknown mother."[14] The suffix *kā* means that the matrix is unknown: as the principle of all *śaktis* of letters and words, or as the mother of universal language, *mātrikā* may function as a principle of delusion and ignorance. The multiplicity of words and phonemes parallels the diversity of representations that lead humans to engage in a dizzying multiplicity of endeavors and activities, thereby covering and ignoring the simplicity and unity of Śiva-Consciousness. *Mātrikā* remains "unknown" inasmuch as the plurality of her śaktic productions prevents most human beings from recognizing their real nature as Self-Consciousness.

However, as *Parāvākśakti, mātrikā* is also a means of liberation. Language, in the highest sense of a network of representations that both divide and express the Real, is therefore identified with a feminine, matricial, and Śaktic reality. The ambiguity of *mātrikā* is exemplified by the conflicting functions of the *śaktis* over which it presides, such as the *ghorās* and the *mahāghorās,* the terrible deities that bring humankind down into blind alleys of worldly obsessions, and the *aghorās,* who lead them back to Absolute Consciousness. In the myriad of śaktic productions that constitutes the world, it is from "words" that impurities result in the form of identification with duality, separation, and a sense of incompleteness.

To the extent that language entails analytic complexity and semantic limitation, it fosters—and in fact, creates—a delusional sense of identity that betrays the integrity of pure Consciousness. A linguistic grid is substituted to reality, in such a way that each and every word constitutes a separate *śakti* functioning as an independent deity that strengthens the centrifugal motion of individualized consciousness. However, when known as rooted in Śiva-Consciousness, *mātrikā* becomes associated with the saving power of letters and words. Indeed, each and every spoken word is potentially a *mantra*. When illuminated from within by a perception of Absolute Consciousness, any discourse radiates as *mantra*. Words that vibrate from the center of consciousness become ipso facto endowed with transmutational power. The meaning attached to the word is, in that sense, less important that the quality of being that it derives from its source of uttering.

In a more strictly technical sense, however, the *mantra* can be defined as a unit of "protective awareness."[15] This means that the *mantra,* besides potentially proceeding from the center of consciousness, enjoys the spiritual and soteriological backing, as it were, of the tradition originated in Śiva-Consciousness. The *mantra* is not a verbal representation of the Supreme, it is the latter itself *as* manifested through phonemes. It, therefore, effects a transmutational centering and rooting of individual consciousness into its source. Flowing from this source, it is also the synthesis of all words and all beings to which words may refer, a synthetic utterance and knowledge of everything there is to utter and to know.[16] As such, it has the power to radiate through levels of reality and actualize śaktic powers that prolong its primordial vibration. Abhinavagupta compares this power to that of a waterwheel:

A waterwheel moves a series of machines connected to it and can set them into operation by the force of its unified impulse. In the same way, by the power of the one continuous act of awareness (*anusamdhāna*) which corresponds to the incessant arising of Mantra, the deities of all Mantras, at one with them, become automatically (*ayatnāt*) propitious.[17]

It is by this same virtue of moving the numerous *śaktis* in accord with its own central vibrating impulse that the *mantra* holds the power of bringing back all subjective and objective phenomena into nondual Consciousness. Given its power of exteriorization as language, the *mantra* is able to reabsorb the world of multiplicity into *samvid-samvitti*. Failing this unifying power of the *mantra*, and its preeminence over the manifold, peripheral tendencies of individualized consciousness, the latter falls under its own spell, so to speak, and exhausts itself into numerous discharges of energy without true Self-awareness. In *Pratyabhijñāhṛidayam* (*The Secret of Self-Recognition*), it is explained that the prisoners of *samsāra* are under the mesmerizing delusion of their own dilapidating powers, and their own dispersing words: "To be a *samsārin* means being deluded by one's own powers because of the ignorance of that [authorship of the fivefold act]."[18] The subjection to the round of existence results from one's inability to bring words to their single source of consciousness. The *mantra*, by contrast, is none other than the central ebb and flow of the Śaktic power of projection of the absolute consciousness of Śiva. To identify with it amounts to a participation in the very surge of the creativeness of the Divine. Thus, the *mantra* allows one to perceive realities in their universal context as manifestations of Consciousness. The *mantra* detaches phenomena from their dispersing fragmentations and nefarious *śaktis*, and merges them with the flow of Śiva-Consciousness.

We have just seen that the main function of the *mantra* is to establish an intimate connection with the source of Consciousness so as to perceive everything within the Light of Śiva. In addition to, or rather in conjunction with, the *mantra*, that is, the verbal utterance that crystallizes and actualizes the blissful energy of Śiva-Śakti, the latter is also accessible through an interiorization of aesthetic pleasures. This is one of the defining characteristics of Tantric Śaivism, and one that distinguishes it from other, more ascetic, perspectives from India. Śaivism insists that all pleasurable enjoyments are instances of contact with Śiva-Consciousness. As we have already intimated in the more general context of our earlier discussion of *śaktopāya*, the crux of the matter lies in one's ability to isolate the pure experience of delight and to abide in it as a manifestation of Śiva-Consciousness. This process presupposes that the practitioner is able to universalize, as it were, such intensely pleasurable experience by bringing it back to its source. The ascetic challenge of this Śaktic path lies in developing one's power to focus on pure Consciousness more than on the object that provides the opportunity for this heightened state of awareness.[19] Indeed, the object of delight tends to pull one toward its own outward reality and away from the experience of consciousness that it triggers: it will remain so as long as liberation from the delusion of mental projections and attachments has not been achieved. The feminine and aesthetic dimension of Śakti appears, therefore, both as an opportunity for objectification and delusion, and as a means of reabsorption into the Supreme Subject.

By contrast, the *mantra* is univocal, its utterance pointing to the Source from which it flows, as a sort of pulsation of consciousness. Indeed, the centering and universalizing of consciousness that it fosters provide the spiritual means to facilitate the aforementioned transmutation of aesthetic perceptions. The *mantra* does precipitate the alchemical spiritualization of phenomenal experiences, because its mode of exteriorization remains independent from any objective productions or external referents: it is pure manifestation of Consciousness without objectification.

## The One and the Unification of the Many

In sharp contrast with the image of the swollen seed that, in Śaivism, presides over Śaktic production, in the Sufism of Ibn al-'Arabī the unfolding of manifestation is the result of a sort of lack or sadness, *kurb*, on the part of God. More specifically, the possibilities of existence held latent in the Essence cause a constriction resulting in a Divine yearning to actualize them into being. In this sense, lack is but the other side of fullness. Sachiko Murata refers to this state in suggestive terms: "It is as if God, prior to creating the universe, has drawn a deep breath. He then feels distressed by holding all the creatures in a non-manifest state, just as a person holding his breath feels constricted."[20] This amounts to saying that the Divine Names, in latency within the Divine Essence, aspire to be differentiated and recognized within a subject-object relationship, as knower and known, or servant and Lord, notwithstanding the scission and therefore imperfection that this relationship must needs entail. The Names are both one with the Essence, and distinct from each other (*tamayyuz*). They are no different from the Essence, while being by definition relational, and therefore relative, or rather "relatively absolute," to use Frithjof Schuon's cogent expression.[21] According to Ibn al-'Arabī:

> The divine names are the *barzakh* between us and the Named.
> They look upon Him since they name Him, and they look upon

us since they bestow upon us effects attributed to the Named. So they make the Named known and they make us known.[22]

This dual knowledge is actualized through the existentiation of a wealth of existent subjects who may be the receptacles of the Names: such is the function of the Breath of the Merciful (*nafas al-rahmān*). Here, a distinction must be drawn between Names and Names of the Names. The former are no different from Divine Attributes—and, in a wider sense, include all realities inasmuch as they refer to the Essence—whereas the latter are the designations of Divine Names that have been revealed by God. Among them, the Name *al-Rahmān*, ordinarily translated as the Merciful, is considered by the tradition, on *Qur'ānic* grounds, to be a virtual equivalent of the Name *Allāh*. On the one hand, the infinite *Rahmah* is none other than the Divine Essence;[23] on the other hand, it is the principle of existentiation (*taqwīn*) through the Breath of the Compassionate. The latter is twofold, denoting as it does an active gift of being through the Breath (*nafas*), but also a passive differentiation through the particular nature of the created reality that is "breathed out." This is what the Sufi tradition denotes by the symbol of the water assuming the color and the size of the recipient. In this case, the recipient is none other than the *mazhar*, or locus of manifestation in which the Divine theophany is mirrored.

The Feminine appears in several dimensions and aspects of this process of Self-disclosure of *Allāh*. These could be summarized by the Arabic terms *dhāt, jamāl,* and *qābiliyyah,* which may be translated as Essence, Beauty, and Receptivity. The Essence has often been symbolized by Sufis, such as Ibn al-Fārid, as a feminine reality variously referred to as Laylā, Salmā, and other female names. This has been so in reference to the liberating infinitude of the Essence, which implies absolute nondelimitation (*mutlaq*). The alchemically transformative and expansively liberating power of femininity for the masculine soul is a powerful symbol—indeed, a terrestrial manifestation of the unbinding reality of the Essence.

At the other end of the range of manifestation, the world of creatures too has often been identified with the feminine by Sufis. This relates to the receptivity of terrestrial and phenomenal realities inasmuch as they receive the existentiating act of the divine "*Kun!*" or "Let it be" from the Breath of the Compassionate. Such is the domain of Existence of which woman becomes a metaphysical symbol through the *Qur'ānic* account of her creation from man. Accordingly, Ibn al-'Arabī situates the masculine in between two feminine realities: "[M]an is placed between the Essence [a feminine noun] from which he is manifested, and woman who is manifested from him."[24] This intermediate status of man, as isthmus or *barzakh*, is akin, as we shall see further, to other realities such as the Breath of the Compassionate, the Prophet, and the Heart.

One can therefore distinguish three degrees of Reality, which may be referred to, most generally, as the Nondelimited, the Supreme Delimitation, and the delimited realities. The locus of transmutation lies in the second degree inasmuch as it relates the highest and the lowest levels and allows for a transforming communication between the two. This is the very point of the fundamental paradox of Ibn al-'Arabī's metaphysics, as so powerfully expressed, in quasi-Śivaist terms, by the following passage from the *Meccan Revelations*:

> God possesses Nondelimited Being, but no delimitation prevents
> Him from delimitation. On the contrary, He possesses all delimita-
> tions, so He is nondelimited delimitation.[25]

The nexus between Nondelimitation and delimitation, or the Absolute and the relative, cannot but present itself in a puzzling, antinomic "formless form" that defies human rationality, and this is the *barzakh*. The *barzakh* is both delimited and nondelimited, human and divine, receptive and active, and such other paradoxical dualities. As Salman Bashier suggestively puts it, the *barzakh* is a "something" that is "nothing": "Ibn al-'Arabī is saying that there *is* something that ties the Real to creation, but that 'this thing *is not* something added to the Real and creation. He is actually stating that there is something and that this something is nothing."[26] We will come back to this point, which is pertinent to the nondual reconciliation of unity and duality through the triad.

The second aspect of Divine Femininity is the quality of Beauty or *jamāl*. On this level, we have already entered the domain of duality, since *jamāl* is always understood, cosmologically, in contradistinction with *jalāl*, or Majesty. According to Ibn al-'Arabī this duality appears at the degree of the Footstool (*kursī*), or the domain of formal manifestation, and not at that of the Throne (*'arsh*), which is marked by the preeminence of Mercy. The entire universe of manifestation is comprised of phenomena pertaining to the qualities of *jalāl* or rigor and *jamāl* or beauty. The first refers to reality in terms of distinction, rigor, separation, discernment, abstraction; thereby alluding to the Real as transcendent, incomparable, and distant. This is the masculine dimension of human-Divine relationship that is epitomized by the incommensurability between the servant and the Lord. The second dimension of reality refers, by contrast, to gentleness, analogy, proximity, all aspects that pertain to beauty as a mediating, inclusive reality. It is this dimension that makes transmutation possible, precisely because it provides us with an ability to relate to Divine Qualities through their manifestation in the cosmos. The qualities of beauty and goodness that are traditionally associated with women are no more and no less than a terrestrial manifestation of this aspect of the Divine. *Jamāl* brings nondelimitation into delimitation in the sense that it presupposes the separateness entailed by delimitations, while introducing into it the unity and inclusiveness akin to analogy. It is through this element of analogy that the relationship inherent to transmutation can enter into play.

Now, what is the source of this analogy? It is not the Essence, which is beyond any relationship, but rather the First Delimitation. It is this Delimitation that makes it possible for further delimitations to be, and to relate analogically to their Divine Source. So if the Nondelimited Essence needs to delimit Itself, as it were, in order to become the cause of all creational delimitations, conversely delimitations need to recognize their analogy with the First Delimitation in order to realize the Essence that it delimits. As delimited realities, creatures need to be transmuted into the Essence, so to speak, through and by the First Delimitation. Furthermore, it is important to note that the latter is both receptive in relation to the Essence and active in relation to further delimitations. Thanks to this dual relationship, the First Determination can function as locus or means of transmutation.

It is at this stage that the notion of receptivity comes to the fore. As Eve is receptive toward Adam inasmuch as she is drawn from him, similarly all spiritual loci of receptivity are passive in relation to the Essence, whether it be the Divine Determination, the Prophet, or the Name of God. This is, for instance, highlighted by the Prophet's quality of illiteracy (al-Ummī), which is functionally akin to the virginity of Mary. When considered from the standpoint of their receptivity, all such realities are feminine. However, the feminine is not only passive or receptive, it is also active and creative, and it is precisely this double feature that distinguishes it from the masculine, which is, by contrast, one-sided. The masculine is either active in relation to the feminine qua masculine, or passive in relation to God qua creature, but not both in the same respect. In contradistinction, the feminine *as* feminine is both passive and active. It is passive as created *from* Adam and active as creative *of* Adam or, in Henry Corbin's words, "such is Eve, the feminine being who, in the image of the divine Compassion, is creatrix of the being by whom she herself was created."[27] This is why in the last chapter of *Bezels of Wisdom*, Ibn al-'Arabī can affirm that the contemplation of God in woman is most perfect. In other words, man as male cannot contemplate God in creation without the theophanic mediation of woman since, left to a contemplation of himself, he can only *either* contemplate passivity—considering himself in relation to God—*or* activity in relation to woman. When contemplating woman, however, he can see a perfect reflection of the Divine Essence as both passive and active, and this is a key to spiritual transmutation since this vision of the Essence in and through woman entails a perpetual interplay between the Real and its central theophany. Beauty is created and it is creative, it reflects God and transforms or redeems the world and the soul. It is the work *of* God and it is the work of His theophanies *on* and *in* the soul.

Here, Ibn al-'Arabī's meditation hinges upon a distinction between "who it is that takes pleasure" and "in whom one takes pleasure."[28] The latter refers to the human experience of sexual pleasure. It is generically accessible to all, but remains confined, for the immense majority of humankind, within the sphere of delimitation, and does not open onto a recognition of God's Self-disclosure. What is lacking in this form of love is a knowledge of the Reality "in whom" pleasure is taken, which is to say, the passive aspect of the experience. Now, the perfection of pleasure, or its utmost spiritualization, would presuppose the combination of activity and passivity. This is encapsulated by a passage by Jandī as follows:

> The *Shaykh* is talking about the witnessing of the Real within the locus in which the man takes pleasure. The man must witness the Real through a single witnessing that brings together the agent and the recipient of the act. At the same time he must witness Him as not confined or delimited through His entification within either of the two, or both together, or the combination of the two, or being free from the combination. On the contrary, he must witness Him as not delimited by any of these modalities and as incomparable with all of them. Then he is the perfect man, the one who takes enjoyment in the Real in every single entity and every single entification.[29]

The transformative ability to see the Nondelimited and the delimited in the same gaze points to what Henry Corbin designated as amphiboly,[30] on the Divine side, and to receptivity on the human side. Amphiboly is an externalization on the part of the Interior (*al-Bātin*), whereas receptivity is an interiorization on the part of mankind as creature, therefore as outer reality. The former occurs primarily (though not exclusively) in and through the human outer form, whereas the latter takes place within the heart, the deepest reality in man and the only locus able to comprehend Divine Infinitude. Corbin's amphiboly, in Arabic *iltibās,* lies at the core of this twofold process. Here, amphiboly refers not to equivocalness, but to the co-presence of the Divine and the human, the hidden and the manifest. The term *iltibās* belongs to the family of words derived from the root denoting clothing, *LBS,* and implies, in our context, that the Divine is as it were clothed in the human, without thereby canceling the demands of its transcendence. This is the mystery of the vision of the Divine in the human garb, to which the *Qur'ān* refers as "the most beautiful form" (*ahsana taqwīm*), a mystery alluded to in a number of *ahadīth*.[31] It must also be noted, in this connection, that the *asmā'*, or revealed Divine Names, are similarly compared by Ibn al-'Arabī to "robes upon the Names."[32] This point highlights the centrality of the *asmā'* in conveying the Presence of the Divine Essence by being the *libās* or garment of the Attributes. It is in response to this donning of the Names that humans must put on the robe of viceregency[33] hence enter a Divine Mould. Sufism refers to this human response through the practice of the spiritual aspirant's (*murīd*) donning a vesture (*khirqah*) at the time of initiation in some Sufi orders. This vestimental symbolism highlights the metaphysical nexus between the Divine Non-Limitedness and human delimitation. The limited as such can only apprehend the Unlimited in the form of *clothing*, whether the latter is contemplated, invoked, or borne.

The aforementioned theophany through *iltibās* is connected to Ibn al-'Arabī's concept of *tahawwul*, or God's transformation through self-disclosure as related to human transformation through states. The following passage summarizes the matter in direct terms: "He has given us news on the tongue of His Messenger concerning his self-transmutation (*tahawwul)* in forms within the places of self-disclosure. That is the root of our transformation in states—both inwardly and outwardly—all of which takes place in Him."[34] The universe is in constant transmutation. *Tahawwul* stems from the same root as *hāl*, a key term in Sufism that refers to spiritual states. A state is a mode of utter receptivity and surrender to God's Act. In operative Sufism, the term is most often used to refer to modalities of spiritual experience that are both temporary and independent from human efforts. The *hāl* pertains to the *waqt*, that is, each instant at which the Breath of the Compassionate breathes the universe into being. Without it, the whole of the universe would fall into nothingness. This is the unending self-disclosure of God that manifests in an indefinite series of states. Ibn al-'Arabī explains this process of transmutation of God's Essence in the following terms:

> The Divinity . . . confronts the creatures through Its own (specific) essence (as Divinity) and It confronts the Essence through Its own essence. That is why It discloses itself (*tajallī*) in many forms, transmuting (*tahawwul*) Itself and undergoing continual change (*tabaddul*) within them.[35]

Mankind plays an inversely analogous role in connecting the manifestation to the Essence through its response to the Self-disclosures of God. This is what classical Sufism refers to as an exchange of qualities between God and humankind, *tabaddul as-sifāt*. On the part of humankind, this amounts to perfect activity (i.e., active remembrance of God), but also, and even more

importantly, pure receptivity to theophanic manifestations in the instant (i.e.,
passive remembrance of God). This is realized, most specifically, through
*dhikr,* or the remembrance of God through the invocation of His Names, the
quintessence of both action and *passion.* Inasmuch as she is identified to *dhikr,*
the soul becomes the isthmus between the Essence and manifestation. This
metaphysical reciprocity of remembrance in *tawhīd* is beautifully expressed in
a *Qur'ān*ic commentary ascribed to Ja'far al-Sādiq:

> The remembrance of God most high, is His Oneness, His prior
> eternity, His will, His power, and His knowledge—never does any
> forgetfulness or unawareness befall Him for they are among human
> qualities. Whoever, then, remembers God, most high, remembers
> Him through His remembrance of him.[36]

Such is the way in which mankind may participate in the transmutation of
God in the universe, and of the universe in God: by responding to God's
transmutation in the multiplicity of states through a transmutation of one's own
self, one's own heart (*qalb*). The Sufi symbols of cup and wine are paramount
here, in that they highlight the receptivity of the heart, which, like the cup, is
able to take the color of the liquid poured into it. The most relevant *Qur'ān*ic
reference for such spiritual reciprocity is to be found in the verse "Then do
ye remember Me; I will remember you" (2:152), which alludes to the deepest
dimension of the invocation, or *dhikrullāh.* This verse entails the triad of the
invoker, the invoked, and the invocation/Invocation. The transmutation of the
soul is carried out through a human invocation of the Divine that is but the
outer and reverse side of the Divine Remembrance of humankind.

Thus, spiritual transmutation is effected through the *barzakh* of *dhikr* as
mediation between *dhākir* and *madhkūr.* Furthermore, it can happen nowhere
but in the heart, which alone has the receptive ability to fluctuate (*taqallub*)
in response to the diversity of divine *tajalliyyāt,* or theophanic manifestations.
This is, for Ibn al-'Arabī, the deepest meaning of the *hadīth qudsī* "My earth
and My heaven embrace Me not, but the heart of My believing servant does
embrace Me."[37] Every creature is receptive (*qābil*) qua creature, but while all
other realities are fixed, as it were, in their capacity to receive specific *tajalliyyāt,*
only the human heart can experience the totality of theophanies insofar as it
is capable of all forms:

> My heart can take on
> any form:
> a meadow for gazelles,
> a cloister for monks,

> For the idols, sacred ground,
> Ka'ba for the circling pilgrim,
> the tables of the Torah,
> the scrolls of the Qu'rân.
> I profess the religion of love;
> wherever its caravan turns along the way,
> that is the belief,
> the faith I keep.[38]

The religion of love, *dīn al-hubb,* is none other than the pure receptivity and transmutation of the heart in its remembrance of God through His Names. It is the *maqām lā maqām,* the "station of no-station," which encompasses all theophanic manifestations.

As a conclusion, we would like to suggest that Sufism and Śaivism approach the transformative virtues of the Divine through the Feminine and the Word in ways that combine parallels and complementarities. While the two traditions understand the feminine from radically different perspectives, they both emphasize its creativeness and reintegrative power.

In Sufism, the feminine points to the Divine Essence (*dhāt*) that defies any conceptual formulation, but also to that facet of the Divine involving beauty, gentleness, and analogy, namely, *jamāl.* More so than the aspect of majesty, *jalāl,* which epitomizes distance, rigor, and incomparability, *jamāl* refers to this dimension of the Divine to which we can relate in terms of our terrestrial experience. As we have seen, this compassionate and feminine dimension of the Divine is a central agent of transmutation operating through a kind of spiritual sympathy.

Kashmiri Śaivism does not focus on such polarities as majesty and beauty but does conceive of the feminine as a dimension that, in the mode of internal self-awareness, results in an extrinsic radiation of the Divine. So it is that the infinite, sovereign, and unfathomable Śiva may be known within the bounds of relative and manifold existence. Through Śakti, Śiva enters the flow and ebb of universal manifestation, thereby making it possible for relative consciousness to be reintegrated within the fold of the Ultimate I. Indeed, Śaktic energy provides the means to free oneself from the binding limitations of existence by means of these very limitations, or rather through the recognition of the presence of the Infinite within the finite.

As for the power of the Word, it derives, in both traditions, from an understanding of sacred words as being ontologically grounded in Divine Reality, and in fact essentially identified with it. In parallel to the feminine, this identification is both creative and reintegrative. The Supreme Word, or Speech, *Vāk,* is both a productive determination of the Absolute Consciousness and the means of liberation through the linguistic crystallizations of this Consciousness in *mantras*. Likewise, the Qur'ānic Name of God, *Allāh*, which many Sufis see as the quintessential content of the Book, is essentially one with the Divine Named Himself. It is by virtue of this ontological identity that the Name can be the prime way of knowing the Named, and of reintegrating the latter through extinction (*fanā*) and permanence (*baqā*).

As it follows from the previous remarks, the main analogy, not to say similarity, between the two traditions, pertains to the transformation of the Ultimate, through śaktic *tattvas* or theophanic Names, in the onto-cosmogonic process that liberates its potentialities. The secret of spiritual deliverance, from a human point of view, lies in welcoming and converting the wherewithal of the transformative creativeness of the Divine. This means recognizing that the creative ebb is also a liberating flow. There is, however, a clear difference of accent between the Sufi view of delimited Nondelimitation and the Śaivite view of bound Unboundedness.

The Śaivite vision is akin to time, or rather to Eternity: it is the frontal eye of Śiva, a lightning-like Now that is the vibratory principle of any energetic production in time. Vibration and pulsation, *spanda,* is energy, and energy unfolds in time, as it were, to bring us back into the eternal instantaneousness of Śiva-Consciousness. The Śivaite world is indeed cyclical. The *mantra* is a vibration of eternity in time, and Śakti is the feminine, productive power that brings time out of the instant of Śiva: she is, in essence, the dance of Śiva, her femininity being only, in a sense, relative since she is essentially none other than the god, in Śiva-Śakti.

By contrast, the Nondelimited Essence of Sufism is like an infinite Space. Delimitation is a Naming of the Essence. It is masculine as determinative of the Essence, and as active in relation to its relative recipients. In the image of the Prophet, it is a *barzakh* between Essence and existence, between the feminine *dhāt* and the world of receptivity.

The Feminine and the Word constitute at the same time manifestations of Reality and ways of knowing It. They are both one with the Supreme and inherently productive of other-than-It. It is in this way that lies the transmutational power which is theirs. Neither monistic nor dualistic, akin neither to one nor to two, the principle of transmutation—inherently akin to the first odd number, i.e., three—is like an isthmus that both distinguishes and unites the transmuting and transmuted realities. But this three is much more accurately defined as neither one nor two, than as a number as such.

In Salman Bashier's words, the *barzakh* is both something and nothing: it is this third thing—Ibn al-'Arabī's *al-shay' al-thālith,* that makes it possible for two to be one without ceasing to be two, nor becoming three. Analogously, Śakti is a *something* as the productive principle of everything, while being *nothing* else than Śiva. She is this virtual nothing that makes everything possible. Her domain of predilection is *bhedābheda*, a distinction without difference, a perplexing paradox that calls for a transmutation of intelligence through the coincidence of opposites, like a station-of-no-station that endlessly reflects the Infinite.

# Epilogue

In his seminal *Sufism and Taoism: A Comparative Study of Key Philosophical Concepts*,[1] Toshihiko Izutsu called for a "meta-historical" metaphysical dialogue, which would, in his opinion, "be crystallized into a *philosophia perennis* in the fullest sense of the term."[2] While the cross-civilizational and interreligious benefits of such an endeavor remain as necessary as ever—and indeed even more urgently so than at the time Izutsu was formulating them—the challenges to this "crystallization" are powerful. Among them, perhaps first and foremost, lies the prevailing historicist thrust of contemporary scholarship, which is highly skeptical of any fundamental doctrinal convergences because it tends to see all metaphysical productions as determined by specific socioeconomic and political circumstances, without which, purportedly, they cannot be understood. Thus, the metahistorical perspective propounded by Izutsu is likely to encounter a high measure of skepticism among scholars whose training prepares them to consider intellectual and spiritual patterns of metaphysical thought within sociocultural contexts only. Whatever one may think of the historicist and analytic leanings of most contemporary scholarship, one cannot but recognize the difficulty of extracting metaphysical concepts from their religious and cultural milieu without jeopardizing their integrity.

It would seem that a balanced approach would be one able to do justice to the complexities and development of specific teachings while reaching a level of theoretical synthesis allowing for meaningful parallels and contrasts. Only such ability to articulate scholarly analysis and comparative synthesis could open the way to the conceptual delineation and "crystallization" of common cross-religious insights. It is our hope that the previous chapters have contributed in some measure to this endeavor while avoiding the pitfall of blurring the intellectual and spiritual identity of the respective viewpoints that we have studied. Our intent has been to shed light on the profoundly diverse, and indeed sometimes diverging, ways in which Reality and appearance have been understood and conceptualized. By the same token, we have no doubt highlighted a number of reoccurring metaphysical patterns while suggesting the inherent *relativity* of these patterns as stemming from their perceived incommensurability with the Reality that they indicate but do not fathom. In the most fundamental and elementary sense, these patterns are situated along a doctrinal spectrum that spans exclusive as well as inclusive notions of That which is deemed *real* in the fullest meaning of the word.

In this respect, the conventional contrast between life-affirming and life-denying religions—which many recent scholars have understandably set aside as largely flawed, provides a useful, if not fully satisfactory, entry into the ways in which the question of reality and appearance may be shown to be relevant to a better understanding of religious phenomena. The fundamental ambiguities of the words *life-affirming* and *life-denying* lie, obviously, in the very use of seemingly unproblematic terms such as *life, denying,* and *affirming*. To say, for example, that Buddhism, taken as a whole, is a life-denying worldview, would only make sense if one were to restrict the meaning of "life" to that aspect of the latter, however central it may be for Buddhists, that is characterized by *tanhā,* or craving. But this identification is obviously questionable, since *tanhā* does not define life as such, let us say for instance, in its organic processes, but rather the psychic tendency to cling to phenomenal experience as such. One may just as legitimately equate "life," by contrast, with that dimension of existence that some Buddhist schools characterize as its most profoundly real dimension, that is, the Buddha Nature, the nature of pure Enlightenment that they perceive as immanent to everything. Similarly, it can be cogently argued that there is no religious tradition, at least among so-called axial traditions, that does not "deny" some aspects of "life," which amounts to saying that there is hardly any religion that does not aim at the realization of a "new life" that is seen as a liberation from the fetters of the "old life." What this means, ultimately, is that such definitions necessarily touch upon our very understanding of what is real and what is apparent or illusory. Given that the complexities of and differences between metaphysical and theological contexts make it difficult, if not impossible, to draw adequate parallels or conjunctions, it can be argued in the wake of John Hick's fruitful insights—but without necessarily following him in his theoretical conclusions—that the concept of Reality, or "the Real," provides, in fact, the most universal and practically relevant approach to a metahistorical comparative metaphysics.[3] This is due, no doubt, to its absolute and relative denotations, which allow for a stratified vision of the universe, one that makes room for both the metaphysical demands of the Ultimate and the ontological claims of the contingent. The dual character of Reality makes it possible to envision, as we have seen, a wide range of doctrinal emphases. These emphases may be deemed mutually contradictory, mostly insofar as they are taken in their conceptual literality, as it were, and arguably less so as they are envisaged in light of their ultimate metaphysical intents. Indeed, this general observation, which would have to be qualified in various ways so as to satisfy all needs of analytical exactness, seems to us to be a key to some of the most acute predicaments of contemporary religious consciousness.

The "postmodern" religious mind seems to be in search of a "formula" for spiritual fulfillment, whether the latter is found in the "absolute" words of scriptures, or experienced in an individual and "informal" space of well-being, balance, and freedom. Now, two conclusions that are pertinent to this quest may be drawn from our readings and reflections. The first suggests, following the teachings of the various paths of contemplative metaphysics, that there is no authentic freedom but through "defining" and "unifying" concepts and forms that facilitate the human movement into a space of inner unboundedness. Thinking, meditating, praying, and acting entail being involved with objective means of orienting oneself toward inner freedom by aligning one's being with Reality, and uprooting or redirecting that which, within, poses an obstacle to this reintegrating alignment. In a way, these conceptual, ritual, and moral means are "appearances," since they are not the Ultimate, but they are appearances of a kind capable of leading mankind to Reality, and they therefore pertain to a coefficient of reality that is higher than that of other phenomena. The second point is that the "absoluteness" of traditional and religious forms—that which makes them different from ordinary phenomena—is not reducible to the status of a mere element in a religious syllabus or spiritual agenda, since it only reaches its ultimate function and goal by actualizing an inner recovery from the delusive tyranny of ego-centered consciousness. In that sense, John Hick's definition of religion as the means of transformation from ego-centeredness to Real-centered[4] is once again quite suggestive of what contemplative metaphysics suggests and aims at, even though it may be argued that it bypasses, in Hick's conceptualization, that which is precisely the very core of the transformative power of contemplative traditions, namely, the nonhuman and transcendent intentionality of their source. At any rate, and by contrast with our previous points, there are at least two deadly risks on the horizon of contemporary religious consciousness.

The first of these risks flows from a metaphysically immature understanding of "freedom" that confuses lack of constraints with genuine inner self-determination, while the second amounts to a blind "servitude" that closes the door of consciousness to the inner space of infinite reality, and, indeed, to unbounded mercy. A penetrating and balanced discrimination between Reality and appearance would give each term its full due in fair metaphysical justice. It would not take the appearance of selfhood for Reality, nor would it confuse Reality with the transformative "appearances" that it has "pedagogically" and mercifully sown along the way. More than ever, a meditation on the subtle, often paradoxical, but always decisively liberating speculations of contemplative intelligence may be the key to avoiding the dead ends of contemporary religion and spirituality.

One of the pitfalls of contemporary religious consciousness lies in its bent to promote, practically if not theoretically, religious phenomena to the status of the ultimate, as if the Absolute could be conflated with the formal ways and demands that religions see as flowing from it and leading to it. This tendency is quite apparent in the various forms of what is commonly, if not satisfactorily, referred to as "fundamentalism." These movements, beyond their extreme formal and contextual diversity, share a central concern focused upon scriptural and dogmatic teachings, taken in their exclusively literal sense, and for placing the strongest emphasis on formal orthopraxy to the point of equating its injunctions, quasi-exclusively, with religion as such. A correlative danger often appears in the paradoxical conjunction of two seemingly contradictory tendencies. One amounts to devaluing terrestrial experience in the name of a transcendent world seen as parallel to the former, but without allowing for any ontological zones of contact between the two. The second lays maximal emphasis on the sociopolitical means of imposing the triumph of the values derived from the "parallel" transcendent world to the point of an ideological fusion of the two. This results in what could be conceptualized as an "abstraction" and an "ideologization" of religion. The contemplative traditions that we have surveyed and pondered do share with such contemporary concerns a sense of the primacy of transcendence—albeit indissociable in fact from immanence—but they radically differ from them by highlighting the prime imperative of an inner realization of transcendence, the external, collective, supports of which they clearly, ideally or normatively, subordinate to a spiritual *metanoia* and to the quest for realized wisdom; without the latter, religious intents and practices may all too often end up mutating into their own ghastly shadows.

As the preceding essays demonstrate, the rich interplay of contemplative concepts of Reality, illusion and appearance, absoluteness and relativity, unknowability and knowledge, essence and form, inwardness and manifestation, leaves us with a complex and balanced view of the unboundedness of Reality, the infinity of its aspects, and the indefinite multiplicity of intellectual and spiritual vantage points. This rich diversity may raise many unresolved questions if one understands "resolution" to mean the production of an all-encompassing rational system. But such is certainly not the case when one realizes that each of these teachings is only a discursive approximation and a means of recognizing and assimilating That which lies beyond its reach and indeed beyond human qua human ken, since "the way that can be spoken of is not the constant [absolute] way."[5]

# Notes

## Introduction

1. "By dint of sacrificing the essential for the urgent one ends up forgetting the urgency of the essential," "Ethics in Process: Turbulence, Uncertainty and Urgency," in *Ethics of the Future*, ed. Enrique Rodriguez Larreta and Cândido Mendes (Rio de Janeiro: Unesco/ISSC/Educam, 1998), 94.

2. "[N]ow, can Metaphysics as we understand it be defined? No, for to define is always to limit, and what is under consideration is, in and of itself, truly and absolutely limitless and thus cannot be confined to any formula or any system whatsoever. Metaphysics might be partially characterized, for example, by saying that it is the knowledge of universal principles, but this is not a definition in the proper sense and in any case only conveys a vague notion." René Guénon, *Studies in Hinduism* (Hillsadle, NY: Sophia Perennis, 2001), 89.

3. Alex Wayman's study of the Buddhist meditation on the symbol of the mirror encompasses a wealth of occurrences and meanings. Foremost among them are three aspects of unity in multiplicity, namely the inalterability of the Enlightened Consciousness reflecting the manifold, the karmic discontinuous continuity after death, and the interdependence of phenomena as "reflecting" each other. Alex Wayman, "The Mirror as a Pan-Buddhist Simile-Metaphor," *History of Religions*, Vol. 13, No. 4 (May 1974), 251–69.

## Chapter 1. Shimmering Reality

1. Let us specify from the outset that contemplative metaphysics and mystical theology are not "irrational" even though they highlight the supra-rational source of spiritual knowledge and the limitations of reason: in fact, any mystical theology makes use of reason when providing doctrinal and theoretical concepts. To be aware of the limitations of reason does not amount to a disqualification of its power and usefulness within the scope of its epistemological jurisdiction. Moreover what we call "rational theology," even though it is by definition a rational discourse, depends on the supra-rational data of revelation for its development.

2. "If you ask of its form, it cannot be stated. It is beyond description. It is neither real nor non-real; neither is it the mixture of the two. Is it separate from the Ātman? It is neither separate, nor yet non-separate ; nor part of the Ātman, yet neither can you say it is not part. It is not the body. It is most wonderful and beyond all description. " Sri Sankarācārya, *Viveka-cūdāmani*, verses 109–11, trans. Svāmī Turīyānanda (Madras: Sri Ramakrishna Math, 1991), 46–47.

3. The fact that the attribution of the *Vivekacūdāmani* to Shankara has been disputed by scholars is not directly relevant to our purpose since this text has been, and continues to be, a classical reference for the perspective of *Advaita*.

4. We need to acknowledge that Shankara adds a third negation to these two: *Māyā* is "neither real, nor unreal, *nor both*," or a mixture of two. In the limits of this chapter we will only touch marginally and, as it were, incidentally upon this third negative characterization.

5. "*Anekāntavāda* may be translated as the 'non-one-sided' or 'many-sided doctrine,' or the 'doctrine of many-sidedness' . . . *Anekāntavāda* is an ontological doctrine. Its fundamental claim, as it eventually came to be understood by the tradition, is that all existent entities have infinite attributes. . . . The apparent contradictions that our perceptions of reality involve—continuity and change, emergence and perishing, permanence and flux, identity and difference—reflect the interdependent, relationally constituted nature of things. Reality is a synthesis of opposites." Jeffery D. Long, *Jainism: An Introduction* (London: I. B. Tauris, 2009), 141.

6. "All of Nāgārjuna's works are broadly soteriological in nature: he is trying to break the habit of reification that is at the root of grasping and craving and hence all suffering." Richard H. Jones, *Nāgārjuna: Buddhism's Most Important Philosopher* (New York: CreateSpace Independent Publishing Platform, 2010), 135.

7. Cf. Arvind Sharma, *The Rope and the Snake: Metaphorical Exploration of Advaita Vedanta* (New Delhi: Manohar, 1997).

8. Śaṅkarācārya, *The Vivekacūdāmani of Śaṅkarācārya Bhagavatpāda: An Introduction and Translation*, trans. John A. Grimes (Ashgate: Aldershot, 2004), 113. "Taking this world as a tree, the seed of this tree of the world is *tamas*." Śaṅkarācārya, *The Vivekacūdāmani*, 64. *Tamas* is the third of the *gunas*—cosmological "strings" with which the entire relative realm, including the Divine Being or *Saguna Brahman*, is woven—the two others being *sattva* and *rajas*. *Sattva* corresponds to light, ascension, and purity, *rajas* to fire, desire, and passion, and *tamas* to heaviness, obscurity, and ignorance. The *Bhagavad Gītā*, by contrast with the *Vivekacūdāmani*, considers all of the three *gunas* to be principles of delusion: "All this universe is deluded by these three states of being/Composed of the qualities./It does not recognize Me,/Who am higher than these, and eternal." *The Bhagavad Gītā*, trans. Winthrop Sargeant (Albany: State University of New York Press, 1994), VII, 13, 331.

9. Śaṅkarācārya, *The Vive*.

10. Although Advaitin writers most often refrain from treating *Māyā* in terms of creation by or from *Ātman*, this is not the case of the *Upanisads*, which frequently refer to *Brahman* as creator: "Unlike Advaita commentators, the Upanisads are not reticent about *brahman* as the creator and are not hesitant to suggest desire and purpose. Aitareya Upanisads (1.1), for example, begins with the act of creation. 'In the

beginning this world was the self (*ātman*), one alone, and there was no other being at all that blinked an eye. He thought to himself:—Let me create the worlds.'" Anantanand Rambachan, *The Advaita Worldview: God, World, and Humanity* (Albany: State University of New York Press, 2006), 92.

11. Sri Shankaracharya, *Daksināmūrti Stotra*, trans. Alladi Mahadeva Sastry (Chennai: Samata Books, 2001), 152.

12. "The Sruti says: By *Māyā*, Siva became two birds always associated together ; the One, clinging to the one unborn (Prakriti), became many as it were." Sri Shankaracharya, *Daksināmūrti Stotra*, VII–27, 158.

13. "*Māyā*, the binding capacity of Hari, and the generator of things external and internal, spreads out like the net of the fisherman, in respect of ignorant *jīvas*, and contracts (in the case of *jīvas* with knowledge) through the will of the Lord. Be this *māyā* real or illusory, (but) contraction and the opposite (expansion) are natural (therefore); and, thus, too (say some)." "Sarvajñātman's *Samksepasārīraka*," in *The Essential Vedānta: A New Source Book of Advaita Vedanta*, ed. Eliot Deutsch and Rohit Dalvi (Bloomington, IN: World Wisdom, 2004), 344.

14. "*Reality* is that which cannot be subrated by any other experiences. . . . *Appearance* is that which can be subrated by other experience. . . . *Unreality* is that which neither can nor cannot be subrated by other experience." Eliot Deutsch, *Advaita Vedānta: A Philosophical Reconstruction* (Honolulu: The University Press of Hawaii, 1969), 18–24. On the basis of such epistemological distinctions, *Māyā* is clearly to be identified with appearance.

15. Sri Shankaracharya, *Daksināmūrti Stotra*, VII–12, 153.

16. Ibid., 154.

17. Ibid., VII–16, 155.

18. The term *svabhāva* (literally "own nature") can be closely approximated by the notion of "essence." David Kalupahana (David Kalupahana, *Buddhist Philosphy: A Historical Analysis* [Honolulu: University of Hawaii Press, 1976], 27) translates it as "inherent nature." Christian Lindtner (Christian Lindtner, *Master of Wisdom: Writings of the Buddhist Master Nāgārjuna* [Emeryville, CA: Dharma Publishing, 1986–97]) translates it by "own being," while Jay Garfield (Jay L. Garfield, *The Fundamental Wisdom of the Middle Way: Nāgārjuna's Mūlamadhyamakakārikā* [Oxford: Oxford University Press, 1995], 89) prefers to render it as "self-nature": "When a Mādhyamika philosopher says of a table that it is empty, that assertion by itself is incomplete. It invites the question, empty of what? And the answer is, empty of inherent existence, or self-nature, or in more Western terms, *essence*. Now, to say that the table is empty is hence simply to say that it lacks essence and importantly *not* to say that it is completely nonexistent."

19. Nāgārjuna, *The Philosophy of the Middle Way (Mūlamadhyamakakārikā)*, ed. and trans. David J. Kalupahana (Albany: State University of New York Press, 1986), 234.

20. "A wrongly perceived emptiness ruins a person of meager intelligence. It is like a snake that is wrongly grasped or knowledge that is wrongly cultivated." Nāgārjuna, *The Philosophy of the Middle Way (Mūlamadhyamakakārikā)*, 335. Cf. also, Nāgārjuna, *Stances du milieu par excellence (Madhyamaka-kārikās)*, ed. and trans. Guy Bugault (Paris: Gallimard, 2002), 309.

21. Nāgārjuna, *The Philosophy of the Middle Way*, 12–13, 17.

22. This has implications on the use of language in the sense that the exclusion of both existence and nonexistence leaves us with a clear sense of the limitations of linguistic categories, thereby opening the way to a transcending of conceptual crystallizations.

23. This is in critical reaction to Abhidharma Buddhists who postulated a continuity of the *dharmas* and their "nature" or *svabhāva*.

24. One of the most famous classical statements of *pratītyasamutpāda* teaches that nothing is caused by itself, by another, by itself and another, and by nothing: "No existents whatsoever are evident anywhere that are arisen from themselves, from another, from both, or from a non-cause." Nāgārjuna, *The Philosophy of the Middle Way*, 105. These four negations amount to an affirmation of the "relative conditioning" of all beings. In summary this foundational passage amounts to (1) the negation of a self-caused cause as God or *causa sui* that would be independent from relations, (2) the idea that a cause would be antecedent in relation to its effect and therefore independent from it, *quod absit*, and (3) the idea of a relationship with nothing, which is an impossibility.

25. *The Connected Discourses of the Buddha: A New Translation of the Samyutta Nikāya*, trans. Bhikkhu Bodhi (Boston: Wisdom Publications, 2000), 12, Nidānasamyutta 1(1) in The Connected Discourses of the Buddha, 533.

26. Nāgārjuna considers that no *nirvāna* would be possible if one were to posit the reality of "essences." "If all this is non-empty, there exists neither arising nor ceasing, [As such,] through relinquishing and ceasing of what does one expect freedom?" *Mūlamadhyamakakārikā* 25:2 in Nāgārjuna, *The Philosophy of the Middle Way*, 356.

27. Śaṅkarācārya, *The Vivekacūdāmani*, 49, 52.

28. Christian Lindtner, *Master of Wisdom*, xx.

29. Mūlamadhyamakakārikā 25:24, in Nāgārjuna, *The Philosophy of the Middle Way*, 369.

30. Mūlamadhyamakakārikā 24:8,9,10, in Nāgārjuna, *The Philosophy of the Middle Way*, 331–33.

31. This is analogous, incidentally, to Shankara's distinction between the real and figurative senses of *Ātman*'s "binding" by *Māyā*: "That *Ātman* does acts, that He bound by them, and that He is released from them, is true only in a figurative sense; it is a mere illusion." Chapter VIII (21), Shankaracharya, *Daksināmūrti Stotra*, 156.

32. "If the concepts 'conditioned co-arising' and "emptiness" don't refer at all to the way the world works, if impermanence, birth-and-death, ignorance, and desirous attachment are not in fact features of unenlightened human existence, then why would the Buddha even bother to claim that they are at the root of our suffering and point toward an effective solution ? Why again, in this case, would Mahāyāna Buddhists bother to argue against theories that espouse some notion of *svabhāva* in the first place, since, if no words refer to reality anyway, there would seem to be nothing about an accurate understanding of human existence at stake in the dispute? If the answer is that the conventional meaning of conditioned co-arising is a more effective means of bringing about enlightenment, then we would seem entitled to ask why it is so?" Douglas L. Berger, "A Reply to Garfield and Westerhoff on 'Acquiring Emptiness,'" *Philosophy East and West* 61, no. 2 (April 2011): 369.

33. "For the Buddha, language derives its 'meaning' (*attha*) when it is able to produce results (*attha*), and thus what is true (*bhuta, taccha*) is that which bears results (*attha-samhita*). The Buddha did not recognize anything that is false to be productive of results. Truth in this sense can be equated with 'meaningful' language. Thus, linguistic expressions that imply permanence and annihilation would be 'meaningless' (*an-attha*) in that they do not communicate anything that in experience (*dhamma*), where experience is understood in terms of the felt results (*attha*) rather than in terms of an indefinable ultimate reality." Nāgārjuna, *Mūlamadhyamakakārikā of Nāgārjuna: The Philosophy of the Middle Way*, trans. David J. Kalupahana (Delhi: Motilal Barnasidass, 2004), 19. "Some more skillful, more illuminating constructions might just be better in bringing us to see that no construction is true. That is the nature of *upāya*." Jay L. Garfield and Jan Westerhoff, "Acquiring the Notion of a Dependent Designation: A Response to Douglas L. Berger," *Philosophy East and West* 61, no. 2 (April 2011): 367.

34. *Mūlamadhyamakakārikā* 24:18, in Nāgārjuna, *The Philosophy of the Middle Way*, 339.

35. *Abhidharma* texts, dating back as early as the third century BC, include abstracts of doctrinal elements from the earlier *sūtras,* the scriptures that are largely comprised of words of the Buddha.

36. *Udāna, Khuddakanikāya, SuttatPitaka,* quoted in Joseph Walser, *Nāgārjuna in Context: Mahāyāna Buddhism and Early Indian Culture* (New York: Columbia University Press, 2005), 177.

37. Nāgārjuna's perspective does not exhaust Buddhism. A degree of "objectification" and "substantialization" is a spiritual possibility, and cannot but appear in a positive light in Buddhism itself, sometimes in direct opposition to the perspective of ultimate emptiness. The emphasis laid by the Chinese *Hua-yen* tradition (seventh-eighth century) on the Buddha Nature (*Tathāgatagarbha*) corresponds to such a possibility. In this case, emptiness itself is considered as a provisional epistemogical mediation that must ultimately give way to a perception and realization of the True Nature in unambiguously affirmative terms: "According to the true ultimate meaning, since deluded thoughts are intrinsically empty, there is nothing that can be negated. All things, being without defilement, are intrinsically the True Nature, and its Marvelous Functioning-in-accord-with-conditions is not only never interrupted, but also cannot be negated. It is only because a class of sentient beings clings to unreal phenomenal appearances, obscures their True Nature, and has difficulty attaining profound enlightenment that the Buddha provisionally negated everything without distinguishing between good and bad, tainted and pure, or the Nature and its phenomenal appearances. Although he regarded the True Nature and its Marvelous Functioning not to be nonexistent, because he provisionally said they were nonexistent, [these teachings] are designated as being of 'hidden intent.' Furthermore, though his intention lays in revealing the Nature, because his words thus negated phenomenal appearances and his intent was not expressed in words, they are referred to as 'hidden.'" (407a7–9; K 121) Tsung-mi, quoted in Peter N. Gregory, "Tsung-mi and the Single Word 'Awareness' (*chih*)," *Philosophy East and West* 35, no. 3 (July 1985): 254. Later *Mahāyāna* highlights a further objectification of *nirvāna* as Amida, the "Other," in *Jodo Shinshu.*

38. An analogous notion, in Buddhism, is that of the *trikāya* or "three bodies" of the Buddha, the highest being identified with the Absolute.

39. This must be qualified by the fact that the Quranic context of definition of *Allāh* is much less ambiguous, or much less fluid, than that of Śiva.

40. Jaideva Singh's Introduction to *Śiva Sūtras: The Yoga of Supreme Identity* (Delhi: Motilal Banarsidass, 1979), xix.

41. "There are simply too many large gaps in the sequence that leads from the Mohenjo-Dara Proto-Śiva through the Vedic Rudra, the *Yajur Vedic Śatarudrīya,* the *Rudra-Śiva* of the *Śvetāśvatara Upaniṣad,* the *aṣṭamūrti* and *pañcavaktra* of the Purānic Śiva, and the notions of early sectarian groups such as the *Pāśupatas,* to the increasingly complex theologies of Śiva in different *āgamic* revelations that finally result, in one branch of the process, in the concept of Śiva as taught by Abhinavagupta. What we do know of this process is that Śiva, from being one in a pantheon of divinities, increasingly became the focus of sectarian groups who worshipped him exclusively." Paul Eduardo Muller-Ortega, *The Triadic Heart of Śiva: Kaula Tantricism of Abhinavagupta in the Non-Dual Shaivism of Kashmir* (Albany: State University of New York Press, 1989), 26.

42. 'Abd al-Karīm al-Jīlī, *Universal Man,* trans. Titus Burckhardt (Roxburgh, Scotland: Beshara Publications, 1983), 57.

43. Let us note that some Mahāyāna texts, such as the classic *Awakening of Faith* by Aśvaghoṣa, written around the beginning of the Christian era, also makes use of this symbolism. This is all the more significant that this text is one which tends to introduce the teachings of *śunyatā* as provisional and situate them within an affirmative context. "[Adoration] to the Dharma whose essence attributes are like the ocean, revealing to us the principle of *anātman* and forming the storage of infinite merits." Aśvaghoṣa, *The Awakening of Faith,* trans. Teitaro Suzuki (Mineola, NY: Dover Publications, 2003), 47.

44. *Tantrāloka* 4.184–86a, in Muller-Ortega, *The Triadic Heart of Śiva,* 146. "It is the powers of the Self (*svaŚakti*) that, emerging from the ocean of consciousness and uniting together in various and sundry ways, create the finite realities."

45. Martin Lings, *What is Sufism?* (Berkeley: University of California Press, 1975), 11.

46. *Futūhāt al-makkiyya* II. 121–25, in William Chittick, *The Sufi Path of Knowledge: Ibn al-'Arabi's Metaphysics of Imagination* (Albany: State University of New York Press, 1989), 345.

47. *Mathnawi* V 2731–32, in William Chittick, *The Sufi Path of Love: The Spiritual Teachings of Rumi* (Albany: State University of New York Press, 1983), 195.

48. Singh, *Śiva Sūtras,* 7.

49. "[The Absolute] is called Maheśvara because of its absolute sovereignty of Will, *sva-tantratā* or *svātantrya.* This absolute Sovereignty or Free Will is not a blind force but the *svabhāva* (own being) of the Universal Consciousness (Cit)." Jaideva Singh, *Pratyabhijñāhṛidayam: The Secret of Self-Recognition* (Delhi: Motilal Banarsidass, 1991), 16.

50. "Just as every drop of water comes to rest in the ocean, so all acts and cognitions [come to rest] in the Great Lord, the ocean of consciousness. Even a little water on the ground drunk by the sun's rays goes, as rain, to the great ocean. Similarly all

knowledge and action in the universe merge in the ocean of Śiva either spontaneously and evidently (*sphutam*), by itself or [indirectly] through a series of other [processes]." Abhinavagupta, *Malini*, quoted in Mark S. G. Dyczkowski, *The Doctrine of Vibration: An Analysis of the Doctrines and Practices of Kashmir Shaivism* (Albany: State University of New York, 1987), 71.

51. Obviously, the Absolute is not "free" not to manifest itself since it would be contradictory with its actual nature. One must therefore distinguish the inner "necessity" inherent to the Absolute from an outer constraint that would weigh upon it.

52. "Here it may be asked 'Why does the Self manifest these *Ābhāsas* [limited manifestations]' Abhinava answers this question by saying that the nature of a thing cannot be questioned. It is absurd to ask why fire burns. To burn is the very nature of fire and so to manifest without what lies within is the very nature of the Self. It is natural for consciousness to assume a variety of forms." Kanti Chandra Pandey, *Abhinavagupta: An Historical and Philosophical Study*, 4th ed. (Varanasi: Chaukhamba Amarabharati Prakashan, 2006), 335.

53. "For non-dualist Kashmir Śaivites . . . the higher Brahman is already full of inner potencies and powers (*Śakti*) and is evolving into the multitude of the created universe through a series of self-transformations (*parināma*)." Natalia Isaeyeva, *From Early Vedanta to Kashmir Shaivism* (Albany: State University of New York Press, 1995), 134–35.

54. "The distinction between the power and its possessor is as imaginary as between the fire and its power to burn." Kanti Chandra Pandey, Introduction, *Īśvara-Pratyabhijñā-Vimarśinī of Abhinavagupta: Doctrine of Divine Recognition*, Volume II (Delhi: Motilal Banarsidass, 1986), x.

55. Muller-Ortega, *The Triadic Heart of Śiva*, 94.

56. "Śakti represents the all-encompassing fullness (*pūrnatā*) of the absolute, the ever-shifting power of awareness actively manifesting as the Circle of Totality (*viśvacakra*). Śiva is the Void (*śūnyatā*) of absolute consciousness—its supportless (*nirālamba*) and thought-free (*nirvikalpa*) nature. Integral and free, Śiva, the abode of the Void, dissolves everything into Himself and brings all things into being." Dyczkowski, *The Doctrine of Vibration*, 119.

57. *Mālinīvijayavārtika* 1/949, in Dyczkowski, *The Doctrine of Vibration*, 119.

58. "*Vimarśa—Vi+mrś*. The root mrś means to touch. *Vimrś* means to touch mentally. It is a highly technical term of this system. Paramaśiva, the ultimate reality is not only *prakāśa* or luminous consciousness, but also *vimarśa*, i.e., consciousness of its consciousness. *Vimarśa* is Self-consciousness or pure I-consciousness of the highest Reality." Singh in *Pratyabhijñāhṛidayam*, 125. Kanti Chandra Pandey characterizes *prakāśa* as pure receptive consciousness and *Vimarśa* as determinate reactive awareness. Kanti Chandra Pandey, *Īśvara-Pratyabhijñā-Vimarśinī of Abhinavagupta: Doctrine of Divine Recognition*, xiv.

59. "The word 'vimarśa' . . . when used with reference to the Universal Self, stands for that power which gives rise to self-consciousness, will, knowledge and action in succession." Pandey, *Īśvara-Pratyabhijna-Vimarsini of Abhinavagupta*, 327.

60. "The self-referential capacity of consciousness is united with all things. From within its very self, this capacity of consciousness differentiates the other, and from the

other it actualizes itself again, It then unifies both of them, the self and the other, and having unified them, it submerges them both back into itself." Abhinavagupta 1:205, in Muller-Ortega, *The Triadic Heart of Śiva*, 96.

61. Abhinavagupta, *Parātrīśikā-Vivarana: The Secret of Tantric Mysticism*, trans. Jaideva Singh, ed. Bettina Baumer (Delhi: Motilal Banarsidass, 1988), 127.

62. "If through this power the yogi realizes the oneness of consciousness and its manifestations, he is elevated, but if he fails to do so, this same power throws him down. Thus the Intermediate power plays a dual role by illumining both the "pure Path' to liberation and the 'Impure Path' of bondage." Dyczkowski, *The Doctrine of Vibration*, 114.

63. Abhinavagupta, *Parātrīśikā-Vivarana*, 127–28.

64. Dyczkowski, *The Doctrine of Vibration*, 116.

65. Pandey, *Abhinavagupta*, 329.

66. *Citi* refers to universal consciousness as a whole, whereas *caitanya* tends to denote its pure, unfragmented, state. Cf. *Pratyabhijñāhrdayam: The Secret of Self-Recognition*, trans. Jaiveda Singh (Delhi: Motilal Banarsidass, 1991), 59.

67. *Pratyabhijñāhṛdayam*, 51.

68. Lin Ma, *Heidegger on East-West Dialogue: Anticipating the Event* (New York: Routledge, 2008), 163.

69. *Jaideva, Śiva Sūtras, 262.*

70. Cf. Utpaladeva, *The Īśvarapratyabhijñākārikā of Utpaladeva with the Author's Vritti*, trans. Raffaele Torella (Delhi: Motilal Banarsidass, 2003), 121.

71. "The absolute oscillates between a 'passion' (*rāga*) to create and 'dispassion' (*virāga*) from the created." Dyczkowski, *The Doctrine of Vibration*, 41.

72. In *Parātrimśikā-laghuvrtti*, Abhinavagupta, contrasting his views with those of Vedānta, opposes the latter's state of repose of *brahman-ātman* to the productive "agitation" of Bhairava-Śiva: "According to us, however, there occurs, beyond that, Bhairava, who manifests the entire universe by means of his activity of churning that state of repose." Muller-Ortega, *The Triadic Heart of Śiva*, 176.

73. Utpaladeva, *The Īśvarapratyabhijñākārikā*, 120.

74. See Utpaladeva, *Les stances sur la reconnaissance du Seigneur avec leur glose, Īśvarapratyabhijñākārikā*, ed. and trans. David Dubois (Paris: L'Harmattan, 2010), 78.

75. "Being essentially reflective awareness (*pratyavamarśa*), consciousness (*citi*) is represented also as 'Supreme Speech.'" Lyne Bansat-Boudon, *An Introduction to Tantric Philosophy: The Paramārthasāra of Abhinavagupta with the Commentary of Yogarāja* (London: Routledge, 2011), 63.

76. "The name *mātrkā* . . . connotes not only the 'mother' of the words, but also of the worlds, inasmuch as the multitude of words entails the multitude of objects by them denoted." Bansat-Boudon, *An Introduction to Tantric Philosophy*, note 443, 107.

77. Torella in *The Īśvarapratyabhijñākārikā*, xvii.

78. Bansat-Boudon, *An Introduction to Tantric Philosophy*, 50.

79. "This I-feeling is the stage of great power, for all mantras arise from and come to rest in it." *Pratyabhijñāhṛdayam: The Secret of Self-Recognition*, 110.

80. Dyczkowski, *The Doctrine of Vibration*, 200.

81. Utpaladeva, *Les Stances sur la Reconnaissace du Seigneur*, 232–33. Amīr ʿAbd al-Kader, *The Spiritual Writings of Amīr ʿAbd al-Kader*, ed. Michel Chodkiewicz (Albany: State University of New York Press, 1982), 17.

82. See, for example, the remarkable *Paths to Transcendence According to Shankara, Ibn al-ʿArabī and Meister Eckhart*, by Reza Shah-Kazemi (Bloomington, IN: World Wisdom, 2006) for a further exploration of these harmonics.

83. Ibn al-ʿArabī, "The Wisdom of Holiness in the Word of Enoch," in *The Bezels of Wisdom: Ibn alʿArabi*, ed. and trans. R. W. J. Austin (New York: Paulist Press, 1980), 85.

84. Ibid.

85. Chittick, *The Sufi Path of Knowledge*, 82.

86. "In the last analysis we see only the properties of the divine names, which are the qualities and attributes intrinsic to Being." Chittick, *The Sufi Path of Knowledge*, 80.

87. Al-Ghazālī, *The Niche of Light*, trans. David Buchman (Provo: Brigham Young University, 1998), 16–17.

88. For further developments on these various degrees and modes of theophany, see "Le Dieu-Un et les dieux multiples," in Henry Corbin, *Le paradoxe du monothéisme* (Paris: L'Herne, 1981), 21–23.

89. Muller-Ortega, *The Triadic Heart of Śiva*, 59.

90. ʿAbd al-Kader, *The Spiritual Writings of the Amīr ʿAbd al-Kader*, 114.

91. Ibn al-ʿArabī, *Bezels of Wisdom*, 275.

92. It must be noted that the reverse position can be at times asserted from another point of view, as when Jīlī affirms that true knowledge is that of the Essence and not of Qualities, because in the former the servant "recognizes that the Divine Essence is his own essence," whereas there is no knowledge of the Qualities since "there is no means ever to exhaust (them.)" al-Jīlī, *Universal Man*, 14. Obviously, Jīlī expresses here a point of view that is closer to Advaita's doctrine of *Ātman* by understanding immanence in a mostly inward way.

93. Hence, the distinction between "Names" and "Names of the Names." "The words which we call divine names are not, strictly speaking the names themselves, but the ʿnames of the namesʾ (*asmā' al-asmā*) which have been revealed by God to His servants through the Koran and other scriptures." Chittick, *The Sufi Path of Knowledge*, 34.

94. "Each thing other than God is a name of God. And since God is Being, every *thing*, every entity, every possible being, is a name of Being." Chittick, *The Sufi Path of Knowledge*, 94.

95. "Every Name implies the Essence as well as the particular aspect it enshrines. Therefore, insofar as it implies the Essence Itself, it partakes of all the Names, whereas, as evincing the particular aspect [of the Essence] it is distinct and unique [relatively]." Ibn al-ʿArabī, *The Bezels of Wisdom*, 88.

96. ʿAbd al-Kader, *The Spiritual Writings*, 114.

97. Al-Ghazālī, *The Niche of Lights*, 12.

98. Cf. for example, Ibn ʿAjība, *Kitāb Miʿrāj al-Tashawwuf ilā Haqā'iq al-Tasawwuf*, ed. and trans. Jean-Louis Michon under the title *L'Ascension du regard vers les réalités du Soufisme* (Paris: Albouraq, 2010), 196.

99. Jīlī considers four degrees of manifestation of the Divine Essence (*dhāt*), which are Divinity (*ulūhiyah*), Unity (*ahadiyah*), Unicity (*wāhidiyah*), and Compassionate Beatitude (*rahmāniyah*). The first two refer to the Essence in Itself, so that it would be more accurate, it seems, to consider them as dimensions of the Divine Reality, rather than degrees of its manifestation. Jīlī explains the distinction between Divinity and Unity as follows:

> The Unity is the most exclusive affirmation of the Essence for Itself, whereas the "Quality of Divinity" is the sublime affirmation of the Essence for Itself and for other than Itself. The distinction between Divinity and Unity corresponds to a recognition of the absolute and infinite dimensions of the Essence. In other words, al-*ahadiyah* is exclusive of everything that is not the Essence. The Name *al-Ahad* means the "One and only One," as clearly expressed in the *Surāh al-Ikhlās*:

> > Say: He is Allah, the One and Only;
> > Allah, the Eternal, Absolute;
> > He begetteth not, nor is He begotten;
> > And there is none like unto Him.
> > (112–1, Yusuf Ali)

This *Surāh* is the best Quranic expression of the exclusive transcendence of the Divine Essence that lies beyond all relationship and comparability. However, the Essence is also infinitely inclusive as well as absolutely exclusive. And it is this infinite dimension of the Divine Essence that is refered to by Jīlī as *ulūhiyah*. Divinity is the synthesis of all the Qualities and Names that are contained in the Essence.

The Unicity (*wāhidiyah*) and Compassionate Beatitude (*rahmāniyah*), by contrast with the Unity and the Divinity, relate to the manifestation of the Essence. The Unicity refers to the inherence of the Essence in all the Names and Qualities while the Compassionate Beatitude "dominates and penetrates the existences and . . . Its principle rules them." Al-Jīlī, *The Universal Man*, 31.

100. Toshihiko Izutsu, *Sufism and Taoism: A Comparative Study of Key Philosophical Concepts* (Berkeley: University of California Press, 1983), 11.

101. Sometimes, the two supreme presences are considered to be the Divinity and the Universal Man (*al-insān al-kāmil*). The latter stands for the Divine Essence, whereas the second represents the synthetic quintessence of Divine Qualities and, thereby, the Prototype of creation.

102. Cf. for example, Titus Burckhardt, *Introduction to Sufi Doctrine* (Bloomington, IN: World Wisdom, 2008), 71. See also Frithjof Schuon, "The Five Divine Presences," in *Form and Substance in the Religions* (Bloomington, IN: World Wisdom, 2002), 51–68.

103. Quran 67:3, translation of Yusuf Ali.

104. "The perfection of the Named is eminently manifested by the fact that He is revealed by His Name to he who ignores Him, so that the Name is to the Named

that which the exterior (*az-zāhir*) is to the interior (*al-bātin*), and in this respect the Name is the Named Himself." al-Jīlī, *Universal Man*, 9.

105. "Each Name and each (Divine) Quality (is) contained in the Name Allāh, (and) it follows that there is no access to the knowledge of God except by way of this Name." al-Jīlī, *Universal Man*, 9.

106. "The entire universe is already contained in the highest consciousness or the highest Self even as the variegated plumage of the peacock is already contained in the plasma of its egg (*mayūrāndarasa-nyāyena*)." *Pratyabhijñāhṛidayam*, 125.

107. Finally, a word must be said of the proportional "presence" and "absence" of God as a personal reality as we move from immanence to transcendence, or from an emphasis on relativity as "not unreal" to one stressing its "nonreal" aspect. From the apparent negation of God in *Madhyamaka* to His universally pervasive and polymorphic presence as "embodied" Śiva in Śaivism the extent to which God is a determining "spiritual reality" varies proportionally to the degree of "non-unreality" conceded to the relative realm. This should come as no surprise since God Himself is by definition "relative," His notion presupposing as it does a relationship with the world of creation and mankind.

108. Nāgārjuna, *The Dispeller of Disputes: Nāgārjuna's Vigrahavyāvartanī*, ed. and trans. Jan Westerhoff (Oxford: Oxford University Press, 2010), 41. "They are to be understood individually by each person, following this direction (*svayam adhigantavyā anayā diśā*): a part [only] can be taught in words (*kimcic chakyam vacanenopdestum*)." Nāgārjuna, *The Dialectical Method of Nāgārjuna: Vigrahavyāvartanī*, trans. Kamaleswar Bhattacharya (Delhi: Motilal Banarsidass, 1998), 137.

109. "That belief which the commonalty of mankind learns is the mould of truth, not truth itself. Complete gnosis is that the truths be uncovered from that mould, as a kernel is taken out of the husk." Al-Ghazālī, *On Knowing Yourself and God*, trans. Muhammad Nur Abdus Salam (Chicago: Great Books of the Islamic World, 2002), 31.

## Chapter 2. Christian and Buddhist Insights into a Metaphysics of Salvation

1. "*Caitanya* (or consciousnes), therefore, connotes absolute freedom in respect of all knowledge and activity (*paripūrnam svātantryam*). The Great Lord, Highest Śiva alone has that (absolute freedom)." *Śiva Sūtras. The Yoga of Supreme Identity. Text of the Sūtras and the Commentary Vimarśinī of Kṣemarāja*, trans. Jaideva Signh (Delhi: Motilal Banarsidass, 1979), 7.

2. "This much at least is clear: that the amalgam of inner piety and outer institution that at a certain stage in their dynamic development was intellectually reified under the term 'religion' and 'religions' was conceived thus because some people (rather inadvertently) fell into the habit of doing so. And the religions have names because we have given names. Once he has become aware of what has happened, man cannot escape choosing between whether or not he will continue to use these particular concepts. To me, for reasons that I have set forth, they seem now clearly

inadequate." Wilfred Cantwell Smith, *The Meaning and End of Religion* (Minneapolis: Fortress Press, 1991), 194.

3. "Scholars might fruitfully historicize and particularize various definitions of Buddhism, might preserve a certain skepticism regarding historical claims to preserve a ahistorical and universal truth, and might seek to reveal the social and political conditions that motivate those claims—but they will need as well to grapple with the tension between academic angles of vision that currently privilege the study of local and historically situated Buddhisms and Buddhist visions of their tradition as crossing or transcending time and space." Karen Derris and Natalie Gummer, *Defining Buddhism(s)* (London: Equinox Publishing, 2007), 6.

4. This is, couched in religious language, the fundamental objection presented to the doctrine of the Trinity by the *Quran.* Thus, we read in 5:73: "They surely disbelieve who say: Lo! Allāh is the third of three; when there is no Allāh save the One Allāh." The status of God as "third" is nothing other than an expression of its dependency on a first and a second, therefore precisely his relativity.

5. *The Mystical Theology,* in Pseudo-Dionysius, *Pseudo-Dionysius: The Complete Works,* trans. Colm Luibheid (New York: Paulist Press, 1987), 135.

6. *The Divine Names* in Pseudo-Dionysius, *Pseudo-Dionysius,* 67.

7. Pseudo-Dionysius, *Pseudo-Dionysius,* 141.

8. Ibid., 61.

9. Ibid., 62.

10. Maximus Confessor, *Chapters on Knowledge,* in *Selected Writings,* trans. George C. Berthold (New York: Paulist Press, 1985), 148.

11. "But God is neither of those who think nor of what is thought for he is beyond them." Confessor, *Chapters on Knowledge,* 148.

12. Pseudo-Dionysius, *Pseudo-Dionysius,* 141.

13. "The 'divine Person' means relation as something subsisting (*relatio ut subsistens*). Otherwise put, it means the relation by way of that substance which is the subsistent hypostasis in the divine nature (*relatio per modum substantiae quae est hypostasis subsistens in natura divina*); though that which subsists in the divine nature is nothing other than the divine nature." *Summa Theologica* I, q. 29, a. 4, in Gilles Emery, *The Trinitarian Theology of St Thomas Aquinas* (Oxford: Oxford University Press, 1993), 116. "Reply to Objection 2: As we say 'three persons' plurally in God, and 'three subsistences,' so the Greeks say 'three hypostases.' But because the word 'substance,' which, properly speaking, corresponds in meaning to 'hypostasis,' is used among us in an equivocal sense, since it sometimes means essence, and sometimes means hypostasis, in order to avoid any occasion of error, it was thought preferable to use 'subsistence' for hypostasis, rather than 'substance.'" q. 29, a. 2, in Thomas Aquinas, *Summa Theologica: Volume 1, part 1,* (New York: Cosimo, 2007), 157.

14. Emery, *The Trinitarian Theology of St Thomas Aquinas,* 91.

15. "From the perspective of its being, like all the other accidental predicates which we attribute to God (such as good, wise, great, and so on), relation does not retain the mode of an existential accident when it is ascribed to God, but exhibits the substantial mode of existence of divinity itself. In God, relation is not something which inheres: it is what God is. Its existence is that of the incomprehensible being which God

is: from this angle, relation is identified with an 'absolute' in God. This identification is hard for us to deal with intellectually, because, in our experience, a relation is not an 'absolute': 'a substance is never a relation.'" Emery, *The Trinitarian Theology*, 94.

16. Frithjof Schuon has coined the expression "relatively Absolute" to refer to the prefiguration of the relative in the Absolute. "We have alluded more than once to the seemingly contradictory, but metaphysically useful and even indispensable, idea of the 'relatively absolute,' which is absolute in relation to what it rules, while pertaining to relativity in relation to the 'Pure Absolute.'" Frithjof Schuon, *In the Face of the Absolute* (Bloomington, IN: World Wisdom, 2014), 79.

17. Significantly, Lossky faults Western Trinitarian theological "reflexes" for giving way to what he considers to be an erroneous and Neoplatonic "apophaticism of the divine-nothingness prior to the Trinity." Vladimir Lossky, *The Mystical Theology of the Eastern Church* (New York: St. Vladimir's Seminary Press, 1976), 65.

18. Ibid.

19. John Anthony McGucki, *The Orthodox Church: An Introduction to its History, Doctrine and Spiritual Culture* (Oxford: Wiley-Blackwell, 2011), 167.

20. "Human thought does not run the risk of going astray if it passes from the consideration of the three persons to that of the common nature. Nevertheless, the two ways [the Western and Eastern] were both equally legitimate so long as the first did not attribute to the essence a supremacy over the three persons." Lossky, *The Mystical Theology of the Eastern Church*, 56.

21. Ibid., 46.

22. John of Damascus, *An Exact Exposition of the Orthodox Faith*, Book I, Chapter VIII, in *The Heart of Catholicism: Essential Writings of the Church from St. Paul to John Paul II*, ed. Theodore E. James (Huntington, IN: Our Sunday Visitor Publishing, 1997), 352.

23. Cf. Saint Gregory Palamas, *The Triads* (New York: Paulist Press, 1983), 97.

24. "The energies hold a middle place: on the one hand they belong to theology, as eternal and inseparable forces of the Trinity existing independently of the creative act; on the other, they also belong to the domain of 'economy,' for it is in His energies that God manifests Himself to His creatures: as St. Basil says, 'they descend even to ourselves.'" Lossky, *The Mystical Theology of the Eastern Church*, 82.

25. Madan Mohan Agrawal, *Essence of Vaisnavism: Philosophy of Bhedābheda* (Delhi: Ajanta, 1992), xiii.

26. In Christianity, one accepts modes for Energies (in the East) but not for the Persons, and one refuses to make degrees out of mode.

27. Michael Comans, *The Method of Early Advaita Vedānta* (Delhi: Motilal Banarsidass, 2000), 217.

28. "St. Irenaeus expresses a similar idea, in a way which is characteristic of the Christian thought of the early centuries: 'for that which is invisible of the Son is the Father, and that which is visible of the Father is the Son.' The Son who renders visible the hidden nature of the Father is here almost identified with the manifesting Energies." Lossky, *The Mystical Theology of the Eastern Church*, 84.

29. See John D. Zizioulas, *Being as Communion* (New York: St. Vladimir's Seminary Press, 1985).

30. See Aristotle Papanikolaou, *Being With God: Trinity, Apophaticism, And Divine-Human Communion* (South Bend: University of Notre Dame Press, 2006), 26.

31. "By combining the first [the Absolute truth] and the fourth [ultimate constituents of experience] of the word *dharma*, we may describe Buddhism as a religious system that defines *dharma* in terms of *dharmas*." Masao Abe, "Buddhism," in *Our Religions*, ed. Arvind Sharma (New York: HarperCollins, 1993), 77.

32. *What the Buddha Taught*, Buddhist Cultural Center, 1996, 53.

33. This restriction means that the view of emptiness is not a view if by this term is meant a philosophical vision or statement preventing or hampering the *realization* of emptiness through a substantialization of its conceptual content. The Buddha taught the doctrine of emptiness as the "exhaustion of all philosophical views," in the sense that the "view of emptiness" would be comparable to a "medicine" that "had cured all the original problems" of a sick man but "remained in the stomach and was not itself expelled," therefore making the disease "much worse." Cf. C. W. Huntington Jr. and Geshe Namgyal Wangchen, *The Emptiness of Emptiness: An Introduction to Early Indian Mādhyamika* (Delhi: Motilal Banarsidass, 1992), 58.

34. These are the Prāsangica and Svātantrika positions. The Prāsangica, with Candrakīrti, is the perspective according to which *pratītya-samutpāda* itself is not a view, whereas the Svātantrika interpretation understands it as the right view. Kalupahana (103) makes the point that the latter is not to be understood, however, as an "absolute truth" but only as a pragmatically effective view. The first interpretation is most radical in applying codependent origination to codependently origination itself, and therefore identifying *nirvāna* with this "negation of negation." The second position makes room for an affirmativeness of codependent arising that does not result in its substantialization. The relativization stops at relativity itself, but without introducing any absolute.

35. Even the early Abhidharmic notion of *dharma*, which is an attempt at defining units of reality that would account for things as they are, strives to avoid any consideration of the latter in terms of substance. That is why the *dharmas* have been characterized as discontinuous and momentary events. They constitute the smallest units of experiential reality, but they are not reducible to conventional objects, in the ordinary sense of "things," since subjective perception is not dissociable from them as units of reality. Richard King, *Indian Philosophy: An Introduction to Buddhist and Hindu Thought* (Edinburgh: Edinburgh University Press, 1999), 116–17.

36. The Buddha presents a rejection of this "distorted vision" in *Sāleyyaka Sutta* (10). The view is characterized negatively as follows: "There is nothing given, nothing offered, nothing sacrificed; no fruit or result of good and bad actions; no this world, no other world; no mother, no father; no beings who are reborn spontaneously; no good and virtuous ascetics and brahmins in the world who have themselves realised by direct knowledge and declare this world and the other world. That is how there are three kinds of mental conduct not in accordance with the *Dhamma*, unrighteous conduct. So, householders, it is by reason of such conduct not in accordance with the *Dhamma*, by reason of such unrighteous conduct that some beings here on the breakup of the body, after death, are reborn in a state of misery, in a bad destination, in the lower world, in hell." Bhikkhu Bodhi, ed., *In the Buddha's Words: An*

*Anthology of Discourses from the Pali Canon* (Somerville, MA: Wisdom Publications, 2005), 158.

37. "Whether Tathagatas arise in the world or not, it still remains a fact, a firm and necessary condition of existence, that all formations are impermanent . . . that all formations are subject to suffering . . . that all things are non-self. A Tathagata fully awakens to this fact and penetrates it. Having fully awakened to it and penetrated it, he announces it, teaches it, makes it known, presents it, discloses it, analyses it and explains it: that all formations are impermanent, that all formations are subject to suffering, that all things are non-self" (3:134). *Anguttara Nikaya, Discourses of the Buddha An Anthology Part I*, selected and translated from the Pali by Nyanaponika Thera and Bhikkhu Bodhi (Kandy, Sri Lanka: Buddhist Publication Society The Wheel Publication, 1970) 155–56.

38. *Udāna, Khuddakanikāya, SuttatPitaka,* quoted in Joseph Walser, *Nāgārjuna in Context: Mahāyāna Buddhism and Early Indian Culture* (New York: Columbia University Press, 2005), 177.

39. See for example, Bhikkhu Thānissaro, *Handful of Leaves*, volume 4 (Sati Center for Buddhist Studies & Metta Forest Monastery, 2004), 120.

40. Cf. Benoytosh Bhattacharya, *An Introduction to Buddhist Esoterism* (Delhi: Motilal Banarsidass, 1980), 128.

41. "[289b] *Samkrta* and *asamskrta* are interdependent in emptiness . . . *Samkrta* and *asamskrta* dharmas exist interdependently (*anyonyāpeksa*): outside of the *samkrtas*, there are no *asamskrtas*, and outside of the *asamkrtas*, there are no *samskrtas*. These two categories include all dharmas. The yogin who considers the faults (*dosa*) of the *samskrtadharmas*, impermanent (*anitya*), painful (*duḥkha*), empty (*śūnya*) etc., knows *ipso facto* the great benefits of the *asamskrtadharmas*." Furthermore, Nāgārjuna explains that "some people, hearing about the defects of the *samskrtadharmas,* become attached (*abhiniveśante*) to the *asamskrtadharmas* and, as a result of this attachment, develop fetters." "[288c] In *nirvāna*, there is no nature of *nirvāna* (*nirvānalaksana*), and the emptiness of *nirvāna* is the emptiness of the absolute (*paramārthaśūnyatā*)." Nāgārjuna, *The Treatise on the Great Virtue of Wisdom*, Volume IV, *Mahāprajñāpāramitāśāstra*. Chapter XLVIII—The Eighteen Emptinesses, trans. Gelongma Karma Migme Chödrön (Wisdom Library: 2001).

42. "It is inappropriate to say that a condition is such by its own nature (*svabhāva*). Instead it becomes a condition depending upon the arising of the effect." Nāgārjuna, *The Philosophy of the Middle Way*, 109.

43. Ibid., 160.

44. Nāgārjuna, *The Dispeller of Disputes*, 53.

45. "*Samsāra* (i.e., the empirical life-death cycle) is nothing essentially different from *nirvāna*. *Nirvāna* is nothing essentially different from *samsāra*," Nāgārjuna, *Mulamadhiyamakakarika*, XXV, 19, trans. K. K. Inada.

46. "The wise must not base their practice
    On getting at the 'emptiness' in what is intrinsically empty.
    In the case of one determined to get at that emptiness itself,
    That wrong is even more extreme than viewing the body as a self."

Nāgārjuna, *Nāgārjuna's Guide to The Bodhisattva Path: Treatise on the Provisions for Enlightenment (The Bodhisambhāra Śāstra by Ārya Nāgārjuna)*, ed. and trans. Bhikshu Dharmamitra (Seattle: Kalavinka Press, 2008), 65.

47. Cf. Brian Edward Brown, *The Buddha Nature. A Study of the Tathāgatagarbha and Ālayavijñāna* (Delhi: Motilal Banarsidas, 1991).

48. "To positively define them (*Tathāgatagarbha* and *Dharmakāya*) as steadfast, eternal, of ultimate existence and intrinsically replete with the infinite Buddha Nature, as well as to designate the Absolute Body (*Dharmakāya*) as the perfection of permanence (*nitya*), pleasure (*sukha*), self (*ātman*), and purity (*śubha*), was a radical departure from, and confrontation with, the classical *Śūnyavāda* of the wisdom (*prajñā*) literature." Brown, *The Buddha Nature,* p.39.

49. "Lord, if there were no Tathagatagarbha, there would be neither aversion towards suffering nor longing, eagerness, and aspiration towards Nirvāna. What is the reason? Whatever be these six perceptions [i.e., the five senses plus the mind], and whatever be this other perception [perhaps intellectual cognition?], these seven natures are unfixed, momentary, and lack experience of suffering; hence these natures are unfit for aversion towards suffering or for longing, eagerness, and aspiration towards Nirvāna. Lord, the Tathāgatagarbha has ultimate existence without beginning or end, has an unborn and undying nature, and experiences suffering; hence it is worthy of the Tathāgatagarbha to have aversion towards suffering as well as longing, eagerness, and aspiration towards Nirvāna." *Lion's Roar of Queen Srimala: A Buddhist Scripture on the Tathagatagabha Theory*, trans. Alex and Hideko Wayman (Delhi: Motilal Banarsidass, 2007), 105.

50. *The Lankāvatāra Sūtra*, trans. Daisetz Teitaro Suzuki (Østermarie, Denmark: Egely Kloster, 2011), 190.

51. *The Awakening of Faith*, trans. D. T. Suzuki, (Dover: New York, 2013), 60.

52. Ibid.

53. Ibid., 74.

54. Peter N. Gregory, *Tsung-mi and the Sinification of Buddhism*, Honolulu: University of Hawai'i Press, 2002.

55. "Therefore we know that this teaching merely destroys feelings of attachment but does not yet clearly reveal the nature that is true and numinous. Therefore the *Great Dharma Drum Sūtra* says: 'All emptiness *sūtras* are expositions that have a remained.' . . . The *Great Perfection of Wisdom Sūtra* says: 'Emptiness is the first gate of the Great Vehicle.'" Tsung-mi, *Inquiry into the Origin of Humanity: An Annotated Translation of Tsung-mi's* Yüan jen lun *with a Modern Commentary*, ed. and trans. Peter N. Gregory (Honolulu: University of Hawai'i Press, 1995), 174–75.

56. "If the mind and its objects are both nonexistent, then who is it that knows they do not exist? Again, if there are no real things whatsoever, then on the basis of what are the illusions made to appear? Moreover, there has never been a case of the illusory things in the world before us being able to arise without being based on something real. If there were no water whose wet nature were unchanging, how could there be the waves of illusory, provisional phenomenal appearances? If there were no mirror whose pure brightness were unchanging, how could there be the reflections of a variety of unreal phenomena? Again, while the earlier statement that the activity of

dreaming and the dream object are equally unreal is indeed true, the dream that is illusory must still be based on someone who is sleeping. Now, granted that the mind and its objects are both empty, it is still not clear on what the illusory manifestations are based. Therefore we know that this teaching merely destroys feelings of attachment but does not yet clearly reveal the nature that is true and numinous." Tsung-mi, *Inquiry into the Origin of Man*, quoted in Peter N. Gregory, *Tsung-mi and the Sinification of Buddhism*, (Honolulu: University of Hawai'i Press, 2002), 236.

57. For a thorough treatment of Tsung-mi's doctrine of the "intents" see Peter N. Gregory's seminal works, *Tsung-mi and the Sinification of Buddhism* (Honolulu: University of Hawai'i Press, 2002) and *Inquiry into the Origin of Humanity: An Annotated Translation of Tsung-mi's* Yüan jen lun *with a Modern Commentary* (Honolulu: University of Hawai'i Press, 1995).

58. Tsung-mi, in Gregory, *Tsung-mi and the Sinification of Buddhism,* 211.

59. Tsung-mi, *Inquiry into the Origin of Humanity,* 108.

60. Ibid., 167.

61. This is in the continuation of early Mahāyāna texts such as the *Ratnagotra,* for which "the *Tathāgatagarbha* represents the true meaning of non-substantiality." Brown, *The Buddha Nature,* 145.

62. Tsung-mi, *Inquiry into the Origin of Humanity,* 174.

63. "According to *dharmadhātu pratītyasamutpāda* countless dharmas (all phenomena in the world) are representations of the wisdom of Buddha without exception. . . . They exist in a state of mutual dependence, interfusion and balance without any contradiction or conflict. . . . 'Perfect interfusion' contains two main connotations. First, as far as a single thing or phenomenon is concerned, it becomes significant only in connection with other things. . . . Second, as far as all things or phenomena are concerned, they are mutually identical and penetrating without any obstruction." Wei Daoru, "A Fundamental Feature of the Huayan Philosophy," in *Reflecting Mirrors: Perspectives on Huayan Buddhism,* ed. Imre Hamar (Wiesbaden: Harrassowitz Verlag, 2007), 189.

64. "If fundamental reality is non-substantial and non-corporeal, then 'emptiness' can express itself in any form, shape or color. Such is the philosophical basis of understanding Pure Land and Amida Buddha." Taitetsu Unno, *Shin Buddhism: Bits of Rubble Turn into Gold* (New York: Doubleday, 2002), 39.

65. "Everything in and out of the universe without exception is interdependently related to every other thing; nothing whatsoever is independently self-existing without relying upon something else. And any relationship is reciprocal and reversible; there can be no unreciprocal and irreversible relationship whatsoever." Masao Abe, *Zen and Comparative Studies* (Honolulu: University of Hawai'i, 1997), 98. " 'Mountains are really mountains, waters are really waters,' *is realized in a thoroughly non-conceptual way* in the absolute present which is beyond and yet embraces, past, present and future." Masao Abe, *Zen and Western Thought* (Honolulu: University of Hawai'i Press, 1985), 17.

66. Toshihiko Izutsu, *Toward a Philosophy of Zen Buddhism* (Boulder: Prajña, 1982), 49.

67. "In Buddhism, *sunyata,* or emptiness as ultimate reality, is entirely unobjectifiable and nonsubstantial in that *sunyata* is neither immanent nor transcendent,

being even beyond the one God." Masao Abe, *Zen and the Modern World: A Third Sequel to Zen and Western Thought* (Honolulu: University of Hawai'i Press, 2003), 27.

68. Abe, *Zen and Western Thought*, 17.

69. "*Samsāra* and *nirvāna* are united through mutual negation at each moment. The unextended, subjective point where *samsāra* and *nirvāna* are mutually united through negation is nothing other than the *moment* (*ksana*). . . . All time of past, present, and future are transcended precisely in the moment of the 'now.'" Abe, "The Problem of Death in East and West," in *Zen and Comparative Studies*, 135.

70. Keiji Nishitani, *Religion and Nothingness* (Berkeley: University of California Press, 1982), 109.

71. "The whole thing centers around the total nullification of individual things in Nothingness and their rebirth from the very bottom of Nothingness again into the domain of empirical reality as concrete individuals, but completely transformed in their inner structure." Izutsu, *Toward a Philosophy of Zen Buddhism*, 30.

72. Abe, *Zen and Western Thought*, 10.

73. The Japanese "*soku*" has been translated by *sive*, not without some ambiguity on account of Spinoza's consecrated use of the Latin term: "When we say 'being-*sive*-nothingness,' or 'form is emptiness; emptiness is form,' we do not mean that what are initially conceived of as being on one side and nothingness on the other have later been joined together. In the context of *Mahāyāna* thought, the primary principle of which is to transcend all duality emerging from logical analysis, the phrase 'being-*sive*-nothingness' requires that one take up the stance of the '*sive*' and from there view being as being and nothingness as nothingness." Nishitani, *Religion and Nothingness*, 97.

74. Izutsu, *Toward a Philosophy of Zen Buddhism*, 29.

75. It must be mentioned that, in doing so, he is just following the traditional account of Chinese Zen Master Ch'ing-yüan Wei-hsin, which distinguishes between "thirty years ago," "after I got an insight into the truth of Zen," and "now." Cf. Izutsu, *Zen and Western Thought*, 4.

76. Let us note that Taoism proposes an ultimate stage of spiritual realization that involves a "forgetting of forgetting" that is not without analogy with the Buddhist "emptying of emptiness": "Yen Hui disregarded human-heartedness and righteousness, and forgot ceremonies and music. He gave up his body and discarded his knowledge. He forgot everything and became one with the infinite. This is the principle of forgetting things. When all things were forgotten, he was thus empty. And yet, compared with the sages, he was still not perfect. The sages forget that they forget, whereas even the great worthies cannot forget that they forget. If Yen Hui could not forget that he forgot, it would seem that something still remained in his mind. That is why he is said to have been often empty." Fung Yu-Lan, *A Short History of Chinese Philosophy* (New York: The Free Press, 1976), 218.

77. Abe, *Zen and Western Thought*, 127.

78. "Thus it can be said: Negation of negation is affirmation of affirmation; double negation is double affirmation; absolute negation is absolute affirmation." Masao Abe, Substance, Process, and Emptiness," in *Zen and Comparative Studies*, 107.

79. Abe, *Zen and Western Thought*, 10.

80. Ibid., 17.

81. Abe, *Zen and Comparative Studies*, 108.

82. Ibid., 109–10.

83. Nāgārjuna, *Nāgārjuna's Guide to the Bodhisattva's Path*, 43.

84. Thus, Hans Waldenfels has alluded to the Buddhist undertones of the reciprocal emptying of God and man in Karl Rahner's theological thought: "The world,
then, is the 'emptiness' of God and man, in it, is that-which-is-not-God. The end, the
high point of the kenosis of God, is realized in two steps, with the radical and total
correspondence of the self-emptying of God and the self-emptying of man." Hans
Waldenfels, *Absolute Nothingness: Foundations for a Buddhist-Christian Dialogue* (New
York: Paulist Press, 1976), 158.

85. Peter Phan, ed., *The Cambridge Companion to the Trinity* (Cambridge: Cambridge University Press, 2011), 4. In a contemporary context, this soteriological, and
indeed historical, focus can even take the form of a negation of the Absolute as such:
"To begin with, I would not speak about 'absolute' truths, even for believers, in the
sense that absolute is that which is disconnected and bereft of all relationship. Truth,
according to the Christian faith, is the love of God for us in Jesus Christ. Therefore,
truth is a relationship. As such each one of us receives the truth and expresses it from
within, that is to say, according to one's own circumstances, culture and situation
in life, etc." Pope Francis, "Letter to a Non-Believer: Pope Francis responds to Dr.
Eugenio Scalfari journalist of the Italian Newspaper *La Repubblica*, From the Vatican,
4 September 2013," *The Holy See*, 4 September 2013, http://w2.vatican.va/content/
francesco/en/letters/2013/documents/papa-francesco_20130911_eugenio-scalfari.html.

86. Izutsu, *Toward a Philosophy of Zen Buddhism*, 49.

87. It is not for nothing that D. T. Suzuki highlights this Patristic *koan* in his
*Introduction to Zen Buddhism*: "A noted Christian Father of the early Middle Ages
once exclaimed: 'O poor Aristotle! Thou who has discovered for the heretics the art
of dialectics, the art of building up and destroying, the art of discussing all things and
accomplishing nothing!' So much ado about nothing, indeed! See how philosophers of
all ages contradict one another after spending all their logical acumen and analytical
ingenuity on the so-called problems of science and knowledge. No wonder the same
old wise man, wanting to put a stop once for all to all such profitless discussions,
has boldly thrown the following bomb right into the midst of those sand-builders:
'*Certum est quia impossible est*'; or, more logically, '*Credo quia absurdum est.*' I believe
because it is irrational; is this not an unqualified confirmation of Zen?" D.T. Suzuki,
*An Introduction to Zen Buddhism* (New York: Grove Press, 2007), 62.

## Chapter 3. On the Good beyond Good and Evil

1. Simone Weil, *Gravity and Grace* (London: Routledge, 2002), 99.

2. "Sometimes the existence of evil is identified with that of a metaphysical
domain of darkness and temptation which exists independently of human sinfulness;

on other occasions we are told that man's sinfulness actualized the potentially evil, i.e. made it tear itself away from the Divine." Gershom Scholem, *Major Trends in Jewish Mysticism*. (New York: Schocken Books, 1995), 236.

3. Moses Nahmanides, quoted in *The Essential Kabbalah: The Heart of Jewish Mysticism*, trans. Daniel Matt (Edison: Castle Books, 1997), 93.

4. Moses Cordovero, *Moses Cordovero's Introduction to Kabbalah: An Annotated Translation of His Or Ne'erav*, trans. Ira Robinson (Hoboken: Ktav Publishing House, 1994), 122.

5. "Thus, the name involves an element of revelation, which is *ipso facto* an element of . . . Stern Judgment or Rigor, which imposes boundaries and limitations and shapes frameworks. In the beginning that precedes all beginnings, before there was any movement, when God was immersed in the recesses of His infinity, the name was integrated within His essence, and Stern Judgment was incorporated within the unity of pure Compassion. No revelation had yet occurred, and no boundary line had yet been drawn to fashion the cosmos and its manifestation." This is based on *Derush Heftzibah* by a major disciple of Isaac Luria, Rabbi Joseph ibn Tabul. Yoram Jacobson, "The Concept of Evil and Its Sanctification in Kabbalistic Thought," in *The Problem of Evil and its Symbols in Jewish and Christian Tradition*, ed. Henning Graf Reventlow and Yair Hoffman (London: T&T Clark International, 2004), 98.

6. Jacobson, "The Concept of Evil," in ibid., 99.

7. "Upon seeing that Adam was created in the supernal image . . . and that he was entirely intellective, like the higher angels, who are angels of compassion, she (Eve) thought, that she would not have any . . . dominion, as the forces of Stern Judgment . . . would not perform their activity, and from them lust is manifested. Therefore she 'squeezed grapes'—she separated . . . and gave . . . [as] the head of the foxes . . . and then there acted . . . the powers—and this is a complete 'cutting off.'" R. Judah Hayyat quoted in ibid., 117.

8. Joseph ben Abraham Gikatilla, *Sha'arei 'Orah*, 2 volumes, ed. Joseph Ben-Shlomo (Jerusalem: Bialik Institute, 1981), 101.

9. Kamalakar Mishra, *Kashmir Śaivism: The Central Philosophy of Tantrism* (Delhi: Indica Books, 2011), 270.

10. Swami Lakshmanjoo, *Kashmir Shaivism: The Secret Supreme*, ed. John Hughes (Culver City, CA: *Universal Shaiva Fellowship*, 2007). 117.

11. "Just as the snake, an object of dread because of its poison, stands as a symbol of evil forces, as long as she lies motionless within us, Kundalinī is related to our obscure, unconscious energies, both poisoned and poisonous. However, once they are awakened and under control, these same energies become effective and confer a true power." Lilian Silburn, *Kundalinī: The Energy of the Depths* (Albany: State University of New York Press, 1988), 15.

12. One may wonder whether there is a nonhuman, or nonconscious evil. The answer is both affirmative and negative given that cosmic imperfections, for instance, are undoubtedly a result of a fragmentation of Śiva's consciousness, but when considered from the latter point of view, they lose their character of "evil" without losing their objective imperfection. The distinction is in part a semantic matter (what do we call evil?) and in part a function of the Śivaite exclusive focus on consciousness.

13. Abhinavagupta, *Fifty Stanzas to Explain Ultimate Realization*, in David Dubois, *Abhinavagupta: La Liberté de la Conscience* (Paris: Almora, 2010), 322.

14. Abhinavagupta writes that "Nothing new is achieved nor is that which in reality is unmanifest, revealed—(only) the idea is eradicated that the luminous being shines not." Quoted in Dyczkowski, *The Doctrine of Vibration*, 194.

15. Ibid.

16. Lakshmanjoo, *Kashmir Shaivism*, 117.

17. Cf. Dubois, *Abhinavagupta*, 295.

18. In the words of Paul Eduardo Muller-Ortega commenting upon Abhinavagupta, "Spiritual ignorance is precisely the attachment to polarities of good and evil, purity and impurity, right and wrong, and life and death. . . . It is precisely the attachment to these polarities that constitutes conventional morality." Muller-Ortega, *The Triadic Heart of Śiva*, 33.

19. Meister Eckhart, *The Essential Sermons, Commentaries, Treatises, and Defense*, ed. and trans. Edmund Colledge, O.S.A., and Bernard McGinn (New York: Paulist Press, 1981), 140.

20. Ibid., 141.

21. Ibid.

22. Ibid., 78.

23. Meister Eckhart. *The Complete Mystical Works of Meister Eckhart*, ed. and trans. Maurice O'C. Walshe (New York: Herder and Herder, 2009), 342.

24. *Futūhāt al-Makkiyya* I 47.2, in Chittick, *The Sufi Path of Knowledge*, 290.

25. "In its essence the possible thing does not possess the property of the Being which is Necessary through Its own Essence, and this is why evil presents itself to the possible thing." *Futūhāt al-Makkiyya* III 315.6, in Chittick, *The Sufi Path of Knowledge*, 291.

26. *Futūhāt* III 510.21, in Chittick, *The Sufi Path of Knowledge*, 293.

27. This is in relation to a passage of the *Qur'ān* in which "good" and "bad" are connected to connotations of smell: "Vile women are for vile men, and vile men for vile women. Good women are for good men, and good men for good women; such are innocent of that which people say: For them is pardon and a bountiful provision." (Qur, 24:26) The terms *khabīth* and *tayyib* that are rendered by "vile" and "good" by Marmaduke Pickthall, and sometimes also by "impure" and "pure," can be understood, as they are by Ibn al-'Arabī, as referring respectively to malodorant and sweet-smelling characteristics.

28. Ibn al-'Arabī, *The Bezels of Wisdom*, 278.

29. Ibid.

30. Ibid., 279.

31. Ibid., 288.

32. "If one of you becomes aware of an evil, let him oppose it by force (literally: 'by his hand'); and if he cannot do that, let him oppose it by speech; and if he cannot do that, let him oppose it by his heart—this is the least which faith demands." 'Abd al-Kader, *The Spiritual Writings*, 147.

33. Ibid., 147.

34. Ibid., 148.

35. Ibid., 149.

36. This is uttterly independent from the question of Divine Omnipotence since the latter refers not to the Impersonal Divine Essence but to the Divine Person whose power is exercised in relation to other-than-God. The Essence is not other than anything.

## Chapter 4. On Hindu *Bhedābheda* and Sufi *Barzakh*

1. Octavio Paz, *The Bow and the Lyre* (Austin: University of Texas Press, 1973), 87.

2. "This [self] was indeed Brahman in the beginning. It knew itself only as 'I am Brahman.' Therefore, it became all. And whoever among the gods had this enlightenment, also became That [Brahman]. It is the same with the seers (rishis), the same with men." Swami Nikhilananda, ed., *The Principal Upanishads* (Mineola, NY: Dover Publications, 2003), 191.

3. Sarvepalli Radhakrishnan and Charles A. Moore, eds., *A Source Book in Indian Philosophy* (Princeton: Princeton University Press, 1967), 94.

4. "Mādhva, like Rāmānuja, holds that knowledge implies a knowing subject or self and a known object or not-self. Knowledge without a knower and a known is inconceivable. Therefore both knowing subjects and known objects must exist. They cannt be reduced to each other. Known objects are as real as knowing subjects. . . . [T]he distinction between the self and the not-self is absolute." Jadunath Sinha, *Indian Realism* (Delhi: Motilal Banarsidass, 1972), 266.

5. Gerald James Larson and Ram Shankar Bhattacharya, *Sāmkhya: A Dualist Tradition in Indian Philosophy*, Encyclopedia of Indian Philosophies, vol. iv (Delhi: Motilal Banarsidass, 1987), 66.

6. Sarvepalli Radhakrishnan, *Indian Philosophy, volume 2* (Delhi: Oxford University Press, 1996), 280.

7. Karl H. Potter, *Presuppositions of Indian Philosophies* (Englewood Cliffs, NJ: Prentice-Hall, 1963), 109.

8. Larson and Bhattacharya, *Sāmkhya*, 79.

9. Mysore Hiriyanna, *The Essentials of Indian Philosophy* (London: George Allen and Unwin, 1985), 114–15.

10. Larson and Bhattacharya, *Sāmkhya*, 80.

11. Radhakrishnan and Moore, *A Source Book*, 679.

12. "(Nor is there any consciousness devoid of objects; for nothing of this kind is ever known. Moreover, the self-luminousness of consciousness has, by our opponent himself, been proved on the ground that its essential nature consists in illumining [revealing] objects; the self-luminousness of consciousness not admitting of proof apart from its essential nature which consists in the lighting up of objects. And as moreover, according to our opponent, consciousness cannot be the object of another consciousness, it would follow that [having neither an object nor itself being an object]." Rāmānuja, *Vedanta-Sutras with Ramanuja's Commentary*, Part III, trans. George Thibaut (Oxford: Clarendon Press, 1904), 52.

13. Radhakrishnan and Moore, *A Source Book*, 687.

14. Ibid., 682.

15. M. A. Alwar, *Essentials of Viśistādvaita* (Bangalore: Shri Kashi Shesha Sastri Religious Trust, 2010), 178–79.

16. Hiriyanna, *The Essentials of Indian Philosophy*, 177.

17. "[For Rāmānuja] the *jīva* is different from God, but not independent of him. It is described as a *prakāra* of God, by which is meant that it is an accessory to him, and not that it is a mode in the sense of being a transformation of him." Ibid., 181.

18. "The real and universal definition of *śeṣa* and *śeṣin* (the subsidiary and the principal) must be expressed as follows: that whose nature lies solely in being valued through a desire to contribute a special excellence to another entity is the *śeṣa*. The other is the *śeṣin* i.e that to which the subsidiary contributes special excellence." Vedarthasamgraha 182, 146, in Jon Paul Sydnor, *Ramanuja and Schleiermacher: Toward a Constructive Comparative Theology*, 2nd ed. (Cambridge: James Clarke, 2012), 43.

19. C. J. Bartley, *The Theology of Rāmānuja: Realism and Religion* (New York: RoutledgeCurzon, 2002), 43.

20. P. T. Raju, *Idealistic Thought of India* (New York: Routledge, [1953] 2013), 156.

21. Ibid.

22. Hiriyanna, *The Essentials of Indian Philosophy*, 178.

23. Ibid.

24. Alwar, *Essentials of Viśistādvaita*, 176–77.

25. P. N. Srinivasachiri, *Ramanuja's Idea of the Finite Self*, quoted in Swami Prabhavananda, *The Spiritual Heritage of India* (Garden City, NY: Doubleday, 1963), 313.

26. "Svetaketu, who is desirous of final release, is at first—by means of the clause 'Thou art that'—instructed to meditate on himself as having his Self in that which truly is; and thereupon the passage 'for him there is delay' only as long as 'I shall not be released, then I shall be united' teaches that for a man taking his stand upon that teaching there will be Release, i.e. union with Brahman—which is delayed only until this mortal body falls away." Rāmānuja, *Vedanta-Sutras with Ramanuja's Commentary*, 204.

27. Prabhavananda, *The Spiritual Heritage of India*, 312.

28. Ibid.

29. Radhakrishnan and Moore, *A Source Book*, 670–71.

30. Andrew J. Nicholson, "Reconciling Dualism and Non-Dualism: Three Arguments in Vijñānabhiksu's *Bhedābheda Vedānta*," *Journal of Indian Philosophy* 35, no. 4 (2007): 382.

31. Andrew J. Nicholson, *Unifying Hinduism. Philosophy and Identity in Indian Intellectual History* (New York: Columbia University Press, 2010), 59.

32. Potter, *Presuppositions*, 157.

33. Mahendranath Sircar, "Reality in Indian Thought," *The Philosophical Review* 42, no. 3 (May 1993): 260.

34. Abhinavagupta, *Abhinavagupta's Śrī Tantrāloka*, Volume I, trans. Satya Prakash D. Singh and Swami Maheshvarananda (New Delhi: Standard Publishing, 2015), 98.

35. "Just as earth, water, etc. get reflected in a clean mirror even so all events and objects of the world get reflected unmixed in the one Lord Himself." Abhinavagupta, *Abhinavagupta's Śrī Tantrāloka*, 86.

36. *Pratyabhijñāhṛidayam*, 52.

37. Singh, *Śiva Sūtras*, 236.

38. Bansat-Boudon, *An Introduction to Tantric Philosophy*, 112–13.

39. Jaiveda Singh in Abhinavagupta, *A Trident of Wisdom: Translation of Parātriśikā-Vivarana*, trans. Jaiveda Singh (Albany: State University of New York Press, 1989), 3.

40. Titus Burckhardt, *Mirror of the Intellect. Essays on Traditional Science and Sacred Art* (Albany: State University of New York Press, 1987), 193.

41. "If a Muslim knew what a idol really was, he would know there is faith in idol worship." Mahmud Shabistarī, *Garden of Mystery: The Gulshan-i Rāz of Mahmud Shabistarī*, trans. Robert Abdul Hayy Darr (Cambridge: Archetype, 2007), 156.

42. "I was a prophet when Adam was between spirit and body." *Hadīth* quoted by al-Hākim, Tayeb Chouiref, *Spiritual Teachings of the Prophet* (Louisville: Fons Vitae, 2011), 206.

43. Muhyī-al-Dīn Ibn al-'Arabī, *The Meccan Revelations: Selected Texts of Al-Futu-hat al-Makkiya*, Presentations and Translations from the Arabic under the direction of Michel Chodkiewicz; in collaboration with William C. Chittick and James W. Morris (New York: Pir Press, 2000), 152.

44. Our translation. From Muhyī al-Dīn ibn 'Arabī, *al-Futūhāt al-Makkīyah*, (Bayrūt: Dar Sādir, 2007).

45. William C. Chittick, *Imaginal Worlds: Ibn Al-'Arabī and the Problem of Religious Diversity* (Albany: State University of New York Press, 1994), 162.

46. Ibid.

47. Al-Jurjānī, *Le Livre des définitions (Kitāb at-Ta'rīfāt)*, ed. and trans. Maurice Gloton, (Beirut: Dar Albouraq, 2005), 108.

48. 'Abd al-Kader, *The Spiritual Writings*, 58.

49. Ibid., 116.

50. "God in His Essence remains incomparable, but He discloses Himself by means of the Barzakh, thus being called similar." Chittick, *Sufi Path of Knowledge*, 126.

51. Ibn al-'Arabī, *Inshā al-dawā'ir*, ed. Nyberg, 22, quoted in 'Abd al-Kader, *Spiritual Writings*, 216.

52. Chittick, *Sufi Path of Knowledge*, 322.

53. Ibid.

54. Ibn al-'Arabī, *Bezels of Wisdom*, 85.

55. Ibid., 113.

56. Arvind Sharma, *Our Religions* (New York: HarperCollins, 1993), 4.

## Chapter 5. Knowing the Unknowable

1. "The concept 'religion,' then, in the West has evolved. Its evolution has included a long-range development that we may term a process of reification: mentally

making religion into a thing, gradually coming to conceive it as an objective systematic entity." Wilfred Cantwell Smith, *The Meaning and End of Religion* (Minneapolis: Fortress Press, 1991), 51.

2. Olivier Roy, *Holy Ignorance: When Religion and Culture Part Ways* (Oxford: Oxford University Press, 2014).

3. René Descartes, *Meditations on First Philosophy: with Selections from the Objections and Replies*, trans. Michael Moriarty (Oxford: Oxford University Press, 2008), 18.

4. René Descartes, *Principles of Philosophy* (New York: Start Publishing, 2012), VII.

5. *Vorlesungen über speculative Dogmatik* 3, Vol. VIII, trans. Joris Geldhof, 339, quoted in Joris Geldhof, "'*Cogitor Ergo Sum*': On the Meaning and Relevance of Baader's Theological Critique of Descartes," *Modern Theology* 21, no. 2 (April 2005): 239.

6. *Vorlesungen über speculative Dogmatik* 3, Vol. VIII, trans. Joris Geldhof, 339, quoted in Geldhof, "'*Cogitor Ergo Sum*'": 241.

7. *Vorlesungen über speculative Dogmatik* 1, Vol. VIII, trans. Joris Geldhof, 110, quoted in Geldhof, "'*Cogitor Ergo Sum*'": 241.

8. Franklin Merrell-Wolff, *Pathways Through To Space: An Experiential Journal* (New York: Three Rivers Press, 1983).

9. Franklin Merrell-Wolff, *Experience and Philosophy* (Albany: State University of New York Press, 1994), 418.

10. Michael Pye, *Skillful Means: A Concept in Mahāyāna Buddhism*, 2nd ed. (London: Routledge, 2003), 9.

11. Abhinavagupta, *Abhinavagupta's Śri Tantrāloka and Other Works*, volume 1, trans. Satya Prakash Singh and Swami Maheshvarananda (New Delhi: Standard Publishers: 2015), 71.

12. Moti Lal Pandit, *The Philosophical and Practical Aspects of Kāśmīra Śaivism* (New Delhi: Munshiram Manoharlal, 2012), 192.

13. Ibid., 82.

14. Pye, *Skilful Means*, 9–10.

15. "Then I listened to the Brahmā's pleading, and out of compassion for beings I surveyed the world with the eye of a Buddha. Surveying the world with the eye of a Buddha, I saw beings with little dust in their eyes and with much dust in their eyes, with keen faculties and with dull faculties, with good qualities and with bad qualities, easy to teach and hard to teach, and some who dwelt seeing fear in blame and in the other world. Just as in a pond of blue or red or white lotuses, some lotuses that are born and grow in the water thrive immersed in the water without rising out of it, and some other lotuses that are born and grow in the water rest on the water's surface, and some other lotuses that are born and grow in the water rise out of the water and stand clear, unwetted by it; so too, surveying the world with the eye of a Buddha, I saw beings with little dust in their eyes and with much dust in their eyes, with keen faculties and with dull faculties, with good qualities and with bad qualities, easy to teach and hard to teach, and some who dwelt seeing fear in blame and in the other world." *Ariyapariyesanā Sutta: The Noble Search* (Sutta 26, i170), in *The Middle Length Discourses of the Buddha: A Translation of the Majjhima Nikāya*, trans. Bhikkhu Ñānamoli and Bhikkhu Bodhi (Somerville, MA: Wisdom Publications, 1995), 262.

16. John W. Schroeder. *Skillful Means: The Heart of Buddhist Compassion* (Honolulu: University of Hawai'i Press, 2001), 2.

17. Ibid., 151.

18. The third body, intermediary between the Nirmāṇakāya and the Dharmakāya, is the Sambhogakāya, or the spiritual or subtle body of bliss in which Buddhas and Bodhisattvas appear.

19. Kūkai, *Kūkai: Major Works*, trans. Yoshito S. Hakeda (New York: Columbia University Press, 1972), 151.

20. Masao Ichishima, "Integration of Sūtra and Tantra," in *Buddhist Thought and Ritual*, ed. David J. Kalupahana (Delhi: Motilal Banarsidass, 1991), 95.

21. Rita M. Gross and Rosemary Radford Ruether, *Religious Feminism and the Future of the Planet: A Buddhist-Christian Conversation* (New York: Continuum, 2001), 76.

22. Miranda Eberle Shaw, *Buddhist Goddesses of India* (Princeton: Princeton University Press, 2006), 169.

23. "At any rate, we would like to hypothesize that the relation between the two tantric principles of 'wisdom' and 'method' is neither one of complementarity, nor polarity, nor even antinomy, but rather one of androcentric hegemony. The translation of *upaya* as 'trick' is thoroughly justified. We can thus in no sense speak of a 'mystic marriage' of *prajna* and *upaya*, and unfortunately we must soon demonstrate that very little of the widely distributed (in the West) conception of Tantrism as a sublime art of love and a spiritual refinement of the partnership remains." Victor and Victoria Trimondi, "The Shadow of the Dalai Lama—Part I—2. Tantric Buddhism," *Trimondi Online Magazine*, www.trimondi.de/SDLE/Part-1-02.htm.

24. Schroeder, *Skillful Means*, 154.

25. The first expression was coined by Toby Mayer, the second by Michel Chodkiewicz. Cf. Toby Mayer, "Theology and Sufism," in *Classical Islamic Theology*, ed. Tim Winter (Cambridge: Cambridge University Press, 2008), 258; and Michel Chodkiewicz. *An Ocean Without Shore: Ibn 'Arabī, the Book and the Law* (Albany: State University of New York Press, 1993), 128.

26. Ibn al-'Arabī, *The Bezels of Wisdom*, 137.

27. Cf. William C. Chittick, "The Ambigity of the Qur'anic Command," in *Between Heaven and Hell: Islam, Salvation, and the Fate of Others*, ed. Mohammad Hassan Khalil (Oxford: Oxford University Press, 2013), 65–86.

28. Chittick, *The Sufi Path of Knowledge*, 352.

29. Ibid.

30. "In God the images of all things are alike, but they are images of unlike things. The highest angel, the soul, and the midge have an equal image in God." Sermon Sixty-Seven in Meister Eckhart, *The Complete Mystical Works of Meister Eckhart*, 342.

31. Chittick, *The Sufi Path of Knowledge*, 349.

32. Ibn al-'Arabī, *The Bezels of Wisdom*, 92.

33. "He lifts the veil between Himself and His servant. The servant sees Him in the form of his own belief, so He is identical to the object of his belief." Ibn al-'Arabī, *The Bezels of Wisdom*, 120, in Chittick, *The Sufi Path of Knowledge* 339.

34. Chittick, *The Sufi Path of Knowledge*, 338.

35. Ibid., 340.

36. *Meccan Revelations*: III 470.16, in Chittick, *The Sufi Path of Knowledge*, 339.

37. Quoted in Sonam Thakchoe, *The Two Truths Debate: Tsongkhapa and Gorampa on the Middle Way* (Somerville, MA: Wisdom Publications, 2007), 74.

38. See Reza Shah-Kazemi's beautifully suggestive "Buddhist *shahādah*": "No conceivable form: only the inconceivable Essence." Reza Shah-Kazemi, *Common Ground Between Islam and Buddhism* (Louisville, KY: Fons Vitae, 2010), 43.

39. Brian Edward Brown, *The Buddha Nature. A Study of the Tathāgatagharba and Ālayavijñāna* (Delhi: Motilal Banarsidass, 1991), 27, note 17.

40. Ibn al-'Arabī, *The Bezels of Wisdom*, 151.

41. Ibid., 85.

42. "The Sense of the Absolute in Religions," in Frithjof Schuon, *Gnosis: Divine Wisdom* (Bloomington, IN: World Wisdom, 2006), 3–16.

## Chapter 6. Transmutation, the Sacred Word, and the Feminine

1. "These two *tattvas* are the interdependent *tattvas*: *śakti-tattva* and *śiva-tattva*. The impression which comes in these two *tattvas* is only I, the pure I, the universal I. It is not 'this universe is my own expansion' or 'I am this whole universe.' No it is just I, pure I, universal I." Lakshmanjoo, *Kashmir Shaivism*, 9.

2. "This churning appears as the gross aspect of vibration, as soon as Śiva differentiates himself from his energy in order to contemplate her." Silburn, *Kundalinī*, 7.

3. Ibid., 207.

4. Bansat-Boudon, *An Introduction to Tantric Philosophy*, 11.

5. *The Yoga of Delight, Wonder, and Astonishment: A Translation of the Vijnana-bhairava*, trans. Jaideva Singh (Albany: State University of New York Press, 1991), 67.

6. Bansat-Boudon, *An Introduction to Tantric Philosophy*, 50.

7. Dyczkowski, *The Doctrine of Vibration*, 188.

8. Isayeva, *From Early Vedanta to Kashmir Shaivism*, 31.

9. Silburn, *Kundalinī*, 11.

10. Abhinavagupta, *Parātrīśikā-Vivarana*, 217.

11. Bansat-Boudon, *An Introduction to Tantric Philosophy*, 199.

12. Ibid.

13. I. K. Taimni, *The Ultimate Reality and Realization—Śiva-Sutra* (Chennai: The Theosophical Publishing House, 2004), 14.

14. Singh, *Śiva Sūtras*, 254.

15. "It is called *mantra*, because it induces *manana* or reflection on the Supreme and because it provides *trāna* or protection from the whirlgig of transmigratory life." Ibid., 253.

16. "At root, the Mantra represents the pure signification of all possible sentences and words relating to the world of particulars." Dyczkowski, *The Doctrine of Vibration*, 201.

17. Ibid.

18. *Pratyabhijñāhṛidayam*, 39.

19. "Clearly, what prevents the yogi from attending to his state of consciousness rather than the circumstances which induce it is the craving for pleasure (*abhilāsa*) born of ignorance—the source of every impurity which clouds consciousness." Dyczkowsky, *The Doctrine of Vibration*, 217.

20. Sachiko Murata, *The Tao of Islam: A Sourcebook on Gender Relationships in Islamic Thought* (Albany: State University of New York Press, 1992), 207.

21. Frithjof Schuon, *Logic and Transcendence: A New Translation with Selected Letters* (Bloomington, IN: World Wisdom, 2009), 27.

22. Chittick, *The Sufi Path of Knowledge*, 39.

23. "Now it is from this all-embracing dimension of divine reality that compassion springs: for it is not just as being or knowledge, presence or immanence, that God encompasses all, it is also as *Rahma*: My *Rahma* encompasses all things. . . . The angels, indeed, give priority to God's *Rahma* over His knowledge (*'Ilm*) when addressing Him as the one who encompasses all things: You encompass all things in *Rahma* and *'Ilm* (40:7)" Reza Shah-Kazemi, *Common Ground Between Islam and Buddhism*, 98.

24. Ibn al-'Arabī, *The Bezels of Wisdom*, 277.

25. Chittick, *The Sufi Path of Knowledge*, 109.

26. Salman Bashier, *Ibn al-'Arabi's Barzakh: The Concept of the Limit and the Relationship between God and the World* (Albany: State University of New York Press, 2004, 139.

27. Henry Corbin, *Creative Imagination in the Sufism of Ibn Arabi*, trans. Ralph Manheim (Princeton: Princeton University Press, 2014), 162.

28. Murata, *The Tao of Islam*, 195.

29. Ibid.

30. "(Ruzbihan's) entire *diarium spirituale* is as it were a series of variations on the theme of the amphiboly (*iltibās*) of the human Image which simultaneously 'is' and 'is not.' All that is sensible, visible and audible is amphiboly, has a double meaning, in that it reveals what is invisible and inaudible, and it is precisely this that constitutes the theophanic function of the beauty of created beings, without it being inconsistent with the divestment of the pure Essence (*tanzīh*)." Henry Corbin, *History of Islamic Philosophy*, (London and New York: Kegan Paul International, 1993), 286.

31. The most strikingly evocative being "Contemplating the face of 'Ali is worship (*'ibadah*)."

32. Chittick, *The Sufi Path of Knowledge*, 34.

33. Murata, *The Tao of Islam*, 70.

34. Chittick, *The Sufi Path of Knowledge*, 16.

35. Ibid., 61.

36. Farhana Mayer, *Spiritual Gems—The Mystical Qur'ān Commentary Ascribed to Ja'far al-Sādiq* (Louisville, KY: Fons Vitae, 2011) 146.

37. Chittick, *The Sufi Path of Knowledge*, 276.

38. Michael Sells, *Mystical Languages of Unsaying* (Chicago: Chicago University Press, 1994), 108.

## Epilogue

1. Toshihiko Izutsu, *Sufism and Taoism: A Comparative Study of Key Philosophical Concepts* (Berkeley: University of California Press, 1983).

2. Ibid., 469.

3. " 'The Real' is then, I suggest, as good a generic name as we have for that which is affirmed in the varying forms of transcendent religious belief. For it is used within the major theistic and non-theistic traditions and yet is neutral as between their very different ways of conceiving, experiencing and responding to that which they affirm in these diverse ways." John Hick, *An Interpretation of Religion—Human Responses to the Transcendent* (New Haven and London: Yale University Press, 2004), 11.

4. "Thus the generic concept of salvation/liberation, which takes a different specific form in each of the great traditions, is that of the transformation of human existence from self-centredness to Reality-centredness." Ibid., 36.

5. Laozi, *Tao Te Ching*, trans. D. C. Lau (Hong Kong: The Chinese University Press, 1996), 3. The character *chang* may mean constant, fixed, but also by extension, and most interestingly for us, absolute: "The Chinese term for 'Tao itself' is *'chang tao'*; the *chang* signifies permanence and constancy. We will call this the absolute Tao, the term *absolute* referring to the claim that this Tao is uncontradictable. As Ch'êng Hao (1032–1085) pithily put it: 'the Tao has no opposite.' " T. P. Kasulis, *Zen Action Zen Person* (Honolulu: University Press of Hawaii, 1981), 30.

# Bibliography

'Abd al-Kader, Amīr. *The Spiritual Writings of Amīr 'Abd al-Kader.* Edited by Michel Chodkiewicz. Albany: State University of New York Press, 1982.

'Abd al-Karīm al-Jīlī, *Universal Man.* Translated by Titus Burckhardt. Roxburgh, Scotland: Beshara Publications, 1983.

Abe, Masao Abe. *Zen and Comparative Studies.* Honolulu: University of Hawai'i Press, 1997.

———. *Zen and the Modern World: A Third Sequel to Zen and Western Thought.* Honolulu: University of Hawai'i Press, 2003.

———. *Zen and Western Thought.* Honolulu: University of Hawai'i Press, 1985.

Abhinavagupta. *A Trident of Wisdom: Translation of Parātrīsikā-Vivarana.* Translated by Jaiveda Singh. Albany: State University of New York Press, 1989.

———. *Abhinavagupta's Śri Tantrāloka and Other Works.* Volume I. Translated by Satya Prakash Singh and Swami Maheshvarananda. New Delhi: Standard Publishers: 2015.

———. *Parātrīsikā-Vivarana: The Secret of Tantric Mysticism.* Translated by Jaideva Singh, edited by Bettina Baumer. Delhi: Motilal Banarsidass, 1988.

Agrawal, Madan Mohan. *Essence of Vaisnavism: Philosophy of Bhedābheda.* Delhi: Ajanta, 1992.

Al-Ghazālī, *On Knowing Yourself and God.* Translated by Muhammad Nur Abdus Salam. Chicago: Great Books of the Islamic World, 2002.

———. *The Niche of Light.* Translated by David Buchman. Provo: Brigham Young University Press, 1998.

Al-Jurjānī. *Le Livre des définitions (Kitāb at-Ta'rīfāt),* Edited and translated by Maurice Gloton. Beirut: Dar Albouraq, 2005.

Alwar, M. A. *Essentials of Viśistādvaita.* Bangalore: Shri Kashi Shesha Sastri Religious Trust, 2010.

Anthony McGucki, John. *The Orthodox Church: An Introduction to its History, Doctrine, and Spiritual Culture.* Oxford: Wiley-Blackwell, 2011.

Aquinas, Thomas. *Summa Theologica: Volume 1, part 1.* New York: Cosimo, 2007.

Bansat-Boudon, Lyne. *An Introduction to Tantric Philosophy: The Paramārthasāra of Abhinavagupta with the Commentary of Yogarāja.* London: Routledge, 2011.

Bartley, C. J. *The Theology of Rāmānuja: Realism and Religion.* New York: Routledge-Curzon, 2002.

Bashier, Salman. *Ibn al-'Arabi's Barzakh: The Concept of the Limit and the Relationship between God and the World.* Albany: State University of New York Press, 2004.

Berger, Douglas L. "A Reply to Garfield and Westerhoff on 'Acquiring Emptiness.'" *Philosophy East and West* 61, no. 2 (April 2011): 368–72.

Bhattacharya, Benoytosh. *An Introduction to Buddhist Esoterism.* Delhi: Motilal Banarsidass, 1980.

Bodhi, Bhikkhu, ed. *In the Buddha's Words: An Anthology of Discourses from the Pali Canon.* Somerville, MA: Wisdom Publications, 2005.

Brown, Brian Edward. *The Buddha Nature. A Study of the Tathāgatagharba and Ālayavijñāna.* Delhi: Motilal Banarsidass, 1991.

Burckhardt, Titus. *Introduction to Sufi Doctrine.* Bloomington, IN: World Wisdom, 2008.

Chittick, William C. "The Ambiguity of the Qur'anic Command." In *Between Heaven and Hell: Islam, Salvation, and the Fate of Others,* edited by Mohammad Hassan Khalil, 65–86. Oxford: Oxford University Press, 2013.

———. *Imaginal Worlds: Ibn Al-'Arabī and the Problem of Religious Diversity.* Albany: State University of New York Press, 1994.

———. *The Sufi Path of Knowledge: Ibn Al-'Arabi's Metaphysics of Imagination.* Albany: State University of New York Press, 1989.

———. *The Sufi Path of Love: The Spiritual Teachings of Rumi.* Albany: State University of New York Press, 1983.

Comans, Michael. *The Method of Early Advaita Vedānta.* Delhi: Motilal Banarsidass, 2000.

Confessor, Maximus. *Chapters on Knowledge,* in *Selected Writings.* Translated by George C. Berthold. New York: Paulist Press, 1985.

Corbin, Henry. *Creative Imagination in the Sufism of Ibn Arabi.* Translated by Ralph Manheim. Princeton: Princeton University Press, 2014.

———. *Le paradoxe du monothéisme.* Paris: L'Herne, 1981.

Cordovero, Moses. *Moses Cordovero's Introduction to Kabbalah: An Annotated Translation of His Or Ne'erav.* Translated by Ira Robinson. Hoboken: Ktav Publishing House, 1994.

Descartes, René. *Meditations on First Philosophy: with Selections from the Objections and Replies.* Translated by Michael Moriarty. Oxford: Oxford University Press, 2008.

———. *Principles of Philosophy.* New York: Start Publishing, 2012.

Deutsch, Eliot. *Advaita Vedānta: A Philosophical Reconstruction.* Honolulu: The University Press of Hawaii, 1969.

———, and Rohit Dalvi, eds. *The Essential Vedānta: A New Source Book of Advaita Vedanta.* Bloomington, IN: World Wisdom, 2004.

Dubois, David. *Abhinavagupta: La Liberté de la Conscience.* Paris: Almora, 2010.

Dyczkowski, Mark S. G. *The Doctrine of Vibration: An Analysis of the Doctrines and Practices of Kashmir Shaivism.* Albany: State University of New York, 1987.

Eckhart, Meister. *The Complete Mystical Works of Meister Eckhart.* Edited and translated by Maurice O'C. Walshe. New York: Herder and Herder, 2009.

———. *The Essential Sermons, Commentaries, Treatises, and Defense,* Edited and translated by Edmund Colledge, O.S.A. and Bernard McGinn. New York: Paulist Press, 1981.

Emery, Gilles. *The Trinitarian Theology of St Thomas Aquinas*. Oxford: Oxford University Press, 1993.

Francis, Pope. "Letter to a Non-Believer: Pope Francis Responds to Dr. Eugenio Scalfari Journalist of the Italian Newspaper 'La Repubblica,' From the Vatican, 4 September 2013." *The Holy See*. 4 September 2013. http://w2.vatican.va/content/francesco/en/letters/2013/documents/papa-francesco_20130911_eugenio-scalfari.html.

Fung, Yu-Lan. *A Short History of Chinese Philosophy*. New York: The Free Press, 1976.

Garfield, Jay L. *The Fundamental Wisdom of the Middle Way: Nāgārjuna's Mūlamadhyamaka-kārikā*. Oxford: Oxford University Press, 1995.

———, and Jan Westerhoff. "Acquiring the Notion of a Dependent Designation: A Response to Douglas L. Berger." *Philosophy East and West* 61, no. 2 (April 2011): 365–67.

Geldhof, Joris. "'*Cogitor Ergo Sum*': On the Meaning and Relevance of Baader's Theological Critique of Descartes." *Modern Theology* 21, no. 2 (April 2005): 237–51.

Gikatilla, Joseph ben Abraham. *Sha'arei 'Orah*, 2 volumes, Edited by Joseph Ben-Shlomo. Jerusalem: Bialik Institute, 1981.

Gregory, Peter N. *Tsung-mi and the Sinification of Buddhism*. Honolulu: University of Hawai'i Press, 2002.

———. "Tsung-mi and the single word 'awareness' (*chih*)," *Philosophy East and West* 35, no. 3 (July 1985): 249–69.

Gross, Rita M., and Rosemary Radford Ruether. *Religious Feminism and the Future of the Planet: A Buddhist-Christian Conversation*. New York: Continuum, 2001.

Hick, John. *An Interpretation of Religion—Human Responses to the Transcendent*. New Haven and London: Yale University Press, 2004.

Hiriyanna, Mysore. *The Essentials of Indian Philosophy*. London: George Allen and Unwin, 1985.

Huntington Jr., C., and Geshe Namgyal Wangchen. *The Emptiness of Emptiness: An Introduction to Early Indian Mādhyamika*. Delhi: Motilal Banarsidass, 1992.

Ibn 'Ajība. *L'Ascension du regard vers les réalités du Soufisme (Kitāb Mi'rāj al-Tashawwuf ilā Haqā'iq al-Tasawwuf)*. Edited and translated by Jean-Louis Michon. Paris: Albouraq, 2010.

Ibn al-'Arabī, Muhyī-al-Dīn. *The Meccan Revelations: Selected Texts of Al-Futuhat al-Makkiya*, Presentations and Translations from the Arabic under the direction of Michel Chodkiewicz; in collaboration with William C. Chittick and James Morris. New York: Pir Press, 2000.

———. *The Bezels of Wisdom: Ibn al-'Arabī*, Edited and translated by R. W. J. Austin. New York: Paulist Press, 1980.

Isaeyeva, Natalia. *From Early Vedanta to Kashmir Shaivism*. Albany: State University of New York Press: 1995.

———. *From Early Vedanta to Kashmir Shaivism: Gaudapada, Bhartrhari, and Abhinavagupta*. Albany: State University of New York Press, 1995.

Izutsu, Toshihiko. *Sufism and Taoism: A Comparative Study of Key Philosophical Concepts*. Berkeley: University of California Press, 1983.

———. *Toward a Philosophy of Zen Buddhism*. Boulder: Prajñā, 1982.

Jones, Richard. *Nāgārjuna: Buddhism's Most Important Philosopher*. New York: CreateSpace Independent Publishing Platform, 2010.

Kalupahana, David J., ed. *Buddhist Thought and Ritual.* Delhi: Motilal Banarsidass, 1991.

Kalupahana, David. *Buddhist Philosophy: A Historical Analysis.* Honolulu: University of Hawaii Press, 1976.

Kasulis, T. P. *Zen Action Zen Person.* Honolulu: University Press of Hawaii, 1981.

King, Richard. *Indian Philosophy: An Introduction to Buddhist and Hindu Thought.* Edinburgh: Edinburgh University Press, 1999.

Kūkai. *Kūkai: Major Works.* Translated by Yoshito S. Hakeda. New York: Columbia University Press, 1972.

Lakshmanjoo, Swami. *Kashmir Shaivism: The Secret Supreme.* Edited by John Hughes. Culver City, CA: Universal Shaiva Fellowship, 2007.

Laozi. *Tao Te Ching.* Translated by D. C. Lau. Hong Kong: The Chinese University Press, 1996.

Larson, Gerald James, and Ram Shankar Bhattacharya. *Sāmkhya: A Dualist Tradition in Indian Philosophy.* Encyclopedia of Indian Philosophies, vol. iv. Delhi: Motilal Banarsidass, 1987.

Lindtner, Christian. *Master of Wisdom: Writings of the Buddhist Master Nāgārjuna,* Emeryville. CA: Dharma Publishing, 1986–97.

Lings, Martin. *What is Sufism?* Berkeley: University of California Press, 1975.

Long, Jeffery D. *Jainism: An Introduction.* London: I. B. Tauris, 2009.

Lossky, Vladimir. *The Mystical Theology of the Eastern Church.* New York: St. Vladimir's Seminary Press, 1976.

Ma, Lin. *Heidegger on East-West Dialogue: Anticipating the Event.* New York: Routledge, 2008.

Mayer, Farhana. *Spiritual Gems—The Mystical Qur'ān Commentary Ascribed to Ja'far al-Sādiq.* Louisville, KY: Fons Vitae, 2011.

Merrell-Wolff, Franklin. *Experience and Philosophy.* Albany: State University of New York Press, 1994.

———. *Pathways through to Space: An Experiential Journal.* New York: Three Rivers Press, 1983.

Mishra, Kamalakar. *Kashmir Śaivism: The Central Philosophy of Tantrism.* Delhi: Indica Books, 2011.

Muller-Ortega, Paul Eduardo. *The Triadic Heart of Śiva: Kaula Tantricism of Abhinavagupta in the Non-Dual Shaivism of Kashmir.* Albany: State University of New York Press, 1989.

Murata, Sachiko. *The Tao of Islam: A Sourcebook on Gender Relationships in Islamic Thought.* Albany: State University of New York Press, 1992.

Nāgārjuna. *Mūlamadhyamakakārikā of Nagarjuna: The Philosophy of the Middle Way.* Translated by David J. Kalupahana. Delhi: Motilal Barnasidass, 2004.

———. *Stances du milieu par excellence (Madhyamaka-kārikās).* Edited and translated by Guy Bugault. Paris: Gallimard, 2002.

———. *The Dialectical Method of Nāgārjuna: Vigrahavyāvartanī.* Translated by Kamaleswar Bhattacharya. Delhi: Motilal Banarsidass, 1998.

———. *Nāgārjuna's Guide to The Bodhisattva Path: Treatise on the Provisions for Enlightenment (The Bodhisambhāra Śāstra by Ārya Nāgārjuna),* Edited and translated by Bhikshu Dharmamitra. Seattle: Kalavinka Press, 2008.

—. *The Dialectical Method of Nāgārjuna: Vigrahavyāvartanī.* Translated by Kamaleswar Bhattacharya. Delhi: Motilal Banarsidass 1998.

—. *The Dispeller of Disputes: Nāgārjuna's Vigrahavyāvartanī,* Edited and translated by Jan Westerhoff. Oxford: Oxford University Press, 2010.

—. *The Philosophy of the Middle Way (Mūlamadhyamakakārikā).* Translated by David J. Kalupahana. Albany: State University of New York Press, 1986.

Nicholson, Andrew J. "Reconciling Dualism and Non-Dualism: Three Arguments in Vijñānabhiksu's Bhedābheda Vedānta." *Journal of Indian Philosophy* 35, no. 4 (2007): 371–403.

—. *Unifying Hinduism. Philosophy and Identity in Indian Intellectual History.* New York: Columbia University Press, 2010.

Nikhilananda, Swami, ed. *The Principal Upanishads.* Mineola, NY: Dover Publications, 2003.

Nishitani, Keiji. *Religion and Nothingness.* Berkeley: University of California Press, 1982.

Palamas, Saint Gregory. *The Triads.* New York: Paulist Press, 1983.

Pandey, Kanti Chandra. *Abhinavagupta: A Historical and Philosophical Study.* 4th ed. Varanasi: Chaukhamba Amarabharati Prakashan, 2006.

—. *Īśvara-Pratyabhijna-Vimarsini of Abhinavagupta: Doctrine of Divine Recognition.* Volume II. Delhi: Motilal Banarsidass, 1986.

Pandit, Moti Lal. *The Philosophical and Practical Aspects of Kāśmīra Śaivism.* New Delhi: Munshiram Manoharlal, 2012.

Papanikolaou, Aristotle. *Being With God: Trinity, Apophaticism, and Divine-Human Communion.* South Bend: University of Notre Dame Press, 2006.

Phan, Peter, ed. *The Cambridge Companion to the Trinity.* Cambridge: Cambridge University Press, 2011.

Potter, Karl. *Presuppositions of Indian Philosophies.* Englewood Cliffs, NJ: Prentice-Hall, 1963.

Prabhavananda, Swami. *The Spiritual Heritage of India.* Garden City, NY: Doubleday, 1963.

*Pratyabhijñāhṛidayam: The Secret of Self-Recognition.* Translated by Jaideva Singh, Motilal Banarsidass, Delhi, 1991.

Pseudo-Dionysius, *Pseudo-Dionysius: The Complete Works.* Translated by Colm Luibheid. New York: Paulist Press, 1987.

Pye, Michael. *Skilful Means: A Concept in Mahāyāna Buddhism.* 2nd ed. London: Routledge, 2003.

Radhakrishnan, Sarvepalli. *Indian Philosophy, volume 2,* Delhi: Oxford University Press, 1996.

—, and Charles A. Moore, eds. *A Source Book in Indian Philosophy.* Princeton: Princeton University Press, 1967.

Raju, P. T. *Idealistic Thought of India.* New York: Routledge, [1953] 2013.

Rāmānuja. *Vedanta-Sutras with Ramanuja's Commentary.* Translated by George Thibaut. Oxford: Clarendon Press, 1904.

Rambachan, Anantanand. *The Advaita Worldview: God, World, and Humanity.* Albany: State University of New York Press, 2006.

Reventlow, Henning Graf, and Yair Hoffman, eds. *The Problem of Evil and its Symbols in Jewish and Christian Tradition*. London: T&T Clark International, 2004.

Rodriguez Larreta, Enrique, and Cândido Mendes, eds. *Ethics of the Future*, Rio de Janeiro: Unesco/ISSC/Educam, 1998.

Roy, Olivier. *Holy Ignorance: When Religion and Culture Part Ways*. Oxford: Oxford University Press, 2014.

Sankarācārya, Sri. *Viveka-cūdāmani*. Translated by Svāmī Turīyānanda. Madras: Sri Ramakrishna Math, 1991.

———. *The Vivekacūdāmani of Śaṅkarācārya Bhagavatpāda: An Introduction and Trans-. lation*. Translated by John A. Grimes. Ashgate: Aldershot, 2004.

Scholem, Gershom. *Major Trends in Jewish Mysticism*. New York: Schocken Books, 1995.

Schroeder, John. *Skillful Means: The Heart of Buddhist Compassion*. Honolulu: University of Hawai'i Press, 2001.

Schuon, Frithjof. "The Five Divine Presences." In *Form and Substance in the Religions*. Bloomington, IN: World Wisdom, 2002.

———. *Form and Substance in the Religions*. Bloomington, IN: World Wisdom, 2002.

———. *Gnosis: Divine Wisdom*. Bloomington, IN: World Wisdom, 2006.

———. *Logic and Transcendence: A New Translation with Selected Letters*. Bloomington, IN: World Wisdom, 2009.

Sells, Michael. *Mystical Languages of Unsaying*. Chicago: Chicago University Press, 1994.

Shabistarī, Mahmud. *Garden of Mystery: The Gulshan-i Rāz of Mahmud Shabistarī*. Translated by Robert Abdul Hayy Darr. Cambridge: Archetype, 2007.

Shah-Kazemi, Reza. *Common Ground between Islam and Buddhism*. Louisville: Fons Vitae, 2010.

———. *Paths to Transcendence According to Shankara, Ibn al-'Arabī and Meister Eckhart*. Bloomington, IN: World Wisdom, 2006.

Shankaracharya, Sri. *Daksināmūrti Stotra*. Translated by Alladi Mahadeva Sastry. Chennai: Samata Books, 2001.

Sharma, Arvind. *The Rope and the Snake: Metaphorical Exploration of Advaita Vedanta*. New Delhi: Manohar, 1997.

Shaw, Miranda Eberle. *Buddhist Goddesses of India*. Princeton: Princeton University Press, 2006.

Silburn, Lilian. *Kundalinī: The Energy of the Depths*. Albany: State University of New York, 1988.

Singh, Jaideva. *Śiva Sūtras: The Yoga of Supreme Identity*. Delhi: Motilal Banarsidass, 1979.

Sinha, Jadunath. *Indian Realism*. Delhi: Motilal Banarsidass, 1972.

Sircar, Mahendranath. "Reality in Indian Thought." *The Philosophical Review* 42, no. 3 (May 1993): 249–71.

Smith, Wilfred Cantwell. *The Meaning and End of Religion*. Minneapolis: Fortress Press, 1991.

Sydnor, Jon Paul. *Ramanuja and Schleiermacher: Toward a Constructive Comparative Theology*. 2nd ed. Cambridge: James Clarke, 2012.

Taimni, I. K. *The Ultimate Reality and Realization—Śiva-Sutra*. Chennai: The Theosophical Publishing House, 2004.

Thakchoe, Sonam. *The Two Truths Debate: Tsongkhapa and Gorampa on the Middle Way.* Somerville, MA: Wisdom Publications, 2007.

*The Bhagavad Gītā.* Translated by Winthrop Sargeant. Albany: State University of New York Press, 1994.

*The Connected Discourses of the Buddha: A New Translation of the Samyutta Nikāya,* Translated by Bhikkhu Bodhi. Boston: Wisdom Publications, 2000.

*The Essential Kabbalah: The Heart of Jewish Mysticism.* Translated Daniel Matt. Edison: Castle Books, 1997.

*The Heart of Catholicism: Essential Writings of the Church from St. Paul to John Paul II.* Edited by Theodore E. James. Huntington, IN: Our Sunday Visitor, 1997.

*The Middle Length Discourses of the Buddha: A Translation of the Majjhima Nikāya.* Translated by Bhikkhu Ñānamoli and Bhikkhu Bodhi. Somerville, MA: Wisdom Publications, 1995.

*The Yoga of Delight, Wonder, and Astonishment: A Translation of the Vijnana-bhairava.* Translated by Jaideva Singh. Albany: State University of New York Press, 1991.

Trimondi, Victor, and Victoria Trimodi. "The Shadow of the Dalai Lama—Part I–2. Tantric Buddhism." *Trimondi Online Magazine. Qur'ān.*trimondi.de/SDLE/Part-1-02.htm.

Tsung-mi. *Inquiry into the Origin of Humanity: An Annotated Translation of Tsung-mi's Yüan jen lun with a Modern Commentary,* Edited and translated by Peter N. Gregory. Honolulu: University of Hawai'i Press, 1995.

Unno, Taitetsu. *Shin Buddhism: Bits of Rubble Turn into Gold.* New York: Doubleday, 2002.

Utpaladeva. *Les stances sur la reconnaissance du Seigneur avec leur glose, Īśvarapratyabhijñākārikā,* Edited and translated by David Dubois. Paris: L'Harmattan, 2010.

———. *The Īśvarapratyabhijñākārikā of Utpaladeva with the Author's Vritti.* Translated by Raffaele Torella. Delhi: Motilal Banarsidass, 2003.

Waldenfels, Hans. *Absolute Nothingness: Foundations for a Buddhist-Christian Dialogue.* New York: Paulist Press, 1976.

Walser, Joseph. *Nāgārjuna in Context: Mahāyāna Buddhism and Early Indian Culture.* New York: Columbia University Press, 2005.

Weil, Simone. *Gravity and Grace.* London: Routledge, 2002.

Zizioulas, John D. *Being as Communion.* New York: St. Vladimir's Seminary Press, 1985.

# Index

'Abd al-Karīm al-Jīlī:
on the super-ontological Essence (*dhāt*)
of God, 21, 41, 49, 219n92, 220n99
and his manifestation, 220–221n104
and the Name Allāh, 221n105
on the Universal Man, 140, 220n99
'Abd al-Qādir al-Jazā'irī, *Amīr*:
on the *barzakh* between the Divine
Reality and the totality of creation
as expressed by *āyat an-Nūr*, 139–140
on the diversity of Names, 39
on the diversity of theophanic
disclosure, 37
on the principle of "discontinuous
continuity," 137, 139
on responding to evil, 110–111
Abe, Masao Abe:
on Buddha-nature, 86
and its differentiation, identification,
and objectification, 87–88
on Buddhism as a religious system
"that defines *dharma* in terms of
*dharma*s," 70, 224n31
on *samsāra* and *nirvāna*, 228n69
on *śunyata* (emptiness), 86–90,
227–228n67
*ābhāsavāda* (thesis of "limited
manifestation"):
Abhinavagupta on the manifestation
of the Self in terms of, 217n52
and the limitless consciousness of
Śiva, 23

Abhinavagupta:
disciples. *See* Kṣemarāja
the impure defined by, 103
the label pantheistic disassociated
from, 98
Śaivite perspective on reality, 20–22,
129, 130, 133, 157, 231n14
on the Self:
manifestation in *Ābhāsas,* 217n52
self-referential capacity of
consciousness, 217–219n60
on Śiva-Śakti Supreme Consciousness,
216–217n50, 234n35
and the emergence of *vimarśa,* 25
and the Heart-*mantra, SAUH,*
191–192, 194–195
and I-ness—or *Aham,* 26–28,
132
and its creative activity, 190
and *parāparāśakti,* 26–27
*parāśakti* identified with, 25–26,
130–131
and *Parātriśikā-Vivarana,* 27
and *parāvāk* (or Supreme Word or
Speech), 30–31, 218n75
and the productive "agitation" of
Bhairava-Śiva, 218n72
*Śri Tantrāloka,* 129, 157, 216n34,
216n44, 217–218n60
Absolute, the:
*Bhedābhedavādins* view of *Brahma-
parināma-vāda,* 118, 125–128